THE TYPOLOGY OF SCRIPTURE:

VIEWED IN CONNEXION WITH THE ENTIRE SCHEME OF

THE DIVINE DISPENSATIONS.

BY

PATRICK FAIRBAIRN,

PROFESSOR OF DIVINITY, FREE CHURCH COLLEGE, ABERDEEN.

In vetere Testamento novum latet et in novo vetus patet.
August. Quæst. in Ex. lxxiii.

SECOND EDITION, MUCH ENLARGED AND IMPROVED.

TWO VOLUMES IN ONE.

PHILADELPHIA:
SMITH & ENGLISH, 36 NORTH SIXTH STREET.
1854.

PREFACE.

THE two volumes here offered to the public, are in substance a republication of those, bearing the same general title, which appeared, the one in 1845, the other in 1847; yet not without considerable differences. The principles brought out on the subject of Typology are, with a few slight modifications, the same in this as in the former edition, and the same view is consequently exhibited of the nature of the connection between the Old and the New Testament dispensations. The portion of the work, however, in which the principles of the subject are formally investigated, has been entirely re-written, and, by means both of omissions and additions, of alterations in thought and style, has been rendered more distinct in statement, and, it is hoped also, more clear and conclusive in argument. The remaining portion of the first volume, which treats in detail of primeval and patriarchal times, has been yet more materially changed, and by much the larger proportion of this part of the volume, as it now stands, differs from the corresponding volume of the former edition. Various fresh topics are here for the first time introduced, and in the discussion of others a more natural and appropriate method has been adopted. By adhering more closely to the guidance of Scripture, and keeping more carefully in view the progression in the Divine plan, a better, and to my own mind at least, a more satisfactory view has been presented of both the religion and the history of the periods before the Law. Several things, which might otherwise appear to be defects in the earlier records of Scripture, and which have often been felt to be somewhat anomalous, are thus seen to be entirely in place, and to have naturally arisen from the method of the Divine procedure.

The second volume differs both less frequently and less materially from the corresponding volume of the former edition. Occasional alterations, however, have been introduced throughout the volume; and several new sections have been added toward the close. A good deal of supplementary matter, closely connected with the main theme, has been thrown into the form of Appendices, a portion of which has already appeared elsewhere, and a portion also belonged to the first edition. But the larger part of an Appendix, in the first volume of that edition, on the restoration of the Jews, that, namely, which treated of the prophecies supposed to refer to the subject, has been omitted here. The chief reason for this omission is, not any change of opinion regarding the interpretation of those prophecies, but a conviction that the subject enters too largely into Old Testament prophecy to be quite satisfactorily discussed in so short a compass. And it is my intention, if time and opportunity are given, to institute a separate inquiry into the nature, function, and characteristics of Prophecy in general, in which occasion will be taken to resume what has been for the present withdrawn.

In making the alterations and improvements above referred to, I have not overlooked either the suggestions that have been privately tendered, or the strictures that have appeared in the public journals. The latter have not certainly been always made in the most genial and courteous spirit; though I feel that, on the whole, much more is due from me of grateful acknowledgment than of reasonable complaint. And as in the historical survey, which forms the Introduction, I have deemed it needful to notice at some length a hostile attack in a periodical on the other side of the Atlantic,

I should not do justice to my own feelings if I did not also refer to a lengthened critique, which appeared in another Transatlantic Periodical—the Princeton Review—not less distinguished by the kindliness of its tone, than by the discriminative spirit of its remarks. It is impossible, in the treatment of such a subject, to give universal satisfaction. And I have no doubt, that even where there is a general acquiescence in the views that are unfolded, there may still appear, notwithstanding the additional pains taken to avoid them, certain faults and imperfections in the mode of execution. But in this respect, as well as others, impartial and competent judges will not refuse a certain measure of indulgence, especially when it is considered how little has been hitherto done for the correct treatment of the Typology of Scripture, and through how many intricate and perplexing topics the path of inquiry necessarily leads. It may justly be deemed matter of thankfulness, if any solid footing has been gained in such a field, and if but a few leading principles have been established with such a degree of certainty, as may be sufficient to pave the way for further investigations.

Fault has in some quarters been found with the extensive range of subjects embraced in the course of discussion, and especially with the large space devoted to the consideration of the Law in the second volume. It might, no doubt, have been possible to have considerably narrowed the field, if the object had been simply to pick out from the earlier dispensations, such portions as more peculiarly possess a typical character. But to have treated the typical in such an isolated manner, would have conduced little either to the proper elucidation of the subject itself, or to the satisfaction and enlightenment of intelligent readers. The Typology of the Old Testament touches at every point on its religion and worship. It is part of a complicated system of truth and duty; and we cannot possibly attain to a correct discernment and due appreciation of the several parts, without contemplating them in the relation they bear both to each other and to the whole.

Some, on the other hand, will probably feel dissatisfied at the omission, or comparatively brief treatment of certain controversial topics, which are agitated in the present day, and which partly depend for their settlement on the view that is taken of subjects belonging to the Old Testament dispensations. The proper object, however, of a work of this nature, is rather to lay a right foundation for the fair and legitimate use of Old Testament materials in matters of controversy, than actually to make that use in every case that might occur. There are cases in which a certain application of the views taken of Old Testament subjects to present controversies, could not fitly be avoided ; but even in these it was necessary to keep within definite limits, to prevent the discussion from becoming unduly protracted.

With these explanations, the Work, in its more enlarged and matured form, is submitted to the judgment of the Public, and commended to the blessing of Him, whose ways it seeks to unfold and vindicate.

PATRICK FAIRBAIRN.

ABERDEEN, *November* 1853.

CONTENTS OF VOLUME FIRST.

BOOK FIRST.

Inquiry into the Principles of Typical Interpretation, with a view chiefly to the determination of the real nature and design of Types, and the extent to which they entered into God's earlier dispensations.

Page

Chap. I. Historical and Critical survey of the past and present state of Theological opinion on the subject, . . . 17

... II. The nature, use, and design of Types considered with an especial reference to what are commonly designated Ritual Types, or the Symbolical Institutions of Old Testament worship, ... 59

... III. The same subject continued, but with a view more especially to the solution of the question, Whether or how far the historical characters and transactions of the Old Testament may be regarded as Typical?—Historical Types, . . 78

... IV. Prophetical Types, or the combination of Type with Prophecy—Alleged double sense of Prophecy, . . . 100

... V. The interpretation of particular Types—specific principles and directions, ... 137

... VI. The place due to the subject of Types as a branch of Theological study, and the advantages arising from its proper cultivation, ... 167

BOOK SECOND.

THE DISPENSATION OF PRIMEVAL AND PATRIARCHAL TIMES.

	Page
Preliminary Remarks,	191

Chap. I. The divine truths embodied in the historical transactions connected with the Fall, being those on which the first Symbolical Religion was based, ... 200

... II. The Tree of Life, ... 214

... III. The Cherubim (and the Flaming Sword), . . . 221

... IV. Sacrificial Worship, ... 248

... V. The Sabbatical Institution, ... 265

... VI. Typical things in history during the progress of the first Dispensation, ... 272

    Sect. I. The Seed of Promise—Abel, Enoch, . . 273

    ... II. Noah and the Deluge, ... 280

    ... III. The New World and its Inheritors—the Men of Faith, ... 288

    ... IV. The change in the Divine Call from the general to the particular—Shem, Abraham, . . . 296

    ... V. The subjects and channels of blessing—Abraham and Isaac, Jacob and the twelve Patriarchs, . 307

    ... VI. The Inheritance destined for the Heirs of Blessing, 342

Appendix A. Typical forms in Nature, ... 379

... B. The Old Testament in the New, ... 382

    I. The Historical and Didactic portions, . . 382

    II. Prophecies referred to by Christ, . . . 389

    III. The deeper principles involved in Christ's use of the Old Testament, ... 394

	Page
IV. The applications made by the Evangelists of Old Testament Prophecies, ...	403
V. Applications in the writings of the Apostle Paul,	410
VI. The applications made in the Epistle to the Hebrews, ...	418
APPENDIX C. The doctrine of a Future State, . . .	425
... D. On Sacrificial Worship, ...	445
... E. Does the original relation of the seed of Abraham to the land of Canaan afford any ground for expecting their final return to it?	450

ERRATA.

At page 66, line 25, *for* " latter" *read* " later"
— 172, — 22, *for* " arguments" *read* " agreements"
— 232, — 19, *for* " inhabitest" *read* " inhabiteth"
— 266, — 2, *for* " in acting" *read* " an acting"
— 308, — 24, *for* " as" *read* " than"
— 450, — 7, *for* " P. 357" *read* " P. 377."

THE TYPOLOGY OF SCRIPTURE.

BOOK FIRST.

INQUIRY INTO THE PRINCIPLES OF TYPICAL INTERPRETATION, WITH A VIEW CHIEFLY TO THE DETERMINATION OF THE REAL NATURE AND DESIGN OF TYPES, AND THE EXTENT TO WHICH THEY ENTERED INTO GOD'S EARLIER DISPENSATIONS.

CHAPTER FIRST.

HISTORICAL AND CRITICAL SURVEY OF THE PAST AND PRESENT STATE OF THEOLOGICAL OPINION ON THE SUBJECT.

THE Typology of Scripture has been one of the most neglected departments of theological science. It has never altogether escaped from the region of doubt and uncertainty; and many still regard it as a field incapable, from its very nature, of being satisfactorily explored, or cultivated so as to yield any sure and appreciable results. Hence, it is not unusual to find those who otherwise are agreed in their views of divine truth, and in the general principles of scriptural interpretation, differing materially in the estimate they have formed of the Typology of Scripture. Where one hesitates, another is full of confidence; and the landmarks that are set up to-day are again shifted to-morrow. With such various and contradictory sentiments prevailing on the subject, it is necessary, in the first instance, to take an historical and critical survey of the field, that we may distinctly perceive what has been done in the past, and what remains yet to be done, in order to the establishment of a well-grounded and scriptural Typology.

I. We naturally begin with the Christian Fathers. Their typological views, however, are only to be gathered from the occasional examples to be met with in their writings; as they nowhere lay down any clear and systematic principles for the regulation of their judgments in the matter. Some exception might, perhaps, be made in respect to Origen. And yet with such vagueness and dubiety has he expressed himself regarding the proper interpretation of Old Testament Scripture, that by some he has been understood to hold, that there is a fourfold, by others a threefold, and by others again only a twofold sense in the sacred text. The truth appears to be, that while he contended for a fourfold *application* of Scripture, he regarded it as susceptible only of a twofold *sense*. And considered generally, the principles of interpretation on which he proceeded were not essentially different from those usually followed by the great majority of the Greek Fathers. But before stating how these bore on the subject now under consideration, it will be necessary to point out a distinction too often lost sight of, both in earlier and in later times, between *allegorical* and *typical* interpretations, properly so called. These have been very commonly confounded together, as if they were essentially one in principle, and differed only in the extent to which the principle may be carried. There is, however, a specific difference between the two, which it is not very difficult to apprehend, and which it is of some importance to notice in connection especially with the interpretations of patristic writers.

An allegory is a narrative, either expressly feigned for the purpose, or—if describing facts which really took place—describing them only for the purpose of representing certain higher truths or principles than the narrative, in its literal aspect, whether real or fictitious, could possibly have taught. The ostensible representation, therefore, is either invented, or at least used, as a mere cover for the higher sense, which may refer to things ever so remote from those immediately described, if only the corresponding relations are preserved. So that allegorical interpretations of Scripture properly comprehend the two following cases, and these only:

1. When the scriptural representation is actually held to have had no foundation in fact—to be a mere mythos, or fabulous description, invented for the sole purpose of exhibiting the mysteries of divine truth ; or, 2. When—without moving any question about the real or fictitious nature of the representation—it is considered incapable as it stands of yielding any adequate or satisfactory sense, and is consequently employed, *precisely as if it had been fabulous*, to convey some meaning of an entirely different and higher kind. The difference between allegorical interpretations, in either of these senses, and those which are properly called typical, cannot be fully manifested till we have ascertained the exact nature and design of a type. It will be enough meanwhile to say, that typical interpretations of Scripture differ from allegorical ones of the first or fabulous kind, in that they indispensably require the reality of the facts or circumstances stated in the original narrative. And they differ also from the other, in requiring, besides this, that the same truth or principle be embodied alike in the type and the antitype. *The typical is not properly a different or higher sense, but a different or higher application of the same sense.*

Returning, then, to the writings of the Fathers, and using the expressions *typical* and *allegorical* in the senses now respectively ascribed to them, there can be no doubt that the Fathers generally were much given both to typical and allegorical explanations, —the Greek Fathers more to allegorical than to typical,—and to allegorical more in the second than in the first sense, described above. They do not appear, for the most part, to have discredited the plain truth or reality of the statements made in Old Testament history. They seem rather to have considered the sense of the latter true and good, as far as it went, but of itself so meagre and puerile, that it was chiefly to be regarded as the vehicle of a much more refined and ethereal instruction. Origen, however, certainly went farther than this, and expressly denied that many things in the Old Testament had any real existence. In his Principia (Lib. iv.) he affirms, that " when the Scripture history could not otherwise be accommodated to the explanation of spiritual things, matters have been asserted which did not take place, nay, which *could* not have taken place ; and others again, which though they might have occurred, yet never actually did so." Again, when speaking of some notices in the life of Rebecca, he says—"In these things, I have often told you, there is not a relation of histories, but a concoction of mysteries."[1] And, in like manner, in his annotations on the first chapters of Genesis, he plainly scouts the idea of God's having literally clothed our first parents with the skins of slain beasts—calls it absurd, ridiculous, and unworthy of God, and declares that in such a case the naked letter is not to be adhered to as true, but exists only for the spiritual treasure which is concealed under it.[2]

Statements of this kind are of too frequent occurrence in the writings of Origen to have arisen from inadvertence, or to admit of being resolved into mere hyperboles of expression. They were, indeed, the natural result of that vicious system of interpretation which prevailed in his age, when it fell, as it did in his case, into the hands of an ardent and enthusiastic follower. At the same time it must be owned, in behalf of Origen, that however possessed of what has been called "the allegorical fury," he does not appear *generally* to have discredited the facts of sacred history; and that he differed from the other Greek Fathers, chiefly in the extent to which he went in decrying the literal sense as carnal and puerile, and extolling the mystical as alone suited for those who had become acquainted with the true wisdom. It would be out of place here, however, to go into any particular illustration of this point, as it is not immediately connected with our present inquiry. But we shall refer to a single specimen of his allegorical mode of interpretation, for the purpose chiefly of shewing distinctly how it differed from what is of a simply typological character. We make our selection from Origen's homily on Abraham's marriage with Keturah (Hom. vi. in Genes.). He does not expressly disavow his belief in the fact of such a marriage having actually taken place in real life, though his language most naturally bears that meaning; but he intimates that this, in common with the other marriages of the patriarchs, contained a sacramental mystery. And what might this be? Nothing less than the sublime truth, "that there is no end to wisdom, and that old age sets no bounds to improvement in knowledge. The death of Sarah (he says) is to be understood as the perfecting of virtue. But he who has attained

---

[1] Opera, vol. ii. p. 88, Ed. Delarue.   [2] Ibid. p. 29.

to a consummate and perfect virtue, must always be employed in some kind of learning—which learning is called by the divine Word, his wife. Abraham, therefore, when an old man, and his body in a manner dead, took Keturah to wife. I think it was better, according to the exposition we follow, that the wife should have been received when his body was dead, and his members were mortified. For we have a greater capacity for wisdom when we bear about the dying of Christ in our mortal body. Then Keturah, whom he married in his old age, is, by interpretation, *incense*, or sweet odour. For he said, even as Paul said, 'We are a sweet savour of Christ.' Sin is a foul and putrid thing; but if any of you in whom this no longer dwells, have the fragrance of righteousness, the sweetness of mercy, and by prayer continually offer up incense to God, ye also have taken Keturah to wife." And on he goes to shew, how many such wives may be taken; hospitality is one, the care of the poor another, patience a third, each christian excellence, in short, a wife; and hence it was, that the patriarchs are reported to have had so many wives, and that Solomon is said to have possessed them even by hundreds, he having received plenitude of wisdom like the sand on the sea-shore, and consequently grace to exercise the greatest number of virtues.

We have here a genuine example of allegorical interpretation, if not actually holding the historical matter to be fabulous, at least treating it as if it were so. It is of no moment, for any purpose which such a mode of interpretation might serve, whether Abraham and Keturah had a local habitation among this world's families, and whether their marriage was a real fact in history, or an incident fitly thrown into a fictitious narrative, constructed for the purpose of symbolizing the doctrines of a divine philosophy. If it had been handled after the manner of a type, and not as an allegory, whatever shade of meaning might have been ascribed to it as a representation of gospel mysteries, the story must have been assumed as real, and the act of Abraham made to correspond with something essentially the same in kind—some sort of union, for example, between parties holding a similar relation to each other, as Abraham did to Keturah. In this, though there might have been an error in the special application that was made of it, there would at least have been some appearance of a probable ground for it to rest upon. But woven into the fine allegorical form it assumes under the hands of Origen, the whole, history and interpretation together, become like "the baseless fabric of a vision." For, what connection, either in the nature of things, or in the actual experience of the Father of the Faithful, can be shewn to exist between the death of one wife and the consummation of virtue in the husband; or the marriage of another and his pursuit of knowledge? Why might not the loss sustained in the first case as well represent the decay of virtue, and the acquisition in the second denote a relaxation in the search after the hidden treasures of wisdom and knowledge? There would evidently be as good reason for asserting the one as the other; and, indeed, with such an arbitrary and elastic style of interpretation, there is nothing, either false or true in doctrine, wise or unwise in practice, which might not claim support in Scripture. The Bible would be made to reflect every hue of fancy, and every shade of belief in those who assumed the office of interpretation; and instead of being rendered serviceable to a higher instruction, it would be turned into one vast sea of uncertainty and confusion.

In proof of this we need only appeal to the use which Clement of Alexandria, Origen's master, has made of another portion of sacred history which treats of Abraham's wives (Strom. L. I. p. 333). The instruction, which he finds couched under the narrative of Abraham's marriage successively to Sarah and Hagar, is, that a Christian ought to cultivate philosophy and the liberal arts before he devotes himself wholly to the study of divine wisdom. The way he takes to make out this is the following:—Abraham is the image of a perfect Christian, Sarah the image of Christian wisdom, and Hagar the image of philosophy or human wisdom (certainly a very ill-favoured likeness!). Abraham lived for a long time in a state of connubial sterility—whence it is inferred that a Christian, so long as he confines himself to the study of divine wisdom and religion alone, will never bring forth any great or excellent fruits. Abraham, then, with the consent of Sarah, takes to him Hagar, which proves, according to Clement, that a Christian ought to embrace the wisdom of this world, or philosophy, and that Sarah, or divine wisdom, will not withhold her consent. Lastly, after Hagar had borne Ishmael to Abraham. he resumed his intercourse with Sarah, and of her begat Isaac; the true import of which is, that a Christian, after having once thoroughly grounded himself in human learning and philosophy, will, if he then devotes himself to the culture of divine wisdom, be capable of propagating the race of true Christians, and of rendering essential service to the church. Thus we have two entirely different senses extracted from similar transactions by the master and the disciple; and still, far from being exhausted, as many more might be obtained, as there are fertile imaginations disposed to use the sacred narrative after the form of their own peculiar conceits.

It was not simply the historical portions of Old Testament Scripture which were thus allegorized by Origen and the other Greek Fathers, who belonged to the same school. A similar mode of interpretation was applied to the ceremonial institutions of the ancient economy; and a higher sense was often sought for in these, than we find any indication of in the epistle to the Hebrews. Clement even carried the matter so far as to apply the allegorical principle to the ten commandments, an extravagance in which Origen did not follow him; though we can scarcely tell why he should not have done so. For, even the moral precepts of the Decalogue touch at various points on the common interests and relations of life; and it was the grand aim of the philosophy, in which the allegorizing then prevalent had its origin, to carry the soul above these into the high abstractions of a contemplative theosophy. The Fathers of the Latin church were much less inclined to such airy speculations, and their interpretations of Scripture, consequently, possessed more of a realistic and unimaginative character. Allegorical interpretations are, indeed, occasionally found in them, but they are more sparingly introduced, and less extravagantly pushed. Typical meanings, however, are as frequent in the one class as in the other, and equally adopted without rule or limit. If in the Eastern church we find such objects as the tree of life in the garden of Eden, the rod of Moses, Moses himself with his arms extended during the conflict with Amalek, exhibited as types of the cross; in the Western church, as represented, for example, by Augustine, we meet with such specimens as the following:—" Wherefore did Christ enter into the sleep of death ? Because Adam slept when Eve was formed from his side, Adam being the figure of Christ, Eve as the mother of the living, the figure of the church. And as she was formed from Adam while he was asleep, so was it when Christ slept on the cross, that the sacraments of the church flowed from his side."[1] So again, Saul is represented as the type of death, because God unwillingly appointed him king over Israel, as he unwillingly subjected his people to the sway of death; and David's deliverance from the hand of Saul foreshadowed our deliverance through Christ from the power of death; while in David's escape from Saul's hand, coupled with the destruction that befel Ahimelech on his account, if not in his stead, there was a prefiguration of Christ's death and resurrection.[2] But we need not multiply examples, or prosecute the subject farther into detail. Enough already has been adduced to shew, that the earlier divines of the Christian church had no just or well-defined principles to guide them in their interpretations of Old Testament Scripture, which could either enable them to determine between the fanciful and the true in typical applications, or guard them against the worst excesses of allegorical license.[3]

---

[1] On Psalm xli.   [2] On Psalm xlii.

[3] Those who wish to read farther regarding the typical and allegorical interpretations of the Fathers may consult Bishop Marsh's Eleventh Lecture on the Interpretation of the Bible, Davidson's Hermeneutics, or Klausen's Hermeneutik, where the subject is treated with some diversity, and also at some length. The major part of our readers perhaps may be of opinion that they have already been detained too long with the subject, believing that such interpretations are for ever numbered among the things that were. So we had ourselves almost begun to think. And yet we have lived to see a substantial revival of the allegorical style of interpretation in a work that has only of late been issuing from the press, and a work that bears the marks of an accomplished and superior mind. We refer to that portion of Mr Worsley's *Province of the Intellect in Religion*, which treats of the *Patriarchs in their Christian import*, and the *Apostles as the completion of the Patriarchs*. It is impossible not to regret that one who can think and write so well, and who has unfolded such spiritual and elevated views of the divine life, should in this part of his scheme of doctrine lay for himself so fanciful a foundation, and while maintaining the reality of the facts recorded in patriarchal and apostolical history, should yet transfigure them into something entirely ideal and visionary. His notion respecting the Patriarchs briefly is, that Abraham, Isaac, and Jacob respectively " present to us the eternal triune object" of worship,— Father, Son, and Holy Ghost; that the marriages of the Patriarchs symbolize God's union with his church, and with each member of it; and especially is this done through the wives and children of Jacob, at least in regard to its practical tendency and sanctifying results. In making out the scheme, the names of the persons are peculiarly dwelt upon as furnishing a sort of key to the allegorical interpretation. Thus Leah, whose name means wearisome and fatiguing labour, was the symbol of " services and

II. Overleaping the dark gulf of the middle ages, we come down to the period of the Reformation. At that memorable era a works which are of little worth in themselves—labours rather of a painful and reluctant duty, than of a free and joyful love." " She sets forth to us that fundamental repulsiveness or stubbornness of our nature, whose proper and ordained discipline is the daily task-work of duty, as done not to man, nor to self, but to God." Afterwards, Leah is identified with the ox, as the symbol of stubbornness and wearisome labour; and so " with Leah the ox symbolizes our task-work of duty, and our capacity for it," while the sheep (Rachel signifying *sheep*), symbolizes " our labours of love, *i. e.* our real rest, and capacity for it."—(P. 71, 113, 128.) One may guess from this specimen what ingenuities require to be plied before the author can get through all the twelve sons of Jacob, so as to make them symbols of the different graces and operations of a Christian life. We object to the entire scheme,—1. Because it is perfectly arbitrary. Though Scripture sometimes warrants us in laying stress on names, as expressive of spiritual ideas or truths connected with the persons they belonged to, yet it is only when the history itself lays stress on them, and even then they never stand alone, as the names often do with Mr Worsley, the *only* keys to the import of the transactions; so that where acts entirely fail, or where they appear to be at variance with the symbolic ideal, the key were still to be found in the name. Scripture nowhere, for example, lays any stress upon the names of Leah and Rachel; while it very pointedly refers to the bad eyes of the one, and the attractive comeliness of the other. And if we *were* inclined to allegorize at all, we should deem it more natural, with Justin Martyr (Trypho, c. 42,) and Jerome (on Hos. xii. 3,) to regard Leah as the symbol of the blear-eyed Jewish church, and Rachel as the beloved church of the gospel. Even this, however, is quite arbitrary, for there is nothing properly in common between the symbol and the thing symbolized—no real bond of connection uniting them together. And if by tracing out such lines of resemblance, we might indulge in a pleasing exercise of fancy, we can never deduce from them a revelation of God's mind and will. 2. But farther, such explanations offend against great fundamental principles—the principle, for example, that the Father cannot be represented as entering into union with the Church, viewed as distinct from the Son and the Spirit; and the principle that a sinful act or an improper relation cannot be the symbol of what is divine and holy. In such a case there never can be any real agreement. Who, indeed, can calmly contemplate the idea of Abraham's connection with Hagar, or Jacob's connection with the two sisters and their handmaids—in themselves both manifestly wrong, and receiving on them the stamp of God's displeasure in providence—should be the chosen symbol of God's own relation to the Church? How very different an allegorizing of this sort is from anything sanctioned in Scripture will be shewn in the sequel. As for the correspondence between the apostles and the patriarchs individually—which Mr Worsley, in his last volume, endeavours to make out as necessary to the full symbolic exhibition of divine truth and righteousness—it appears to us so entirely destitute even of the semblance of verisimilitude, that any refutation is unnecessary. The mere facts that, according to his scheme, Peter, the first of the apostles, answers to Simeon, the least favourably known and most unimportant of the heads of Israel, and Andrew to Judah; while Simon Zelotes, the all but unknown apostle, represents a higher phase of the Christian life than Simon the son of Jonas—such facts shew how fanciful the scheme is which Mr Worsley has here been labouring to build, and how completely the evangelical narrative has been made to assume the form of his own preconceived notions.

mighty advance was made, not only beyond the ages immediately preceding, but also beyond all that had passed from the commencement of Christianity, in the sound interpretation of Scripture. The original text then at last began to be examined with something like critical exactness, and a steadfast adherence was generally professed, and in good part also maintained, to the natural and grammatical sense. The leading spirits of the Reformation were here also the great authors of reform. Luther denounced mystical and allegorical interpretations as "trifling and foolish fables, with which the Scriptures were rent into so many and diverse senses, that silly poor consciences could receive no certain doctrine of any thing."[1] Calvin, in like manner, declares that "the true meaning of Scripture is the natural and obvious meaning, by which we ought resolutely to abide;" and speaks of the "licentious system" of Origen and the allegorists, as "undoubtedly a contrivance of Satan to undermine the authority of Scripture, and to take away from the reading of it the true advantage."[2] In some of his interpretations, especially on the prophetical parts of Scripture, he even went to an extreme in advocating what he here calls the natural and obvious meaning, and thereby missed the more profound import, which, according to the elevated and often enigmatical style of prophecy, it was the design of the Spirit to convey. On the other side, in spite of their avowed and generally followed principles of interpretation, the writers of the Reformation-period not unfrequently fell into the old method of allegorizing, and threw out typical explanations of a kind that cannot stand a careful scrutiny. It were quite easy to produce examples of this from the writings of those who lived at and immediately subsequent to the Reformation; but it would be of no service as regards our present object, since their attention was comparatively little drawn to the subject of types; and none of them attempted to construct any distinct typological system.

III. We pass on, therefore, to a later period—about the middle of the seventeenth century—when the science of theology began to be studied more in detail, and the types consequently received a more formal consideration. About that period arose

---

[1] On Gal. iv. 26.   [2] On Gal. iv. 22.

what is called the Cocceian school, which, though it did not revive the double sense of the Alexandrian (for Cocceius expressly disclaimed any other sense of Scripture than the literal and historical one), yet was chargeable in another respect with a participation in the caprice and irregularity of the ancient allegorists. Cocceius himself, less distinguished as a systematic writer in theology than as a Hebrew scholar and learned expositor of Scripture, left no formal enunciation of principles connected with typical or allegorical interpretations; and it is chiefly from his annotations on particular passages, and the more systematic works of his followers, that these are to be gathered. How freely, however, he was disposed to draw upon Old Testament history for types of Gospel things, may be understood from a single example—his viewing what is said of Asshur going out and building Nineveh, as a type of the Turk or Mussulman power, which at once sprang from the kingdom, and shook the dominion of Antichrist (cur. Prior in Gen. x. 11.) He evidently conceived that *every* event in Old Testament history, which in any way resembled something under the New, was to be regarded as typical. And that, even notwithstanding his avowed adherence to but one sense of Scripture, he could occasionally adopt a second, appears alone from his allegorical interpretation of the eighth Psalm; according to which the *sheep* there spoken of, as being put under man, are Christ's flock—the *oxen*, those who labour in Christ's service—the *beasts of the field*, such as are strangers to the city and kingdom of God, barbarians and savages—the *fowl of the air and fish of the sea*, persons at a still greater distance from godliness; so that, as he concludes, there is nothing so wild and intractable on earth but it shall be brought under the rule and dominion of Christ.

It does not appear, however, that the views of Cocceius differed materially from those which were held by some who preceded him; and it would seem rather to have been owing to his eminence generally as a commentator than to any distinctive peculiarity in his typological principles, that he came to be so prominently identified with the school, which from him derived the name of Cocceian. If we turn to one of the earlier editions of Glass's Philologia Sacra, published before Cocceius commenced his critical labours (the first was published before he was born), we shall find the principles of allegorical and typical interpretations laid down with a latitude which Cocceius himself could scarcely have quarrelled with. Indeed, we shall find few examples in his writings that might not be justified on the principles stated by Glass; and though the latter, in his section on allegories, has to throw himself back chiefly on the Fathers, he yet produces some quotations in support of his views, both on these and on types, from some writers of his own age. There seems to have been no essential difference between the typological principles of Glass, Cocceius, Witsius, and Vitringa; and though the first wrote some time before, and the last about half a century later than Cocceius, no injustice can be done to any of them by classing them together, and referring indifferently to their several productions. Like the Fathers, they did not sufficiently distinguish between allegorical and typical interpretations, but regarded the one as only a particular form of the other, and both as equally warranted by New Testament Scripture. Hence, the rules they adopted were to a great extent applicable to what is allegorical in the proper sense, as well as typical, though for the present we must confine ourselves to the typical department. They held, then, that there was a twofold sort of types, the one *innate*, consisting of those which Scripture itself has expressly asserted to possess a typical character; the other *inferred*, consisting of such as, though not specially noticed or explained in Scripture, were yet, on probable grounds, inferred by interpreters as conformable to the analogy of faith, and the practice of the inspired writers in regard to similar examples.[1] This latter class were considered not less proper and valid than the other; and pains were taken to distinguish them from those which were sometimes forged by Papists, and which were at variance with the analogies just mentioned. Of course, from their very nature they could only be employed for the support and confirmation of truths already received, and not to prove what was in itself doubtful. But not on that account were they to be less carefully searched for, or less confidently used, because thus only, it was maintained, could Christ be found in all Scripture, which all testifies of him.

It is evident alone, from this general statement, that there was

---

[1] Philologia Sac. Lib. II. P. I. Tract. II. sect. 4. Vitringa Obs. Sac. Vol. II. Lib. VI. c. 20. Witsius De Œconom. Lib. IV. c. 6.

something vague and loose in the Cocceian system, which left ample scope for the indulgence of a luxuriant fancy. Nor can we wonder that, in practice, a mere resemblance, however accidental or trifling, between an occurrence in Old, and another in New Testament times, was deemed sufficient to constitute the one a type of the other. Hence, in the writings of the very able and learned men above referred to, we find the name of Abel (emptiness) viewed as prefiguring our Lord's humiliation; the occupation of Abel, Christ's office as the Shepherd of Israel; the withdrawal of Isaac from his father's house to the land of Moriah, Christ's being led out of the temple to Calvary; Adam's awaking out of sleep, Christ's resurrection from the dead; Samson's meeting a young lion by the way, and the transactions that followed, Christ's meeting Saul on the road to Damascus, with the important train of events to which it led; David's gathering to himself a party of the distressed, the bankrupt, and discontented, Christ's receiving into his Church publicans and sinners. And many others of a like nature.

Multitudes of examples perfectly similar—that is, equally destitute of any proper foundation in principle—are to be found in writers of our own country, such as Mather,[1] Keach,[2] Worden,[3] J. Taylor,[4] Guild,[5] who belonged to the same school of interpretation, and who nearly all lived toward the latter part of the seventeenth century. Excepting the two first, they make no attempt to connect their explanations with any principles of interpretation, and these two very sparingly. Their works were all intended for popular use, and rather exhibited by particular examples, than theoretically expounded the nature of their views. They, however, agreed in admitting *inferred* as well as *innate* types, but differed —more perhaps from constitutional temperament than on theoretical grounds—in the extent to which they severally carried the liberty they claimed to go beyond the explicit warrant of New Testament Scripture. Mather in particular, and Worden, usually confine themselves to such types as have obtained special notice of some kind from the writers of the New Testament; though

---

[1] The Figures and Types of the Old Testament.
[2] Key to open the Scripture Metaphors and Types.
[3] The Types unveiled, or the Gospel picked out of the Legal Ceremonies.
[4] Moses and Aaron.   [5] Moses unveiled.

they held the principle, that "where the analogy was evident and manifest between things under the law and things under the gospel, the one were to be concluded (on the ground simply of that analogy) to be types of the other." How far this warrant from analogy was thought capable of leading, may be learned from Taylor and Guild, especially from the latter, who has no fewer than forty-nine typical resemblances between Joseph and Christ, and seventeen between Jacob and Christ, not scrupling to swell the number by occasionally taking in acts of sin, as well as circumstances of the most trifling nature. Thus, Jacob's being a supplanter of his brother, is made to represent Christ's supplanting death, sin, and Satan; his being obedient to his parents in all things, Christ's subjection to his heavenly Father and his earthly parents; his purchasing his birthright by red pottage, and obtaining the blessing by presenting savoury venison to his father, clothed in Esau's garment, Christ's purchasing the heavenly inheritance to us by his red blood, and obtaining the blessing by offering up the savoury meat of his obedience, in the borrowed garment of our nature, &c.

Now, we may affirm of these, and many similar examples occurring in writers of the same class, that the analogy they found upon was a merely *superficial* resemblance found between things in the Old and other things in the New Testament Scriptures. But with such a loose and shifting foundation, it was manifestly left open to any one to introduce the most frivolous conceits, and to caricature rather than vindicate its grand theme. Then, if such weight was fitly attached to mere resemblances between the Old and the New, even when they were altogether of a slight and superficial kind, why should not profane as well as sacred history be ransacked for them? What, for example, might prevent Romulus (seeing that God is in all history) assembling a band of desperadoes, and founding a world-wide empire on the banks of the Tiber, from serving, as well as David in the circumstances specified above, to typify the procedure of Christ in calling to him publicans and sinners at the commencement of his kingdom? As many points of resemblance might be found in the one case as in the other; and the two transactions in ancient history, as here contemplated, stood much on the same footing as regards the appointment of God; for both alike were the offspring of human policy, struggling against outward difficulties, and endeavouring with such materials as were available to supply the want of better resources. And thus, by pushing the matter beyond its just limits, we reduce the sacred to a level with the profane, and, at the same time, throw an air of uncertainty over the whole aspect of its typical character.[1]

That the Cocceian mode of handling the typical matter of ancient Scripture so readily admitted of the introduction of trifling, far-fetched, and even altogether false analogies, was one of its capital defects. It had no essential principles or fixed rules by which to guide its interpretations—set up no proper landmarks along the field of inquiry—left room on every hand for arbitrariness and caprice to enter. It was this, perhaps, more than anything else, which tended to bring typical interpretations into disrepute, and disposed men, in proportion as the exact and critical study of Scripture came to be cultivated, to regard the subject of its typology as hopelessly involved in conjecture and uncertainty. Yet this was not the only fault inherent in the typological system now under consideration. It failed, more fundamentally still, in the idea it had formed of the connection between the Old and the New in God's dispensations—between the type and the thing typified—which it made chiefly to consist in mere external resemblances, to the comparative neglect of the great fundamental principles which are common alike to all dispensations, and in which the more vital part of the connection must be sought. It was this more radical error, which in fact gave rise to the greater portion of the extravagances that disfigured the typical illustrations of our older divines; for it naturally led them to make account of resemblances that were sometimes trivial, and sometimes only apparent. And not only so; but it also led them to misapprehend the immediate object and design of the types in their relation to the Old Testament worshippers. While these

---

[1] In the reference made above to the beginnings of David's kingdom, it will be understood that the characters he associated with himself are simply viewed in the light contemplated by the writers we now contend against. My own conviction is, that 1 Sam. xxii. 2, if rightly interpreted, would present those who gathered themselves to David as spiritually the better sort in Israel—those who were partly made bankrupt by oppression, and partly were grieved and vexed in their minds at the existing state of things.

as types speak a language that can be distinctly and intelligently understood only by us, who are privileged to read their meaning in the light of gospel realities, they yet had, *as institutions in the existing worship, or events in the current providence of God*, a present purpose to accomplish, apart from the prospective reference to future times, and we might almost say, as much as if no such reference had belonged to them.

IV. These inherent errors and imperfections in the typological system of the Cocceian school, were not long in leading to its general abandonment. But theology had little reason to boast of the change. For the system that supplanted it, without entering at all into a more profound investigation of the subject, or attempting to explain more satisfactorily the grounds of a typical connection between the Old and the New, simply contented itself with admitting into the rank of types what had been expressly treated as such in the Scripture itself, to the exclusion of all besides. This seemed to be the only safeguard against error and extravagance.[1] And yet, we fear, other reasons of a less justifiable kind contributed not a little to produce the result. An unhappy current had begun to set in upon the Protestant Church, in some places, while Cocceius still lived, and in still more soon after his death, which disposed many of her more eminent teachers to slight the evangelical element of Christianity, and, if not utterly to lose sight of Christ himself, at least to disrelish and repudiate a system which delighted to find traces of Him in every

[1] The following critique of Buddeus, which belongs to the earlier part of last century, already points in this direction: "It cannot certainly be denied that the Cocceians, at least some of them, have carried this matter too far. For, besides that they *everywhere* seem to find images and types of future things, where other people can discern none, when they come to make the application to the antitype, they not unfrequently descend to minute and even trifling things, nay, advance what is utterly insignificant and ludicrous, exposing holy writ to the mockery of the profane. And here it may be proper to notice the fates of exegetical theology; since that intemperate rage for allegories which appeared in Origen and the Fathers, and which had been condemned by the schoolmen, was again, after an interval, though under a different form, produced anew upon the stage. For this typical interpretation differs from the allegorical only in the circumstance, that respect is had in it to the future things which are adumbrated by the types; and so, the typical may be regarded as a sort of allegorical interpretation. But in either way the amplest scope is afforded for the play of a luxuriant fancy and a fertile invention."—I. F. Buddei Isagoge II. hist. Theolog. 1830.

part of revelation. It was the redeeming point of the older typology, which should be allowed to go far in extenuating the occasional errors connected with it, that it kept the work and kingdom of Christ ever prominently in view, as the grand scope and end of all God's dispensations. It *felt*, if we may so speak, correctly, whatever it may have wanted in the requisite depth and precision of *thought*. But towards the end of the seventeenth and the beginning of the eighteenth century, a general coldness very commonly discovered itself, both in the writings and the lives of even the more orthodox sections of the Church. The living energy and zeal which had achieved such important results a century before, either inactively slumbered, or spent itself in doctrinal controversies ; and the faith of the Church was first corrupted in its simplicity, and then weakened in its foundations by the pernicious influence of a widely cultivated, but esssentially anti-Christian philosophy. In such circumstances Christ was not allowed to maintain his proper place in the New Testament, and it is not to be wondered at if he should have been nearly banished from the Old.

Vitringa, who lived when this degeneracy from better times had made considerable progress, attributed to it much of that distaste which was then beginning to prevail in regard to typical interpretations of Scripture. With special reference to the work of Spencer on the Laws of the Hebrews—a work not less remarkable for its low-toned, semi-heathen spirit, than for its varied and well-digested learning—he lamented the inclination that appeared to seek for the grounds and reasons of the Mosaic institutions in the mazes of Egyptian idolatry, instead of endeavouring to discover in them the mysteries of the Gospel. These, he believed, the Holy Spirit had plainly intimated to be couched there, and they shone, indeed, so manifestly through the institutions themselves, that it seemed impossible for any one to perceive the type, who recognised the antitype. Nor could he conceal his fear, that the talent, authority, and learning of such men as Spencer would gain extensive credit for their opinions, and soon bring the Typology of Scripture, as he understood it, into general contempt.[1] In this apprehension he was certainly not mistaken.

[1] Obs. Sac. Vol. II. p. 460, 461.

Another generation had scarcely passed away when Dathe published his edition of the Sacred Philology of Glass, in which the section on types, to which we have already referred, was quietly dropt out, as relating to a subject no longer thought worthy of a recognised place in the science of an enlightened theology. The rationalistic spirit, in the strength of its anti-Christian tendency, had now discarded the *innate*, as well as the *inferred* types of the older divines; and the convenient principle of *accommodation*, which was at the same time introduced, furnished an easy solution for those passages in New Testament Scripture, which seemed to indicate a typical relationship between the past and the future. It was only an adaptation, called forth by Jewish prejudice or conceit, of the facts and institutions of an earlier age to things essentially different under the Gospel; but now, since the state of feeling that gave rise to it no longer existed, deservedly suffered to fall into desuetude. And thus the bond was virtually broken by the hand of these rationalizing theologians between the Old and the New in Scripture, and the records of Christianity, when scientifically interpreted, were found to have marvellously little in common with those of Judaism.

In Britain various causes contributed to hold in check this downward tendency, and to prevent it from reaching the same excess of dishonour to Christ, which it soon attained on the Continent. Even persons of a cold and philosophical temperament, such as Clarke and Jortin, not only wrote in defence of types, as having a certain legitimate use in Revelation, but also admitted more within the circle of types than Scripture itself has expressly applied to Gospel times.[1] They urged, indeed, the necessity of exercising the greatest caution in travelling beyond the explicit warrant of Scripture; and in their general cast of thought they undoubtedly had more affinity with the Spencerian than the Cocceian school. Yet a feeling of the close and pervading connection between the Old and the New Testament dispensations restrained them from discarding the more important of the inferred types. Jortin especially falls so much into the current of the older writers, that he employs his ingenuity in reckoning up

---

[1] Clarke's Evidences, p. 420, sq. Jortin's Remarks on Ecclesiastical History, Vol. I. p. 138—152.

so many as forty particulars in which Moses typically prefigured Christ. A work composed about the same period as that to which the Remarks of Jortin belong, and one that has had more influence than any other in fashioning the typological views generally entertained in Scotland — the production of a young dissenting minister in Dundee (Mr M'Ewen)[1]—is still more free in the admission of types not expressly sanctioned in the Scriptures of the New Testament. The work itself being posthumous, and intended for popular use, contains no investigation of the grounds on which typical interpretations rest, and harmonises much more with the school that had flourished in the previous century, than that to which Clarke and Jortin belonged. As indicative of a particular style of biblical interpretation, it may be classed with the older productions of Mather and Taylor, and partakes alike of their excellencies and defects.

There was, therefore, a considerable unwillingness in this country to abandon the Cocceian ground on the subject of types. The declension came in gradually, and its progress was rather marked by a tacit rejection in practice of much that was previously held to be typical, than by the introduction of views avowedly different. It became the practice of theologians to look more into the general nature of things for the reasons of Christianity, than into the pre-existing elements and characteristics of former dispensations, and to account for the peculiarities of Judaism by its partly antagonistic, partly homogeneous relation to Paganism, rather than by any concealed reference it might have to the coming realities of the Gospel. As an inevitable consequence, the typological department of theology fell into general neglect, from which the Old Testament Scriptures themselves did not altogether escape. Those portions of them especially which narrate the history, and prescribe the religious rites of the ancient Church, were but rarely treated in a manner that bespoke any confidence in their fitness to minister to the spiritual discernment and faith of Christians. It seems, partly at least, to have been owing to this growing distaste for Old Testament inquiries, and

---

[1] Grace and Truth, or the Glory and Fulness of the Redeemer displayed, in an attempt to explain the Types, Figures, and Allegories of the Old Testament, by the Rev. W. M'Ewen.

this general depreciation of its Scriptures, that what is called the Hutchinsonian school arose in England—which, by a sort of recoil from the prevailing spirit, ran into the opposite extreme of searching for the elements of all knowledge, human and divine, in the writings of the Old Testament. This school possesses too much the character of an episode in the history of biblical interpretation in this country, and was itself too strongly marked by a spirit of extravagance, to render any formal account of it necessary here. It was, besides, chiefly of a physico-theological character, combining the elements of a natural philosophy with the truths of revelation, both of which it sought to extract from the statements, and sometimes even from the words and letters of Scripture. The most profound meanings were consequently discovered in the text of Scripture, in respect alike to the doctrines of the Gospel and the truths of science. One of the maxims of its founder was, that "every passage of the Old Testament looks backward and forward, and every way, like light from the sun; not only to the state before and under the law, but under the Gospel, and nothing is hid from the light thereof."[1] When such a depth and complexity of meaning was supposed to be involved in every passage, we need not be surprised to learn, respecting the exactness of Abraham's knowledge of future events, that he knew from preceding types and promises, that "one of his own line was to be sacrificed, to be a blessing to all the race of Adam;" and not only so, but that when he received the command to offer Isaac, he proceeded to obey it, "not doubting that Isaac was to be that person who should redeem man."[2]

The cabalistic and extravagant character of the Hutchinsonian system, if it had any definite influence on the study of types and other cognate subjects, could only tend to increase the suspicion with which they were already viewed, and foster a disposition to agree to whatever might keep investigation within the bounds of sobriety and discretion. Accordingly, while nothing more was done to unfold the essential and proper ground of a typical connection between Old and New Testament things, and to prevent abuse by making the subject more thoroughly understood in its fundamental principles, the more scientific students

---

[1] Hutchinson's Works, Vol. I. p. 202. [2] Ibid. Vol. VII. p. 325.

of the Bible came, by a sort of common consent, to acquiesce in the opinion, that those only were to be reckoned types to which Scripture itself, by express warrant, or at least by obvious implication, had assigned that character. We may take Bishop Marsh as the ablest and most systematic expounder of this view of the subject. He says,—" There is no other rule by which we can distinguish a real from a pretended type, than that of Scripture itself. There are no other possible means by which we can know that a previous design and a pre-ordained connection existed. Whatever persons or things therefore, recorded in the Old Testament, were expressly declared by Christ or by his apostles to have been designed as prefigurations of persons or things relating to the New Testament, such persons or things so recorded in the former, are types of the persons or things with which they are compared in the latter. But if we assert that a person or thing was designed to prefigure another person or thing, where no such prefiguration has been declared by divine authority, we make an assertion for which we neither have, nor can have, the slightest foundation."[1] This is certainly a very authoritative and peremptory decision of the matter. But the principle involved in this statement, though seldom so oracularly announced, has long been practically received. It was substantially adopted by Macknight, in his Dissertation on the Interpretation of Scripture, at the end of his Commentary on the Epistles, before Bishop Marsh wrote, and it has been followed since by Vanmildert and Conybeare in their Bampton Lectures, by Nares in his Warburtonian Lectures, by Chevalier in his Hulsean Lectures, by Horne in his Introduction, and a host of other writers.

Judging from an article in the American Biblical Repository, which appeared in the number for January 1841, it would appear that the leading authorities on the other side of the Atlantic concur in the same general view. The reviewer himself advocates the opinion that " no person, event, or institution, should be regarded as typical, but what may be proved to be such from the Scriptures," meaning by that their explicit assertion in regard to the particular case. And in support of this opinion he quotes, besides English writers, the words of two of his own countrymen,

[1] Lectures, p. 373.

Professors Stowe and Moses Stuart, the latter of whom says,— "That just so much of the Old Testament is to be accounted typical as the New Testament affirms to be so, and *no more*. The fact, that any thing or event under the Old Testament dispensation was designed to prefigure something under the New, can be known to us only by revelation; and of course all that is not designated by divine authority as typical, can never be made so by any authority less than that which guided the writers of the New Testament."[1]

Now, the view embraced by this school of interpretation lies open to one objection, in common with the school that preceded it. While the field, as to its extent, was greatly circumscribed, and in its boundaries ruled as with square and compass, nothing was done in the way of investigating it internally, or of unfolding the grounds of connection between type and antitype. Fewer points of resemblance are usually presented to us between the one and the other by the writers of this school than are found in works of an older date; but the resemblances themselves are quite as much of a superficial and outward kind. The real harmony and connection between the Old and the New in the divine dispensations, stood precisely where it was. But other defects adhere to this modern typological system. The leading excellence of the system that preceded it was the constant reference it supposed the Scriptures of the Old Testament to bear toward Christ and the Gospel dispensation; and the practical disavowal of this may be said to constitute the great defect of the more exact and leaner system, which has now obtained the general suffrage of the learned. It drops a golden principle for the sake of avoiding a few lawless aberrations. With the narrow limits it sets to our inquiries, we cannot indeed wander far into the regions of extravagance. But in the very prescription of these limits, it wrongfully withholds from us the key of knowledge, and shuts us up to evils scarcely less to be deprecated than those it seeks to correct. For it destroys to a large extent the bond of connection between the Old and the New Testament Scriptures, and thus deprives the Christian Church of much of the instruction in divine things which they were designed to impart. Were men accustomed, as

---

[1] Stuart's Ernesti, p. 13.

they should be, to search for the germs of Christian truth in the earliest Scriptures, and to regard the inspired records of both covenants as having for their leading object " the testimony of Jesus," they would know how much they were losers by such an undue contraction of the typical element in Old Testament Scripture. And in proportion as a more profound and spiritual acquaintance with the divine Word is cultivated, will the feeling of dissatisfaction grow in respect to a style of interpretation, that so miserably dwarfs and cripples the relation which the preparatory bears to the final in God's revelations.

It is necessary, however, to take a closer view of the subject. The principle on which this typological system is based, is, that nothing less than inspired authority is sufficient to determine the reality and import of any thing that is typical. But we can see no solid ground for such a principle. No one holds the necessity of inspiration to explain each particular prophecy, and decide even with certainty on its fulfilment, and why should it be reckoned indispensable in the closely related subject of types? This question was long ago asked by Witsius, and yet waits for a satisfactory answer. A part only, it is universally allowed, of the prophecies which refer to Christ and his kingdom have been specially noticed and interpreted by the pen of inspiration. So little necessary, indeed, was inspiration for such a purpose, that even before the descent of the Holy Spirit at Pentecost, our Lord reproved his disciples as "fools and slow of heart to believe *all* that the prophets had spoken." And from the close analogy between the two subjects—for what is a type but a prophetical act or institution?—we might reasonably infer the same liberty to have been granted, and the same obligation to be imposed, in regard to the typical parts of ancient Scripture. But we have something more than a mere argument from analogy to guide us to this conclusion. For, the very same complaint is brought by an inspired writer against private Christians concerning their slowness in understanding the typical, which our Lord brought against his disciples in respect to the prophetical portions of ancient Scripture. In the epistle to the Hebrews a sharp reproof is administered for the imperfect acquaintance believers among them had with the typical character of Melchizedec, and subjects of a like nature—thus placing it beyond a doubt that it is both the duty and the privilege of the Church, with that measure of the Spirit's grace which it is the part even of *private* Christians to possess, to search into the types of ancient Scripture, and come to a correct understanding of them. To deny this, is plainly to withhold an important privilege from the church of Christ; to dissuade from it, is to encourage the neglect of an incumbent duty.

But the unsoundness of the principle, which would thus limit the number of types to those which New Testament Scripture has expressly noticed and explained, becomes still more apparent when it is considered what these really are, and in what manner they are introduced. Leaving out of view the tabernacle, with its furniture and services, which, as a whole, is affirmed in the epistles to the Hebrews and the Colossians to have been of a typical nature, the following examples are what the writers now referred to usually regard as having something like an explicit sanction in Scripture:—1. Persons or characters; Adam (Rom. v. 11, 12; 1 Cor. xv. 22); Melchizedec (Heb. vii.); Sarah and Hagar, Ishmael and Isaac, and by implication Abraham (Gal. iv. 22—35); Moses (Gal. iii. 19, Acts iii. 22—26); Jonah (Matth. xii. 40); David (Ezek. xxxvii. 24, Luke i. 32., &c.); Solomon (2 Sam. vii.); Zerubbabel and Joshua (Zech. iii. iv. Hag. ii. 23). 2. Transactions or events; the preservation of Noah and his family in the ark (1 Pet. iii. 20); the redemption from Egypt and its passover-memorial (Luke xxii. 15, 16, 1 Cor. v. 7); the exodus (Matth. ii. 15); the passage through the Red sea, the giving of manna, Moses's veiling of his face while the law was read; the water flowing from the smitten rock; the serpent lifted up for healing in the wilderness, and some other things that befel the Israelites there (1 Cor. x. John iii. 14, v. 33, Rev. ii. 17).[1]

---

[1] We don't vouch, of course, for the absolute completeness of the above list. Indeed, it is scarcely possible to know what would be regarded as a complete list—some feeling satisfied with an amount of recognition in Scripture which seems quite insufficient in the eyes of others. There have been those who, on the strength of Gen. xlix. 24, would insert Joseph among the specially mentioned types, and claim also Sampson, on account of what is written in Judges xiii. 5. But scriptural warrants of such a kind are out of date now—they can no longer be regarded as current coin. On the other hand, there are not a few who deem the scriptural warrant insufficient for some of those we have specified, and think the passages, where they are noticed, refer to them merely in the way of illustration. The list, however, comprises what are usually regarded as

Now, let any person of candour and intelligence take his Bible, and examine the passages to which reference is here made, and then say, whether the manner in which these typical characters and transactions are there introduced, is such as to indicate, that these alone were held by the inspired writers to be prefigurative of similar characters and transactions under the gospel? as if in naming them they meant to exhaust the typical bearing of Old Testament history? On the contrary, we deem it impossible for any one to avoid the conviction, that in whatever respect these particular examples may have been adduced, it is simply *as examples* adapted to the occasion, and taken from a vast storehouse, where many more were to be found. They have so much at least the appearance of having been selected merely on account of their suitableness to the immediate end in view, that they cannot fairly be regarded otherwise than as specimens of the class they belong to. And if so, they should rather have the effect of prompting farther inquiry than of repressing it; since, instead of themselves comprehending and bounding the whole field of typical matter, they only exhibit practically the principles on which others of a like description are to be discovered and explained.

Indeed, were it otherwise, nothing could be more arbitrary and inexplicable than the Typology of Scripture. For, what is there to distinguish the characters and events, which Scripture has thus particularized, from a multitude of others, to which the typical element might equally have been supposed to belong? Is there anything on the face of the inspired record to make us look on *them* in a singular light, and attribute to them a significance altogether peculiar respecting the future affairs of God's kingdom? So far from it, that we instinctively feel, if these really possessed a typical character, so also must others, which hold an equally, or perhaps even more prominent place in the history of God's dispensations. Can it be seriously believed, for example, that Sarah and Hagar stood in a typical relation to gospel times, while no such place was occupied by Rebekah, as the spouse of Isaac, and the mother of Jacob and Esau? What reason can we imagine for Melchizedec and Jonah having been

historical types, having the authority of Scripture, by writers belonging to the school of Marsh. The arguments of those who would discard them altogether, shall be considered under next division.

constituted types—persons to whom our attention is comparatively little drawn in Old Testament history—while such leading characters as Joseph, Sampson, Joshua, are omitted? Or, for selecting the passage through the Red sea, and the incidents in the wilderness, while no account should be made of the passage through Jordan, and the conquest of the land of Canaan?

We can scarcely conceive of a mode of interpretation which should deal more capriciously with the word of God, and make so anomalous a use of its historical matter. Instead of investing these with a homogeneous character, it arbitrarily selects a few out of the general mass, and sets them up in solitary grandeur, like mystic symbols in a temple, fictitiously elevated above the sacred materials around them. The exploded principle, which sought a type in *every* notice of Old Testament history, had at least the merit of uniformity to recommend it, and could not be said to deal partially, however often it might deal fancifully, with the facts of ancient Scripture. But according to the plan now under review, for which the authority of inspiration itself is claimed, we perceive nothing but arbitrary distinctions and groundless preferences. And though unquestionably it were wrong to expect in the word of God the precise method and order, which might naturally have been looked for in a merely human composition, yet as the product, amid all its variety, of one and the same Spirit, we *are* warranted to expect that there shall be a consistent agreement among its several parts, and that distinctions shall not be created in the one Testament, which in the other seem destitute of any just foundation or apparent reason.

But then, if a greater latitude is allowed, how shall we guard against error and extravagance? Without the express authority of Scripture, how shall we be able to distinguish between a happy illustration and a real type? In the words of Bishop Marsh: "By what means shall we determine, in any given instance, that what is *alleged* as a type, was really *designed* for a type? The only possible source of information on this subject is Scripture itself. The only possible means of knowing that two distant, though similar historical facts, were so connected in the general scheme of divine Providence, that the one was designed to prefigure the other is the authority of that book, in which the scheme of divine Providence is unfolded."[1] This is an objection, indeed, which strikes at the root of the whole matter, and its validity can only be ascertained by a thorough investigation into the fundamental principles of the subject. That Scripture is the sole rule, on the authority of which we are to distinguish what is properly typical from what is not, we readily grant—though not in the straitened sense contended for by Bishop Marsh and those who hold similar views, as if there were no way for Scripture to furnish a sufficient direction on the subject, except by specifying every particular case. It is possible, surely, that in this, as well as in other things, Scripture may unfold certain fundamental views or principles, of which it makes but a few individual applications, and for the rest leaves them in the hand of spiritually enlightened consciences. The more so, as it is one of the leading peculiarities of New Testament Scripture rather to develope great truths, than to dwell on minute and isolated facts. It is a presumption against, not in favour of, the system we now oppose, that it would shut up the Typology of Scripture, in so far as connected with the characters and events of sacred history, within the narrow circle of a few scattered and apparently random examples. And the attempt to rescue it from this position, if in any measure successful, will also serve to exhibit the unity of design which pervades the inspired records of both covenants, the traces they contain of the same divine hand, the subservience of the one to the other, and the mutual dependence alike of the Old upon the New, and of the New upon the Old.

V. We have still, however, another stage of our critical survey before us, and one calling in some respects for careful discrimination and inquiry. The style of interpretation which we have connected with the name of Marsh could not, in the nature of things, afford satisfaction to men of thoughtful minds, who must have something like equitable principles as well as external authority to guide them in their interpretations. Such persons could not avoid feeling that, if there was so much in the Old Testament bearing a typical relation to the New, as was admitted on scriptural authority by the school of Marsh, there must be

[1] Lectures, p. 372.

considerably more; and also, that underneath that authority there must be a substratum of fundamental principles capable of bearing what Scripture itself has raised on it, and whatever besides may fitly be conjoined with it. But some, again, might possibly be of opinion that the authority of Scripture cannot warrantably carry us so far, and that both scriptural authority, and the fundamental principles involved in the nature of the subject, apply only in part to what the followers of Marsh regarded as typical. Accordingly, among more recent inquirers we have examples of each mode of divergence from the formal rules laid down by the preceding school of interpretation. The search for first principles has disposed some greatly to enlarge the typological field, and it has disposed others greatly to curtail it.

1. Of the former class the chief examples are to be found in Germany; as it was there also that the new and more profound spirit of investigation began to develope itself. Near the commencement of the present century the religions of antiquity became there, as they had never been before, the subject of learned inquiry, and a depth of meaning was discovered in the myths and external symbols of these, which in the preceding century was not so much as dreamt of. Creuzer, in particular, by his great work (Symbolik) created quite a sensation in this department of learning, and opened up what seemed to be an entirely new field of research. He was followed by Baur (Symbolik und Mythologie), Görres (Mythengeschichte), Müller, and others of less note, each endeavouring to proceed farther than his predecessors into the explication of the religious views of the ancients, by weaving together, and interpreting what is known of their historical legends and ritual services. These inquiries were at first conducted merely in the way of antiquarian research and philosophical speculation; and the religion of the Old Testament was deemed, in that point of view, too unimportant to be made the subject of special consideration. Creuzer only here and there throws out some passing allusions to it. Even Baur, though a theologian, enters into no regular investigation of the symbols of Judaism, while he expatiates at great length on all the varieties of Heathenism. By and bye, however, a better spirit appeared. Mosaism, as the religion of the Old Testament is called, had a distinct place allotted it by Görres among the ancient religions of

Asia. And at last it was itself treated at great length, and with consummate ability and learning, in a separate work—the *Symbolik des Mosaischen Cultus* of Bähr (published in 1837-9.) This is still the great work in Germany on the meaning of the Mosaic symbols, although it is pervaded by fundamental errors of the gravest kind (on which we shall afterwards have occasion to remark), and not unfrequently falls into fanciful views on particular parts. Some of these have been corrected by Hengstenberg in the second volume of his *Authentie des Pentateuchus*, who has also furnished many good typical illustrations in his Christology and other exegetical works. Tholuck, in his Commentary on the Hebrews, has followed in the same tract, generally adopting the explanations of Hengstenberg, and still more recently (chiefly since the publication of our first edition), further contributions have been made by Kurtz, Baumgarten, Delitzsch. Even De Wette, in his old age, caught something of this new spirit; and after many an effort to depreciate apostolic Christianity by detecting in it symptoms of Judaical weakness and bigotry, he made at least one commendable effort in the nobler direction of elevating Judaism by pointing to the manifold germs it contained of a spiritual Christianity. In a passage quoted by Bähr (vol. i. p. 16, from an article of De Wette on the "Characteristik des Hebraismus"), he says,—" Christianity sprang out of Judaism. Long before Christ appeared, the world was prepared for his appearance: *the entire Old Testament is a great prophecy, a great type of him who was to come, and has come.* Who can deny that the holy seers of the Old Testament saw in spirit the advent of Christ long before he came, and in prophetic anticipations, sometimes more, sometimes less clear, descried the new doctrine? The typological comparison, also, of the Old Testament with the New, was by no means a mere play of fancy; nor can it be regarded as altogether the result of accident, that the evangelical history, in the most important particulars, runs parallel with the Mosaic. Christianity lay in Judaism as leaves and fruits do in the seed, though certainly it needed the divine sun to bring them forth."

Such language, and especially from such a quarter, indicates a decided change. Yet it must not be supposed, on reading so strong a testimony, as if every thing were already conceded; for what by such writers as De Wette is granted in the general, is often denied or explained away in the particular. Nor has any systematic treatise (so far as we know) yet appeared on the Continent, unfolding the grounds of a typological connection between the things of the Old and those of the New Testament dispensations, and laying its foundations broad and deep in the great principles of God's administration. Bähr confines himself almost entirely to the mere interpretation of the symbols of the Mosaic dispensation, and, therefore, even when his views are correct, has only supplied some materials for the construction of a sound typological system. Tholuck and other learned men still note it as a defect in their literature, that they are without any work on the subject suited to the existing position and demands of theological science.

It is to be observed, however, that this new current opinion among the better part of theologians on the Continent, leads them to find the typical element widely diffused through the historical and prophetical, as well as the more strictly religious portions of the Old Testament. No one who is in any degree acquainted with the exegetical productions of Hengstenberg and Olshausen, now made accessible to English readers, can have failed to perceive this, from the tone of their occasional references and illustrations. Their unbiassed exegetical spirit rendered it impossible for them to do otherwise; for the same connection, they perceived, runs like a thread through the whole, and binds all together. Indeed, the only formal attempt made to work out a new system of typological interpretation—the small treatise of Olshausen (published in 1824, and consisting only of 124 widely printed pages), entitled, *Ein Wort uber tiefern Schriftsinn*, has respect almost exclusively to the historical and prophetical parts of ancient Scripture. When he comes distinctly to unfold what he calls the deeper exposition of Scripture, he contents himself with a brief elucidation of the following points:—That Israel's relation to God is represented in Scripture as forming an image of all and each of mankind, in so far as the divine life is possessed by them—that Israel's relation to the surrounding heathen in like manner imaged the conflict of all spiritual men with the evil in the world—that a parallelism is drawn between Israel and Christ as the one who completely realized what Israel should have been—and that all real children of God again image what, in the whole, is found imperfectly in Israel and perfectly in Christ, (p. 87-110.)

The positions, it must be confessed, indicate a considerable degree of vagueness and generality; and the treatise, as a whole, is defective in first principles and logical precision, as well as fulness of investigation. Klausen, in the following extract from his Hermeneutik, pp. 334–345, has given a fair outline of Olshausen's views: "We must distinguish between a false and a genuine allegorical exposition, which latter has the support of the highest authority, though it alone has it, being frequently employed by the inspired writers of the New Testament. The fundamental error in the common allegorizing, from which all its arbitrariness has sprung, bidding defiance to every sound principle of exposition, must be sought in this, that a double sense has been attributed to Scripture, and one of them consequently a sense entirely different from that which is indicated by the words. Accordingly, the characteristic of the genuine allegorical exposition must be, that it recognises no sense besides the literal one—none differing from this in nature, as from the historical reality of what is recorded; but only a *deeper-lying sense* (ὑπόνοια,) bound up with the literal meaning by an internal and essential connection—a sense given along with this and in it; so that it must present itself whenever the subject is considered from the higher point of view, and is capable of being ascertained by fixed rules. Hence, if the question be regarding the fundamental principles, according to which the connection must be made out between the deeper apprehension and the immediate sense conveyed by the words, these have their foundation in the law of general harmony, by which all individuals, in the natural as well as in the spiritual world, form *one* great organic system—the law by which all phenomena, whether belonging to a higher or a lower sphere, appear as copies of what essentially belongs to their respective ideas; so that the whole is represented in the individual, and the individual again in the whole. This mysterious relation comes most prominently out in the history of the Jewish people and their worship. But something analogous everywhere discovers itself; and in the manner in which the Old Testament is expounded in the New, we are furnished with the rules for all exposition of the Word, of nature, and of history."

The vague and unsatisfactory character of this mode of representation, is evident almost at first sight; the elements of truth contained in it are neither solidly grounded nor sufficiently guarded against abuse; so that, with some justice, Klausen remarks, in opposition to it,—" The allegorizing may perhaps be applied with greater moderation and better taste than formerly; but against the old principle, though revived as often as put down, viz. that every sense which can be found in the words has a right to be regarded as the sense of the words, the same exceptions will always be taken." If the Typology of Scripture cannot be rescued from the domain of allegorizings, it will be impossible to secure for it a solid and permanent footing. We must have done with what can be fitly called allegorizings, or a nearer and deeper sense. We simply add, that Klausen himself has no place in his Hermeneutics for typical, as distinguished from allegorical interpretations. In common with Hermeneutical writers generally, he regards these as substantially the same in kind; and the one only as the excess of the other. *Some* application he would allow of Old Testament Scripture to the realities of the Gospel, in consideration of what is said by inspired writers of the relation subsisting between the two; but he conceives that relation to be of a kind which scarcely admits of being brought to the test of historical truth, and that the examples furnished of it in the New Testament arose from necessity rather than from choice. Dr Davidson (in his Hermeneutics), we are glad to see, proceeds farther, justifies and approves of typical interpretations; though he still also speaks of allegorical interpretations, not as essentially different from typical, but only as " an excessive use of the true spiritual interpretation contained in the New Testament." (Pp. 68, 69).

2. But we must now refer more particularly to the sentiments of that class, whom the new turn of thought and inquiry has led greatly to curtail the typical matter of Scripture—to whom, undoubtedly, Klausen belongs. Here, however, we do not need to go to writers in a foreign tongue for our authorities; we have them in our own. Thus in the Connection and Harmony of the Old and New Testament, by Dr L. Alexander, 1841, while he fol-

lows Bähr in the mode of explaining some of the leading symbols of the Old Testament, and finds in them typical representations of the realities of the gospel, he declares himself opposed to any further extension of the typical matter of the Old Testament. Nothing in his view is typical which does not possess the character of a " divine institution ;" or, as he more formally defines it, " symbolical institutes expressly appointed by God, to prefigure to those among whom they were set up certain great transactions in connection with that plan of redemption which, in the fulness of time, was to be unfolded to mankind." Hence all of what are called the historical types, even those which Marsh and his followers were wont to allow on account of the special explanations given of them in the New Testament, are entirely discarded ; the use made of them in the New Testament is held to be " for illustration merely, and not for the purpose of building anything on them ;" it does not properly constitute them types.

This view has recently been taken up, and at much greater length defended, in a periodical work, which, though a production of America, is not unknown in this country—the Ecclesiastical and Literary Journal of Mr Lord. The part to which we more particularly refer is an article that appeared in No. XV., containing an elaborate review of the first edition of the Typology, and endeavouring to overthrow the views maintained in it, as " a monstrous scheme," not only " without the sanction of the word of God," but " one of the boldest and most effective contrivances for its subversion." This certainly is strong language, yet it is only a fair specimen of the harsh and contemptuous phraseology which pervades the article, and which too commonly characterizes both the pen and the school of the writer. We have no intention of taking any particular notice either of these or of the palpable misrepresentations with which they are not unfrequently accompanied. We mean simply to examine the grounds on which the reviewer principally rests his opposition to our typological principles, and succeeds so entirely to his own satisfaction in cutting off much from the typical category in Scripture that we hold to belong to it.

The process, indeed, is a very brief and simple one. He first sets forth a delineation of the nature and characteristics of a type, so tightened and compressed as to admit of nothing but what pertained to "the tabernacle worship, or the propitiation and homage of God;" this, in his judgment, embraces the entire sphere of the typical. And having thus oracularly settled the chief point (for he seems to think anything in the shape of proof quite unnecessary), it becomes an easy matter to discard whatever else may be called typical; for it is put to flight the moment he presents his exact definitions, and can only be considered typical by persons of dreamy intellect, who are utter strangers to clearness of thought and precision of language. In this way it is possible, we admit, and also not very difficult, to make out a scheme and establish a nomenclature of one's own; but the question is, does it accord with the representations of Scripture? and will it serve, in respect to these, as a guiding and harmonizing principle? We might, in a similar way, draw out a series of precise and definite characteristics of Messianic prophecy—such as, that it must avowedly bear the impress of a prediction of the future—that it must clearly and distinctly point to the person or times of Messiah—that it must be conveyed in language capable of no ambiguity or double reference—and then, with this sharp weapon in our hand, proceed summarily to lop off all supposed prophetical passages in which these characteristics are wanting—holding such, if applied to Messianic times, to be mere accommodations, originally intended for one thing, and afterwards loosely adapted to another. The rationalists of a former generation were great adepts in this mode of handling prophetical Scripture, and by the use of it dexterously got over nearly one-half of the passages which in the New Testament are represented as finding their fulfilment in Christ. But we have yet to learn, that by so doing they succeeded in throwing any satisfactory light on the interpretation of Scripture, or in placing on a Scriptural basis the connection between the Old and the New in God's dispensations.

How closely the principles of Mr Lord lead him to tread in the footsteps of these effete interpreters, will appear presently. But we must first lodge our protest against his account of the essential nature and characteristics of a type, as entirely arbitrary and unsupported by Scripture. The things really possessing this character, he maintains, must have had the following distinctive marks: They must have been specifically constituted types by God; must have been known to be so constituted, and contemplated as such by those who had to do with them ; and must have been continued till the coming of Christ, when they were abrogated or superseded by something analogous in the Christian dispensation. These are his essential elements in the constitution of a type ; and an assertion of the want of these forms the perpetual refrain, with which he disposes of those characters and transactions, that in his esteem are falsely accounted typical. We demur to every one of them in the sense understood by our opponent, and challenge him, or any other person, to produce any scriptural proof of them, as applying to the strictly religious symbols of the Old Testament worship, and to them alone. These were not specifically constituted types, or formally set up in that character, no more than such transactions as the deliverance from Egypt, or the preservation of Noah in the deluge, which he denies to have been typical. In the manner of their appointment, viewed by itself, there is no more to indicate a reference to the Messianic future in the one than in the other. Neither were they for certain known to be types, and used as such by the Old Testament worshippers. They unquestionably were not in the time of our Lord ; and how far they may have been so at any previous period, is a matter only of doubtful speculation, and nowhere of express revelation. Nor, finally, was it by any means an invariable and indispensable characteristic, that they should have continued in use till they were superseded by something analogous in the Christian dispensation. They might have partly stood ; the redemption from Egypt, for example, did stand, in a transaction which was incapable of being so continued. It was a creative act, bringing Israel as a people of God into formal existence, and as such capable only of being commemorated, but not of being repeated, or rendered in itself perpetual. It *was* commemorated, however, in the passover-feast. In that feast the Israelites continually freshened the remembrance of it anew on their hearts. They in spirit re-enacted it as a thing that required to be ever renewing itself in their personal experience, precisely as Christians do now through the Supper in regard to the one great redemption-act of Christ upon the cross. This also, considered simply as an act in God's administration, is incapable of being repeated ; it can only be commemorated, and in its effects spiritually applied to the conscience. Yet so far from being thereby bereft of an antitypical character, it is the central antitype of the gospel. Why should it be otherwise in respect to the type? The analogy of things favours it; and the testimony of Scripture not doubtfully requires it.

To say nothing of other passages of Scripture which bear less explicitly, though to our mind very materially upon the subject, our Lord himself, at the celebration of the last passover, declared to his disciples, "With desire I have desired to eat this passover with you before I suffer; for I say unto you, I will not any more eat thereof, until it be fulfilled in the kingdom of God." (Luke xxii. 15, 16.) There is a prophecy (what else can the words mean?) as well as a memorial in this commemorative ordinance, —a prophecy, because it is the rehearsal of a typical transaction, which is now, and only now, going to meet with its full realisation. Such appears to me the plain and unsophisticated import of our Lord's words. And the Apostle Paul is, if possible, still more explicit: "For even Christ our passover is sacrificed for us; therefore let us keep the feast," &c. (1 Cor. v. 7, 8.) What, we again ask, are we to understand by these words, if not that there is in the design and appointment of God an ordained connection between the sacrifice of Christ and the sacrifice of the Passover, so that the one, as the means of redemption, takes the place of the other? In any other sense the language would be only fitted to mislead, by begetting apprehensions regarding a mutual correspondence and connection which had no existence. But what says our opponent? "Christ is indeed said to be our *passover*, but it is by a metaphor, and indicates only, that it is by his blood we are saved from everlasting death, as the first-born of the Hebrews were saved by the blood of the paschal lamb from death by the destroying angel." Why could not the apostle have so expressed himself if that was all he meant? If there was no real connection between the earlier and the later event, and the one stood as much apart from the other as the lintels of Goshen in themselves did from the cross of Calvary, why employ language that forces upon every unbiassed mind the reality of a proper connection? Simply, we believe, because it actually existed; and our "exegetical conscience" refuses to be satisfied with Mr Lord's mere metaphor. But when he states further, that the passover, having been "appointed with a reference to the exemption of the first-born of the Israelites from the death that was to be inflicted on the first-born of the Egyptians, it cannot be a type of Christ's death for the sins of the world, as that would imply that Christ's death also was *commemorative* of the preservation from an analogous death,"—a child might tell him, that he confounds between the passover as an original redemptive transaction, and as a commemorative ordinance, pointing back to the original institution, and perpetually rehearsing it. It is as a *festal solemnity* alone that there can be anything commemorative belonging either to the Paschal sacrifice or to Christ's. Viewed, however, as redemptive acts, there *was* a sufficient analogy between them: the one redeemed the firstborn of Israel (the élite of its families), and the other redeems " the Church of the first-born, whose names are written in heaven."

There is the same sort of trifling with the testimony of Scripture in most of the other instances examined by the reviewer. Christ, for example, calls himself, with pointed reference to the manna, " the bread of life ;" and in Rev. ii 17, an interest in his divine life is called " an eating of the hidden manna ;" but it is only " by a metaphor," precisely as Christ elsewhere calls himself the vine, or is likened to a rock. As if there were no difference between an employment of these natural emblems and the identifying of Christ with the supernatural food given to support his people, after a typical redemption, and on the way to a typical inheritance. It is not the simple reference to a temporal good on which, in such a case, we rest the typical import, but this in connection with the whole of the relations and circumstances in which the temporal was given or employed. Jonah was not, it is alleged, a type of Christ ; for he is not called such, but only " a sign ;" neither was Melchizedec called by that name. Well, but Adam *is* called a type ($\tau \acute{\upsilon} \pi o \varsigma \ \tau o \tilde{\upsilon} \ \mu \acute{\epsilon} \lambda \lambda o \nu \tau o \varsigma$, Rom. v. 14), and baptism *is* called the antitype to the deluge ($\mathring{o} \ \varkappa \alpha \grave{\iota} \ \mathring{\eta}\mu\alpha\varsigma \ \mathring{\alpha}\nu\tau\acute{\iota}\tau\upsilon\pi o\nu \ \nu \tilde{\upsilon} \nu \ \sigma \acute{\omega} \zeta \epsilon \iota \ \beta \acute{\alpha} \pi \tau \iota \sigma \mu \alpha$, 1 Pet. iii. 21). True, but then, we are told, the word in these passages only means a similitude ; it does not mean type or antitype in the proper sense. What, then, *could* denote it ? Is there any other term more properly fitted to express the idea ? And if the precise term, when it *is* employed, still does not serve, why object in other cases to the want of it ? Strange, surely, that its presence and its absence should be alike grounds of objection. But if the matter is to come to this mere stickling about words, shall we have any types at all ? Are even the tabernacle and its institutions of worship called by that name? Not once; but, inversely, the designation of *antitypes* is in one passage applied to them: "The holy places made with hands, the antitypes of the true," (ἀντίτυπα τῶν ἀληθινῶν, Heb. ix. 24.) So little does Scripture, in its teachings on this subject, encourage us to hang our theoretical explanations on a particular epithet! It varies the mode of expression with all the freedom of common discourse, and even, as in this last particular instance, inverts the current phraseology; but still, amid the variety, it indicates with sufficient plainness a real economical connection between the past and the present in God's dispensations,—such as is commonly understood by the terms type and antitype; and it is not for want of scriptural evidence if any fail to perceive it.

Our reviewer furnishes us still further with a specimen of his dialectical skill, in the remarks he makes on the passage in Galatians respecting Sarah and Isaac on the one side, and Hagar and Ishmael on the other. He begins, as usual, with telling us, that there is nothing typical expressed in the characters and relations there mentioned; for they are not any of them called types; nor, we may add, if they had been, would it have brought us a whit nearer the mark. "It is only said," he continues, "that that which is related of Hagar and Sarah is exhibited allegorically; that is, that there are other things that, used as allegorical representatives of Hagar and Sarah, exhibit the same facts and truths. The object of the allegory is to exemplify *them* by analogous things; not *by* them to exemplify something else, to which they present a resemblance. It is *they* that are said to be allegorized, that is, represented by something else; not something else that is allegorized by them. They are accordingly said to be the two covenants, that is, like the two covenants; and Mount Sinai is used to represent the covenant that genders to bondage; and Jerusalem from above, that is, the Jerusalem of Christ's kingdom, the covenant of freedom or grace. And they accordingly are employed [by the apostle] to set forth the character and condition of the bond and the free woman, and their offspring. He attempts to illustrate the lot of the two classes who are under law and under grace; first, by referring to the different relations to the covenant, and different lot of the children of the bond and the free woman; and then, by using Mount Sinai to exemplify the character and condition of those under the Mosaic law, and the heavenly Jerusalem, to exemplify those who are under the gospel. The places from which the two covenants are proclaimed are thus used to represent those two classes ; not Hagar and Sarah to represent those places, or the covenants that are proclaimed from them." Now, this parade of petty criticism—professing to explain all, and yet leaving the main thing totally unexplained—is introduced, let it be observed, to expose an alleged " singular neglect of discrimination" in the use we had made of the passage. We had, it seems, been guilty of the extraordinary mistake of supposing Hagar and Sarah to be themselves the representatives in the apostle's allegorization, and not, as we should have done, the objects represented. Does any of our readers, with all the advantage of the reviewer's explanation, recognise the importance of this distinction ? Or can he tell how it serves to explicate the apostle's argument ? His mind must be differently constituted from ours if it has not well-nigh driven from his mind any distinct conception of the real subject of discourse. In itself it might have been of no moment, though it is of some for the apostle's argument, whether Hagar and Sarah be said to represent the two covenants of law and grace, or the two covenants be said to represent them ; as in Heb. ix. 24, it is of no moment whether the earthly sanctuary be called the antitype of the heavenly, or the heavenly of the earthly. There is in both cases alike a mutual representation, or relative correspondence; and it is the *nature* of the correspondence, inferior and preparatory in the one case, spiritual and ultimate in the other, which is chiefly important. It is *that* (though entirely overlooked by the reviewer) which makes the apostle's appeal here to the historical transactions in the family of Abraham suitable and appropriate to the object he has in view.

We shall gather into a few sentences what, at different places in the former edition, we actually said respecting this passage in Galatians. We first stated, in a quotation from Bishop Marsh, that though the apostle here calls his reference to the historical transactions an allegorizing of them, he did not convert them into allegory in the ordinary sense. He did not treat them as fabulous ; he did nothing more, in fact, than represent one class of characters and relations as types, and the other as antitypes. As Tholuck also justly remarks in regard to it, that the allegorizing presented is "nothing else than the typical meaning, and the typical exposition here also admits of a perfect justification."[1] Then, secondly, in opposition to Dr Alexander, we affirmed that the apostle's reference to the things connected with Hagar and Sarah could not have been for illustration merely, or with the design simply of presenting an apt similitude; it must have proceeded on the ground of a real, valid, and divinely-appointed connection between the things compared. For how else could the apostle have introduced it with a call to the Galatians to hear the law?" "Tell me, ye that desire to be under the law, do ye not hear the law?" Could he have honestly made such an appeal in respect to a mere play of fancy, or anything not strictly binding on the conscience? It is a summons to hear the authoritative word of God; which necessarily implies, that the transactions referred to in the case of Hagar and of Sarah were of the nature of a revelation, purposely ordered and arranged to teach on the narrower and lower sphere of domestic life, what was afterwards to take place nationally and spiritually in connection with the covenants of law and grace. But this, in our view, is all one with saying that the one was expressly designed to be to the spiritual eye a type and foreshadowing of the other. Lastly, as to the specific import of the passage, we had substantially said before, and we now repeat, that the tenor of the apostle's statement, and the place it holds in his train of argument, not only warrant, but even oblige us to regard the two mothers as the representatives of the two covenants, rather than inversely; for it is by the mothers and their natural offspring he intends to throw light on the covenants and their respective tendencies and results. It was the earlier that exemplified and illustrated the later, not the later that exemplified and illustrated the earlier; otherwise the reference of the apostle is misplaced, and the reasoning he founds on it manifestly inconclusive.

One specimen more of our reviewer's criticism, and we shall leave him. Among the passages of Scripture we had referred to, as indicating a typical relationship between the old and the new in God's dispensations, is Matth. ii. 15, where the Evangelist speaks of Christ being in Egypt till the death of Herod, " that it

---

[1] Das Alte Testament im Neuen, p. 38.

might be fulfilled which was spoken of the Lord by the prophet, saying, Out of Egypt have I called my Son." The allusion to this passage in our introductory chapter was never meant to convey the idea that it was the only Scriptural authority for concluding a typical relationship to have subsisted between Israel and Christ. And any one reading for information, and not for objection, might have found in other parts of the work a good deal of Scriptural authority besides this, bearing on the subject. It was, however, referred to as one of the passages most commonly employed by typological writers in proof of such a relationship, and in itself most obviously implying it. But what says our reviewer? " The language of Matthew does not imply that it (the passage in Hosea) was a prophecy of Christ; he simply states, that Jesus continued in Egypt till Herod's death, so that that occurred in respect to him which had been spoken by Jehovah by the prophet, Out of Egypt have I called my Son; or, in other words, so that that was accomplished in respect to Christ which had been related by the prophet of Israel." Had we not good reason for saying that our author's principles inevitably led him, as an interpreter of Scripture, to tread in the footsteps of the rationalists? One might suppose that it was a comment of Paulus or Kuinoel that we were here presented with, and we transfer the paraphrase of the latter to the bottom of the page, to shew how entirely they agree in spirit.[1] If the Evangelist simply meant what is ascribed to him, was he so unskilled in the ordinary use of language as not to be able plainly to express it? Or, if the words he employs distinctly indicate such a connection between Christ and Israel, as gave to the testimony in Hosea the force of a prophecy (which must be the impression of every unbiassed reader), what shall we say of the arbitrary and sophistical sense, which the reviewer thinks himself entitled to put even on the words of inspiration? And this, too, from one who hardly knows how to express his astonishment that such a work as the Typology should have appeared " at a period when the principles of language are more thoroughly investigated than in any former age, and the whole body of the learned hold, that the sacred volume, like other writings, is to be interpreted by the laws of

---

[1] Ut adeo hic recte possit laudari, quod dominus olim interprete propheta dixit, nempe: ex Ægypto vocavi filium meum.

philology!" "Physician, heal thyself!" It is no solitary example of rationalistic interpretation of which our reviewer has here been guilty. The antagonistic position he has taken up against all historical and prophetical types of necessity requires a similar mode of getting rid of a great many other applications of the Old Testament in the New. But as we mean to treat of this separately, and at some length, in a subsequent part of the work, we shall not further refer to it here. And, in conclusion, we trust we have said enough to shew that, while we hold the school of Marsh to have erred by way of defect in limiting the typical matter of ancient Scripture to what has been specially noticed as typical in Scripture itself, it was still fully justified in finding express warrant in Scripture for a good deal of such matter beyond the province of religious symbol and sacrificial worship. There are principles of interpretation authorised and sanctioned in New Testament Scripture, which furnish ample ground for maintaining the existence of a typical connection, to a considerable extent, between the old and the new, in respect also to the historical and prophetical portions of the old,—a typical connection substantially alike, though, we do not say in all respects perfectly agreeing, to that attaching to the institutions and services of religion. Even among these there were some shades of diversity as to the precise form and kind of correspondence between type and antitype; and other diversities naturally arose when the connection passed into the region of history and prophecy. This was implied in the first edition of the Typology. But, I admit, it was not with sufficient distinctness exhibited. And, among the improvements introduced into the present edition, will be found both a more clear and orderly enunciation of the fundamental principles of the subject, and a more discriminating exhibition of the differences between one portion of what is typical and another.

CHAPTER SECOND.

THE NATURE, USE, AND DESIGN OF TYPES CONSIDERD WITH AN ESPECIAL REFERENCE TO WHAT ARE COMMONLY DESIGNATED RITUAL TYPES, OR THE SYMBOLICAL INSTITUTIONS OF OLD TESTAMENT WORSHIP.

IN entering on the formal investigation of this subject, we shall not attempt, what we have already found to prove so fruitless in the hands of another, to begin with a precise definition of a type. The points that would require to be embraced by it are of too complex and varied a character to admit of being distinctly expressed in a brief enunciation. But there are two principal ideas more or less clearly indicated in the definitions commonly adopted, which unfold what is of primary moment, and comprise all that is necessary as a foundation for farther inquiry. Understanding the word *type* in the theological sense—for as employed in Scripture the original word is undoubtedly used with greater latitude[1]—it is admitted by general consent, first, that in the character, action, or institution, which is denominated the *type*, there must be a resemblance in form or spirit to what answers to it under the Gospel; and secondly, that it must not be *any* character, action, or institution, occurring in Old Testament Scripture, but such only as had their ordination of God, and were designed by Him to foreshadow and prepare for the better things of the Gospel. For, as Bishop Marsh has justly remarked, " to constitute one thing the type of another, something more is wanted than mere resemblance. The former must not

---

[1] Heb. viii. 5; Phil. iii. 17; 1 Thes. i. 7; 1 Pet. v. 3; Rom. vi 17. In these passages τύπος, type, very nearly corresponds in meaning to our words *model, pattern*, or *exemplar* generally. And this is what is usually called the Scriptural, as opposed to the theological sense of the word. It might more properly, perhaps, be called the general as distinguished from the more specific theological meaning, which, if not actually expressed, is sometimes, at least in substance, indicated in Scripture, as at Rom. v. 14; Heb. ix. 24; 1 Pet. iii. 21.

only resemble the latter, but must have been *designed* to resemble the latter. It must have been so designed in its original institution. It must have been designed as something preparatory to the latter. The type as well as the antitype must have been pre-ordained; and they must have been pre-ordained as constituent parts of the same general scheme of divine Providence. It is this *previous design* and this *pre-ordained* connection [together, of course, with the resemblance], which constitute the relation of type and antitype".[1] We insert, *together with the resemblance;* for, while stress is justly laid on the previous design and pre-ordained connection, the resemblance also forms an indispensable element in this very connection, and is, in fact, the point that involves the more peculiar difficulties belonging to the subject, and calls for the closest investigation.

I. We begin, therefore, with the other point—the previous design and pre-ordained connection necessarily entering into the relation between type and antitype. A relation so formed, and subsisting to any extent between Old and New Testament things, evidently pre-supposes and implies two important *facts*. It implies, first, that the realities of the Gospel, which constitute the antitypes, are the ultimate objects which were contemplated by the mind of God, when planning the economy of his successive dispensations. And it implies, secondly, that to prepare the way for the introduction of these ultimate objects, he placed the Church under a course of training, which included instruction by types, or designed and fitting resemblances of what was to come. Both of these facts are so distinctly stated in Scripture, and, indeed, so generally admitted, that it will be unnecessary to do more than present a brief outline of the proof on which they rest.

1. In regard to the first of the two facts, we find the designation of "the ends of the world" applied in Scripture to the Gospel-age;[2] and that not so much in respect to its posteriority in point of time, as to its comparative maturity in regard to the things of salvation—the higher and better things having now come, which had hitherto appeared only in prospect or existed but

---

[1] Marsh's Lectures, p. 371.   [2] 1 Cor. x. 11; Heb. xi. 40.

in embryo. On the same account the Gospel dispensation is called " the dispensation of the fulness of times ;"[1] indicating, that with it alone the great objects of faith and hope, which the Church was from the first destined to possess, were properly brought within her reach. Only with the entrance also of this dispensation does the great mystery of God, in connection with man's salvation, come to be disclosed, and the light of a new and more glorious era at last breaks upon the Church. " The day-spring from the height," in the expressive language of Zacharias, then appeared, and made manifest what had previously been wrapt in comparative obscurity, what had not even been distinctly conceived, far less satisfactorily enjoyed.[2] Here, therefore, in the sublime discoveries and abundant consolations of the Gospel, is the *reality*, in its depth and fulness, while, in the earlier endowments and institutions of the Church, there was no more than a shadowy exhibition and a partial experience;[3] and as a necessary consequence, the most eminent in spiritual light and privilege before, were still decidedly inferior even to the less distinguished members of the Messiah's kingdom.[4] In a word, the blessed Redeemer, whom the Gospel reveals, is Himself the beginning and the end of the scheme of God's dispensations ; in Him is found alike the centre of Heaven's plan, and the one foundation of human confidence and hope. So that *before* his coming into the world, all things of necessity pointed toward him ; types and prophecies bore testimony to the things that concerned his work and kingdom ; the children of blessing were blessed in anticipation of his looked for redemption ; and *with* his coming, the

[1] Eph. i. 10.

[2] Luke i. 78 ; 1 John ii. 8 ; Rom. xvi. 25, 26 ; Col. i. 27 ; 1 Cor. ii. 7, 10.

[3] Col. ii. 17 ; Heb. viii. 5.

[4] Matth. xi. 11, where it is said respecting John the Baptist, "notwithstanding he that is least ($\dot{o}$ $\mu\iota\kappa\rho\acute{o}\tau\epsilon\rho\sigma$) in the kingdom of heaven, is greater than he." The older English versions retained the comparative, and rendered " he that is *less* in the kingdom of heaven"—(Wickliffe, Tyndale, Cranmer, the Geneva); and so also Winer Greek Gr. § 36, 3, " he who occupies some lower place in the kingdom of heaven." Lightfoot, Hengstenberg, and many others approve of this *milder* sense, as it may be called ; but Alford in his recent commentary adheres still to the stronger, " the *least ;*" and so does Stier in his *Reden Jesu*, who, in illustrating the thought, goes so far as to say, " a mere child that knows the catechism, and can say the Lord's prayer, both knows and has more than the Old Testament can give, and so far stands higher and nearer to God than John the Baptist." One cannot but feel that this is putting something like a strain on our Lord's declaration.

grand reality itself came, and the higher purposes of Heaven entered on their fulfilment.[1]

2. The other fact pre-supposed and implied in the relation between type and antitype, namely, that God subjected the Church to a course of preparatory training, including instruction by types, before he introduced the realities of his final dispensation, is written with equal distinctness in the page of inspiration. It is scarcely possible, indeed, to dissociate even in idea the one fact from the other; for, without such a course of preparation being perpetually in progress, the long delay which took place in the introduction of the Messiah's kingdom would be quite inexplicable. Accordingly, the Church of the Old Testament is constantly represented as having been in a state of comparative childhood, supplied only with such means of instruction, and subjected to such methods of discipline as were suited to so imperfect and provisional a period of her being. Her law, in its higher aim and object, was a schoolmaster to bring men to Christ (Gal. iii. 24); and every thing in her condition—what it wanted, as well as what it possessed, what was done for her, and also what remained undone—concurred in pointing the way to Him, who was to come with the better promises and the perfected salvation (Heb. vii. viii. ix.) Such is the plain import of a great many Scriptures bearing on the subject.

It is to be noted, however, in regard to this course of preparation, continued through so many ages, that every thing in the mode of instruction and discipline employed ought not to be regarded as employed simply for the sake of those who lived during its continuance. It was, no doubt, primarily introduced on their account, and must have been wisely adapted to their circumstances, as under preparation for better things to come. But, at the same time, it must also, like the early training of a well educated youth, have been fitted to tell with beneficial effect on the spiritual life of the Church in her more advanced state of existence, after she had actually attained to those better things themselves. The man of mature age, when pursuing his way amid the perplexing cares and busy avocations of life, finds himself continually indebted to the lessons he was taught and the

---

[1] Rev. i. 8; Luke ii. 25; Acts x. 43, iv. 12; Rom. iii. 25; 1 Pet. i. 10-12, 20.

skill he has acquired during the period of his early culture. And, in like manner, it was undoubtedly God's intention that his method of procedure toward the Church in her state of minority, not only should minister what was needed for her immediate instruction and improvement, but should also furnish materials of edification and comfort for believers to the end of time. If the earlier could not be made perfect without the things belonging to the later Church (Heb. xi. 40), so neither, on the other hand, can the later profitably or even safely dispense with the advantage she may derive from the more simple and rudimentary things that belonged to the earlier. The Church, considered as God's nursery for training souls to a meetness for immortal life and blessedness, is substantially the same through all periods of her existence ; and the things which were appointed for the behoof of her members in one age, had in them also something of lasting benefit for those on whom the ends of the world are come (1 Cor. x. 6, 11.)

It is farther to be noted, that in this work of preparation for the more perfect future, arrangements of a typical kind, being of a somewhat recondite nature, necessarily occupied a relative and subsidiary, rather than the primary and most essential place. The church enjoyed from the first the benefit of direct and explicit instruction, imparted either immediately by the hand of God, or through the instrumentality of his accredited messengers. From this source she always derived her knowledge of the more fundamental truths of religion, and also her more definite expectations of the better things to come. The fact is of importance, both as determining the proper place of typical acts and institutions, and as indicating a kind of extraneous and qualifying element, that must not be overlooked in judging of the condition of believers under them. Yet they were not, on that account, rendered less valuable or necessary as constituent parts of a preparatory dispensation. For, it was through them, as temporary expedients, and by virtue of the resemblances they possessed to the higher things in prospect, that the realities of Christ's kingdom obtained a kind of present realization to the eye of faith. What, then, was the nature of these resemblances ? Wherein precisely did the similarity which formed more especially the preparatory element in the Old, as compared with the New, really lie ? This is the point that mainly calls for elucidation.

II. It is the second point we were to investigate, as being that which would necessarily require the most lengthened and careful examination. And the general statement we submit respecting it is, that two things were here essentially necessary : *there must have been in the Old the same great elements of truth as in the things they represented under the New ; and then, in the Old, these must have been exhibited in a form more level to the comprehension, more easily and distinctly cognizable by the minds of men.*

1. There must have been, first, the same great elements of truth—for the mind of God, and the circumstances of the fallen creature, are substantially the same at all times. What the spiritual necessities of men now are, they have been from the time that sin entered into the world. Hence the truth revealed by God to meet these necessities, however varying from time to time in the precise amount of its communications, and however differing also in the external form under which it might be presented, must have been, so far as disclosed, essentially one in every age. For, otherwise, what anomalous results would follow ? If the principles unfolded in God's communications to men, and on which he regulates his dealings toward them, were materially different at one period from what they are at another, then either the wants and necessities of men's natural condition must have undergone a change, or—these being the same, as they undoubtedly are—the character of God must have altered — he cannot be the immutable Jehovah. Besides, the very idea of a course of preparatory dispensations were, on the supposition in question, manifestly excluded ; since that could have no proper ground to rest on, unless there was a deep-rooted and fundamental agreement between what was temporary and what was final and ultimate in the matter. The primary and essential elements of truth, therefore, which are embodied in the facts of the Gospel, and on which its economy of grace is based, cannot, in the nature of things, be of recent origin—as if they were altogether peculiar to the New Testament dispensation, and had

only begun with the entrance of it to obtain a place in the government of God. On the contrary, their existence must have formed the ground-work, and their varied manifestation the progress of any preparatory dispensations that might be appointed. And whatever ulterior respect the typical characters, actions, or institutions of those earlier dispensations might carry to the coming realities of the Gospel, their more immediate intention and use must have consisted in the exhibition they gave of the vital and fundamental truths, common alike to all dispensations.

2. If a clear and conclusive certainty attaches to this part of our statement, it does so in even an increased ratio to the other. Holding that the same great elements of truth must of necessity pervade both type and antitype, we must unquestionably hold, that in the former they were more simply and palpably exhibited —presented in some shape in which the human mind could more easily and distinctly apprehend them—than in the latter. It would manifestly have been absurd to admit into a course of preparation for the realities of the Gospel, certain temporary exhibitions of the same great elements of truth that were to pervade these, unless the preparatory had been of more obvious meaning, and of more easy comprehension, than the ultimate and final. The transition from the one to the other must clearly have involved a rise in the mode of exhibiting the truth from a lower to a higher territory—from a form of developement more easily grasped, to a form which should put the faculties of the mind to a greater stretch. For thus only could it be wise or proper to set up preparatory dispensations at all. These, manifestly, had been better spared, if the realities themselves lay more, or even so much within the reach and comprehension of the mind, as their temporary and imperfect representations.

Standing, then, on the foundation of these two principles, as necessarily forming the essential elements of the resemblance that subsisted between the Old and the New in God's dispensations, we may now proceed to consider how far they can legitimately carry us in explaining the subject in hand ; or, in other words, to answer the question, how on such a basis the typical things of the past could properly serve as preparatory arrangements for the higher and better things of the future ? We shall endeavour to answer this question, in the first instance, by making application of our principles to the symbolical institutions of the Mosaic dispensation, which are usually denominated the *ritual* or *legal* types. For, in respect to these we have the advantage of the most explicit assertion in Scripture of their typical character; and we are also furnished with certain general descriptions of their nature as typical, which may partly serve as lights to direct our inquiries, and partly provide a test by which to try the correctness of our results.

Viewing the institutions of the dispensation brought in by Moses as typical, we look at them in what may be called their *secondary* aspect; we consider them as *prophetic symbols of the better things to come in the Gospel.* But this evidently implies that in another and more immediate respect they were merely symbols, that is, outward and sensible representations of Divine truth, in connection with an existing dispensation and a religious worship. It was only from their being this, in the one respect, that they could, in the other, be prophetic symbols, or types, of what was afterwards to appear under the Gospel; on the ground already stated, that the preparatory dispensation to which they belonged was necessarily inwrought with the same great elements of truth, which were afterwards, in another form, to pervade the Christian. Had there not been the identity of the truths here supposed, assimilating the two dispensations to each other amid all their outward diversities, the earlier would rather have blocked up than prepared and opened the way for the latter. A partial exhibition of a *truth*, or an embodiment of it in things comparatively little, easily grasped by the understanding, and but imperfectly satisfying the mind, may certainly make way for its exhibition in some more complete and perfect manner:—The mind thus familiarized to it in the little, may both have the desire created, and the capacity formed for beholding its developement in things of a far higher and nobler kind. But a partial or defective representation of an *object*, apart from any principles common to both, must rather tend to pre-occupy the mind, and either entirely prevent it from anticipating, or fill it with mistaken and prejudiced notions of, the reality. If such a representation of the mere objects of the Gospel had been all that was aimed at in the symbolical institutions of the Old Testament—if their direct, immediate, and only use had been to serve, as pictures, to prefigure and presentiate to the soul the future realities of the divine kingdom—then, who could wonder if these realities should have been wholly lost sight of before, or misbelieved and repudiated when they came? For, in that case, the preparatory dispensation must have been far more difficult for the worshipper than the ultimate one. The child must have had a much harder lesson to read, and a much higher task to accomplish, than the man of full-grown and ripened intellect. And divine wisdom must have employed its resources, not to smooth the Church's path to an enlightened view, and a believing reception of the realities of the Gospel, but to shroud them in the most profound and perplexing obscurities.

Every serious and intelligent believer will shrink from this conclusion. But if he does so, he will soon find, that there is only one way of effectually escaping from it; and that is, by regarding the symbolical institutions of the Old Covenant as not simply or directly representations of the realities of the Gospel, but in the first instance as parts of an existing dispensation, and, as such, expressive of certain great and fundamental truths, which could even then be distinctly understood and embraced. This was what might be called their more *immediate and ostensible* design. Their *further and prospective* reference to the higher objects of the Gospel, was of a more indirect and occult nature; and stood in the same essential truths being exhibited by means of present and visible, but inferior and comparatively inadequate objects. So that in tracing out the connection from the one to the other, we must always begin with inquiring, What, *per se*, was the native import of each symbol? What truths did it symbolize merely as part of an existing religion? and from this proceed to unfold how it was fitted to serve as a guide and a stepping-stone to the glorious events and issues of Messiah's kingdom. This—which it was the practice of the older typological writers in great measure to overlook—is really the foundation of the whole matter; and without it every typological system must either contract itself within very narrow bounds, or be in danger of running out into superficial or fanciful analogies. The Mosiac ritual had at once a shell and a kernel,—its shell, the outward rites and observances it enjoined; its kernel, the spiritual relations which these indicated and the spiritual truths which they embodied and expressed. Substantially, these truths and relations were, and must have been, the same for the Old that they are for the New Testament worshippers; for the spiritual wants and necessities of both are the same, and so also is the character of God, with whom they have to do. *There*, therefore, in that fundamental agreement, that internal and pre-established harmony of principle, we are to find the bond of union between the symbolical institutions of Judaism and the permanent realities of Messiah's kingdom. One truth in both—but that truth existing first in a lower, then in a higher stage of developement; in the one case, as a precious bud embosomed and but partially seen amid the imperfect relations of flesh and time; in the other expanded under the bright sunshine of heaven into all the beauty and fruitfulness of which it is susceptible.

To make our meaning perfectly understood, however, we must descend from the general to the particular, and apply what has been stated to a special case. In doing so, we shall go at once to what may justly be termed the very core of the religion of the Old Covenant—the right of expiatory sacrifice. That this was typical, or prophetically symbolical of the death of Christ, is testified with much plainness and frequency in New Testament Scripture. Yet, independently of this connection with Christ's death, it had a meaning of its own, which it was possible for the ancient worshipper to understand, and, so understanding, to present through it an acceptable service to God, whether he might perceive or not the further respect it bore to a dying Saviour. It was in its own nature a symbolical transaction, embodying a threefold idea; first, that the worshipper having been guilty of sin, had forfeited his life to God; then, that the life so forfeited must be surrendered to divine justice; and finally, that being surrendered in the way appointed, it was given back to him again by God, or he became re-established, as a justified person, in the divine favour and fellowship. How far a transaction of this kind, done symbolically and not really—by means of an irrational creature substituted in the sinner's room, and unconsciously devoted to lose its animal, in lieu of his intelligent and rational life—might commend itself as altogether satisfactory to his view; or how far he might see reason to regard it as but a provisional arrangement, proceeding on the contemplation of something more perfect yet to come—these are points which might justly be raised, and will indeed call for future discussion, but they are somewhat extraneous to the subject itself now under consideration. We are viewing the right of expiatory sacrifice simply as a constituent part of ancient worship—a religious service, which formally, and without notification from itself of anything farther being required, presented the sinner with the divinely appointed means of reconciliation and restored fellowship with God. In this respect it symbolically represented, as we have said, a threefold idea, which if properly understood and realized by the worshipper, he performed, in offering it, an acceptable service. And when we rise from the symbolical to the typical view of the transaction—when we proceed to consider the right of expiation as bearing a prospective reference to the redemption of Christ, we are not to be understood as ascribing to it some new sense or meaning; we merely express our belief that the complex capital idea which it so impressively symbolized, finds its only true, as from the first, its destined realization, in the work of salvation by Jesus Christ. For, in him alone was there a real transference of man's guilt to one able and willing to bear it—in his death alone, the surrender of a life to God, such as could fitly stand in the room of that forfeited by the sinner—and in faith alone on his death, a full and conscious appropriation of the life of peace and blessing obtained by him for the justified. So that here only it is we perceive the idea of a true, sufficient, and perfect sacrifice converted into a living reality—such as the holy eye of God, and the troubled conscience of man, can alike rest on with perfect satisfaction. And while there appear precisely the same elements of truth in the ever-recurring sacrifices of the Old Testament, and in the one perfect sacrifice of the New, it is seen, at the same time, that what the one symbolically represented, the other actually possessed; what the one could only exhibit as a kind of acted lesson for the present relief of guilty consciences, the other makes known to us, as a work finally and for ever accomplished for all who believe in the propitiation of the cross.

The view now given of the symbolical institutions of the Old Testament, as prophetic symbols of the realities of the Gospel, is in perfect accordance with the general descriptions we have of their nature in Scripture itself. These are of two classes. In the one they are declared to have been *shadows* of the better things of the Gospel; as in Heb. x. 1, where the law is said to have had " a shadow, and not the very image of good things to come ;" in ch. viii. 5, where the priests are described as " serving unto the example (copy) and shadow of heavenly things ;" and again in Col. ii. 16, where the fleshly ordinances in one mass are denominated " shadows of good things to come," while it is added, " the body is of Christ." Now, that the tabernacle, with the ordinances of every kind belonging to it, were shadows of Christ and the blessings of his kingdom, can only mean that they were obscure and imperfect resemblances of these; or that they embodied the same elements of divine truth, but wanted what was necessary to give them proper form and consistence as parts of a final and abiding dispensation of God. And when we go to inquire, wherein did the obscurity and imperfection consist, we are always referred to the carnal and earthly nature of the Old as compared with the New. The tabernacle itself was a material fabric, constructed of such things as this present world could supply, and hence called " a worldly sanctuary ;" while its counterpart under the Gospel is the eternal region of God's presence and glory, neither discernible by fleshly eye, nor made by mortal hands. In like manner, the ordinances of worship connected with the tabernacle were all ostensibly directed to the preservation of men's present existence, or the advancement of their wellbeing as related to an outward sanctuary and a terrestrial commonwealth; while in the Gospel it is the soul's relation to the sanctuary above, and its possession of an immortal life of blessedness and glory, which all is directly intended to provide for. In these differences between the Old and the New, which bespeak so much of inferiority on the part of the former, we perceive the darkness and imperfection which hung around the things of the ancient dispensation, and rendered them shadows only of those which were to come. But still shadows are resemblances. Though unlike in one respect, they must be like in another. And as the unlikeness stood in the dissimilar nature of the things immediately handled and perceived—in the different *materiel*, so to speak, of the two dispensations, wherein should the resemblance be found but in the common truths and relations alike pervading both ? By means of an earthly tabernacle, with its appropriate services, God manifested toward his people the same principles of government, and required from them substantially the same disposition and character that he does now under the higher dispensation of the Gospel. For, look beyond the mere outward diversities, and what do you see? You see in both alike a pure and holy God, enshrined in the recesses of a glorious sanctuary—unapproachable by sinful flesh but through a medium of powerful intercession and cleansing efficacy—yet when so approached, ever ready to receive and bless with the richest tokens of his favour and lovingkindness as many as come in the exercise of genuine contrition for sin, and longing for restored fellowship with the God they have offended. The same description applies equally to the service of both dispensations; for in both the same impressions are conveyed of God's character respecting sin and holiness, and the same gracious feelings necessarily awakened in the bosom of sincere worshippers in regard to them. But then, as to the means of accomplishing this, there was only, in the one case, a shadowy exhibition of spiritual things through earthly materials and temporary expedients, while, in the other, the naked realities appear in the one perfect sacrifice of Christ, the rich endowments of grace, and the glories of an everlasting kingdom.

The other general description given in New Testament Scripture of the prophetic symbols or types of the old dispensation does not materially differ from the one now considered, and, when rightly understood, leads to the same result. According to it the religious institutions of earlier times contained the *rudiments* or elementary principles of the world's religious truth and life. Thus in Col. ii. 20, the now antiquated ordinances of Judaism are called " the rudiments of the world;" and in Gal. iv. 3, the church, while under these ordinances, is said to have been " in bondage under the elements or rudiments of the world." The expression also, which is found in ch. iii. 24 of this Epistle to the Galatians, " the law was our schoolmaster to bring us to Christ," conveys much the same idea; since it is the special business of a schoolmaster to communicate to those under his charge the rudiments of learning, by which their minds may in due time be prepared for the higher walks of science and literature. The law certainly did this, to a considerable extent, by direct instruction in the great principles of truth and duty. But it did so not less by means of its symbolical institutions and ordinances, which were in themselves inherently defective, and yet in their spirit and design entirely analogous to the higher things of the Gospel. The animal, the fleshly, the material, the temporal, was what alone appeared in them, when viewed in respect merely to their ostensible character and object; all, however, moulded and arranged, so as to exhibit ideas and relations that reached far beyond these, and could only, indeed, find their suitable developement in things spiritual, heavenly, and eternal. The church had then to be dealt with after the manner of a child. But the child must have instruction administered to him in a form adapted to his juvenile capacities. If he is to be prepared for apprehending the outlines and proportions of the globe, these must be presented to his view on diagrams of a few spans long. Or, if he is to be made acquainted with the laws and principles which bear sway throughout the material universe, he must again see them exemplified in miniature among the small and familiar objects of every day life. In like manner, the church of the Old Testament, while in bondage to fleshly institutions and services, yet received through these the rudiments of all divine truth and wisdom. In a form which the eye of a spiritual babe could scan, and its hand, in a manner, grasp, she had constantly exhibited before her the essential truths and principles of God's everlasting kingdom. And nothing more was needed than that the instruction thus imparted should have been impartially received and properly cultivated, in order to fit the disciple of Moses for passing with intelligence and delight from his rudimental tutelage, under the *shadows* of good things, into the free use and enjoyment of the things themselves.

The general descriptions, then, given of the symbolical institutions and services of the Old Testament, in their relation to the Gospel, perfectly accord with the principles we have advanced. And viewed in the light now presented, we at once see the essential unity that subsists between the Old and the New dispensations, and the nature of that progression in the divine plan, which rendered the one a fitting preparation and stepping-stone to the other. In its fundamental elements the religion of both covenants is thus found to be identical. Only it appears under the old covenant as on a lower platform, disclosing its ideas, and imparting its blessings through the imperfect instrumentalities of fleshly relations and temporal concerns; while under the new every thing rises heavenwards, and eternal realities come distinctly and prominently into view. But as ideas and relations are more palpable to the mind, and lie more within the grasp of its comprehension, when exhibited on a small scale, in corporeal forms, amid familiar and present objects, than on a scale of large dimensions, which stretches into the unseen, and embraces alike the divine and human, time and eternity; so the economy of outward symbolical institutions was in itself simpler than the Gospel, and, as a lower exhibition of divine truth, prepared the way for a higher. But they did this, let it be observed, in their character merely *as symbolical institutions*, or parts of a dispensation then existing, not as typically foreshadowing the things belonging to a higher and more spiritual dispensation yet to come. It was comparatively an easy thing for the Jewish worshipper to understand how, from time to time, he stood related to a visible sanctuary and an earthly inheritance, or to go through the process of an appointed purification by means of water and the blood of slain victims applied externally to his body:—much more easy than for the Christian to apprehend distinctly his relation to an heavenly sanctuary, and realize the cleansing of his conscience from all guilt by the inward application of the sacrifice of Christ and the regenerating grace of the Holy Spirit. But for the Jewish worshipper to do both his own and the Christian's part—both to read the meaning of the symbol as expressive of what was already laid open to his view, and to descry its concealed reference to the yet undiscovered realities of a better dispensation, would have required a reach of discernment and a strength of faith far beyond what is now needed in the Christian. For this had been, not like him to discern the heavenly, when the heavenly had come, but to do it amid the obscurities and imperfections of the earthly; not simply to look with open eye into the deeper mysteries of God's kingdom, when these mysteries are fully disclosed, but to do so while they were still buried amid the thick folds of a cumbrous and overshadowing drapery.

Yet let us not be mistaken. We speak merely of what was strictly required, and what might ordinarily be expected of the ancient worshipper, in connection with the institutions and services of his symbolical religion, taken simply by themselves. We do not say that there *never was*, much less that there *could not be*, any proper insight obtained by the children of the old covenant into the future mysteries of the Gospel. There were special gifts of grace then, as well as now, occasionally imparted to the more spiritual members of the covenant, which enabled them to rise to unusual degrees of knowledge; and it is a distinctive property of the spiritual mind generally to be dissatisfied with the imperfect, to seek and long for the perfect. Even now, when the comparatively perfect has come, what spiritual mind is not often conscious to itself of a feeling akin to melancholy, when it thinks of the yet abiding darkness and disorders of the present, or does not fondly cling to every hopeful indication of a brighter future? But even the *best* things of the old covenant bore on them the stamp of imperfection. The temple itself, which was the peculiar glory and ornament of Israel, still in a very partial and defective manner realised its own grand idea of a people dwelling with God, and God dwelling with them; and hence, because of that inherent imperfection (it was plainly declared), a higher and better mode of accomplishing the object should one day take its place (Jer. iii. 16, 17). So, too, the palpable disproportion already noticed in the rite of expiatory sacrifice between the rational life forfeited through sin, and the merely animal life substituted in its room, seemed to proclaim the necessity of a more adequate atonement for human guilt, and could not but dispose intelligent worshippers to give more earnest heed to the announcements of prophecy regarding the coming purposes of heaven. But yet, when we have admitted all this, it by no means follows that the people of God generally, under the old covenant, could attain to very definite views of the realities of the Gospel; nor does it furnish us with any reason for asserting that such views must ever of necessity have mingled with the service of an acceptable worshipper. For, his was the worship of a preparatory dispensation. It must, therefore, have been simpler and easier than what was ultimately to supplant it. And this, we again repeat, it could only be by being viewed in its more obvious and formal aspect, as the worship of an existing religion, which provided for the time then present a fitting medium of access to God, and hallowed intercourse with heaven. The man who humbly availed himself of what was thus provided to meet his soul's necessities, stood in faith, and served God with acceptance—though still with such imperfections in the present, and such promises for the future, that the more always he reflected, he would become the more a child of desire and hope.[1]

We have spoken as yet only of the symbolical institutions and services of the Old Testament; and of these quite generally, as one great whole. For it is carefully to be noted, that the Scriptural designations of rudiments and shadows, which we have shewn to be the same as typical, when properly understood, are applied to the entire mass of the ancient ordinances in their prospective reference to Gospel realities. And yet, while New Testament Scripture speaks thus of the whole, it deals very sparingly in particular examples; and if it furnishes, in its language and allusions, many valuable hints to direct inquiry, it still contains remarkably few detailed illustrations. It nowhere tells us, for example, what was either immediately symbolized, or prophetically shadowed forth, by the Holy Place in the tabernacle, or the shew-bread, or the golden candlestick, or the ark of the cove-

---

[1] If any one will take the trouble to look into the older writers, who formally examined the typical character of the ancient symbolical institutions, he will find them entirely silent in regard to the points chiefly dwelt upon in the above discussion. Lowman, for example, on the Rational of the Hebrew Worship, and Outram de Sac. Lib. i. c. 18, where he comes to consider the nature and force of a type, give no proper or satisfactory explanation of the questions, wherein precisely did the resemblance stand between the type and the antitype, or how should the one have prepared the way for the other. We are told frequently enough, that the "Hebrew ritual contained a plan, or sketch, or pattern, or shadow of Gospel things:" that "the type adumbrated the antitype by something of the same sort with that which is found in the antitype," or "by a symbol of it," or "by a slender and shadowy image of it," or "by something that may somehow be compared with it," &c. But we look in vain for anything more specific. Townley, in his Reasons of the Laws of Moses, still advances no farther in the Dissertation he devotes to the Typical Character of the Mosaic Institutions. Even Olshausen, in the treatise formerly noticed (Ein Wort über tiefern Schriftsinn), when he comes to unfold what he calls his deeper exposition, confines himself to a brief illustration of the few general statements formerly mentioned. See p. 44.

nant, or, indeed, by anything connected with the tabernacle, excepting its more prominent offices and ministrations. Even the Epistle to the Hebrews, which enters with such comparative fulness into the connection between the Old and the New, and which is most express in ascribing a typical value to all that belonged to the tabernacle, can yet scarcely be said to give any detailed explanation of its furniture and services beyond the rite of expiatory sacrifice, and the action of the high priest in presenting it, more particularly on the great day of atonement. So that those who insist on an explicit warrant and direction from Scripture in regard to each particular type, will find their principle conducts them but a short way even through that department, which, they are obliged to admit, possesses throughout a typical character. A general admission of this sort can be of little use, if one is restrained on principle from touching most of the particulars; one might as well maintain that these did not in any degree partake of the typical element. So, indeed, Bishop Marsh has substantially done; for, " that such explanations," he says, referring to particular types, " are in various instances given in the New Testament, no one can deny. And if it was deemed necessary to explain one type, where could be the expediency or moral fitness of withholding the explanation of others? Must not, therefore, the *silence* of the New Testament in the case of any *supposed* type, be an argument against the existence of that type?"[1] Undoubtedly, we reply, if the Scriptures of the New Testament professed to illustrate the whole field of typical matter in God's ancient dispensations; but by no means, if, as is really the case, they only take it up in detached portions, by way of occasional example; and still less if the effect would be practically to exclude from the character of types many of the very institutions and services which are declared to have been all " shadows of good things to come, whereof the body is Christ." How we ought to proceed in applying the general views that have been unfolded to the interpretation of such parts of the Old Testament symbols as have not been explained in New Testament Scripture, will no doubt require careful consideration. But that we are both warranted and bound to give them a Christian interpretation, is manifest from the

[1] Lectures, p. 392.

general character that is ascribed to them. And the fact that so much of what was given to Moses as " a testimony (or evidence) of those things which were to be spoken after" in Christ, remains without any particular explanation in Scripture, sufficiently justifies us in expecting that there may also be much typical, though unexplained matter, in the other, the historical department of the subject, which we now proceed to investigate.

CHAPTER THIRD.

THE SAME SUBJECT CONTINUED, BUT WITH A VIEW MORE ESPECIALLY TO THE SOLUTION OF THE QUESTION, WHETHER OR HOW FAR THE HISTORICAL CHARACTERS AND TRANSACTIONS OF THE OLD TESTAMENT MAY BE REGARDED AS TYPICAL?—HISTORICAL TYPES.

In the preceding chapter we have seen in what sense the religious institutions and services of the old covenant were typical. They were constructed and arranged so as to express symbolically the great truths and principles of a spiritual religion—truths and principles which were common alike to Old and New Testament times, but which, from the nature of things, could only find in the New their proper developement and full realisation. On the limited scale of the earthly and perishable—in the construction of a material tabernacle, and the suitable adjustment of bodily ministrations and sacrificial offerings,—there was presented a palpable exhibition of those great truths respecting sin and salvation, the purification of the heart, and the dedication of the person and the life to God, which in the fulness of time were openly revealed and manifested on the grand scale of a world's redemption, by the mediation and work of Jesus Christ. In that pre-arranged and harmonious, but still inherently defective and imperfect exhibition of the fundamental ideas and spiritual relations of the Gospel, stood the real nature of its typical character.

Nor, we may add, was there anything arbitrary in so employing the things of flesh and time to shadow forth, under a preparatory dispensation, the higher realities of God's everlasting kingdom. It has its ground and reason in the organic arrangements or appearances of the material world. For these are so framed as to be ever giving forth representations of divine truth, and are a kind of ceaseless regeneration, in which, through successive stages, new and higher forms of being are continually springing out of the lower. It is on this constitution of nature that the figurative language of Scripture is based. And it was only building on a foundation that already existed, and which stretches far and wide through the visible territory of creation, when the outward relations and fleshly services of a symbolical religion were made to image and prepare for the more spiritual and divine mysteries of Messiah's kingdom. Hence, also, some of the more important symbolical institutions were expressly linked (as we shall see) to appropriate seasons and aspects of nature.

But was symbol alone thus employed? Might there not also have been a similar employment of many circumstances and transactions in the province of sacred history? Might not God have, in many respects, disposed the events of his providence, and appointed the external relations of his people, as well as framed the institutions of his worship, so as to give, by means of them, like exhibitions of the better things of the Gospel? If the revelation of the Lord Jesus Christ, with the blessings of his great salvation, was the object mainly contemplated by God from the beginning of the world, and with which the Church was ever travailing in birth—if, consequently, the previous dispensations were chiefly designed to lead to, and terminate upon, Christ and the things of his salvation:—what can be more natural than to suppose that the evolutions of providence throughout the period during which the salvation was preparing, should have concurred with the symbols of worship in imaging and preparing for what was to come? It is possible, indeed, that the connection here, between the past and the future, might be somewhat more varied and fluctuating, and in several respects less close and exact, than in the case of a compact system of religious symbols of worship, appointed to last till they were superseded by the better things of the New dispensation. This is only what might be expected from the respective natures of the two departments referred to. But that a connection, similar in kind, had a place in the one as well as in the other, we think not only in itself probable, but capable of being satisfactorily established. And in support of it we advance the following considerations:—First, That the historical relations and circumstances recorded in the Old Testament, and typically interpreted in the New, had very much the same resemblances and the same defects in respect to the realities of the Gospel, which we have found to belong to the ancient symbolical institutions of worship; Secondly, That such historical types were absolutely necessary, in considerable number and variety, to render the earlier dispensations thoroughly preparative in respect to the coming dispensation of the Gospel: And, thirdly, that Old Testament Scripture itself contains undoubted indications, that much of its historical matter stood related to some higher ideal, in which the truths and relations exemplified in them were again to meet and receive a new but more perfect developement.

I. The first consideration is, that the historical relations and circumstances recorded in the Old Testament, and typically interpreted in the New, had very much the same resemblances and defects, in respect to the Gospel, which we have found to belong to the ancient symbolical institutions of worship. Thus—to refer to one of the earliest events in the world's history so interpreted—the general deluge, that destroyed the old world, and preserved Noah and his family alive, is represented as standing in a typical relation to Christian baptism (1 Pet. iii. 21). It did so, as will be explained more at large hereafter, from its having destroyed those who, by their corruptions, destroyed the earth, and saved for a new world the germ of a better race. Doing this in the outward and lower territory of the world's history, it served substantially the same purpose that Christian baptism does in a higher; since this is designed to bring the individual that receives it under those vital influences that purge away the corruption of a fleshly nature, and cause the seed of a divine life to take root and grow for the occupation of a better inheritance. In like manner, Sarah, with her child of promise, the special and peculiar gift of heaven, and Hagar, with her merely natural and fleshly offspring, are explained as typically foreshadowing, the one a spiritual church, bringing forth real children to God, in spirit and destiny as well as in calling, the heirs of his everlasting kingdom; the other, a worldly and corrupt church, whose members are in bondage to the flesh, having but a name to live, while they are dead. (Gal. iv. 22, 31.) In such cases, it is clear that the same kind of resemblances, coupled also with the same kind of differences, appear between the preparatory and the final, as in the case of the symbolical types. For here also the ideas and relations are substantially one in the two associated transactions; only in the earlier they appear ostensibly connected with the theatre alone of an earthly existence, and with respect to seen and temporal results; while in the later it is the higher field of grace and the interests of a spiritual and immortal existence that come directly into view.

Or, look again to the use made of the events that befel the Israelites on their way to the land of Canaan, as regards the state and prospects of the Church of the New Testament on its way to Heaven. Look at this, for example, as unfolded in the third and fourth chapters of the epistle to the Hebrews, and the essential features of a typical connection will at once be seen. For, the exclusion of those carnal and unbelieving Israelites, who fell in the wilderness, is there exhibited, not only as affording a reasonable presumption, but as providing a valid ground for asserting, that persons similarly affected now toward the kingdom of glory cannot attain to Heaven. Indeed, so complete in point of principle is the identity of the two cases, that the same expressions are applied to both alike, without intimation of any differences existing between them: " the Gospel is preached" to the one class as well as to the other; God gives to each alike " a promise of rest," while they equally "fall through unbelief," having hardened their hearts against the word of God. Yet there were the same differences in kind as we have noted between the type and the antitype in the symbolical institutions of worship—the visible and earthly being employed in the one to exhibit such relations and principles as in the other appear in immediate connection with what is spiritual and heavenly. In the type we have the prospect of Canaan, the Gospel of an *earthly* promise of rest, and, because not believed, issuing in the loss of a *present* life of honour and blessing; in the antitype, the prospect of a *heavenly* inheritance, the Gospel promise of an *everlasting* rest, bringing along with it, in the experience of such as reject it, the fearful loss of *eternal* blessedness and glory.

Again, and with reference to the same period in the Church's history, it is said in John iii. 14-15, " As Moses lifted up the serpent in the wilderness, so must the Son of Man be lifted up, that whosoever believeth in him should not perish, but have everlasting life." The language here certainly does not necessarily betoken by any means so close a connection between the

Old and the New, as in the cases previously referred to ; nor are we disposed to assert that the same connection in all respects really existed. The historical transaction in this case had at first sight the aspect of something occasional and isolated, rather than of an integral and essential part of a great plan. And yet the reference in John, viewed in connection with other passages of Scripture bearing on the subject, sufficiently vindicates for it a place among the earlier exhibitions of divine truth, planned by the foreseeing eye of God with special respect to the coming realities of the Gospel. As such it entirely accords in nature with the typical prefigurations already noticed. In the two related transactions there is a fitting correspondence as to the relations maintained: in both alike a wounded and dying condition in the first instance, then the elevation of an object apparently inadequate, yet really effectual, to accomplish the cure, and this through no other medium on the part of the affected, than their simply looking to the object so presented to their view. But with this pervading correspondence, what marked and distinctive characteristics! In the one case a dying body, in the other a perishing soul. There an uplifted serpent, of all instruments of healing from a serpent's bite the most unpromising ; here the exhibition of one condemned and crucified as a malefactor, of all conceivable persons apparently the most impotent to save. There, once more, the fleshly eye of nature deriving from the outward object visibly presented to it the healing virtue it was ordained to impart ; and here the spiritual eye of the soul, looking in steadfast faith to the exalted Redeemer, and getting the needed supplies of his life-giving and regenerating grace. In both the same elements of truth, the same modes of dealing, but in the one developing themselves on a lower, in the other on a higher territory ; in the former having immediate respect only to things seen and temporal, and in the latter to what is unseen, spiritual, and eternal. And when it is considered how the divine procedure, in the case of the Israelites, was in itself so extraordinary and peculiar, so unlike God's usual methods of dealing in providence, and yet directly bore only on their inferior and perishable interests, it seems to be, without any adequate reason, to want, in a sense, its due explanation, until it is viewed as a dispensation specially designed to prepare the way for the higher and better things of the Gospel.

Similar explanations might be given of the other historical facts recorded in Old Testament Scripture, and invested with a typical reference in the New. But enough has been said to shew the essential similarity in the respect borne by them to the better things of the Gospel, and of that borne by the ritual types of the law. The ground of the connection in the one class, precisely as in the other, stands in the substantial oneness of the ideas and relations pervading the earlier and the later transactions, as corresponding parts of related dispensations; or in the identity of truth and principle appearing in both, as different, yet mutually dependent parts of one great providential scheme. In that internal agreement and relationship, rather than in any mere outward resemblances, we are to seek the real bond of connection between the Old and the New.

At first sight, perhaps, a connection of this nature may appear to want something of what is required to satisfy the conditions of a proper typical relationship. And there are two respects more especially, in which this deficiency may seem to exist.

1. It has been so much the practice to look at the connection between the Old and the New in an external aspect, that one naturally fancies the necessity of some more palpable and arbitrary bond of union to link together type and antitype. The one is apt to be thought of as a kind of pre-ordained pantomime of the other—like those pre-figurative actions which the prophets were sometimes instructed, whether in reality or in vision, to perform (as Isaiah in ch. xx, or Ezekiel in ch. xii.), meaningless in themselves, yet very significant as foreshadowing intimations of coming events in providence. Such prophecies in action, certainly, had something in common with the typical transactions now under consideration. They both alike had respect to other actions or events yet to come, without which, pre-ordained and foreseen, they would not have taken place. They both also stood in a similar relation of littleness to the corresponding circumstances they foreshadowed—exhibiting on a comparatively small scale what was afterwards to realize itself on a large one, and thereby enabling the mind more readily to anticipate the approaching future, or more distinctly to grasp it after it had come. But they differed in this, that the typical actions of the prophets had respect *solely* to the coming transactions they prefigured,

and but for these would have been foolish and absurd; while the typical actions of God's providence, as well as the symbolical institutions of his worship, had a moral meaning of their own, independently of the reference they bore to the future revelations of the Gospel. To overlook this independent moral element, is to leave out of account what should be held to constitute the very basis of the connection between the past and the future. But if, on the other hand, we make due account of it, we establish a connection, which, in reality, is of a much more close and vital nature, and one, too, of far higher importance, than if it consisted alone in points of outward resemblance. For it implies not only that the entire plan of salvation was all along in the eye of God, but that, with a view to it, he was ever directing his government, so as to bring out in successive stages and operations the very truths and principles, which were to find in the realities of the Gospel their more complete manifestation. He shewed, that he saw the end from the beginning by interweaving with his providential arrangements the elements of the more perfect, the terminal plan. And, therefore, to lay the ground-work of the connection between the preparatory and the final in the elements of truth and principle common alike to both, instead of placing it in merely formal resemblances, is but to withdraw it from a less to a more vital and important part of the transactions—from the outer shell and appearance, to the inner truth and substance of the history; so that we can discern, not only some perceptible coincidences between the type and the antitype, but the same fundamental character, the same spirit of life, the same moral import and practical design.

To render this more manifest, as it is a point of considerable moment in our inquiry, let us compare an alleged example of historical type, where the resemblance between it and the supposed antitype is of an ostensible, but still only of an outward kind, with one of those referred to above—the brazen serpent, for example, or the deluge. In this latter example there was scarcely *any* outward resemblance presented to the Christian ordinance of baptism; as in no proper sense could Noah and his family be said to have been literally baptized in the waters. But both this and the other historical transaction presented strong lines of resemblance, of a more inward and substantial kind, to the things connected with them in the Gospel—such as enable us to recognize without difficulty the impress of one divine hand in the two related series of transactions, and to contemplate them as corresponding parts of one grand economy, rising gradually from its lower to its higher stages of developement. Take, however, as an example of the other class, the occupation of Abel as a shepherd, which by many, among others by Witsius, has been regarded as a prefiguration of Christ in his character as the great Shepherd of Israel. A superficial likeness, we admit; but what is to be found of real unity and agreement ? What light does the one throw upon the other ? What expectation beforehand could the earlier beget of the later, or what confirmation afterwards can it supply ? Admitting that the death of Abel somehow foreshadowed the infinitely more precious blood to be shed on Calvary, what distinctive value could the sacrifice of life in his case derive from the previous occupation of the martyr ? Christ, certainly, died as the spiritual shepherd of souls, but Abel was not murdered on account of having been a keeper of sheep ; nor had his death any necessary connection with his having followed such an employment. For what purpose, then, press points of resemblance so utterly disconnected, and dignify them with the name of typical prefigurations ? resemblances, worthless even if real, and from their nature incapable of affording any insight into the mind and purposes of God ? But when, on the contrary, we look into the past records of God's providence, and find there in the dealings of his hand and the institutions of his worship a coincidence of principle and economical design with what appears in the dispensation of the Gospel, we cannot but feel that we have something of real weight and importance to grapple with. And if, farther, we have reason to conclude, not only that agreements of this kind existed, but that they were all skilfully planned and arranged—the earlier with a view to the later, the earthly and temporal for the spiritual and heavenly—we find ourselves possessed of the essential elements of a typical connection. But we *have* reason so to conclude, as has partly been shewn already, and will still farther be shewn in the sequel.

2. Granting, however, what has now been stated—granting that the connection between type and antitype is more of an internal than of an external kind, it may still be objected, in regard to the

historical types, that they wanted for the most part something of the necessary correspondence with the antitypes; the one did not occupy under the Old the same relative place that the other did under the New—existing for a time as a shadow until it was superseded and displaced by the substance. Perhaps not; but is such a close and minute correspondence absolutely necessary? Or is it to be found even in the case of all the symbolical types? With them also considerable differences appear; and we look in vain for anything like a fixed and absolute uniformity. The correspondence assumed the most exact form in the sacrificial *rites of the tabernacle worship. There*, certainly, part may be said to have answered to part; there was priest for priest, offering for offering, death for death, and blessing for blessing—throughout, an inferior and temporary substitute in the room of the proper reality, and continuing till it was superseded and displaced by the latter. We find a relaxation, however, in this closely adjusted relationship, whenever we leave the immediate province of sacrifice; and in many of the things expressly denominated shadows of the Gospel, it can hardly be said to have existed. In regard, for example, to the ancient festivals, the new moons, the use or disuse of leaven, the defilement of leprosy and its purification, there was no such precise and definite superseding of the Old by something corresponding under the New—nothing like office for office, action for action, part for part. The symbolical rites and institutions referred to were typical—not, however, as representing things that were to hold specifically and palpably the same place in Gospel times—but rather as embodying in set forms and ever-recurring bodily services the truths and principles, that in naked simplicity and by direct teaching, were to pervade the dispensation of the Gospel.

There is quite a similar diversity in the case of the historical types. In some of them the correspondence was very close and exact; in others more loose and general. Of the former class was the calling of Israel as an elect people, their relation to the land of Canaan, as their covenant-portion, their redemption from the yoke of Egypt, and their temporary sojourn in the wilderness as they travelled to inherit it—all of which continued (the two latter by means of commemorative ordinances) till they were superseded by corresponding but higher objects under the Gospel.

In respect to these we can say, the new dispensation presents people for people, redemption for redemption, inheritance for inheritance, and one kind of wilderness-training for another; objects precisely corresponding in the relations they severally occupied, and the one preserving their existence or transmitting their efficacy, till they were supplanted by the other. But we do not pretend to see the same close connection and the same exact correspondence between the Old and the New in all, or even the greater part of the historical transactions of the past, which we hold to have been typical; nor are we warranted to look for it. The analogy of the symbolical types would lead us to expect, along with the more direct typical arrangements, many acts and institutions of a somewhat incidental and subordinate kind, in which a typical representation should be given of ideas and relations, that could only find in the realities of the Gospel their full and proper manifestation. If they were not appointed as temporary substitutes for these realities, and kept in operation or perpetually commemorated, till the better things took their place, they were still moulded after the form and pattern of the better. They were designed by God, not, it may be, to present to men's minds the events and objects of the Gospel, but at least to acquaint them with its elements of truth, and to familiarize them with its spiritual ideas, its modes of procedure and principles of working. And in this they plainly possessed the more essential part of a typical connection.

II. Enough, however, for the first point. We proceed to the second; which is, that such historical types as those under consideration, were absolutely necessary, in considerable number and variety, to render the earlier dispensations thoroughly preparative in respect to the coming dispensation of the Gospel. This was necessary, first of all, from the typical character of the position and worship of the members of the old covenant. The main things respecting them being, as we have seen, typical, it was inevitable but that many others of a subordinate and collateral nature should be the same; for otherwise they would not have been suitably adapted to the dispensation to which they belonged.

But we have something more than this general correspondence or analogy to appeal to. For, the nature of the historical types themselves, as already explained, implies their existence in considerable number and variety. The representation they were designed to give of the fundamental truths and principles of the Gospel, with the view of preparing the church for the new dispensation, would necessarily have been incomplete and inadequate, unless it had embraced a pretty extensive field. The object of their appointment would have been but partially reached, if they had consisted only of the few straggling examples which have been particularly mentioned in New Testament Scripture. Nor, unless the history in general of Old Testament times, in so far as its recorded transactions bore on them the stamp of God's mind and will, had been pervaded by the typical element, could it have in any competent measure fulfilled the design of a preparatory economy. So that whatever distinctions it may be necessary to draw between one part of the transactions and another, as to their being in themselves sometimes of a more essential, sometimes of a more incidental character, or in their typical bearing being more or less closely related to the realities of the Gospel, their very place and object in a shadowy dispensation required them to be extensively typical. To be spread over a large field, and branched out in many directions, was as necessary to their typical, as to their more immediate and temporary design.

Thus the one point grows by a sort of natural necessity out of the other. But the argument admits of being considerably strengthened by the manner in which the historical types that *are* specially mentioned in New Testament Scripture are there referred to. So far from being represented as singular in their typical reference to Gospel times, they have uniformly the appearance of being only selected for the occasion. Nay, the obligation on the part of believers generally to seek for them throughout the Old Testament Scriptures, and apply them to all the purposes of Christian instruction and improvement, is distinctly asserted in the epistle to the Hebrews; and the capacity to do so is represented as a proof of full-grown spiritual discernment (Heb. v. 11-14). There is, therefore, a sense in which the saying of Augustine,—" The Old Testament, when rightly understood, is one great prophecy of the New,"[1] is strictly true even in regard to those parts of ancient Scripture, which, in their direct and immediate bearing, partake least of the prophetical. Its records of the past are, at the same time, pregnant with the germs of a corresponding but more exalted future. The relations sustained by its more public characters, the parts they were appointed to act in their day and generation, the deliverances that were wrought for them and by them, and the chastisements they were from time to time given to experience, did not begin and terminate with themselves. They were parts of an unfinished and progressive plan, which finds its destined completion in the person and kingdom of Christ; and only when seen in this prospective reference do they appear in their proper magnitude and their full significance.

Christ, then, is the end of the history as well as of the law, of the Old Testament. It had been strange, indeed, if it were otherwise; strange if its historical transactions had not been ordained by God, in another manner than the common events of history, to bear a prospective reference to the Gospel scheme. For what is this scheme itself, in its fundamental character, but a grand historical developement? What are the doctrines it teaches, the blessings it imparts, and the promises it unfolds of everlasting glory, but the reflection and fruit of its recorded facts—the facts, namely, of the incarnation and life, the death and resurrection, of the Lord Jesus Christ? These are the foundation on which all rests, the root from which everything springs in Christianity. And shall it, then, be imagined, that the earlier facts in the history of related and preparatory dispensations did not point, like so many heralds and forerunners, to these unspeakably greater ones to come? If a prophecy lay concealed in their symbolical rites, could it fail to be found also in the historical transactions, that were often so closely allied to these, and always coincident with them in purpose and design? Assuredly not. In so far as God spake in the transactions, and gave discoveries by them of his truth and character, they typically bore respect to the one "pattern-man," and the terminal kingdom of righteousness and blessing,

---

[1] Vetus Testamentum recte intelligentibus prophetia est Novi Testamenti (Contra Faust. L. xv. 2.) And again, Ille apparatus veteris Testamenti in generationibus, factis etc. parturiebat esse venturum (Ib. L. xix. 31.)

of which he was to be the head and centre. Here only the history of God's earlier dispensations attained its proper end, as in this also the history of the world finds its grand turning-point.[1]

III. The thought, however, may very naturally occur, that if the historical matter of the Old Testament possess as much as we represent of a typical character, some plain indications of its being so should be found in Old Testament Scripture itself. We should scarcely need to draw our proof of the existence and nature of the historical types entirely from the writings of the New Testament. It was with the view of meeting this thought that we advanced our third statement; which is, that Old Testament Scripture does contain undoubted marks and indications of its historical personages and events being related to some higher ideal, in which the truths and relations exhibited in them were again to meet, and obtain a more adequate developement. The proof of this is to be sought chiefly in the prophetical writings of the Old Testament, in which the more select instruments of God gave expression to the Church's faith respecting both the past and the

---

[1] Some notice was taken toward the close of the Introduction of the change that has for some time been in progress on the Continent regarding the Typology of Scripture generally. In connection with the particular branch of it considered above, the following quotation (given by Hartmann in his Verbinnung des Alten Test. mit den Newen, p. 6, from a German periodical) may serve both as a specimen of the improved tone of thinking on the subject of Old Testament history, and its connection with the Gospel. "Must not Judaism be of great moment to Christianity, since both stand in brotherly and sisterly relations to each other? The historical books of the Hebrews are also religious books; the religious import is involved in the historical. The history of the people, as a divine leading and management in respect to them, was at the same time a training for religion, precisely as the Old Testament is a preparation for the New." To the same effect also Jacobi, as quoted by Sack, Apologetik, p. 356, on the words of Christ, that "as the serpent was lifted up, *must* the Son of Man be lifted up," ($ὑψωθῆναι δεῖ$): "History is also prophecy. The past contains within itself the future as an embryo, and at certain points, discernible by the spiritual eye, the greater, as in an image, is seen represented in the smaller, the internal in the external, the present or future in the past. Here there is nothing whatever arbitrary; throughout there is a divine *must*, connection, and arrangement, pregnant with mutual relations." More recently still Hofmann, in his Weissagung und Erfüllung, has given peculiar prominence to this view of Old Testament history; though he has nearly neutralized the benefit by the false views with which he has mixed it up. To these we shall probably refer afterwards. It is well, however, to hear him speaking of "the whole Old Testament history being a *vaticinium reale* respecting the New," and of history and prophecy being the two great component-factors in a preparatory economy.

future in his dispensations. And in looking there we find, not only that an exalted personage, with his work of perfect righteousness, and his kingdom of consummate bliss and glory, was seen to be in prospect, but also that the expectations cherished of what was to be, took very commonly the form of a new and higher exhibition of what had been. In giving promise of the better things to come, prophecy to a large extent availed itself of the characters and events of history. But it could only do so on the twofold ground, that it perceived in these essentially the same elements of truth and principle which were to appear in the future; and in that future anticipated a nobler exhibition of them than had been given in the past. And what was this but, in other words, to declare their typical meaning and design? The truth of what we say will more fully appear when we come to treat of the combination of type with prophecy—which, on account of its importance, we reserve for the subject of a separate chapter. Meanwhile, it will be remembered how even Moses speaks before his death of "the prophet which the Lord their God should raise up from among his brethren like to himself" (Deut. xviii. 18)—one that should hold a like position and do a similar work, but each in its kind more perfect and complete—else, why look out for another? In like manner David connects the historical appearance of Melchizedec with the future head of God's Church and kingdom, when he announces him as a priest after the order of Melchizedec (Ps. cx. 4); he foresaw that the relations of Melchizedec's time should be again revived in this divine character, and the same part fulfilled anew, but raised, as the connection intimates, to a higher sphere, invested with a heavenly greatness and a world-wide significance and power. So again we are told (Mal. iii., 1, iv. 5) another Elias should arise in the brighter future, to be succeeded by a more glorious manifestation of the Lord, to do what had never but very imperfectly been done before; namely, to provide for himself a true spiritual priesthood, a regenerated people, and an offering of righteousness. But the richest proofs are furnished by the latter portion of Isaiah's writings. For, there we find the prophet intermingling so closely together the past and the future, that it is often difficult to tell of which he actually speaks. He passes from Israel to the Messiah, and again from the Messiah to Israel, as if the one were but a new, a higher and perfect developement of what belonged to the other. And the Church of the future is constantly represented under the relations of the past, only freed from the imperfections that attached to these, and rendered in every respect blessed and glorious.

Such are a few specimens of the way in which the more spiritual and divinely enlightened members of the old covenant saw the future imaged in the past or present. They discerned the essential oneness in truth and principle between the two; but, at the same time, were conscious of such inherent imperfections and defects attaching to the past, that they felt it required a more perfect future to render it properly worthy of God, and fully adequate to the wants and necessities of his people. And there is one entire book of the Old Testament which owes in a manner its existence, as it now stands, to this likeness in one respect, but diversity in another, between the past and the future things in God's administration. We refer to the Book of Psalms. The pieces of which this book consists are in their leading character devotional summaries, expressing the pious thoughts and feelings which the consideration of God's ways, and the knowledge of his revelations, were fitted to raise in reflecting and spiritual bosoms. But the singular thing is, that they are this for the New, as well as for the Old Testament worshipper. They are still incomparably the most perfect expression of the religious sentiment, and the best directory to the soul in its thoughts and communings about divine things, which is anywhere to be found. There is not a feature in the divine character, not a spiritual principle or desire in the mind of an enlightened Christian, or an aspect of the life of faith, to which expression, more or less distinct, is not given in this invaluable portion of ancient Scripture. How could such a book have come into existence, centuries before the Christian era, but for the fact, that the Old and the New dispensations—however they may have differed in outward form, and however the ostensible transactions in the one case may have been inferior to what they were to be in the other—were founded on the same relations, and pervaded by the same essential truths and principles? No otherwise could the Book of Psalms have served as the great hand-book of devotion to the members of both covenants. *There* the disciples of Moses and Christ meet as on common ground—the one still readily and gratefully using the fervid and deep-toned utterances which the other had breathed forth ages before, and bequeathed as a legacy to succeeding generations. And though it was comparatively carnal institutions under which the holy men lived and worshipped, who indited those divine songs ; though it was transactions which directly bore only on their earthly and temporal condition, that formed the immediate ground and occasion of the sentiments they uttered ; yet, where in all Scripture can the believer, who now " worships in spirit and in truth," more readily find for himself the words that shall fitly express his loftiest conceptions of God, embody his most spiritual and enlarged views of the divine government, or tell forth the feelings and desires of his soul even in many of its most lively and elevated moods ?

But with this fitting adaptation in the Psalms to the thoughts and feelings of the Christian, what a difference still exists between the Psalms and the epistles of the New Testament ! With all that discovers itself in the Psalms of a vivid apprehension of God, and of a habitual confidence in his faithfulness and love, there still is apparent something of awe and restraint upon the soul ; it never rises into the filial cry of the Gospel, Abba, Father. There is a fitfulness also in its movements, as of one dwelling in a dusky and changeful atmosphere. Continually, indeed, do we see the Psalmist flying, in distress and trouble, under the shelter of the Almighty, and trusting in his mercy for deliverance from the guilt of sin. Even in the worst times he still prays and looks for redemption. But *the* redemption which dispels all fear, and satisfies the soul with the highest good, he knew not, excepting as a bright day-star glistening in the far-distant horizon. He knew it as a thing that should assuredly be brought in for the Church of God ; and could tell somewhat of the mighty and glorious personage destined in the divine counsels to accomplish it—of his unparalleled struggles in the cause of righteousness, and of his final triumphs, resulting in the extension of his kingdom to the farthest bounds of the earth. But no more—the veil still hangs ; expectation still waits and longs ; and it is only for the believer of other times to say, " Mine eyes have seen thy salvation ;" " I have a desire to depart, and to be with Christ;" or again, " Behold what manner of love the Father hath bestowed upon us, that we should be called the Sons of God ; and it doth not yet appear what we shall be, but we know, that when he appears, we shall be like him, for we shall see him as he is."

Such is the agreement, and such also the difference between the Old and the New. " *There* we see the promise and prelude of the blessings of salvation ; *here*, these blessings themselves, far surpassing all the previous foreshadowings of them. There, a fiducial resting in Jehovah ; here, an unspeakable fulness of spiritual and heavenly blessings from the opened fountain of his mercy. There, a confidence that the Lord would not abandon his people ; here, the Lord himself assuming their nature, the God-man, connecting himself in organic union with humanity, and sending forth streams of life through its members. There, in the back-ground, night, only relieved by the stars of the word of promise and operations of grace in suitable accordance with it ; here, in the back-ground, day, still clouded, indeed, by our human nature, which is not yet completely penetrated by the Spirit, and is ever anew manifesting its sinfulness, but yet such a day as gives assurance of the cloudless sunshine of eternity, of which God himself is the light."[1]

The whole of the argument maintained in this and the preceding chapters, respecting the typical character of God's earlier dispensations, admits of confirmation and support from the existence of typical forms in nature, which present in this respect a striking analogy between the natural and the religious departments of God's working. A brief outline of the kind of illustration that might be obtained here, is given in another place, as it has only a collateral bearing on the main subject.[2] But let us not close this elementary discussion without reflecting for a moment on the skilful adjustment which appears in the earlier dispensations of God, as regards the progressive character of his divine plan. The plan so considered certainly presents something strange and mysterious to our view, especially in the extreme slowness of its progression ; since it required the postponement of the work of redemption for so many ages, and kept the church during these in a state of comparative ignorance in respect to the great objects of her faith and hope. Yet what is it but an application to the world's history of what is constantly proceeding before our eyes in each man's personal history, whose term of probation upon earth

---

[1] Delitzsch, Biblisch-prophetische Theologie, p. 232.   [2] See Appendix A.

is, in many cases half, in nearly all a third part consumed, before the individual attains to a capacity for the objects and employments of manhood? Constituted as we personally are, and as the world also is, progression of some kind is indispensable to happiness and well-being; and the majestic slowness that appears in the plan of God's administration of the world, is but a reflection of the nature of its divine author, with whom a thousand years are as one day. Starting, then, with the assumption, that the divine plan behoved to be of a progressive character, the nature of the connection we have found to exist between its earlier and later parts, discovers the perfect wisdom and foresight of God. The terminating point in the plan was what is called emphatically "the mystery of godliness,"—God manifest in the flesh for the redemption of a fallen world, and the establishment through all its borders of a kingdom of righteousness, that should not pass away. It was necessary that some intimation of this ulterior design should be given from the first, that the church might know whither to direct her expectations. Accordingly, the prophetic Word began to utter its predictions with the very entrance of sin. The first promise was given on the spot that witnessed the fall; and that a promise which contained, within its brief but pregnant meaning, the whole burden of redemption. As time rolled on, prophecy continued to add to its communications, having still for its grand scope and aim "the testimony of Jesus." And at length so express had its tidings become, and so plentiful its revelations, that when the purpose of the Father drew near to its accomplishment, the remnant of sincere worshippers were like men standing on their watch-towers, waiting and looking for the long-expected consolation of Israel; nor was there anything of moment in the personal history or work of the Son, of which it could not be written, It was so done, that the Scriptures might be fulfilled.

It is plain, however, on a little consideration, that something more was needed than the simple announcements of prophecy. The church required training as well as teaching, and training of a very peculiar kind; for she had to be formed for receiving things "which men had not heard, nor had the ear perceived, neither had the eye seen—the things which God had prepared for those that waited for him." (Isa. lxiv. 4.) "The new dispensation was to be wholly made up of things strange and wonderful;

all that is seen and heard of it is contrary to carnal wisdom. The appearance of the Son of God in a humble condition—the discharge by him in person of a Gospel ministry, with its attendant circumstances—his shame and sufferings—his resurrection and ascension into heaven—the nature of the kingdom instituted by him, which is spiritual—the blessings of his kingdom, which are also spiritual—the instruments employed for advancing the kingdom, men devoid of worldly learning, and destitute of outward authority—the gift of the Holy Spirit, the calling of the Gentiles, the rejection of so many among the Jewish people :—these, among other things, were indeed such as the carnal eye had never seen, and the carnal ear had never heard ; nor could they without express revelation, by any thought or natural ingenuity on the part of man, have been foreseen or understood."[1] But lying thus so far beyond the ken of man's natural apprehensions, and so different from what they were disposed of themselves to expect, if all that was done beforehand respecting them had consisted in the necessarily partial and obscure intimations of prophecy, there could neither have been any just anticipation of the things to be revealed, nor any suitable training for them ; the change from the past to the future must have come as an irruption, and men could only have been brought by a sort of violence to submit to it.

To provide against this, there was required, as a proper accompaniment to the intimations of prophecy, the training of preparatory dispensations, that the past history and established experience of the church might run, though on a lower level, yet in the same direction with her future prospects. And what her circumstances in this respect required, the wisdom and foresight of God provided. He so skilfully modelled for her the institutions of worship, and so wisely arranged the dealings of his providence, that there was constantly presented to her view in the outward and earthly things with which she was there conversant, the cardinal truths and principles of the coming dispensation. In every thing she saw and handled, there was something to mould her spirit into accordance with the realities of the Gospel ; so that if she could not be said to live *directly* under "the powers of the world to come," she yet shared their *secondary* influence, being placed amid the signs and shadows of the true, and conducted

[1] Vitringa on Isa. lxiv. 4.

through earthly transactions that bore on them the image of the heavenly.

It is to this preparatory training, as being on the part of God sufficiently protracted and complete, that we are to regard the apostle as chiefly referring, when he speaks of Christ having appeared, "when the fulness of the time was come" (Gal. iv. 4). Chiefly, though not by any means exclusively. For there is a manifold wisdom in all God's arrangements. In the moral as well as in the physical world he is ever making numerous operations conspire to the production of one result, and one result to serve many important ends. It is, therefore, a most fit and proper object of inquiry to search and consider how many lines there were in the world's condition, that opportunely met at the time of Christ's appearing, and together rendered it above all others the best suited for the institution of his kingdom, and most advantageous for the diffusion of its truths and blessings among the nations of the earth. But whatever light may be gathered from these external researches, it should never be forgotten that God's own record must furnish the main grounds for determining the special fitness of the selected time, and the position of his church the paramount reason. In everything that essentially affects the interests of the church, therefore pre-eminently in what concerns the manifestation of Christ, which is the centre-point of all that touches her interests, the state and condition of the church herself is ever the first thing contemplated by the eye of God; the rest of the world holds but a secondary and subordinate place. And so, when we are told that Christ appeared in the fulness of time, the fact, of which we are mainly assured, is, that all was done which was fit and necessary to be done for bringing the church into a state of preparedness for the time of his appearing. Not only had the period anticipated by prophecy arrived, and believing expectation, mounting on the ladder of prophecy, reached its proper height, but also the long series of preliminary arrangements and dealings was now complete, which were designed to make the church familiar with the fundamental truths and principles of Messiah's kingdom, and prepare her for the erection of this kingdom with its divine realities and eternal prospects. Nor do we need to make any exception to this in behalf of the long period that reached from the Babylonish exile to the advent of

Christ; for however this may seem at first sight to have been a period chiefly of disaster and inaction, it is found on more careful consideration to have been, in other respects, one of active and powerful influence—one peculiarly fitted to complete the training of the covenant-people, and dispose aright both their minds and their persons for the new era that awaited them.

It is true that we search in vain for the general and widespread success, which we might justly expect to have arisen from the plan of God, and to have made conspicuously manifest its infinite wisdom. With the exception of a comparatively small number, the professing church was found so completely unprepared for the doctrine of Christ's kingdom, as to reject it with disdain, and oppose it with unrelenting violence. But this neither proves the absence of the design, nor the unfitness of the means for carrying it into effect. It only proves how insufficient the best means are of themselves to enlighten and sanctify the human mind, when it becomes set upon objects that fall in with its own carnal views and prejudices—proves how the heart may remain essentially untaught, even after undergoing the most perfect course of instruction, and may remain wedded to error and corruption. But while we cannot overlook the fatal ignorance and perversity that pervaded the mass of the Jewish people, we are not to forget that there still was among them a pious remnant, "the election according to grace," who, as the church in the world, so they in the church ever occupy the foremost place in the mind and purposes of God. In the bosom of the Jewish church, as is justly remarked by Thiersch, there lay a domestic life so pure, noble, and tender, that it could yield such a person as the holy Virgin, and could furnish an atmosphere in which the Son of God might grow up sinless from childhood to manhood. There was Simeon and Anna, Zacharias and Elizabeth, Mary and Joseph, the company of apostles, the converts, no small number after all, who flocked to the standard of Jesus, as soon as the truths of his salvation came to be fully known and understood, and the believing Jews and proselytes scattered abroad, who, in almost every city, were ready to form the nucleus of a Christian church, and greatly facilitated its extension in the world. Did not the course of God's preparatory dispensations reach its end in regard to these? We have only to look for the answer to the style of argument and address used by the apostles. How much do both their language and their ideas savour of the sanctuary! How constantly do they throw themselves back for illustration and support, not only on the prophecies, but also on the sacred annals and institutions of the Old Testament! They spake and reasoned on the assumption, that the revelations of the Gospel were but a new and higher exhibition of the principles, which appeared alike in the events of their past history and the services of their religious worship. An appropriate language was already furnished by means of these to their hand, through which they could discourse aright of spiritual and divine things. But more than that, as they had no new language to invent, so they had no new ideas to discover, or unheard-of principles to promulgate. The scheme of truth, which they were called to expound and propagate, had its foundations already laid in the whole history and constitution of the Jewish commonwealth. In labouring to establish it, they felt that they were treading in the footsteps, and, on a higher vantage-ground, maintaining the faith of their illustrious fathers. In short, they appear as the heralds and advocates of a cause, which, in its essential principles, had its representation in all history, and gathered as into one glorious orb of truth the scattered rays of light and consolation which had been emanating from the ways of God since the world began. Thus wisely were the different parts of the divine plan adjusted to each other; and, for the accomplishment of what was required, the training by means of types could no more have been dispensed with, than the glimpse-like visions and hopeful intimations of prophecy.

CHAPTER FOURTH.

PROPHETICAL TYPES, OR THE COMBINATION OF TYPE WITH PROPHECY—
ALLEGED DOUBLE SENSE OF PROPHECY.

A TYPE necessarily possesses something of a prophetical character, and differs in degree rather than in kind from what is usually designated prophecy. The one images or prefigures, while the other foretels, coming realities. In the one case representative acts or symbols, in the other verbal delineations, serve the purpose of indicating beforehand what God was designed to accomplish for his people in the approaching future. The difference is not such as to affect the essential nature of the two subjects, as alike connecting together the Old and the New in God's dispensations. In distinctness and precision, however, simple prophecy has greatly the advantage over informations conveyed by type. For prophecy, however it may differ in its general characteristics from history, as it naturally possesses something of the directness, so it may also attain to something of the exactness of historical description. But types having a significance or moral import of their own, apart from anything prospective, must, in their prophetical aspect, be somewhat less transparent, and possess more of a complicated character. Still the relation between type and antitype, when pursued through all its ramifications, may produce as deep a conviction of design and pre-ordained connection, as can be derived from simple prophecy and its fulfilment, though, from the nature of things, the evidence in the latter case must always be more obvious and palpable than in the former.

But the possession of the same common character is not the only link of connection between type and prophecy. Not only do they agree in having both a prospective reference to the future, but they are often also combined into one prospective exhibition of the future. Prophecy, though it sometimes is of a quite simple, and direct nature, is far from being always so; and can scarcely ever be said to delineate the future with the precision and exactness that history employs in recording the past. In many portions of it there is a certain degree of complexity, if not dubiety, and that mainly arising from the circumstances and transactions of the past being in some way interwoven with its anticipations of things to come. Here, however, we approach the confines of a controversy on which some of the greatest minds have expended their talents and learning, and with such doubtful success on either side, that the question is still perpetually brought up anew for discussion, whether there is or is not a double sense in prophecy? That some portion of debateable ground will always remain connected with the subject appears to us more than probable. But, at the same time, we are fully persuaded that the portion admits of being greatly narrowed in extent, and even reduced to such small dimensions, as not materially to affect the settlement of the main question, if only the typical element in prophecy is allowed its due place and weight. This we shall endeavour, first of all, to exhibit in the several aspects in which it actually presents itself; and shall then subjoin a few remarks on the views of those who espouse either side of the question, as it is usually stated.

From the general resemblance between type and prophecy, we are prepared to expect that they may sometimes run into each other; and especially, that the typical in action may in various ways form the ground-work and the materials, by means of which the prophetic in word gave forth its intimations of the coming future. And this, it is quite conceivable, may have been done under any of the following modifications. 1. A typical action might, in some portion of the prophetic word, be historically mentioned, and hence the mention being that of a prophetical circumstance or event, would come to possess a prophetical character. 2. Or something typical in the past or the present might be represented in a distinct prophetical announcement, as going to appear again in the future; thus combining together the typical in act, and the prophetical in word. 3. Or, the typical, not expressly and formally, but in its essential relations and principles, might be embodied in an accompanying prediction, which foretold things corresponding in nature, but far higher and greater in importance. 4. Or, finally, the typical might itself be still future, and in a prophetic word might be partly described, partly pre-supposed, as a typical ground for the delineation of other things still more distant, to which, when it occurred, it was to stand in the relation of type to antitype. We could manifestly have no difficulty in conceiving such combinations of type with prophecy, without any violence done to their distinctive properties, or any invasion made on their respective provinces—nothing, indeed, happening but what might have been expected from their mutual relations, and their fitness for being employed in concert to the production of common ends. And we shall now shew how each of the suppositions has found its verification in the prophetic Scriptures.[1]

I. The first supposition is that of a typical action being historically mentioned in the prophetic word, and the mention, being that of a prophetical circumstance or event, thence coming to possess a prophetical character. There are two classes of Scriptures which may be said to verify this supposition; one of which is of a somewhat general and comprehensive nature, so that the fulfilment is not necessarily confined to any single person or period, though it could not fail, in an especial manner, to appear in the personal history of Christ. To this class belonged such recorded experiences as the following—"The zeal of thine house hath eaten me up" (Ps. lxix. 9, comp. with John ii. 17); "He that eateth bread with me hath lifted up his heel against me" (Ps. xli. 9, comp. with John xiii. 18); "They hated me without a cause" (Ps. lxix. 4. comp. with John xv. 25); "The stone which the builders rejected is become the head of the corner" (Ps. cxviii. 22, comp. with Matth. xxi. 42, 1 Pet. ii. 6, 7.) These passages are all distinctly referred to Christ in the Gospels, and the things that befel him are expressly said, or plainly indicated to have happened, that such scriptures might be fulfilled. Yet

---

[1] It is proper to state, however, that we cannot present here anything like a full and complete elucidation of the subject; and we therefore mean to supplement this chapter by an appendix on the Old Testament in the New, in which the subject will both be considered from a different point of view, and followed out more into detail. See Appendix B.

as originally penned they assume the form of historical statements, rather than of prophetical announcements—recorded experiences on the part of those who indited them, and experiences of a kind, that in one form or another, could scarcely fail to be often recurring in the history of God's church and people. As such it might have seemed enough to say, that they contained general truths which were exemplified also in Jesus, when travailing in the work of man's redemption. But the convictions of Jesus himself and the inspired writers of the New Testament go beyond this; they perceive a closer connection—a prophetical element in the passages, which must find its due fulfilment in the personal experience of Christ. And this the passages contained, simply from their being in their immediate and historical reference, descriptive of what belonged to characters—David and Israel—that bore typical relations to Christ ; so that their being descriptive in the one respect necessarily implied their being prophetic in the other. What had formerly taken place in the experience of the type, must substantially renew itself again in the experience of the great antitype—whatever other and inferior renewals it may find besides.

To the same class also may be referred the passage in Ps. lxxviii. 2, " I will open my mouth in a parable (lit. similitude); I will utter dark sayings (lit. riddles) of old," which in Matth. xiii. 35 is spoken of as a prediction that found, and required to find, its fulfilment in our Lord's using the parabolic mode of discourse. As an utterance in the seventy-eighth Psalm the word simply records a fact, but a fact essentially connected with the discharge of the prophetical office, and, therefore, substantially indicating what must be met with in Him, in whom all prophetical endowments were to have their highest manifestation. Every prophet may be said to speak in similitudes or parables in the sense here indicated, which is comprehensive of all discourses upon divine things, delivered in figurative terms or an elevated style, and requiring more than common discernment to understand it aright. The parables of our Lord formed one species of it, but not by any means the only one. It was the common prophetico-poetical diction, which was characterized, not only by the use of measured sentences, but also by the predominant employment of external forms and natural similitudes. But, marking as it did, the possession of a prophetical gift, the record of its employment by Christ's prophetical types and forerunners was a virtual prediction, that it should be ultimately used in some appropriate form by himself.

The other class of passages which comes within the terms of *the first supposition, is of a more specific* and formal character. It coincides with the class already considered, in so far as it consists of words originally descriptive of some transaction or circumstance in the past, but afterwards regarded as prophetically indicative of something similar under the Gospel. Such is the word in Hos. xi. 1, " I called my son out of Egypt," which, as uttered by the prophet, was unquestionably meant to refer historically to the fact of the Lord's goodness in delivering Israel from that land of bondage and oppression. But the Evangelist Matthew expressly points to it as a prophecy, and tells us, that the infant Jesus was for a time sent into Egypt, and again brought out of it, that the word might be fulfilled. This arose from the typical connection between Christ and Israel. The Scripture fulfilled was prophetical, simply because the circumstance it recorded was typical. But in so considering it, the Evangelist puts no new strain upon its terms, nor introduces any sort of double sense into its import. He merely points to the prophetical element involved in the transaction it relates, and thereby discovers to us a bond of connection between the Old and the New in God's dispensations, necessary to be kept in view for a correct apprehension of both.

The same explanation in substance may be given of another example of the same class—the word in Exod. xii. 46, " A bone of him shall not be broken," which in John xix. 36 is represented as finding its fulfilment in the remarkable preservation of our Lord's body on the cross from the common fate of malefactors. The Scripture in itself was a historical testimony regarding the treatment the Israelites were to give to the paschal lamb, which, instead of being broken into fragments, was to be preserved entire, and eaten as one whole. It could only be esteemed a prophecy from being the record of a typical or prophetical action. But, when viewed in that light, the Scripture itself stands precisely as it did, without any recondite depth or subtile ambiguity being thrown into its meaning. For the prophecy in it is found, not by extracting from its words some new and hidden sense, but merely by noting the typical import of the circumstances, of which the words in their natural and obvious sense are descriptive.

How either Israel or the paschal lamb should have been in such a sense typical of Christ, that what is recorded of the one could be justly regarded as a prophecy of what was to take place in the other, will be matter for future inquiry, and, in connection with some other prophecies, will be partly explained in the appendix already referred to in this chapter. It is the *principle*, on which the explanation must proceed, to which alone for the present we desire to draw attention, and which, in the cases now under consideration, simply recognises the prophetical element involved in the recorded circumstance or transaction of the past. Neither is the Old Testament Scripture, taken by itself, prophetical, nor does the New Testament Scripture invest it with a force and meaning foreign to its original purport and design. The Old merely records the typical fact, which properly constitutes the whole there is of prediction in the matter, while the New reads forth its import as such, by announcing the co-relative events or circumstances in which the fulfilment should be discovered. And nothing more is needed for perfectly harmonising the two together, than that we should so far identify the typical transaction recorded with the record that embodies it, as to perceive, that when the Gospel speaks of a Scripture fulfilled, it speaks of that Scripture in connection with the prophetical character of the subject it relates to.

There is nothing, surely, strange or anomalous in this. It is but the employment of a metonymy of a very common kind, according to which what embodies or contains any thing is viewed as in a manner one with the thing itself—as when the earth is made to stand for the inhabitants of the earth, a house for its inmates, a cup for its contents, a word descriptive of events past or to come, as if it actually produced them.[1] Of course, the validity of such a mode of explanation depends entirely upon the reality of the connection between the alleged type and antitype—between the

---

[1] So, for example, in Hos. vi. 5, "I have hewed them by the prophets;" Gen. xxvii. 37, "Behold I have made him thy lord;" xlviii. 22, "I have given thee one portion above thy brethren, which I took out of the hand of the Amorite"—each ascribing to the word spoken the actual doing of that which it only declared to have been done.

earlier circumstance or object described, and the later one to which the description is prophetically applied. On any other ground such references as those in Matthew to Hosea, and in John to Exodus, can only be viewed as fanciful or strained accommodations. But the matter assumes another aspect if the one was originally ordained in anticipation of the other, and so ordained, that the earlier should not have been brought into existence if the later had not been before in contemplation. Seen from this point of view, which we hold to be the one taken by the inspired writers, the past appears to run into the future, and to have existed mainly for it. And the record or delineation of the past is naturally and justly, not by a mere fiction of the imagination, seen to possess the essential character of a prediction. Embodying a prophetical circumstance or action, it is itself named by one of the commonest figures of speech, a prophecy.

II. Our second supposition was that of something typical in the past or present being represented in a distinct prophetical announcement as going to appear again in the future—the prophetical in word being thus combined with the typical in act into a prospective delineation of things to come. This supposition also includes several varieties, and in one form or another has its exemplifications in many parts of the prophetic word. For it is in a manner the native tendency of the mind, when either of itself forecasting, or under the guidance of a divine impulse anticipating and disclosing the future, to see this future imaged in the past, to make use of the known in giving shape and form to the unknown; so that the things which *have* been, are then usually contemplated as in some respect types of what *shall* be, even though in the reality there may be considerable differences of a formal kind between them.

How much it is the native tendency of the mind to work in this manner, when itself endeavouring to descry the events of the future, is evident from the examples, transmitted to us by the most cultivated minds, of human divination. Thus the Pythoness in Virgil, when disclosing to Æneas what he and his posterity might expect in Latium, speaks of it merely as a repetition of the scenes and experiences of former times. "You shall not want Simois, Xanthus, or the Grecian camp. Another Achilles, also of divine offspring, is already provided for Latium."¹ In like manner Juno, in the vaticination put into her mouth by Horace, respecting the possible destinies of Rome, declares, that in the circumstances supposed, " the fortune of Troy again reviving, should again also be visited with terrible disaster, and that even if a wall of brass were thrice raised around it, it should be thrice destroyed by the Greeks."² In such examples of pretended divination, no one, of course, imagines it to have been meant that the historical persons and circumstances mentioned were to be actually reproduced in the approaching or contemplated future. All we are to understand is, that others of a like kind—holding similar relations to the parties interested, and occupying much the same position—were announced beforehand to appear ; and so, would render the future a sort of repetition of the past ; or the past a kind of typical foreshadowing of the future.

As an example of divine predictions precisely similar in form, we may point to Hos. viii. 13, where the prophet, speaking of the Lord's purpose to visit the sins of Israel with chastisement, says, " They shall return to Egypt." The old state of bondage and oppression should come back upon them ; or the things going to befal them of evil should be after the type of what their forefathers had experienced under the yoke of Pharaoh. Yet that the new should not be by any means the exact repetition of the old, as it might have been conjectured from the altered circumstances of the time, so it is expressly intimated by the prophet himself a few verses afterwards, when he says, " Ephraim shall return to Egypt, and they shall eat unclean things in Assyria" (chap ix. 3) ; and again in ch. xi. 5, " He shall not return into the land of Egypt, but the Assyrian shall be his king." He shall return to Egypt and still not return ; in other words, the Egypt-state shall come back on him, though the precise locality and external circumstances shall differ. In like manner Ezekiel in ch. iv. foretels, in his own peculiar and mystical way, the return of the Egypt-state ; and in

---

[1] Non Simois tibi, nec Xanthus, nec Dorica castra
Defuerint. Alius Latio jam partus Achilles,
Natus et ipse dea.—Æn. vi. 88-90.

[2] Trojæ renascens alite lugubri
Fortuna tristi clade iterabitur etc.—Carm. L. III. 3, 61-68.
See also Seneca Medea, 374, etc.

ch. xx. speaks of the Lord as going to bring the people again into the wilderness; but calls it "the wilderness of the peoples," to indicate that the dealing should be the same only in character with what Israel of old had been subjected to in the wilderness, not a bald and formal repetition of the story.

Indeed, God's providence knows nothing in the sacred any more than in the profane territory of the world's history, of a literal reproduction of the past. And when prophecy threw its delineations of the future into the form of the past, and spake of the things yet to be as a recurrence of those that had already been, it simply meant that the one should be after the type of the other, or should in spirit and character resemble it. By type, however, in such examples as those just referred to, is not to be understood type in the more special or theological sense in which the term is commonly used in the present discussions, as if there was anything in the past that of itself gave prophetic intimation of the coming future. It is to be understood only in the general sense of a pattern-form, in accordance with which the events in prospect were to bear the image of the past. The prophetical element, therefore, did not properly reside in the historical transaction referred to in the prophecy, but in the prophetic word itself, which derived its peculiar form from the past, and through that a certain degree of light to illustrate its import. There were, however, other cases in which the typical in circumstance or action—the typical in the proper sense—was similarly combined with a prophecy in word; and in them we have a twofold prophetic element—one more concealed in the type, and another more express and definite in the word, but the two made to coalesce in one prediction.

Of this kind is the prophecy in Zech. vi. 12, 13, where the prophet takes occasion, from the building of the literal temple in Jerusalem under the presidency of Joshua, to foretel a similar, but higher and more glorious work in the future: "Behold the man, whose name is the Branch; and he shall grow up out of his place, and he shall build the temple of the Lord; even he shall build the temple of the Lord," &c. The building of the temple was itself typical of the incarnation of God in the person of Christ, and of the raising up in him of a spiritual house that should be "an habitation of God through the Spirit." (John ii. 19; Matth. xvi. 18; Eph. ii. 20, 22.) But the prophecy thus involved in the action is expressly uttered in the prediction, which at once explained the type, and sent forward the expectations of believers toward the contemplated result. Similar, also, is the prediction of Ezekiel, in chap. xxxiv. 23, in which the good promised in the future to a truly penitent and believing people, is connected with a return of the person and times of David : " And I will set up one shepherd over them, and he shall feed them, even my servant David ; he shall feed them, and he shall be their shepherd." And the closing prediction of Malachi, " Behold, I will send you Elijah the prophet before the coming of the great and dreadful day of the Lord." David's kingdom and reign in Israel were from the first intended to foreshadow those of Christ ; and the work also of Elias, as preparatory to the Lord's final reckoning with the apostate commonwealth of Israel, bore a typical respect to the work of preparation that was to go before the Lord's personal appearance in the last crisis of the Jewish state. Such might have been probably conjectured or dimly apprehended from the things themselves ; but it became comparatively clear, when it was announced in explicit predictions, that a new David and a new Elias were to appear. The prophetical element was there before in the type ; but the prophetical word brought it distinctly and prominently out ; yet so as in no respect to materially change or complicate the meaning. The specific designation of " David my servant," and " Elijah the prophet," are in each case alike intended to indicate, not the literal reproduction of the past, but the full realization of all that the past typically foretokened of good. It virtually told the people of God, that in their anticipations of the coming reality, they might not fear to heighten to the uttermost the idea which those honoured names were fitted to suggest ; their anticipations would be amply borne out by the event, in which still higher prophecy than Elijah's, and unspeakably nobler service than David's, was to be found in reserve for the church.[1]

[1] Those who contend for the actual re-appearance of Elijah, because the epithet of " the prophet,"they think, fixes down the meaning to the personal Elijah, may as well contend for the re-appearance of David as the future king ; for " David my servant" is as distinctive an appellation of the one, as " Elijah the prophet" of the other. But in reality they are thus specified as both exhibiting the highest known ideal—the one of king-like service, the other of prophetic work as preparatory to a divine manifestation. And in thinking of *them* the people could get the most correct view they were capable of entertaining of the predicted future.

III. We pass on to our third supposition, which may seem to be nearly identical with the last, yet belongs to a stage further in advance. It is that the typical, not expressly and formally, but in its essential relations and principles, might be embodied in an accompanying prediction, which foretold things corresponding in nature, but of higher moment and wider import. So far this supposed case coincides with the last, that in that also the things predicted might be, and, if referring to gospel times, actually were higher and greater than those of the type. But it differs, in that this superiority did not there, as it does here, appear in the terms of the prediction, which simply announced the recurrence of the type. And it differs still farther, in that there the type was expressly and formally introduced into the prophecy, while here it is tacitly assumed, and only its essential relations and principles are applied to the delineation of some things analogous and related, but conspicuously loftier and greater. In this case, then, the typical transactions furnishing the materials for the prophetical delineation, must necessarily form the back-ground, and the explanatory prediction the foreground of the picture. The words of the prophet must describe not the typical past, but the corresponding and grander future,—describe it, however, under the form of the past, and in connection with the same fundamental views of the divine character and government. So that there must here also be but one sense, though a twofold prediction— one more vague and indefinite, standing in the type or prophetic action, the other more precise and definite, furnished by the prophetic word, and directly pointing to the greater things to come.

The supposition now made is actually verified in a considerable number of prophetical Scriptures. Connected with them, and giving rise to them, there were certain circumstances and events so ordered by God as to be in a greater or less degree typical of others under the Gospel. And there was a prophecy connecting the two together, by taking up the truths and relations embodied in the type, and expanding them so as to embrace the higher and still future things of God's kingdom,—thus at once indicating the typical design of the past, and announcing in appropriate terms the coming events of the future.

Let us point, in the first instance, to an illustrative example, in which the typical element, indeed, was comparatively vague and general, but which has the advantage of being the first, if we mistake not, of this species of prophecy, and in some measure gave the tone to those that followed. The example we refer to is the song of Hannah (1 Sam. ii. 1-10) indited by that pious woman under the inspiration of God, on the occasion of the birth of Samuel. The history leaves no room to doubt that this was its immediate occasion; yet, if viewed in reference to that occasion alone, how comparatively trifling is the theme! How strained and magniloquent the expressions! Hannah speaks of her "mouth being enlarged over her enemies," of "the bows of the mighty men being broken," of the "barren bearing seven," of the "full hiring themselves out for bread," and other things of a like nature—all how far exceeding, how completely caricaturing the occasion, if it has respect merely to the fact of a woman, hitherto reputed barren, becoming at length the joyful mother of a child! Were the song a mere inflation in the style of common eastern poetry, we might not be greatly startled at such grotesque exaggerations; but being a portion of that word, which is all given by inspiration of God, and is as silver tried in a furnace, we must disband from our mind any idea of extravagance or conceit. Indeed, from the whole strain and character of the song, it is evident, that though occasioned by the birth of Samuel, it was so far from having exclusive reference to that event, that the things concerning it formed one only of a numerous and important class pervading the providence of God, and closely connected with his highest purposes. In a spiritual respect it was a time of mournful barrenness and desolation in Israel; "the word of the Lord was precious, there was no open vision;" and iniquity was so rampant as even to be lifting up its insolent front, and practising its foul abominations in the very precincts of the Sanctuary. How natural, then, for Hannah, when she had got that child of desire and hope, which she had devoted from his birth as a Nazarite to the Lord's service, and feeling her soul moved by a prophetic impulse, to regard herself as specially raised up to be "a sign and a wonder" to Israel, and to do so particularly in respect to that principle in the divine government, which had so strikingly developed itself in her experience, but which was destined to receive its grandest manifestation in the work and kingdom, which were to be more peculiarly the Lord's! Hence, instead of looking simply to her individual case, and marking the operation of the Lord's hand in what merely concerned her personal history, she wings her flight aloft, and surveys the wide field of God's providential dealings; noting especially, as she proceeds, the workings of that pure and gracious sovereignty which delights to exalt an humble piety, while it brings down the proud and rebellious. And as every exercise of this principle is but part of a grand series, which culminates in the dispensation of Christ, her song runs out at the close into a sublime and glowing delineation of the final results to be achieved by it in connection with his righteous administration. "The adversaries of the Lord shall be broken to pieces; out of heaven shall he thunder upon them; the Lord shall judge the ends of the earth; and he shall give strength unto his king, and exalt the horn of his anointed."[1]

This song of Hannah, then, plainly consists of two parts, in the one of which only—the concluding portion—it is properly prophetical. The preceding stanzas are taken up with unfolding, from past and current events, the grand spiritual idea; the closing ones carry it forward in beautiful and striking application to the affairs of Messiah's kingdom. In the earlier part it presents to us the germ of sacred principle unfolded in the type; in the latter, it exhibits this rising to its ripened growth and perfection in the final exaltation and triumph of the king of Zion. The two differ in respect to the line of things immediately contemplated—the facts of history in the one case, in the other the anticipations of prophecy; but they agree in being alike pervaded by one and the same great principle, which, after floating down the

---

[1] The last clause might as well, and indeed better, have been rendered, "Exalt the horn of his Messiah." Even the Jewish interpreter, Kimchi, understands it as spoken directly of the Messiah, and the Targum paraphrases, "He shall multiply the kingdom of Messiah." It is the first passage of Scripture where the word occurs in its more distinctive sense, and is used as a synonyme for the consecrated or divine king. It may seem strange that Hannah should have been the first to introduce this epithet, and to point so directly to the destined head of the divine kingdom: it will even be inexplicable, unless we understand her to have been raised up for a "sign and a wonder" to Israel, and to have spoken as she was moved by the Holy Ghost. But the other expressions, especially "the adversaries of the Lord shall be destroyed, and the ends of the earth shall be judged," shew that it really was of the kingdom with such a head that she spoke. And the idea of Grotius and the Rationalists, that she referred in the first instance to Saul, is entirely groundless.

stream of earthly providences, is represented as ultimately settling and developing itself with resistless energy in the affairs of Messiah's kingdom. And as if to remove every shadow of doubt as to this being the purport and design of Hannah's song, when we open the record of that better era, which she only saw glistening as a distant star in the horizon, we find the Virgin Mary, in her song of praise at the announcement of Messiah's birth, re-echoing the sentiments, and sometimes even repeating the very words of the mother of Samuel—" My soul doth magnify the Lord, and my spirit hath rejoiced in God my Saviour. For he hath regarded the low estate of his handmaiden. He hath shewed strength with his arm: he hath scattered the proud in the imagination of their hearts. He hath put down the mighty from their seats, and exalted them of low degree. He hath filled the hungry with good things; and the rich he hath sent empty away. He hath holpen his servant Israel, in remembrance of his mercy, as he spake to our fathers, to Abraham and to his seed for ever." Why should the Spirit, breathing at such a time on the soul of Mary, have turned her thoughts so nearly into the channel that had been struck out ages before by the pious Hannah? Or why should the circumstances connected with the birth of Hannah's Nazarite offspring have proved the occasion of strains, which so distinctly pointed to the manifestation of the King of Glory, and so closely harmonized with those actually sung in celebration of the event? Doubtless to mark the connection really subsisting between the two. It is the Spirit's own intimation of his ulterior design in transactions long since past, and testimonies delivered centuries before—namely, to herald the coming of Messiah, and make the church familiar with the form and character of his spiritual dispensation.[1]

[1] The view now given of Hannah's song presents it in a much higher, as we conceive it does also in a truer light, than that exhibited by Bishop Jebb, who speaks of it in a style that seems scarcely compatible with any proper belief in its inspiration. The song appears, in his estimation, to have been the mere effusion of Hannah's private, and, in great part, unsanctified feelings. " We cannot but feel," he says, " that her exultation partook largely of a spirit far beneath that which enjoins the love of our enemies, and which forbids personal exultation over a fallen foe." He regards it as " unquestionable, that previous sufferings had not thoroughly subdued her temper—that she could not suppress the workings of a retaliative spirit,—and was thus led to dwell, not on the peaceful glories of his (Samuel's) priestly and prophetic rule, but on his

Hannah's song was the first specimen of that combination of prophecy with type, which is now under consideration; but it was soon followed by others, in which both the prophecy was more extended, and the typical element in the transactions that gave rise to it, was more marked and specific. The examples we refer to are to be found in the Messianic psalms, which also resemble the song of Hannah in being of a lyrical character, and thence admitting of a freer play of feeling on the part of the individual writer than could fitly be introduced into simple prophecy. But this again principally arose from the close connection typically between the present and the future, whereby the feelings originated by the one naturally incorporated themselves with the delineation of the other. And as it was the institution of the temporal kingdom in the person and house of David which here formed the ground and the occasion of the prophetic delineation, there was no part of the typical arrangements under the ancient dispensation which more fully admitted, or, to prevent misapprehension, more obviously required the accompaniment of a series of lyrical prophecies, such as that contained in the Messianic psalms.

For, the institution of a temporal kingdom in the hands of an Israelitish family involved a very material change in the external framework of the theocracy; and a change that of itself was fitted to rivet the minds of the people more to the earthly and visible, and take them off from the invisible and divine. The constitution under which they were placed before the appointment of a king—though it did not absolutely preclude such an appointment—yet seemed as if it would rather suffer than be improved by so broad and palpable an introduction of the merely human element. It was till then a theocracy in the strictest sense; a commonwealth, that had no recognized head but God, and placed every thing essentially connected with life and wellbeing under his immediate presidence and direction. The

future triumphs over the Philistine armies" (Sacred Literature, p. 397). If such were indeed the character of Hannah's song, we may be assured it would not have been so closely imitated by the blessed Virgin. But it is manifestly wrong to regard Hannah as speaking of her merely personal enemies—her language would otherwise be chargeable with vicious extravagance, as well as unsanctified feeling. She identifies herself throughout with the Lord's cause and people; and it is simply her zeal for righteousness which expresses itself in a spirit of exultation over prostrate enemies.

land of the covenant was emphatically God's land[1]—the people that dwelt in it were *his* peculiar property and heritage[2]—the laws which they were bound to obey were his statutes and judgments[3]—and the persons appointed to interpret and administer them were *his* representatives, and on this account even sometimes bore his name.[4] It was the peculiar and distinguishing glory of Israel as a nation, that they stood in this near relationship to God, and that which more especially called forth the rapturous eulogy of Moses,[5] "Happy art thou, O Israel, who is like unto thee! The eternal God is thy refuge, and underneath are the everlasting arms." It was a glory, however, which the people themselves were too carnal for the most part to estimate aright, and of which they never appeared more insensible, than when they sought to be like the Gentiles, by having a king appointed over them. For, what was it but in effect to seek, that they might lose their peculiar distinction among the nations? that God might retire to a greater distance from them, and might no longer be their immediate guardian and sovereign?

Nor was this the only evil likely to arise out of the proposed change. Every thing under the old covenant bore reference to the future and more perfect dispensation of the Gospel; and the ultimate reason of any important feature or material change in respect to the former, can never be understood without taking into account the bearing it might have on the future state and issues of things under the Gospel. But how could any change in the constitution of ancient Israel, and especially such a change as the people contemplated, when they desired a king after the manner of the Gentiles, be adopted without altering matters in this respect to the worse? The dispensation of the Gospel was to be, in a peculiar sense, the "kingdom of heaven, or of God," having for its high end and aim the establishment of a near and blessed intercourse between God and men. It realizes its consummation, when the vision seen by John, and described

---

[1] Lev. xxv. 23; Ps. x. 16; Isa. xiv. 25; Jer ii. 7, &c.
[2] Ex. xix. 5; Ps. xciv. 5; Jer. ii. 7; Joel iii. 2.
[3] Ex. xv. 26; xviii. 16; etc.
[4] Ex. xxii. 28; Ps. lxxxii. 6.
[5] Deut. xxxiii. 26, 29.

after the precise pattern of the constitution set up in the wilderness, comes into fulfilment—when " the tabernacle of God is with men, and he dwells with them." Of this consummation it was a striking and impressive image that was presented in the original structure of the Israelitish commonwealth, wherein God himself sustained the office of king, and had his peculiar residence and appropriate manifestations of glory in the midst of his people. And when they, in their carnal affection for a worldly institute, clamoured for an earthly sovereign, they not only discovered a lamentable indifference towards what constituted their highest honour, but betrayed also a want of discernment and faith in regard to God's prospective and ultimate design in connection with their provisional economy. They gave conclusive proof that " they did not see to the end of that which was to be abolished," and preferred a request, which, if granted according to their expectation, would in a most important respect have defeated the object of their theocratic constitution.

We need not, therefore, be surprised that God should have expressed his dissatisfaction with the proposal made by the people for the appointment of a king to them, and should have regarded it as a substantial rejection of himself, that he should not reign over them. (1 Sam. viii. 7). But why then did he afterwards accede to it? And why did he make choice of the things connected with it, as an historical occasion and a typical ground for shadowing forth the nature and glories of Messiah's kingdom? The divine procedure in this, though apparently capricious, was in reality marked by the highest wisdom, and affords one of the finest examples to be found in Old Testament history of that overruling providence, by which God often averted the evil which men's devices tended to produce, and rendered them subservient to the greatest good.

The appointment of a king, as the earthly head of the commonwealth, we have said, was not absolutely precluded by the theocratic constitution. It was from the first contemplated by Moses as a thing which the people would probably desire, and in which they were not to be gainsayed, but were only to be directed into the proper method of accomplishing it (Deut. xvii. 14–20). It was even possible—if the matter was rightly gone about, and the divine sanction obtained respecting it—to turn it to profitable account, in familiarising the minds of men with what was destined to form the central idea of the Messiah's kingdom—the personal indwelling of the divine in the human nature—and so, to acquire for it the character of an important step in the preparatory arrangements for the kingdom. This is what was actually done. After the people had been solemnly admonished of their guilt in requesting the appointment of a king on *their* worldly principles, they were allowed to raise one of their number to the throne—not, however, as absolute and independent sovereign, but only as the deputy of Jehovah; that he might simply rule in the name, and in subordination to the will, of God.[1] For this reason his throne was called "the throne of the Lord;"[2] on which, as the queen of Sheba expressed it to Solomon, he was "set to be king for the Lord his God;"[3] and the kingly government itself was afterwards designated "the kingdom of the Lord."[4] For the same reason, no doubt, it was that Samuel "wrote in a book the manner of the kingdom, and laid it up before the Lord;"[5] that the protest concerning its derived and vicegerent nature might be perpetuated. And to render the divine purpose in this respect manifest to all who had eyes to see and ears to hear, the Lord allowed the choice first to fall on one who—as the representative of the people's carnal wisdom and prowess—was little disposed to rule in humble subordination to the will and authority of Heaven, and was therefore supplanted by another who should act as God's representative, and bear distinctively the name of *his servant*.[6]

It was, therefore, in this second person, David, that the kingly administration in Israel properly began; he was the root and founder of the kingdom—as a kingdom, in which the divine and human stood first in an official, as they were ultimately to stand in a personal union. And to make the preparatory and the final in this respect properly harmonise and adapt themselves to each other, the Lord, in the first instance, ordered matters connected with the institution of the kingly government, so as to render the beginning an image of the end—typical throughout of Mes-

---

[1] See Warburton's Legation of Moses, B. V. sect. 3.   [2] 1 Chron. xxix. 23.
[3] 2 Chron. ix. 8.   [4] 2 Chron. xiii. 8.   [5] 1 Sam. x. 2.
[6] This appellation is used of David far more frequently than of any other person. Upwards of thirty times it is expressly coupled with David; and in the Psalms he is ever speaking of himself as the Lord's servant.

siah's work and kingdom. And then, lest the typical bearing of things should be lost sight of in consequence of their present interest or importance, he gave in connection with them the word of prophecy, which, proceeding on the ground of their typical import, pointed the expectations of the Church to corresponding, but far higher and greater things still to come. In this way, what must otherwise have tended to veil the purpose of God, and obstruct the main design of his preparatory dispensation, was turned into one of the most effective means of revealing and promoting it. The earthly head, that now under God stood over the members of the commonwealth, instead of overshadowing his authority, only presented this more distinctly to their view, and served as a stepping-stone to faith, in enabling it to rise nearer to the apprehension of that personal indwelling of Godhead—the real Immanuel—which was to constitute the foundation and the glory of the Gospel dispensation. Not only was the work of God's preparatory arrangements not arrested, and the prospective anticipation of the future not marred, but occasion was taken to unfold this future in its more essential features with an air of individuality and distinctness, with a variety of detail and vividness of colouring not to be met with in any other portions of prophetic Scripture.

We refer for illustration to a single example of this combination of prophecy with type (others will be noticed, and in a somewhat different connection, in the Appendix)—the second Psalm. The production as to form is a kind of inaugural hymn, intended to celebrate the appointment and final triumph of Jehovah's king. The heathen nations are represented as foolishly opposing it (v. 1, 2); they agree among themselves, if the appointment should be made, practically to disown and resist it (v. 3); the Almighty however, perseveres in his purpose, scorning the rebellious opposition of such impotent adversaries (v. 4); the eternal decree goes forth, that the anointed king is enthroned on Zion; that being Jehovah's son, he is made the heir of all things, even to the uttermost bounds of the habitable globe (v. 5–9). And in consideration of what has thus been decreed and ratified in Heaven, the Psalm concludes with a word of friendly counsel and admonition to earthly potentates and rulers, exhorting them to submit in time to the sway of this glorious king, and forewarning them of the inevitable ruin of resistance. That in all this we can trace the lines of Messiah's history, is obvious at a glance. Even the older Jewish doctors, as we learn by the quotation from Solomon Jarchi, given by Venema, agreed that " it should be expounded of King Messiah ;" but he adds, " in accordance with the literal sense, and that it may be used against the heretics (*i. e.* Christians), it is proper to explain it as relating to David himself." Strange, that this idea, the offspring of Rabbinical artifice, seeking to withdraw an argument from the cause of Christianity, should have so generally commended itself to Christian interpreters ! But if by *literal sense* is to be understood the plain and natural import of the words employed, what ground is there for such an interpretation ? David was not opposed in his appointment to the throne of Israel by heathen nations or rulers, who knew and cared comparatively little about it ; nor was his being anointed king coincident with his being set on the holy hill of Zion ; nor, after being established in the kingdom, did he ever dream of pressing any claims of dominion on the kings and rulers of the earth : his wars were uniformly wars of defence, and not of conquest. So palpable, indeed, is the discordance between the lines of David's history, and the lofty terms of the psalm, that the opinion which ascribes it in the literal sense to David, may now be regarded as comparatively antiquated ; and some even of those who formerly espoused it (such as Rosenmüller), have at length owned, that " it cannot well be understood as applying either to David or to Solomon, much less to any of the later Hebrew kings, and that the judgment of the more ancient Hebrews is to be followed, who considered it as a celebration of the mighty king that they expected under the name of the Messiah."

But has the Psalm, then, no connection with the life and kingdom of David ? Unquestionably it has ; and a connection so close, that what took place in him was at once the beginning and the image of what, amid higher relations, and on a more extended scale, was to be accomplished by the subject of the Psalm. While the terms in which the king and the kingdom there celebrated are spoken of, stretch far above the line of things that belonged to David, they yet bear throughout the mark and impress of these. In both alike we see a sovereign choice and fixed appointment, on the part of God, to the office of king among men—an opposition of the most violent and heathenish nature to withstand and nullify the appointment—the gradual and successive overthrow of all the obstacles raised against the purpose of Heaven, and the extension of the sphere of empire (still partly future in the case of Messiah) till it reached the limits of the divine grant. The lines of history in the two cases are entirely parallel; there is all the correspondence we expect between type and antitype; but the prophecy which marks the connection between them, while it was occasioned by the purpose of God respecting David, and derived from his history the particular mould in which it was cast, was applicable only to Him, who, to the properties of a human nature and an earthly throne, was to add those also of the heavenly and divine.

We shall not here go further into detail respecting this class of prophecies, which belong chiefly to the Psalms; but we must remark, that as it was their object to explain the typical character of David's calling and kingdom, and to connect this with the higher things to come, we may reasonably expect there will be some portions in the Messianic psalms, which are alike applicable to type and antitype; and also entire psalms, in which there may be room for doubting to which of the two they may most fitly be referred. In some the distinctive, the superhuman and divine properties of the Messiah's person and kingdom are so broadly and characteristically delineated, (as in Ps. ii. xxii. xlv. lxxii. cx), that it is impossible by any fair interpretation of the language to understand the description of another than Christ. But there are others, in which the merely human elements are so strongly depicted (such as Ps. xl. lxix. cix.), that not a few of the traits might doubtless be found in the bearer also of the earthly kingdom; while still the excessive darkness of the picture, as a whole, on the one side, and the magnitude of the results and interests connected with it, on the other, shut us up to the conclusion that Christ, in his work of humiliation and his kingdom of blessing and glory, is the real subject of the prophecy. Viewed as an entire and prospective delineation, the theme is still one, and the sense not manifold but simple. There are again others, however, of which Ps. xli. may be taken as a specimen, in which the delineation throughout is as applicable to the bearer of the earthly, as to that of the heavenly kingdom; so that if regarded as a prophecy at all, it can only be in the way explained under our first supposition, as an historical description of things that happened under typical relations, which imparted to them a prophetical element.

Such varieties are no more than what might have been expected in the class of sacred lyrics now under consideration; and the rather so, as they were composed for the devotional use of the church at a time when she required as well to be refreshed and strengthened by the faith of the typical past, as to be cheered and animated by the hope of the still grander antitypical future. It was necessary that she should be taught so to look for the one as not to lose sight of the other; but rather, in what had already occurred, to find the root and promise of what was to be hereafter. The word of Nathan to David (2 Sam. vii. 4–16), which properly began the series, and laid the foundation for further developements, presented the matter in this light. David is there associated with his filial successor, as alike connected with the institution of the kingdom in its primary and inferior aspect; and the high honour was conceded to his house of furnishing the royal dynasty that was destined to preside for ever in God's name over the affairs of men. But this *for ever*, emphatically used in the promise, evidently pointed to a time when the relations of the kingdom in its then provisional and circumscribed form, should give way to others immensely greater and higher. It pointed to a commingling of the divine and human, the heavenly and the earthly, in another manner than could possibly be realised in the case either of David himself, or of any ordinary descendant from his loins. And it became one of the leading objects of David's prophetical calling, and of those who were his immediate successors in the prophetical function, to unfold, after the manner already described, something of that ulterior purpose of heaven, which, though included, was still but obscurely indicated in the fundamental prophecy of Nathan.[1]

---

[1] According to the view now given, there is no need for that alternating process which is so commonly resorted to in the explanation of Nathan's prophecy, by which this one part is made to refer to Solomon and his immediate successors, and that other to Christ. There is no need for formally splitting it up into such portions, each pointing to different quarters, nor can the understanding satisfactorily rest in them. The prophecy is to be taken as an organic whole, as the kingdom also is, of which it speaks. David reigned in

IV. But we have still to notice another possible combination of type with prophecy. It is possible, we said, that the typical transactions might themselves be still future; and might, in a prophetic word, be partly described, partly presupposed, as a ground for the delineation of other things still more distant, in respect to which they were to hold a typical relation. The difference between this and the last supposition is quite immaterial in so far as any principle is involved. It makes no essential change in the nature of the relation, that the typical transactions forming the groundwork of the prophetical delineation should have been contemplated as future, and not as past or present. It is true that the prophet was God's messenger, in an especial sense, to the men of his own age, and as such usually delivered messages, which were called forth by what had actually occurred, and bore its peculiar impress. But he was not necessarily tied to that. As from the present he could anticipate the still undeveloped future, so there was nothing to hinder—if the circumstances of the Church might require it—that he should also at times realise as present a nearer future, and from that anticipate another more remote. In doing so he would naturally transport himself into the position of those who were to witness that nearer future, which would then be contemplated as holding much the same relation typically to the higher things in prospect, as in the case last considered: that is, the matter-of-fact prophecy involved in the typical transactions viewed as already present, would furnish to the prophet's eye the form and aspect under which he would exhibit the corresponding events yet to be expected.

The only addition which the view now suggested makes to the one generally held, is, that we suppose the prophet, while he spake as from the midst of circumstances future, though not dis-

---

the Lord's name, and the Lord, in the fulness of time, was born to occupy David's throne—a mutual interconnection. The kingdom throughout is God's, only existing in an embryo state, while presided over by David and his merely human descendants; and rising to its ripened form, as soon as it passes into the hands of one who, by virtue of his divine properties, was fitted to bear the glory. The prophecy, therefore, is to be regarded as a general promise of the connection of the kingdom with David's person and line, including Christ as belonging to that line, after the flesh; but in respect to the element of eternity, the absolute perpetuity, guaranteed in the promise, not only admitting, but requiring the possession of a nature in Christ, higher unspeakably than he could derive from David.

tant, recognised in these something of a typical nature; and on the basis of that as the type unfolded the greater and more distant antitype. There is plainly nothing incredible or even improbable in such a supposition, especially if the nearer future already lay within the vision of the Church. The circumstances, however, giving rise to prophecies of this description could not be expected to be of very frequent occurrence. They could only be expected in those more peculiar emergencies when it became needful for the Church's warning or consolation to overshoot, as it were, the things more immediately in prospect, and fix the eye on others more remote in point of time, though in nature most closely connected with them.

Now, at one remarkable period of her history, the Old Testament Church was certainly in such circumstances—the period preceding and during the Babylonish exile. From the time that this calamity had become inevitable, the prophets, as already noticed, had spoken of it as a second Egypt—a new bondage to the power of the world, from which the Church required to be delivered by a new manifestation of redemptive grace. But a second redemption after the manner of the first would obviously no longer suffice to restore the heart of faith to assured confidence, or fill it with satisfying expectations of coming good. The redemption from Egypt, with all its marvellous accompaniments and happy results, had still failed to provide an effectual security against sweeping desolation. And if the redemption from Babylon might have brought, in the fullest sense, a restoration to the land of Canaan, and the re-establishment of the temple-service; yet if this were all the spirit of prophecy could descry of coming good, there must still have been room for fear to enter; there could scarcely fail even to be sad forebodings of new desolations likely to rise and undo the work of the new redemption. At such a period, therefore, the prophet had a double part to perform, when charged with the commission to comfort the people of God. He had, in the first instance, to declare the fixed purpose of God to visit Babylon for her sins, and thereby afford a door of escape for the captive children of the covenant, that as a people saved anew they might return to their ancient heritages. But he had to do more than this. He had to take his station, as it were, on the floor of that nearer redemption, and from thence direct the eye of hope to another and higher, of which it was but the imperfect shadow—a redemption which should lay the foundation of the Church's wellbeing so broad and deep, that the former troubles could no longer return, and heights of prosperity and blessing should be reached entirely unknown in the past. Thus alone could a ground of consolation be provided for the people of God, really adequate to the emergencies of that dismal time, when all that was of God seemed ready to perish, under the combined force of internal corruption and outward violence.

It was precisely in this way that the Prophet Isaiah sought to comfort the church of God by inditing the latter portion of his writings (ch. xl.-lxvi.), in which we have the most important example of the class of prophecies now under consideration. The central object in the whole of this magnificent chain of prophecy, is the appearance, work, and kingdom of the Lord Jesus Christ— his spirit and character, his sufferings and triumphs, the completeness of his redemption, the safety and blessedness of his people, the certain overthrow of his enemies, and the final glory of his kingdom. The manner in which this prophetic discourse is entered on, might alone satisfy us that such is in reality its main theme. For, the voice which there meets us, of one crying in the wilderness, is that to which, according to all the evangelists, John the Baptist appealed, as announcing beforehand his office and mission to the church of God. And if the forerunner is found at the threshold, who should chiefly occupy the interior of the building but He, whom John was specially sent to make known to Israel? The substance of the message also, as there briefly indicated, entirely corresponds; for, it speaks not, as is often loosely represented, of the people's return to Jerusalem, but of the Lord's return to the people; it announces a coming revelation of his glory, which all flesh should see; and proclaims to the cities of Judah the tidings, Behold your God! We are not to be understood as meaning, that the Lord might not in a sense be said to come to his people, when in their behalf he brought down the pride of Babylon, and laid open for them a way of return to their native land. A reference to this more secret and preparatory revelation of himself may certainly be understood, both here and in several kindred representations that follow; yet not as their direct and immediate object, but rather as something pre-supposed, similar in kind, though immensely inferior in degree to the proper reality. There are passages, indeed, so general in the truths and principles they enunciate, that they cannot with propriety be limited to one period of the church's history any more than to another. And again, there are others, especially the portion reaching from ch. xliv. 24 to xlviii. 22, as also ch. li., lii., which refer more immediately to the events connected with the deliverance from Babylon, as things in themselves perfectly certain, and fitted to awaken confidence in regard to the greater things that were yet destined to be accomplished. He who could speak of Babylon as already prostrate in the dust, though no shade had yet come over the lustre of her glory—who, at the very moment she was the scourge and terror of the nations, could picture to himself the time when she should be seen as a spoiled and forlorn captive—who could behold the once weeping exiles of Judea, escaped from her grasp, and sent back with honour to revive the glories of Jerusalem, while the proud destroyer was left to sink and moulder into irrecoverable ruin—He, who could foresee all this as in a manner present, and commit to his Church the prophetic announcement generations before it had been fulfilled, might well claim from his people an implicit faith, when giving intimation of a work still to be done, the greatness of which should surpass all thought, as its blessings should extend to all lands (ch. xlv. 17, 22, xlix. 18-26). Thus, the deliverance accomplished from the yoke of Babylon formed a fitting prelude and stepping-stone to the main subject of the prophecy—the revelation of God in the person and work of his Son. The certainty of the one—a certainty soon to be realized—was a pledge of the ultimate certainty of the other; and the character also of the former, as a singular and unexpected manifestation of the Lord's power to deliver his people and lay their enemies in the dust, was a prefiguration of what was to be accomplished once for all in the salvation to be wrought out by Jesus Christ.[1]

---

[1] The same view substantially of this portion of Isaiah's writings was given by Vitringa, who thus sums up the leading topics of discourse:—"The great mystery of the manifestation of the kingdom of God and his righteousness in the world through the Messiah, his forerunner, and apostles, with the revival of an elect church, then reduced to a very small number, with its more remarkable preceding signs, and the means that should be subservient to the whole work of grace,—among which preceding signs the

There are few portions of Old Testament prophecy, which altogether resemble the one we have been considering. Perhaps that which approaches nearest to it, in the mode of combining type with prophecy, is the thirty-fourth chapter of Isaiah, which is not a direct and simple delineation of the judgments that were destined to alight upon Idumea, but rather an ideal representation of the judgments preparing to alight on the enemies generally of God's people, founded upon the approaching desolations of Edom, which it contemplates as the type of the destruction that awaits all the adversaries. Still more similar, however, is our Lord's prophecy regarding the destruction of Jerusalem and his own final advent to judge the world in the twenty-fourth chapter of St Matthew's Gospel; in which, undoubtedly, the nearer future is regarded as the type of the higher and more remote. It would almost seem as if the two events were, to a certain extent, thrown together in the prophetic delineation; for the efforts that have been made to separate the portions strictly applicable to each, have never wholly succeeded; and more, perhaps, than any other part of prophetic Scripture is there the appearance here of something like a double sense. What reasons may have existed for this we can still but imperfectly apprehend. One principal reason, we may certainly conclude, was, that it did not accord with our Lord's design, as it would not have consisted with his people's good, to have exhibited very precise and definite prognostics of his second coming. The exact period behoved to be shrouded almost to the very last in mystery, and it seemed to divine wisdom the fittest course to order the circumstances connected with the final act of judgment on the typical people and territory, so as to serve, at the same time, for signs and tokens of the last great act of judgment on the world at large. As the acts themselves corresponded, so there should also be a correspondence in the manner of their accomplishment; and to contemplate the one as imaged in the other, without being able in

deliverance from Babylon by Cyrus, in connection with the destruction of Babylon itself, as typical of the overthrow of all idolatrous and Satanic power, are chiefly dwelt upon, in like manner, as the conviction both of Jews and Gentiles concerning the vanity of idols and the truth of God and his spiritual worship, hold the most prominent place among the concurrent means."

all respects to draw the line very accurately between them, was the whole that could safely be permitted to believers.

The result, then, of the preceding investigation is, that there is in Scripture a fourfold combination of type with prophecy. In the first of these the prophetic import lies in the type, and in the word only as descriptive of the type. In the others there was not a double sense, but a double prophecy—a typical prophecy in action, coupled with a verbal prophecy in word; not uniformly combined, however, but variously modified; in one class a distinct typical action having associated with it an express prophetical announcement; in another, the typical lying only as the background on which the spirit of prophecy raised the prediction of a corresponding but much grander future; and in still another, the typical belonging to a nearer future, which was realised as present, and taken as the occasion and groundwork of a prophecy respecting a future greater, and also more distant. It is in this last department alone that there is anything like a mixing up of two subjects together, and a consequent difficulty in determining when precisely the language refers to the nearer, and when to the more remote transactions. Even then, however, only in rare cases; and with this slight exception, there is nothing that carries the appearance of confusion or ambiguity. Each part holds its appropriate place, and the connection subsisting between them, in its various shapes and forms, is such as might have been expected in a system so complex and many-sided as that to which they belonged.

II. We proceed now to offer some remarks on the views generally held on the subject of the prophecies which have passed under our consideration. They fall into two opposite sections. Overlooking the real connection in such cases between type and prophecy, and often misapprehending the proper import of the language, the opinion contended for, on the one side, has been, that the predictions contain a double sense—the one primary and the other secondary, or the one literal and the other mystical; while, on the contrary side, it has been maintained that the predictions have but one meaning, and when applied in New Testament Scripture, in a way not accordant with that meaning, it is held to be a simple accommodation of the words. A brief examination of the two opposing views will be sufficient for our purpose.

1. And, first, in regard to the view which advocates the theory of the double sense. Here it has been laid down as a settled canon of interpretation, that " the same prophecies frequently refer to different events, the one near and the other remote—the one temporal the other spiritual, and, perhaps, eternal ; that the expressions are partly applicable to one and partly to another ; and that what has not been fulfilled in the first, we must apply to the second." If so, the conclusion seems inevitable, that there must be a painful degree of uncertainty and confusion resting on such portions of prophetic Scripture. And the ambiguity thus necessarily pervading them, must, one would think, have rendered them of comparatively little value, whether originally as a ground of hope to the Old Testament church, or now as an evidence of faith to the New.

Great ingenuity was certainly shewn by Warburton in labouring to establish the grounds of this double sense, without materially impairing in any respect the validity of the prophecy. The view advocated by him, however, lies open to two serious objections, which have been powerfully urged against it, especially by Bishop Marsh, and which have demonstrated its arbitrariness. 1. In the first place, while it proceeds upon the supposition, that the double sense of prophecy is quite analogous to the double sense of allegory, there is in reality an essential difference between them. " When we interpret a prophecy, to which a double meaning is ascribed, the one relating to the Jewish, the other to the Christian dispensation, we are in either case concerned with an interpretation of *words*. For the same words which, according to one interpretation, are applied to one event, are, according to another interpretation, applied to another event. But in the interpretation of an allegory, we are concerned only in the *first* instance with an interpretation of words ; the *second* sense, which is usually called the allegorical, being an interpretation of *things*. The interpretation of the words gives nothing more than the plain and simple narratives themselves (the allegory generally assuming the form of a narrative) ; whereas the *moral* of the allegory is learnt by an application of the things signified by those words to other things which resemble them, and which the former were intended to suggest. There is a fundamental difference, therefore, between the interpretation of an allegory, and the interpretation of a prophecy with a double sense."[1] 2. The view of Warburton is, besides, liable to the objection, that it not only affixes a necessary darkness and obscurity to the prophecies having the double sense, but also precludes the existence of any other prophecies more plain, direct, and explicit—until at least the dispensation, under which the prophecies were given, and for which the double sense specially adapted them, was approaching its termination. He contends that the veiled meaning of the prophecies was necessary, in order at once to awaken some general expectations among the Jews of better things to come, and, at the same time, to prevent these from being so distinctly understood as to weaken their regard to existing institutions. It is fatal to this view of the matter, that in reality many of the most direct and perspicacious prophecies concerning the Messiah were contemporaneous with those, which are alleged to possess the double meaning and the veiled reference to the Messiah. If, therefore, the divine method were such as to admit only of the one class, it must have been defeated by the other. And it must also have been, not so properly a ground of blame as a matter of necessity, arising from the very circumstances of their position, that the Jews " could not stedfastly look to the end of that which was to be abolished" (2 Cor. iii. 13). The reverse, however, was actually the case ; for the more clearly they perceived the meaning of the prophecies, and the end of their symbolical institutions, the more heartily did they enter into the design of God, and the more nearly attain the condition which it became them to occupy.

These objections, however, apply chiefly to that vindication of the double sense which came from the hand of Warburton, and was interwoven with his peculiar theory. The opinion has since been advocated in a manner that guards it against both objections, and is put, perhaps, in its most approved form by Davison. " What," he asks, " is the double sense ? Not the convenient latitude of two unconnected senses, wide of each other, and giving room to a fallacious ambiguity, but the combination of two

---

[1] Marsh's Lectures, p. 441.

related, analogous, and harmonizing, though disparate subjects, each clear and definite in itself; implying a twofold truth in the prescience, and creating an aggravated difficulty, and thereby an accumulated proof in the completion. For a case in point: to justify the predictions concerning the kingdom of David in their double force, it must be shewn of them, that they hold in each of their relations, and in each were fulfilled. So that the double sense of prophecy, in its true idea, is a check upon the pretences of a vague and unappropriated prediction, rather than a door to admit them. But this is not all. For if the prediction distribute its sense into two remote branches or systems of the divine economy; if it shew not only what is to take place in distant times, but describe also different modes of God's appointment, though holding a certain and intelligent resemblance to each other; such prediction becomes not only more convincing in the argument, but more instructive in the doctrine, because it expresses the correspondence of God's dispensations in their points of agreement, as well as his foreknowledge."[1]

This representation so far coincides with the one given in the preceding pages, that it virtually recognises a combination of type with prophecy; but differs, in that it supposes both to have been included in the prediction, the one constituting the primary, the other the secondary sense of its terms. And, undoubtedly, according to this scheme, as well as our own, the correspondence between God's dispensations might be sufficiently exhibited, both in regard to doctrine and general harmony of arrangement. But when it is contended further, that prophecy with such a double sense, instead of rendering the evidence it furnishes of divine foresight more vague and unsatisfactory, only supplies an accumulated proof of it by creating an aggravated difficulty in the fulfilment, it seems to be forgotten that the terms of the prediction, to admit of such a duplicate fulfilment, must have been made so much more general and vague. But it is the precision and definiteness of the terms in a prediction, which, when compared with the facts in providence that verify them, chiefly produce in our minds a conviction of divine foresight and direction. And in so far as prophecies might have been constructed to comprehend

---

[1] Davison on Prophecy, p. 196.

two series of disparate events, holding in each of the relations, and in each fulfilled, it could only be by dispensing with the more exact criteria, which we cannot help regarding in such cases as the most conclusive evidence of prophetic inspiration.

But as it was by no means the sole object of prophecy to provide this evidence, so predictions without such exact criteria are certainly not wanting in the word of God. There are prophecies which were not so much designed to foretel definite events, as to unfold great prospects and results, in respect to the manifestation of God's purposes of grace and truth toward men. Such prophecies were of necessity general and comprehensive in their terms, and admitted of manifold fulfilments. It is of them that we would understand the singularly pregnant and beautiful remark of Lord Bacon in the Second Book of the Advancement of Learning, that " divine prophecies, being of the nature of their Author, with whom a thousand years are but as one day, are therefore not fulfilled punctually at once, but have springing and germinant accomplishment ; though the height or fulness of them may refer to some one age." The very first prophecy ever uttered to fallen man—the promise given of a seed through the woman that should bruise the head of the serpent ; and that afterwards given to Abraham of a seed of blessing, may be referred to as illustrative of the principle ; since in either case—though not by virtue of a double sense, but of a wide and comprehensive import—a fulfilment from the first was constantly proceeding, while " the height and fulness" of the predicted good could only be reached in the redemption of Christ and the glories of his kingdom.

To return, however, to the matter at issue, we have yet to press our main objection to the theory of the double sense of prophecy ; we dispute the fact on which it is founded, that there really *are* prophecies (with the partial exceptions already noticed) predictive of similar, though disparate series of events, strictly applicable to each, and in each finding their fulfilment. This necessarily forms the main position of the advocates of the double sense ; and when brought to particulars, they constantly fail to establish it. The terms of the several predictions are sure to be put to the torture in order to get one of the two senses extracted from them. And the violent interpretations resorted to for the purpose of effecting this, afford one of the most striking proofs of the blinding influence which a theoretical bias may exert over the mind. Such Psalms, for example, as the second and forty-fifth, which are so distinctly characteristic of the Messiah, that some learned commentators have abandoned their early predilections to interpret them wholly of him, are yet ascribed by the advocates of the double sense as well to David as to Christ. Nay, by a singular inversion of the usual meaning of words, they call the former the literal, and the latter their figurative or secondary sense,—although this last is the only one the words can strictly bear.

There is no greater success in most other cases; we shall confine ourselves to one. "Thou shalt not leave my soul in hell, neither wilt thou suffer thine Holy One to see corruption: thou wilt make known to me the path of life; in thy presence is fulness of joy; and at thy right hand are pleasures for evermore." These words in the sixteenth Psalm were applied by the apostle Peter to Christ, as finding in the events of his history their only proper fulfilment. David, he contends, could not have been speaking directly of himself, since he had seen corruption; and instead of regaining the path of life, and ascending into the presence of God (namely, in glorified humanity), had suffered, as all knew, the common lot of nature. And so, the apostle infers, the words should be understood more immediately of Christ, in whose history alone they could properly be said to be accomplished. Warburton, however, inverts this order. Of the deliverance from hell, the freedom from corruption, and the return to the paths of life, he says, "Though it literally signifies security from the curse of the law upon transgressors, viz. immature death, yet it may very reasonably be understood in a spiritual sense of the resurrection of Christ from the dead; in which case the words or terms translated *soul* and *hell* are left in the meaning they bear in the Hebrew tongue of *body* and *grave!*" He does not, of course, deny that Peter claimed the passage as a prophecy of Christ's resurrection; but maintains that he does so, "no otherwise than by giving it a secondary or spiritual sense." In such a style of interpretation, one cannot but feel as if the terms *primary* and *secondary*, *literal* and *spiritual*, had somehow come to exchange places; since the plain import of the words carries us directly to

Christ, while only by a strained and inadequate meaning can they be adapted to David.

Such, indeed, is usually the case in the instances referred to by the advocates of this theory. The double sense they contend for does not strictly hold in both of the relations; and very commonly what is contended for as the immediate and primary, is the sense that is least accordant with the grammatical import of the words. We, therefore, reject it as a satisfactory explanation of a numerous class of prophecies, and on three several grounds: First, because it so ravels and complicates the meaning of the prophecies to which it is applied, as to involve us in painful doubt and uncertainty regarding their proper application. Secondly, should this be avoided, it can only arise from the prophecies being of so general and comprehensive a nature, as to be incapable of a very close and specific fulfilment. And, finally, when applied to particular examples, the theory practically gives way, as the terms employed in all the more important predictions are too definite and precise to admit of more than one proper fulfilment.

2. We turn now, in the last place, to the mode of prophetical interpretation which has commonly prevailed with those who have ranged themselves in opposition to the theory of the double sense. The chief defect in this class of interpreters consists in their having failed to take sufficiently into account the connection subsisting between the Old and the New Testament dispensations. They have hence generally given only a partial view of the relations involved in particular prophecies, and not unfrequently have confined the application of these to circumstances which only supplied the occasion of their delivery, and the form of their delineations. The single sense contended for has thus too often differed materially from the real sense. And many portions of the Psalms and other prophetical Scriptures, which in New Testament Scripture itself are applied to gospel-times, have been stript of their evangelical import, on the ground that the writer of the prophecy must have had in view some events immediately affecting himself or his country, and that no further use, except by way of accommodation, can legitimately be made of the words he uttered.

Such, for example, has been the way that the remarkable prophecy in Isaiah, respecting the son to be born of a virgin (ch. vii. 14–16), has often been treated. The words of the prophecy are, " Behold the virgin conceiveth and beareth a son, and she shall call his name Immanuel. Butter [rather milk] and honey shall he eat, when he shall know (or that he may know) to refuse what is evil and choose what is good ; for before this child shall know to refuse the evil, and to choose the good, the land shall become desolate, by whose two kings thou art distressed." We may be said to have two inspired commentaries on this prediction, one in the Old, and another in the New Testament. The prophet Micah, the contemporary of Isaiah, evidently referring to the words before us, says, immediately after announcing the birth of the future ruler of Israel at Bethlehem, " Therefore will he give them up, until the time that she who shall bear hath brought forth" (v. 3). The peculiar expression, " she who shall bear" points to the already designated mother of the divine king, but only in this prediction of Isaiah designated as the virgin ; so that, in the language of Rosenmüller, " both predictions throw light on each other. Micah discloses the divine origin of the person predicted ; Isaiah the wonderful manner of his birth." The other allusion in inspired Scripture is by St Matthew, when, relating the miraculous circumstances of Christ's birth, he adds, " Now all this was done, that it might be fulfilled which was spoken of the Lord by the prophet, saying, Behold a virgin shall be with child," &c. And the prophecy, as Bishop Lowth has well stated, " is introduced in so solemn a manner ; the sign is so marked, as a sign selected and given by God himself, after Ahaz had rejected the offer of any sign of his own choosing out of the whole compass of nature ; the terms of the prophecy are so peculiar, and the name of the child so expressive, containing in them much more than the circumstances of the birth of a common child required, or even admitted ; that we may easily suppose, that in minds prepared by the general expectation of a great deliverer to spring from the house of David, they raised hopes far beyond what the present occasion suggested ; especially when it was found, that in the subsequent prophecy, delivered immediately afterward, this child, called Immanuel, is treated as the Lord and Prince of Judah (ch. viii. 8–10). Who could this be, other than the heir of the throne of David? under which character a great and even a divine person had been promised."

These things leave little doubt as to the real bearing of the prophecy. But as originally delivered, it is connected with two peculiarities—the one that it is given as a sign to the house of David, then represented by the wicked Ahaz, and trembling for fear on account of the combined hostility of Syria and Israel— the other that it is succeeded by a word to the prophet concerning a son to be born to him by the prophetess, which should not be able to cry, My Father, before the king of Assyria had spoiled both the kingdoms of Syria and Israel (ch. viii. 1–4). And it has been thought, from these peculiarities, that it was really this son of the prophet that was meant by the Immanuel, as this alone could be a proper sign to Ahaz of the deliverance that was to be so speedily granted to him from the object of his dread. So Grotius, who holds that St Matthew only applied it mystically to Christ, and a whole host of interpreters since, of whom many can think of no better defence for the Evangelist than that, as the words of the prophet were more elevated and full than the immediate occasion demanded, they might be said to be fulfilled in what more nearly accorded with them. Apologies of this kind, it is easy to be seen, will not avail much in the present day to save the common discernment, to say nothing of the inspired authority of the Evangelist. But there is really no need for them. It is quite arbitrary to suppose that the child to be born of the prophetess (an ideal child, we should suppose, conceived and born in prophetic vision—since otherwise it must have been born in fornication) is to be identified with the virgin's son; the rather so, as an entirely different name is given to it (Maher-shalal-hash-baz)—an ideal, but descriptive name, and pointing simply to the spoliation that was to be effected on the hostile kingdoms. Immanuel has another, a higher import, and bespeaks what the Lord should be to the covenant-people, not what he should do to the enemies. Nor is the other circumstance, of the word being uttered as a sign to the house of David, any reason for turning it from its natural sense and application. A sign in the ordinary sense had been refused, under a pretence of pious trust in God, but really from a feeling of distrust and reliance on mere earthly confidences. And now the Lord gives a sign in a peculiar sense—much as Jesus met the craving of an adulterous generation for a sign from heaven, by giving the sign of the prophet Jonas—the reverse of what they either wished or expected—a sign, not from heaven, but from the lower parts of the earth. So here, by announcing the birth of Immanuel, the prophet gave a sign suited to the time of backsliding and apostacy in which he lived. For it told the house of David that, wearying God as they were doing by their sins, he would vindicate his cause in a way they little expected or desired; that he would provide for the occupancy of the throne over his land and people by raising up a child of divine, as well as human properties; but that, meanwhile, every thing should go to desolation and ruin—first, indeed, in the allied kingdoms of Israel and Syria (v. 16), but afterwards also in the kingdom of Judah (v. 17-25); so that the destined possessor of the throne, when he came, should find all in a prostrate condition, and grow up like one in an impoverished and stricken country, where only the natural products of milk and honey were to be found (comp. v. 16 with 22); like one that should be fed with the simple fare of a cottage shepherd. Thus understood, the whole is entirely natural and consistent; and the single sense of the prophecy proves to be identical, as well with the native force of the words, as with the interpretations of inspired men.

We have selected this as one of the most common and plausible specimens of the false style of interpretation to which we have referred. It is needless to adduce more, as the explanations given in the earlier part of the chapter have already met many of them by anticipation; and the supplementary treatise in the Appendix will supply what further is needed. If but honestly and earnestly dealt with, the Scripture has no reason to fear, in this or in other departments, the closest investigation; the more there is of rigid inquiry, displacing superficial considerations, the more will its inner truth and harmony appear.

CHAPTER FIFTH.

THE INTERPRETATION OF PARTICULAR TYPES—SPECIFIC PRINCIPLES AND DIRECTIONS.

It was one of the objections we urged against the typological views of our older divines, that their system admitted of no fixed or definite rules being laid down for guiding us to the knowledge and interpretation of particular types. Every thing was left to the discretion or caprice of the individual who undertook to investigate them. The few directions that were sometimes given upon the subject were too vague and general to be of any material service. That the type must have borne, in its original design and institution, a pre-ordained reference to the Gospel antitype—that there is often more in the type than in the antitype, and more in the antitype than the type—that there must be a natural and appropriate application of the one to the other—that the wicked as such, and acts of sin as such, must be excluded from the category of types—that one thing is sometimes the type of different and even contrary things, though in different respects—and that there is sometimes an interchange between the type and the antitype of the names respectively belonging to each:—These rules of interpretation, which are the whole that Glassius and other hermeneutical writers furnish for our direction, could not go far, either to restrain the license of conjecture, or to mark out the particular course of thought and inquiry that should be pursued. They can scarcely be said to touch the main difficulties of the subject, and throw no light on its more distinguishing peculiarities. Nor, indeed, could any other result have been expected. The rules could not be precise or definite, when the system on which they were founded was altogether loose and indeterminate. And only with the laying of a more solid and stable foundation could directions for the practical treatment of the subject come to possess any measure of satisfaction or explicitness.

Even on the supposition that some progress has now been made in laying such a foundation, we cannot hold out the prospect, that no room shall be left for dubiety, and that all may be reduced to a kind of dogmatical precision and certainty. It would be unreasonable to expect this, considering both the peculiar character and the manifold variety of the field embraced by the Typology of Scripture. That there may still be particular cases in which it will be questionable whether anything properly typical belonged to them, and others in which a diversity of view may be allowable in explaining what is typical, seems to us by no means improbable. And in the specific rules or principles of interpretation that follow, we do not aim at dispelling every possible doubt and ambiguity connected with the subject, but only at fixing its more prominent and characteristic outlines. We believe, that with ordinary care and discretion, they will be sufficient to guard against material error.

I. The first principle we lay down has respect merely to the amount of what is typical in Old Testament Scripture; it is, that *nothing is to be regarded as typical of the good things under the Gospel, which was itself of a forbidden and sinful nature.* Something approximating to this has been mentioned among the too general and obvious directions which philological writers have been accustomed to give upon the subject. It is, indeed, so much of that description, that though in itself a principle most necessary to be observed and acted on, yet we should have refrained from any express announcement or formal proof of it here, were it not still frequently set at nought in theological discussions, as well as popular discourses.

The ground of the principle, as we have given it, lies in the connection which the type has with the antitype, and consequently with God. The antitype standing in the things which belong to God's everlasting kingdom, is necessarily of God; and so, by a like necessity, the type, which was intended to foreshadow and prepare for it, must have been equally of him. Whether a symbol in religion, or a fact in providence, it must have borne upon it the divine sanction and approval; otherwise, there could have been no proper connection between the ultimate reality and its preparatory exhibitions. So far as the institutions of religion are concerned, this is readily admitted; and no one would think of contending for the idolatrous rites of worship which were sometimes introduced into the services of the sanctuary, being ranked among the shadows of the better things to come.

But there is not the same readiness to perceive the incongruity of admitting to the rank of types, actions which were as far from being accordant with the mind of God, as the impurities of an idolatrous worship. Such actions might, no doubt, differ in one respect from the forbidden services of religion; they might in some way be overruled by God for the accomplishment of his own purposes, and thereby be brought into a certain connection with himself. This was never more strikingly done than in respect to the things which befel Jesus—the great antitype—which were carried into effect by the operation of the fiercest malice and wickedness, and yet were the very things which the determinate counsel and foreknowledge of God had appointed before to be done. It is one thing, however, for human agents and their actions being controlled and directed by God, so as, amid all their impetuosity and uproar, to be constrained to work out his righteous purposes ; but another thing for them to stand in such close relationship to him, that they become express and authoritative revelations of his will. This last is the light in which they must be contemplated, if a typical character is ascribed to them. For the time, during which typical things lasted, they stood as temporary representations under God's own hand of what he was going permanently to establish under the Gospel. And, therefore, as amid those higher transactions, where the *antitype* comes into play, we exclude whatever was the offspring of human ignorance or sinfulness ; so in the earlier and inferior transactions, which were *typical* of what was to come, we must, in like manner, exclude the workings of all earthly and sinful affections. The typical and the antitypical alike must bear on them the image and superscription of God.

Violations of this obvious principle are much less frequently met with now, than they were in the theological writings of last century. Still, however, instances are occasionally forcing themselves on one's notice. And in popular discourses, none perhaps occurs more frequently than that connected with Jacob's melancholy dissimulation and cunning policy for obtaining the blessing. His receiving the blessing, we are sometimes told, in the garments of Esau, which his mother arrayed him with, " is to be viewed as a faint shadow of our receiving the blessing from God in the garments of Jesus Christ, which all the children of the promise wear. It was not the feigned venison, but the borrowed garments, that procured the blessing. Even so, we are not blessed by God for our good works, however pleasing to him, but for the righteousness of our Redeemer." What a confounding of things that differ! The garments of the "profane" Esau made to image the spotless righteousness of Jesus! And the fraudulent use of the one by Jacob, viewed as representing the believer's simple and confiding trust in the other! Between things so essentially different, there can manifestly be nothing but superficial resemblances, which necessarily vanish the moment the real facts of the case rise into view. It was not Jacob's imposing upon his father's infirmities either with false venison, or with borrowed garments, which in reality procured for him the blessing. The whole that can be said of these is, that in the actual circumstances of the case, they had a certain influence, of an instrumental kind, in leading Isaac to pronounce it. But what had been thus spoken on false grounds and under mistaken apprehensions, might surely have been recalled, when the truth came to be known. The prophet Nathan, at a later age, found no difficulty in revoking the word he had too hastily spoken to David respecting the building of the temple, though it had been elicited by something very different from falsehood—simply by an exciting and unexpected display of goodness (2 Sam. vii. 3). And in the case now referred to, if there had been nothing more in the matter than the mock venison and the hairy garments of Esau, there can be little doubt that the blessing that had been pronounced, would have been instantly revoked, and the curse which Jacob dreaded uttered in its stead. In truth, Isaac erred in what he purposed to do, not less than Jacob in beguiling him to do what he had not purposed. He was going to utter in God's name a prophetic word, which, if it had been uttered as he intended, would have contravened the oracle originally given to

Rebekah concerning the two children, even before their birth—that the elder should serve the younger. And there were not wanting indications in the spirit and behaviour of the sons, after they had sprung to manhood, which might have led a mind of spiritual discernment to descry in Jacob, rather than Esau, the heir of blessing. But living as Isaac had done for the most part in a sort of luxurious ease, in his declining years especially yielding too much to the fleshly indulgences assiduously ministered to by the hand of Esau, the eye of his mind, like that of his body, grew dim, and he lost the correct perception of the truth. But when he saw how the providence of God had led him to bestow the blessing, otherwise than he himself had designed, the truth rushed at once upon his soul. "He trembled exceedingly"—not simply, nor perhaps chiefly, because of the deceit that had been practised upon his blindness, but because of the worse spiritual blindness which had led himself so grievously to misapprehend the purpose of God. And hence, even after the discovery of Jacob's fraudulent behaviour, he declared with the strongest emphasis, "Yea, and he shall be blessed."

Thus, when the real circumstances of the case are considered, there appears no ground whatever for connecting the improper conduct of Jacob with the mode of a sinner's justification. The resemblances that may be found between them are quite superficial or arbitrary. And such always are the resemblances which appear between the workings of evil in man, and the good that is in God. The two belong to essentially different spheres, and a real analogy, or a divinely ordained connection cannot possibly unite them together. The principle, however, may be carried a step farther. As the operations of sin cannot prefigure the actings of righteousness, so the direct results and consequences of sin cannot justly be regarded as typical representations of the exercises of grace and holiness. When, therefore, (to refer again to the history of Jacob) the things that befel him in God's providence, on account of his unbrotherly and deceitful conduct, are represented as typical foreshadowings of Christ's work of humiliation—Jacob's withdrawal from his father's house, prefiguring Christ's leaving the region of glory and appearing as a stranger on the earth—Jacob's sleeping on the naked ground with nothing but a stone for his pillow, Christ's descent into the lowest depths of poverty and shame, that he might afterwards be exalted to the head-stone of the corner, and so forth[1]—in such representations there is manifestly a stringing together of events which have no fundamental agreement, and are without any common relations. In the one case Jacob was merely suffering the just reward of his misdeeds, while the Redeemer, in the other and alleged parallel transactions, was voluntarily giving the highest display of the holy love that animated his bosom for the good of men. And whatever there might be in certain points of an outward and formal resemblance between them, it is in the nature of things impossible that there could be a real harmony and connection.

It is to be noted, however, that we apply the principle now under consideration to the extent merely of denying a typical connection between what in former times appeared of evil on the part of man, and the good subsequently introduced by God. And we do so on the ground that such things only as he sanctioned and approved in the past, could foreshadow the higher and better things which were to be sanctioned and approved by him in the future. But as all the manifestations of truth have their corresponding and antagonist manifestations of error, it is perfectly warrantable and scriptural to regard the form of evil which, from time to time, confronted the type, as itself the type of something similar, which should afterwards arise as a counter form of evil to the antitype. Antichrist, therefore, may be said to have had his types as well as Christ. Hagar was the type of a carnal church, in bondage to the elements of the world, and producing a seed after the flesh, as Sarah was of a spiritual church, possessing the freedom and enjoying the privileges of the children of God. Egypt, Edom, Assyria, Babylon without, and Saul, Ahithophel, Absalom, and others within the Old Testament church, have each their counterpart in the things belonging to the history of Christ and his church of the New Testament. In strictness of speech it is the other class of relations alone which were settled and ordained by God; but as God's acts and operations in his church never fail to call into existence the world's enmity and opposition, so the forms which this assumed in earlier times might well be regarded as prophetic of those, which were after-

---

[1] Kanne's Christus in Alten Testament, Th. ii., p. 133, &c.

wards to appear. And if so with the evil itself, still more with the visitations of severity sent to chastise the evil; for these come directly from God. The judgments, therefore, he inflicted on iniquity in the past, typified like judgments on all similar aspects of iniquity in the future. And the period when the good shall reach its full developement and final triumph, shall also be that in which the work of judgment sheds upon the evil perpetual desolation.

II. We pass on to another, which must still also be a somewhat negative principle of interpretation, viz. that in determining the existence and import of particular types, we must be guided, *not so much by any knowledge possessed, or supposed to be possessed, by the ancient worshippers concerning their prospective fulfilment, as from the light furnished by their realization in the great facts and revelations of the Gospel.*

Whether we look to the symbolical or the historical types, neither their own nature, nor God's design in appointing them, could warrant us in drawing very definite and conclusive inferences regarding the insight possessed by the Old Testament worshippers into their prospective or Gospel import. The one formed part of an existing religion, and the other of a course of providential dealings; and in that more immediate respect there were certain truths they embodied, and certain lessons they taught for those who had directly to do with them. Their fitness for unfolding such truths and lessons formed, as we have seen, the ground-work of their typical connection with Gospel-times. But though they must have been understood in that primary aspect by all sincere and intelligent worshippers, these did not necessarily perceive their further reference to the things of Christ's kingdom. Nor does the reality or the precise import of their typical character depend upon the correctness or the extent of the knowledge held respecting it by the members of the Old Covenant. For the connection implied in their possessing such a character between the preparatory and the final dispensations was not of the Church's forming, but of God's; and the greater part of the design which he intended these to serve with ancient believers, may have been accomplished, though they knew little, and perhaps in some cases nothing, of the germs that lay concealed in them of better things to come. These germs *were* concealed in all typical events and institutions, not directly exhibited—since the events and institutions had a significance and use for the time then present, apart from what might be evolved in the future purposes of God. Now, we are expressly told, even in regard to direct prophecies of gospel-times, that not only the persons to whom they were originally delivered, but the very individuals through whom they were communicated, did not always or necessarily understand their precise meaning. Sometimes, at least, they had to assume the position of inquirers, in order to get the more exact and definite information which they desired (Dan. xii. 8 ; 1 Pet. i. 12), and it would seem from the case of Daniel, that even then they did not always obtain it. The prophets were not properly the authors of their own predictions, but spake as they were moved by the Holy Ghost. *Their* knowledge, therefore, of the real meaning of the prophecies they uttered, was an entirely separate thing from the prophecies themselves ; and if we knew what it was, it would still by no means conclusively fix their full import. Such being the case in regard even to the persons who uttered the *spoken and direct* prophecies of the Old Testament, how preposterous would it be to make the insight obtained by believers generally into the *indirect and veiled* prophecies, (as the types may be called), the ground and standard of the gospel-truth they embodied ? In each case alike, it is the mind of God, not the discernment or faith of the ancient believer, that we have properly to do with.

Obvious as this may appear to some, it has been very commonly overlooked ; and typical explanations have in consequence too often taken the reverse direction of what they should have done. Writers in this department are constantly telling us, how formerly the eye of faith looked through the present to the future, and finding in that the reason why our present should be descried in the remote past. Thus Adam is represented in a popular work as having " believed the promise concerning Christ, in whose commemoration he offered continual sacrifice ; and in the assurance thereof he named his wife *Eve*, that is to say *life*, and he called his son *Seth*, *settled*, or persuaded in Christ."[1] Another exalts in like manner the faith of Zipporah, and regards her,

[1] Fisher's Marrow of Modern Divinity, P. 1, c. 2.

when she said to Moses, " A bloody husband thou art, because of the circumcision," as announcing " through one of her children, the Jehovah as the future Redeemer and bridegroom."[1] Another presents Moses to our view as wondering at the great sight of the burning bush, " *because* the great mystery of the incarnation and sufferings of Christ was there represented ; a great sight he might well call it, when there was represented *God manifest in the flesh*, suffering a dreadful death, and rising from the dead."[2] And Owen, speaking of the Old Testament believers generally, says, " Their faith in God was not confined to the outward things they enjoyed, but on Christ in them, and represented by them. They believed that they were only resemblances of him and his mediation, which, when they lost the faith of, they lost all acceptance with God in their worship."[3] Writers of a different class, and of later date, have followed substantially in the same track. Warburton maintains with characteristic dogmatism, that the transaction with Abraham, in offering up Isaac, was a typical action, in which the patriarch had scenically represented to his view the sufferings, death, and resurrection of Christ ; and that on any other supposition, there can be no right understanding of the matter.[4] Dean Graves expresses his concurrence in this interpretation, as does also Mr Faber, who says, that " Abraham must have clearly understood the nature of that awful transaction by which the day of Christ was to be characterised, and could not have been ignorant of the benefits about to be procured by it."[5] And, to mention no more, Chevallier intimates a doubt concerning the typical character of the brazen serpent, because " it is not plainly declared, either in the Old or the New Testament, to have been ordained by God purposely to represent to the Israelites the future mysteries of the Gospel revelation." [6]

---

[1] Kanne's Christus in Alt. Test. I. p. 100.

[2] History of Redemption, by Jonathan Edwards. Period I. p. 4.

[3] Owen on Heb. viii. 5. In another part of his writings, however, we find him saying, " Although those (Old Testament) things are now full of light and instruction to us, evidently expressing the principal works of Christ's mediation, yet they were not so unto them. The meanest believer may now find out more of the work of Christ in the types of the Old Testament, than any prophet or wise man could have done of old."— On the Person of Christ, ch. 8.

[4] Legation of Moses, B. vi. sec. 5.

[5] Treatise on the Three Dispensations, Vol. ii. p. 57.   [6] Historical Types, p. 221.

These quotations sufficiently shew, how current the opinion has been, and still is, that the persons who lived amid the types must have perfectly understood their typical character, and that by *their* knowledge in this respect, we are bound in great measure, if not entirely, to regulate ours. It is, however, a very difficult question, and one (as we have already had occasion to state) on which we should seldom venture to give more than an approximate deliverance, how far the realities typified even by the more important symbols and transactions of ancient times were distinctly perceived by any individual who lived prior to their actual appearance. The reason for this uncertainty and probable ignorance is the same with that, which has been so clearly exhibited by Bishop Horsley, and applied in refutation of an infidel objection, in the closely related field of prophecy. It was necessary, for the very ends of prophecy, that a certain disguise should remain over the events it foretold, till they became facts in providence; and therefore, "whatever private information the prophet might enjoy, the Spirit of God would never permit him to disclose the ultimate intent and particular meaning of the prophecy."[1] Types being a species of prophecy, and from their nature less precise and determinate in meaning, they must certainly have been placed under the veil of a not inferior disguise. Whatever insight more advanced believers might have had into their ultimate design, it could neither be distinctly announced, nor, if announced, serve as a sufficient directory for us; it could only furnish, according to the measure of light it contained, comfort and encouragement to themselves. And whether that measure might be great or small, vague and general, or minute and particular, we should not be bound, even if we knew it, to abide by its rule; for here, as in prophecy, the judgment of the early Church "must still bow down to time as a more informed expositor."

That the sincere worshippers of God in former ages, especially such as possessed the higher degrees of spiritual thought and discernment, were acquainted not only with God's general purpose of redemption, but also with some of its more prominent features and results, we have no reason to doubt. It is impossible to read those portions of Old Testament Scripture which disclose the feelings and expectations of gifted minds, without being con-

[1] Horsley's Works, vol. i. p. 271—273.

vinced, that considerable light was sometimes obtained respecting the work of salvation. We shall find an opportunity for inquiring more particularly concerning this, when we come to treat, in a subsequent part of our investigations, respecting the connection between the moral legislation, and the ceremonial institutions of Moses. But that the views even of the better part of the Old Testament worshippers must have been comparatively dim, and that their acceptance as worshippers did not depend upon the clearness of their discernment in regard to the person and kingdom of Christ, is evident from what was stated in our second chapter as to the relatively imperfect nature of the earlier dispensations, and the childhood-state of those who lived under them. It was the period, when, as is expressly stated in the epistle to the Hebrews (ch. ix. 8), "the way into the holiest of all was not yet made manifest;" or, in other words, when the method of salvation was not fully disclosed to the view of God's people. And though we may not be warranted to consider what is written of the closing age of Old Testament times as a fair specimen of their general character, yet we cannot shut our eyes to the fact, that not only did much prevailing ignorance then exist concerning the better things of the new covenant, but that instances occur even of genuine believers, who still betrayed an utter misapprehension of their proper nature. Thus Nathanael was pronounced "an Israelite indeed, in whom there was no guile," while he obviously laboured under inadequate views of Christ's person and work. And no sooner had Peter received the peculiar benediction bestowed, on account of his explicit confession of the truth, than he gave evidence of his ignorance of the design, and his repugnance to the thought, of Christ's sufferings and death. Such things occurring on the very boundary-line between the Old and the New, and after the clearer light of the New had begun to be partially introduced, render it plain, that they may also have existed, and in all probability did generally prevail, even among the believing portion of Israel in remoter times.

But this being the case, it would manifestly be travelling in the wrong direction, to make the knowledge, which was possessed by ancient believers regarding the prospective import of particular types, the measure of ours. The providential arrangements and religious institutions which constitute the types, had an end to serve, independently of their typical design, in ministering to the present wants of believers, and nourishing in their souls the life of faith. Their more remote and typical import was for us, even more than for those, who had immediately to do with them. It does not rest upon the more or less imperfect information such persons might have had concerning it; but chiefly on the light furnished by the records of the New Testament, and thence reflected on those of the Old. "It is Christ who holds the key of the types, not Moses;" and instead of making every thing depend upon the still doubtful inquiry, what did pious men of old descry of Gospel realities through the shadowy forms of typical institutions? we must repair to these realities themselves, and by the light radiating from them over the past, as well as the present and future things of God, read the evidence of that "testimony of Jesus," which lies written in the typical, not less than in the prophetical portions of ancient Scripture.

III. But if in this respect we have comparatively little to do with the views of those who lived under former dispensations, there is another respect, in which we have much to do with them. And our next principle of interpretation is, that we must always, in the first instance, *be careful to make ourselves acquainted with the truths or ideas exhibited in the types, considered merely as providential transactions or religious institutions.* In other words, we are to find in what they were in their immediate relation to the patriarchal or Jewish worshipper, the foundation and substance of what they typically present to the Christian Church.

There is no contrariety between this principle and the one last announced. We had stated, that in endeavouring to ascertain the reality and the nature of a typical connection between Old and New Testament affairs, we are not to reason downward from what might be known of this in earlier times, but rather upward from what may now be known of it, in consequence of the clearer light and higher revelations of the Gospel. What we farther state is, that the religious truths and ideas which were embodied in the typical events and institutions of former times, must be regarded as forming the ground and limit of their prospective reference to the affairs of Christ's kingdom. That they had a moral, political, or religious end to serve for the time then present, so far from interfering with their destination to typify the spiritual things of the Gospel, forms the very sum and substance of their typical bearing. Hence their character in the one respect, the more immediate, may justly be regarded as the essential key to their character in the other and higher respect.

This principle of interpretation grows so necessarily out of the views advanced in the earlier and more fundamental parts of our inquiry, that it must here be held as in a manner proved. Its validity must stand or fall with that of the general principles we have sought to establish, as to the relation between type and antitype. That relation, it has been our object to shew, rests on something deeper than merely outward resemblances. It rests rather on the essential unity of the things so related, on their being alike embodiments of the same principles of divine truth; but embodiments in the case of the type, on a lower and earthly scale, and as a designed preparation for the higher developement afterwards to be made in the Gospel. That, therefore, which goes first in the nature of things, must also go first in any successful effort to trace the connection between them. And the question, What elements of divine truth are symbolized in the type? must take precedence of the other question, How did the type foreshadow the greater realities of the antitype? For it is in the solution we obtain for the one, that a foundation is to be laid for the solution of the other.

It is only by keeping steadfastly to this rule that we shall be able, in the practical department of our inquiry, to direct our thoughts to substantial, as opposed to merely superficial and fanciful resemblances. The palpable want of discrimination in this respect, between what is essential and what is only accidental, formed one of the leading defects in our older writers. And it naturally sprung from too exclusive a regard to the antitype, as if the things belonging to *it* being fully ascertained, we were at liberty to connect it with every thing formally resembling it in ancient times, whether really akin in nature to it or not. Thus, when Kanne, in a passage formerly referred to, represents the stone which Jacob took for his pillow at Bethel, as a type of Christ in his character, as the foundation-stone of his church, there is, no doubt, a kind of outward similarity, so that the same language may, in a sense, be applied to both; but there is no common principle uniting them together. The use which Jacob made of the stone was quite different from that in respect to which Christ is exhibited as the stone laid in Zion—laid not for the repose or slumber, but for the stability and support of a ransomed people. The strength and durability of a rock were essentially needed for this; but they contributed nothing to the fitness of what Jacob's necessities drove him to employ as a temporary pillow. It was his misfortune, not his privilege, to be obliged to resort to a stone for such a purpose.

We had occasion formerly to describe in what manner the lifting up of the brazen serpent in the wilderness might be regarded as typical of the lifting up of a crucified Redeemer; by shewing how the inferior objects and relations of the one had their correspondence in the higher objects and relations of the other![1] But suppose we should proceed in the opposite direction, and should take these higher objects and relations of the antitype as the rule and measure of what we are to expect in the type; then, having a far wider and more complicated subject for our starting-point, we should naturally set about discovering many slight and superficial analogies in the type, to bring it into a fuller correspondence with the antitype. This is what many who have treated of the subject actually do. And hence we find them expatiating upon the metal of which the serpent was formed, and which, from being inferior to some others, they regarded as foreshadowing Christ's outward meanness, while in its solidity they descried his divine strength, and in its dim lustre the veil of his human nature![2] What did it avail to the Israelite, or for any purpose the serpent had to serve, of what particular stuff it was made? A dead and senseless thing in itself, it must have been all one for those who were called to look to it, whether the material was brass or silver, wood or stone. And yet, as if it were not enough to make account of these trifling accidents, others were sometimes invented, for which there is no foundation in the inspired narrative, to obtain for the greater breadth of the one subject a corresponding breadth in the other. Thus Guild represents the serpent as not having been forged by man's hand or hammer, but by a mould, and in the fire, to image the divine con-

---

[1] Chap. iii. p. 81.   [2] Guild's Moses Unveiled, and Watson's Holy Eucharist.

ception of Christ's human nature; and Justin Martyr, with still greater license, supposes the serpent to have been made in the form of a cross, the more exactly to represent a suffering Redeemer. Suppose it had been modelled after this form, would it have been rendered thereby a more effective instrument for healing the diseased? Or, would one essential idea have been added to what either an Israelite or a Christian were otherwise at liberty to associate with it? All such puerile straining of the subject arose from an inverted order being taken in tracing the connection between the spiritual reality and the ancient shadow. It would no longer be thought of, if the principle of interpretation here advanced were strictly adhered to; that is, if the typical matter of an event or institution were viewed simply as standing in the truths or principles which it brought distinctly into view; and if these were regarded as actually comprising all that in each particular case could legitimately be applied to the antitypical affairs of Christ's kingdom.

The judicious application of this principle will serve also to rid us of another class of extravagances, which are of frequent occurrence in writers of the Coccejan school, and which mainly consist, like those already noticed, of external resemblances, deduced with little or no regard to any real principle of agreement. We refer to the customary mode of handling typical persons or characters, with no other purpose apparently than that of exhibiting the greatest possible number of coincidences between these and Christ. As many as forty of such have been reckoned between Moses and Christ, and even more between Joseph and Christ. Of course, a great proportion of such resemblances are of a quite superficial and trifling nature, and are of no moment, whether they happen to be perceived or not. For any light they throw on the purposes of Heaven, or any advantage they yield to our faith, we gain nothing by admitting them, and we lose as little by rejecting them. They would never have been sought for had the real nature of the connection between type and antitype been understood, and the proper mode of exhibiting it been adopted: nor would typical persons or individuals, sustaining a typical character through the whole course and tenor of their lives, have been supposed to exist. It was to familiarise the Church with great truths and principles, not to occupy her thoughts with petty agreements and fanciful analogies, that she was kept so long conversant with preparatory dispensations. And as that end might have been in part served by a single transaction, or a special appointment in a life-time; so, whenever it was served, it must have been by virtue of its exhibiting important aspects of divine truth; such as were to re-appear in the person and work of Christ. It is not, in short, individuals throughout the entire compass of their history, but individuals in certain divinely appointed offices or relations, in which we are to seek for what is typical in this province of sacred history.[1]

IV. Another conclusion flowing not less clearly than the foregoing from the views already established, and which we propose as our next leading principle of interpretation, is, that while the symbol or institution constituting the type has properly *but one radical meaning, yet the fundamental idea or principle exhibited in it may often be capable of more than one application to the realities of the Gospel;* that is, it may bear respect to, and be developed in, more than one department of the affairs of Christ's kingdom. But in illustrating this proposition, we must take in succession the several parts of which it consists.

1. The first part asserts each type to be capable of but one radical meaning. It has a definite way of expressing some fundamental idea—that, and no more. Were it otherwise, we should find any consistent or satisfactory interpretation of typical things quite impracticable, and should often lose ourselves in a sea of uncertainty. An example or two may serve to shew how far this

---

[1] Scarcely any of the late works on the types, published in this country, are free from the extravagances we have referred to respecting personal types. They assume, however, the most extreme form in the German work of Kanne, published in 1818. There the mere similarity of names is held as a conclusive proof of a typical connection; so that Miriam, the sister of Moses, was a type of Mary, for the Jews call the former Maria, as well as the latter. The work is full of such puerilities. It is the same tendency, however, to rest in merely superficial resemblances which led Schöttgen, for example, in his Horæ Heb. on 1 Cor. x. 2, and leads some still, to hold that the Israelites must have been "bedewed and refreshed" by the cloud. It is true the sacred narrative is silent about that, nor is any support to be found for it in the Jewish writings; but it seemed to the learned author necessary to make out a typical relation to baptism, and so he regards it as in a manner self-evident. On the same ground, of course, Noah and his family must have been all sprinkled or dipped in the flood, since this too was the type of baptism!

has actually been the case in the past. Glassius makes the deluge to typify both the preservation of the faithful through baptism, and the destruction of the wicked in the day of judgment; and the rule under which he adduces this example is, that "a type may be a figure of two, and even contrary things, though in different respects."[1] In like manner, Taylor, taking the full liberty of such a canon, when interpreting the passage of the Israelites through the Red sea as a type of baptism, sees in that event, first, "the offering of Jesus Christ to their faith, through the Red sea, of whose death and passion they should find a sure and safe way to the celestial Canaan;" and then this other truth, that "by his merit and mediation he would carry them through all difficulties and dangers, as deep as the bottom of the sea, unto eternal rest."[2] In this last specimen the Red sea is viewed as representing at the sametime, and in relation to the same persons, both the atoning blood of Christ and the outward trials of life. The other example is not so palpably incorrect, nor does it in fact go to the entire length, which the rule it is designed to illustrate properly warrants; for the action of the waters in the deluge is considered by it, with reference to different persons, as well as in different respects. It is at fault, however, in making one event typical of two diverse and unconnected results. Many other examples might be produced of similar false interpretations from what has been written of the tabernacle and its services, equally indicative, on the part of the writers, of a capricious fancy, but utterly destitute in themselves of any solid foundation.

Our previous investigations, we trust, have removed this prolific source of ambiguity and confusion. For, if we have not entirely failed of our object, we have proved that the typical transactions and symbols of the Old Testament are by no means so vague and arbitrary as to be capable of bearing senses altogether variable and inconsistent. Viewed as a species of language, which they really were—a speaking by action instead of words—they could only reach the end they had to serve by giving forth a distinct and intelligible meaning. Such language can no more do

---

[1] Philolog. Sac. Lib. II. p. 1. Trac. II. sec. 4, § 8. He quotes from Cornelius à Lepide, but adopts the rule as good.
[2] Moses and Aaron, p. 237.

this than oral or written discourse, if constructed so as to be susceptible of the most diverse and even opposite senses. By the necessities of the case, therefore, we are constrained to hold, that whatever instruction God might design to communicate to the church, either in earlier or in later times, by means of the religious institutions and providential arrangements of past times, it must have been such as admits of being derived from them by a fixed and determinate mode of interpretation. To suppose that their virtue consisted in some capacity to express meanings quite variable and inconsistent with each other, would be to assimilate them to the uncertain oracles of heathenism. *Their* excellence, on the contrary, lay in the truth and importance of some one meaning, which it was their destination, not always, it may be, with equal distinctness, but still always without ambiguity, to unfold.

2. This is to be understood in the strictest sense of such typical acts and symbols, as, from their nature, were expressive of a simple, uncompounded idea. In that case, it would be an incongruity to make what was one in the type present, like a revolving light, a changeful and varying aspect toward the antitype. But the type itself might possibly be of a complex nature; that is, it might embody a process which branched out into two or more lines of operation, and so combined two or more related ideas together. In such a case there will require to be a corresponding variety in the application that is made from the type to the antitype. The twofold, or perhaps still more complicated idea contained in the one must have its counterpart in the other, as much as if each idea had received a separate representation; though due regard must be paid to the connection, which they appear to have one with another, as component elements of the same type. For example, the event of the deluge, recently adverted to, which at once bore on its bosom an elect seed, in safe preservation for the peopling of a new world, and overwhelmed in perdition the race of ungodly men who had corrupted the old, unquestionably involves a complex idea. It embodies in one great act a double process—a process, however, which was accomplished simultaneously in both its parts; since the doing of the one carried along with it the execution of the other. In thinking, therefore, of the New Testament antitype, we must have respect not only to the

two ideas themselves severally represented, but also to their relation to each other; we must look for some spiritual process, which in like manner combines a work of preservation with a work of destruction. In the different fates of the righteous and the wicked, the one as appointed to salvation, and the other to perdition, we have certainly a twofold process and result; but have we the two in a similar combination? We certainly have them so combined in the personal history and work of Christ, as his triumph and exaltation inevitably involved the bruising of Satan; and the same shall also be found in the final judgment, when by putting down for ever all adverse authority and rule, Christ shall raise his church to the dominion and the glory. If the typical connection between the deluge and God's grander works of preservation and destruction, is put in either of these lights, the objection we lately offered to the interpretation of Glassius will be obviated, and the requirements of a scriptural exegesis satisfied. A like combination of two ideas is found in the application made of the deluge by the Apostle Peter to the ordinance of baptism, as will be shewn in due time. And there are, besides, many things connected with the tabernacle and its services—for example, the use made in them of symbolical numbers, the different kinds of sacrifice, the ritual of cleansing—which are usually so employed as to convey a complex meaning, and a meaning that of necessity assumes different shades, according to the different modifications introduced into the symbolical materials. Such differences, however, can only be of a minor kind; they can never touch the fundamental character of the typical phenomena so as to render them expressive in one relation of something totally unlike to what they denoted in another. A symbolical act or institution can as little be made to change its meaning arbitrarily, as a term in language. Its precise import must always be determined first by an intelligent consideration of its inherent nature, and then by the connection in which it stands.

3. It is one thing, however, to maintain that a type, either as a whole, or in its component parts, can express only one meaning; and another, to allow more than one application of it to the affairs of Christ's kingdom. Not only is there an organic connection between the old and the new dispensations, giving rise to the relation of type and antitype, but also an organic connection be-

tween one part and another of the Gospel dispensation; in consequence of which the ideas and principles exhibited in the types may find their realisation in more than one department of the Gospel system. The types, as well as the prophecies, hence often admit of "a springing and germinant accomplishment." They do so, especially in those things which concern the economical relation subsisting between Christ and his people; by reason of which he is at once the root out of which they grow, and the pattern after which their condition and destiny is to be formed. If on this account it be necessary that in all things he should have the pre-eminence, it is not less necessary that they should bear his image, and share in his heritage of blessing. So closely are they identified with him in their present experience and their future prospects, that they are now spoken of as having "fellowship with him in his sufferings," being "planted with him in the likeness of his death," and again, "planted with him in the likeness of his resurrection," "sitting with him in heavenly places," having "their life hid with him in God," and being at last raised to "inherit his kingdom, and sit with him upon his throne." In short, the church as a whole is formed after his likeness, while again, in each one of her members is reproduced an image of the whole. Therefore, the principles and ideas, which by means of typical ordinances and transactions were perpetually exhibited before the eye of the Old Testament church, while they must find their grand developement in Christ himself, must also have further developements in the history of his church and people. They have respect to *our* relations and experiences, *our* state and prospects, in so far as these essentially coincide with Christ's; for so far, the one is but a partial renewal, or a prolonged existence of the other.

There are things of a typical nature, it is proper to add, which in a more direct and special manner bear respect to the church and people of Christ. The rite of circumcision, for example, the passage through the Red Sea, the judgments in the wilderness, the eating of manna, and many similar things, must obviously have their antitypes in the heirs of salvation rather than in him, who, in this respect, stood alone; he was personally free from sin, and did not himself need the blessings he provided for others. So that, when the apostle writes of the ordinances of the law, that they were " shadows of good things to come, but the body is of Christ" (Col. ii. 17), he is not to be understood as meaning that Christ personally and alone is the object they prospectively contemplated, but Christ together with his body the church—the events and interests of the Gospel dispensation. In this collective sense Christ is mentioned also in 1 Cor. xii. 12, and Gal. iii. 16. Nor is it by any means an arbitrary sense; for it is grounded in the same vital truth, on which we have based the admissibility of a twofold application or bearing of typical things, viz. the organic union subsisting between Christ and his redeemed people— " he in them and they in him."

V. Another principle of interpretation arising out of the preceding investigations, and necessary to be borne in mind for the right understanding of typical symbols and transactions, is, that *due regard must be had to the essential difference between the nature of type and antitype.* For, as the typical is divine truth on a lower stage, exhibited by means of outward relations and terrestrial interests, so, when making the transition from this to the antitypical, we must expect the truth to appear on a loftier stage, and, if we may so speak, with a more heavenly aspect. What in the one bore immediate respect to the bodily life, must in the other be found to bear immediate respect to the spiritual life. While in the one it is seen and temporal objects that ostensibly present themselves, their proper counterpart in the other are the unseen and eternal:—*there,* the outward, the present, the worldly; *here,* the inward, the future, the heavenly.

A change and advance of the kind here supposed, enters into the very vitals of the subject, as unfolded in the earlier part of our inquiry. The reason why typical symbols and institutions were employed by God in his former dealings with his church, arose from the adoption of a plan, which indispensably required that very progression in the mode of exhibiting divine truth. The world was treated for a period as a child that must be taught great principles, and prepared for events of infinite magnitude and eternal interest, by the help of familiar and sensible objects, which lay fully open to their view, and came within the grasp of their comprehension. But now that we have to do with the things themselves, for which those means of preparation were instituted, we must take care, in tracing the connection between the one and the other, to keep steadily in view the essential difference between the two periods, and with the rise in the divine plan give a corresponding rise to the application we make of what belonged to the ancient economy. To proceed without regard to this—to look for the proper counterpart of any particular type in the same class of objects and interests, as that to which the type itself immediately referred, would be to act like those Judaizing Christians, who, after the better things had come, held fast at once by type and antitype, as if they belonged to one sphere, and consisted of the same materials. It would be to remain at the old foundations, while the scheme of God has risen to a higher place, and laid a new world, as it were, open to our view. If, therefore, we enter aright into the change which has been effected in the position of the divine kingdom, and give to that its proper weight in determining the connection between type and antitype, we must look for things in the one, similar, indeed, to those in the other, but, at the same time, proportionally higher and greater; and, in particular, must remember, that according to the rule, internal things now take the place of external, and spiritual of bodily.

Much discretion, however, which it is impossible to bound by such precise and definite rules as might meet all conceivable cases, will be necessary in applying the principle now stated to individual examples. In the majority of cases there will be no difficulty; for the distinction we mention between the Old and the New is so manifest as to secure a certain degree of uniformity even among those who are not remarkable for discrimination. And, indeed, the writers most liable to err in other respects, persons of delicate sensibilities and spiritual feeling, are less in danger of erring here, as they have usually a clear perception of the more inward and elevated character of the Gospel dispensation. The point, in regard to which they are most likely to err concerning it, and that which really forms the chief difficulty in applying the principle now under consideration, arises from what may be called the mixed nature of the things belonging to Messiah's kingdom. As contradistinguished from those of earlier dispensations, and rising above them, we denominate the realities of the Gospel spiritual, heavenly, eternal. And yet they are not totally disconnected with the objects of flesh and time. The centre-point of the whole, Jesus Christ, not only sojourned in bodily form upon the earth, but had certain conditions to fulfil of an outward and bodily kind, which were described beforehand in prophecy, and may also, of course, have had their typical adumbrations. In the case of the Church, too, her life of faith is not altogether of an inward nature, and confined to the hidden man of the heart. It touches continually on the corporeal and visible; and certain events essentially connected with her progress and destiny—such as the miraculous gifts of the Spirit, the calling of the Gentiles, the persecutions of the world, the doom of Antichrist—could not take place without assuming an outward and palpable form. What then, it may be asked, becomes of the characteristic difference between the Old and the New, so far as such things are concerned? Must not type and antitype still be found substantially on the same level?

No; the only legitimate conclusion is, that there are cases in which the difference is less broadly marked; but it still exists. The operations, experiences, and blessings peculiar to the dispensation of the Gospel, are not all of an entirely inward and spiritual nature, but they all bear directly on the interests of a spiritual salvation, and the realities of a heavenly and eternal world. The members of Christ's kingdom, so long as they are in flesh and blood, must have their history interwoven on every side with the relations of sense and time, and be themselves dependent upon outward ordinances for the existence and nourishment of their spiritual life. Yet whatever is external in their privileges and condition, has its internal side and even its avowed reason in things pertaining to the soul's salvation, and the coming inheritance of glory. So that the spiritual and heavenly is here always kept prominently in view, as the end and object of all; while in Old Testament times every thing was veiled under the sensible relations of flesh and time, and, excepting to the divinely illuminated eye, seemed as if it did not look beyond them.

For example, the deluge and baptism so far agree in form, that they have both an outward operation; but the operation, in the one case, has to do directly with the preservation and destruction of an earthly life; while in the other it bears immediately upon the life of immortality in the soul. The crucifixion of Christ and the slaying of the paschal lamb, were alike outward transactions; but the direct and ostensible result contemplated in the first, was salvation from the condemnation and punishment of sin; in the second, escape from corporeal death, and deliverance from the yoke of an earthly bondage. In like manner, it might be said to be as much an outward transaction for Christ to ascend personally into the presence of the Father, as for the High-priest to go within the veil with the blood of the yearly atonement; but to rectify men's relation to a worldly sanctuary and an earthly inheritance, was the immediate object sought by this action of the high-priest, while the appearance of Christ in the heavenly places was to secure for his people access to the everlasting kingdom of light and glory. In such cases the common property of a certain outwardness in the acts and operations referred to, is far from placing them on the same level; a higher element still appears in the one as compared with the other. But if, on the other hand, we should say, as has often been said, that Isaac's bearing the wood for the altar typified Christ's bearing his cross to Calvary, we bring together two circumstances which do stand precisely upon the same level, alike outward in themselves, and the one no more than the other involving any rise to a higher sphere of truth. Else, how should a common man, Cimon the Cyrenian, have shared with Christ in the bearing of the burden?

But the most pernicious examples of this false style of typical applications are to be found in the Grotian school of interpretation, whose low and carnal tone is continually betraying itself in a tendency to depress and lower the spiritual truths of the Gospel to a conformity with the simple letter of Old Testament Scripture. The Gospel is read, not only through a Jewish medium, but also in a Jewish sense, and nothing but externals admitted in the New, wherever there is descried, in the form of the representation, any reference to such in the Old. It is one of the few services which neological exegesis has rendered to the cause of divine truth, that by a process of exhaustion it has nearly emptied this meagre style of interpretation of the measure of plausibility it originally possessed. But it is still occasionally followed, in the particular respect now under consideration, by theological writers of a higher stamp. Thus, the doctrine of election, as unfolded in the epistles of the New Testament, is held by the advocates of a modified Arminianism to be improperly understood of an appointment to personal salvation and an eternal life, on the special ground that the election of the Jewish people was only their calling as a nation to outward privileges and a temporal inheritance. Nay, we reply, this is rather a reason why election in the Christian sense must go farther and deeper. For, the proper counterpart under the Gospel to those external relations of Judaism is the gift of grace and the heirship of glory—the lower in the one case shadowing the higher in the other—the outward and temporal representing the spiritual and eternal. Even Macknight, who cannot certainly be charged with any excess of the spiritual element in his interpretations, perceived the necessity of making, as he expresses it, "the natural seed the type of the spiritual, and the temporal blessings the emblems of the eternal." Hence, he justly regards the outward professing church in the one case, with its election to the earthly Canaan, as answering in the other, to the "invisible church, consisting of believers of all nations, who, partaking the nature of God by faith and holiness, are truly the sons of God, and have the inheritance of his blessing."[1]

[1] On Rom. ix. 8. For the other side see Whitby on the same chapter, and on 1 Pet. ii. 9; Graves' Works, vol. iii. p. 233. Archbishop Whately, in his Essays on the Peculiarities of the Gospel, p. 95, gives the representation a somewhat different turn from Whitby and Graves. He regards the Israelites as not having been " elected absolutely and infallibly to enter the promised land, to triumph over their enemies, and live in security, wealth, and enjoyment; but only to the privilege of having these blessings placed *within their reach*, on the condition of their obeying the law which God had given them." Whence, he infers, Christians are only elected, in the same sense, to the privileges of a Gospel condition and the *promise* of final salvation. In regard to election in the Gospel sense, such a representation vanishes before a few plain texts— such as " Many are called, but few are chosen ;" " elect according to the foreknowledge of God the Father, through sanctification of the Spirit, unto obedience and sprinkling of the blood of Jesus ;" " according as he hath chosen us in him before the foundation of the world . . having predestinated us unto the adoption of children by Jesus Christ to himself." If such passages do not imply election to a state of personal salvation, it is not in the power of language to express the idea. In regard to the Israelites, we maintain that the election and the promise were also made absolutely—" to thy seed will I give this land "—and the proper inference respecting those, who afterwards perished in the wilderness, without being permitted to enter the land, is simply, that they were not of that portion of the seed who were elect, according to the foreknowledge of God, to

The characteristic differences, with their respective limitations and apparent anomalies, may be briefly stated thus:—It belongs properly to the New dispensation to reveal divine and spiritual things distinctly to the soul, while in the Old they are presented under the veil of something outward and earthly. The spiritual and divine itself, which always, as a living under-current, ran beneath this exterior veil, might, even during the existence of the Old, come directly into view; but whenever it did so, there was no longer a figure or type of the true, but the true itself. Thus, in so far as the seed of Israel were found an election of God, actually partaking of the grace and blessing of the covenant—in so far as they were a royal priesthood, circumcised in heart to the Lord, they shewed themselves to be possessed of the reality of a justified condition and a regenerated life. The exhibitions that may have been given by any of them of such a state, were not typical in the sense of foreshadowing something higher and better under the Gospel; and if those, in whom they appeared, are spoken of as types, it must be as specimens, not as adumbrations—patterns of what is common to the children of faith in every age. The only connection possible in such a case, is that which subsists between type and impression, exemplar and copy, not that between type and antitype.

Turning to the things of the New dispensation, we have simply to reverse the statement now made. While here the spiritual and divine are exhibited in unveiled clearness, it is quite conceivable that they may at times have appeared under the distinctive guise of the Old, imbedded in fleshly and material forms. Especially might this be expected to happen at the beginning of the Gospel, when the transition was in the course of being made from the Old to the New, as the Messiah came forth to lay the foundations of his spiritual and everlasting kingdom on the external theatre of a present world. It was natural at such a time for God graciously to accommodate his ways to a weak faith, and facilitate its exercise, by making the things that appeared under

the possession of the land. It is true, they might justly be said to have lost it for disobeying the law, but viewed in respect to their connection with the calling and promise of God, it was their want of faith to connect them with these, their unbelief, which was the immediate cause of their perdition.

the New, wear the very livery of those that prefigured them under the Old. This is precisely what was done in some of the more noticeable parts of Christ's earthly history. But in so far as it *was* done; that is, in so far as some outward transaction in the Old re-appeared in a like outward transaction in the New, their relation to each other could not properly be that of type and antitype, but only of exemplar and copy—unless the New Testament transaction, while it bore a formal resemblance to that of the Old, was itself at the same time the sensible exponent of some higher truth. If it were this, then the relation would still be substantially that of type and antitype. And such, indeed, it is, in the few cases which actually fall within the range of these remarks, and which, when superficially viewed, seem at variance with the principle of interpretation we are seeking to establish.

Let us, in conclusion, glance at the cases themselves. The recal of the infant Jesus from the land of Egypt, after a temporary sojourn there, is regarded by the evangelist Matthew as the correlative in New Testament times to the deliverance of Israel under the Old. It is impossible to overlook the indication of a similar connection, though none of the evangelists have expressly noticed it, between Israel's period of trial and temptation for forty years in the wilderness, and Christ's withdrawal into the wilderness to be tempted forty days of the devil. The evangelist John sets the singular and apparently accidental preservation of Christ's limbs on the cross, beside the prescription regarding the Paschal Lamb, not to let a bone of him be broken, and sees in the one a divinely appointed compliance with the other (ch. xix. 36). And in the epistle to the Hebrews (ch. xiii. 12), the crucifixion of Jesus beyond the gates of Jerusalem is represented, not indeed as done to establish a necessary, but still as exhibiting an actual correspondence with the treatment of those sin-offerings which were burned without the camp. There can be no doubt, that in each of these instances of formal agreement between the Old and the New, the transactions look as if they were on the same level, and appear equally outward in the one as in the other. Shall we say, then, that on this account they do not really stand to each other in the relation of type and antitype? Or, that there was some peculiarity in the later transactions, which still, amid the apparent sameness, raised them to a sufficient elevation above the earlier? This last supposition we conceive to be the correct one.

In the first instance, it was not unnatural, when there was so little faith in the Church, and when such great things were in the course of being accomplished, that certain outward and palpable correspondences, such as we have noticed, should have been exhibited. It was a kind and gracious accommodation, on the part of God, to the ignorance and weakness of the times. The people were almost universally looking in the wrong direction for the things connected with the person and kingdom of Messiah; and he mercifully controlled in various respects the course and progress of events, so as, in a manner, to force on their notice the marvellous similarity of his working now to what he had done in the days of old. He did what was fitted to impress visibly upon the darker features of the evangelical history his own image and superscription, and to mark them out to men's view as wrought according to the law of a foreseen and pre-established harmony. Yet we should not expect such obvious and palpable marks of agreement to be commonly stamped by the hand of God upon the new things of his kingdom, as compared with the old; we should rather regard them as a sort of extraordinary and peculiar helps granted to a weak and unenlightened faith at the commencement of the kingdom. And even when so granted, we should not expect them to constitute the whole of the matter, but should suppose something farther to be veiled under them than immediately meets the eye—a deeper agreement, of which the one outwardly appearing was little more than the sign and herald.

This supposition gathers strength when we reflect that the outward agreement, however manifest and striking in some respects, is still never so uniform and complete as to convey the impression that the entire stress lay there, or that it was designed to be anything more than a stepping-stone for the mind to rise higher. Thus, while the child Jesus was for a time located in Egypt, and again brought out of it by the special providence of God, like Israel in its youth; yet what a difference between the two cases—in the length of time spent in the transactions, and the whole circumstances connected with their accomplishment! Jesus and Israel alike underwent a period of temptation in a wilderness before entering on their high calling; but again, how widely different in the precise region selected for the scene of trial, and the time during which it was continued! Christ's crucifixion beyond the gates of Jerusalem, and the preservation of his limbs from external violence, exhibited a striking resemblance to peculiarities in the sacrifices of the passover and sin-offering—enough to mark the overruling agency of God; but in other outward things there were scarcely less marked discrepancies—nothing, for example, in the sacrifices referred to, corresponding with the pierced side of Jesus, or his suspension on the cross; and nothing again in Jesus formally answering to the sacrificial rites of the imposition of hands, the sprinkling of blood, or the burning of the carcase. These, and other defects that might be named in the external correspondence between the New and the Old, plainly enough indicates that the outward agreement was, after all, not the main thing, nor the thing that properly constituted the typical connection between them. Else, where such agreement failed, the connection must have failed too; and in many respects Christ should not have been the "body" of the ancient shadows, in more, perhaps, than those in which he actually was. Who would not shrink from alleging this? But we can find no consistent reason for denying it, except on the ground that the occasional outward coincidences between our Lord's personal history and things in God's earlier dispensations, were the *signs* of a typical relationship rather than that relationship itself—a likeness merely on the surface, that gave notice of a deeper and more essential agreement.

This peculiarity in some of the typical applications of Scripture, has its parallel in the applications also sometimes made of the prophecies. We merely point for examples to the employment by St John, ch. xix. 37, of Zech. xii. 10, "They shall look on me whom they have pierced," or by St Matthew in ch. ii. 23, viii. 17 of other prophetical testimonies, and refer to the explanations given of them in our appendix. In such cases it is obvious, on a little reflection, that the outward and corporeal things with which the word of prophecy is immediately connected, fell so far short of their full meaning, that if they were fitly regarded as a fulfilment of what had been spoken, it was more because of the index they afforded to other and greater things yet to come, than of what they themselves actually were. It was like pointing to the little cloud in the horizon, which may be scarcely worth noticing in itself, but which assumes another aspect when it is discerned to be the sign and the forerunner of rising vapours and torrents of approaching rain. The beginning and the end, the present sign and the coming reality, are then seen blending together, and forming but one object.

CHAPTER SIXTH.

THE PLACE DUE TO THE SUBJECT OF TYPES AS A BRANCH OF THEOLOGICAL STUDY, AND THE ADVANTAGES ARISING FROM ITS PROPER CULTIVATION.

The loose and incorrect views which have so long prevailed regarding the types, and which have latterly assumed a form, that tends at once to circumscribe their number and lessen their importance, have told so adversely on the subject, that little more than a nominal place has been assigned it in our more recent theological systems. For any real value to be attached to it in the order of God's revelations, or any light it is fitted to throw, when rightly understood, on the interpretation of Scripture, we search in vain amid the writings of our leading hermeneutical and systematic divines. The treatment it has most commonly received at their hands is rather negative than positive. They appear greatly more concerned about the abuses to which it may be carried, than the advantages to which it may be applied. And were it not for the purpose of exploding errors, delivering cautions, and disowning unwarrantable conclusions, it is too plain the subject would scarcely have been deemed worthy of any separate and particular consideration.

If the discussion pursued through the preceding chapters has been conducted with any success, it must have tended to beget a quite different feeling upon the subject. Various points of moment connected with the purposes of God and the interpretation of Scripture must have suggested themselves to the reflective reader, as capable both of receiving fresh light, and acquiring new importance from a well-grounded system of Typology. One entire branch of the subject—its connection with the closely related field of prophecy—we have already, on account of its special importance, considered in a separate chapter. At present we shall look to some other points of a more general kind, which have, however, an essential bearing on the character of divine revelation, and which will enable us to bring out, in a variety of lights, the soundness and importance of the views we have been endeavouring to establish.

I. We mark, first, an *analogy in God's methods of preparatory instruction*, as adopted by him at different, but somewhat corresponding periods of the Church's history. In *one* brief period of its existence the Church of the New Testament might be said to stand in a very similar relation to the immediate future, that the Church of the Old Testament generally did to the more distant future, of gospel-times. It was the period of our Lord's earthly ministry, during which the materials were in preparation for the actual establishment of his kingdom, and his disciples were subjected to the training which was to fit them for taking part in its affairs. The process that had been proceeding for ages with the Church had, in *their* experience, to be virtually begun and completed in the short space of a few years. And we are justly warranted to expect, that the method adopted during this brief period of special preparation toward the first members of the New Testament Church, should present some leading features of resemblance to that pursued with the Old Testament Church as a whole, during her immensely more lengthened period of preparatory training.

Now, the main peculiarity, as we have seen, of God's method of instruction and discipline in respect to the Old Testament Church, consisted in the use of symbol and action. It was chiefly by means of historical transactions and symbolical rites that the ancient believers were taught what they knew of the truths and mysteries of grace. For the *practical* guidance and direction of their conduct they were furnished with means of information the most literal and express; but in regard to the *spiritual* concerns and objects of the Messiah's kingdom, all was couched under veil and figure. The instruction given addressed itself to the eye rather than to the ear. It came intermingled with the things they saw and handled; and while it necessarily made them familiar with the elements of gospel-truth, it not less necessarily left them in comparative ignorance as to the particular events and operations in which the truth was to find its ultimate and proper realisation.

How entirely analogous was the course pursued by our Lord with his immediate disciples during the period of his earthly ministry! The direct instruction he imparted to them was, with few exceptions, confined to lessons of moral truth and duty—freeing the law of God from the false glosses of a carnal and corrupt priesthood, which had entirely overlaid its meaning, and disclosing the pure and elevated principles on which his kingdom was to be founded. But in regard to what might be called the mysteries of the kingdom—the constitution of Christ's person, the peculiar character of his work for and in the souls of men, and the connection of all with a higher and future world—no direct instruction of any moment was imparted up to the very close of Christ's earthly ministry. On one or two occasions, when he sought to convey some definite information upon such points, the disciples either completely misunderstood his meaning, or shewed themselves incapable of profiting by his instructions (Matth. xvi. 21-23; Luke xviii. 34; John ii. 19-22, vi.) So that in the last discourse he held with them before his sufferings, he spoke of the many things he had yet to say to them, but which, as they still could not bear them, had to be reserved to the teaching of the Holy Spirit, who was afterwards to lead them into all the truth. Were they, therefore, left without instruction of any kind respecting those higher truths and mysteries of the kingdom? By no means; for throughout the whole period of their connection with Christ, they were constantly receiving such instruction as could be conveyed through action and symbol; or more correctly, through action and allegory, which was here made to take the place of symbol, and served substantially the same design.

The public life of Jesus was full of action, and in that, to a large extent, consisted its fulness of instruction. Every miracle he performed was a type in history; for, on the outward and visible field of nature, it revealed the divine power he was going to manifest, and the work he came to achieve in the higher field of grace. In every act of healing men's bodily diseases, and supplying of men's bodily wants, there was an exhibition to the eye of sense at once of his purpose to bring salvation to their souls, and of the principles on which he should proceed in doing so. In like manner, when he resorted to the parabolic method of instruction, what was it but another employment of the familiar and sensible things of nature, under the form of allegory, to convey still further instruction respecting the spiritual and divine things of his kingdom? There was in the procedure something of judgment to his adversaries, who had failed to profit, as they ought, by his more simple and direct teaching (Matth. xiii. 11–15). But for his own disciples, it formed a cover, through which he could present to them a larger amount of spiritual truth, and give them a more correct idea of his kingdom, than it was possible, as yet, for them to obtain in any other way. Every parable contained an allegorical representation of some particular aspect of the kingdom, which, like the types of an earlier dispensation, only needed to be illuminated by the facts of Gospel history, to render it a clear and intelligible image of spiritual and divine realities. In all, the outward and earthly was made to present the form of the inward and heavenly.

Thus, the special training of our Lord's disciples very closely corresponded to the course of preparatory dispensations through which the church at large was conducted before the time of his appearing. Such an analogy, pursued in circumstances so altered, and through periods so widely different, bespeaks the consistent working and presiding agency of Him, "who is the same yesterday, to-day, and for ever." It furnishes also a ready and effective answer to the Socinian argument against the peculiar doctrines of the Gospel, on account of the comparative silence maintained respecting them in the direct instructions of Christ. "Can such doctrines," they have sometimes asked, "enter so essentially, as is alleged, into the original plan of Christianity, when its divine author himself says so little about them? When in all he taught his disciples we look in vain for any explicit or systematic exhibition of them?" Look, we reply, to the analogy of God's dealings with his church, and let that supply the answer. Christ and the mysteries of his redemption were the end of all the earlier proceedings of God, and of the institutions of worship he gave to his church; and yet many centuries of preparatory instruction and discipline were permitted to elapse before the objects themselves were brought distinctly into view. Should it then be deemed strange or unaccountable that the persons immediately chosen by Christ to announce them, were made to undergo a brief but perfectly similar preparatory course, under the eye of their divine Master? The *facts* of Christianity are the basis of its *doctrines;* and until those facts had become matter of history, the doctrines could neither be explicitly taught, nor clearly understood. They could only be obscurely represented to the mind through the medium of typical actions, symbolical rites, or parabolical narratives. And it results as much from the essential nature of things as from the choice of its divine author, that the mode of instruction, which was continued through the lengthened probation of the Old Testament church, should have found its parallel in " the beginning of the Gospel of Jesus Christ."

II. But there is an *analogy of faith and practice* which is of still greater importance than any analogy that may appear in the methods of instruction. However important it may be to note resemblances in the mode of communicating divine truth, at one period as compared with another, it is more so to know that the truth, however communicated, has always been found one in its tendency and working; that the earlier and the later, the Old and the New Testament churches, though differing widely in light and privilege, yet breathed the same spirit, walked by the same rule, possessed and manifested the same elements of character. A correct acquaintance with the Typology of Scripture alone explains, how, with such palpable differences subsisting between them, there should still have been such essential uniformity in the result.

In the writings of the New Testament, especially in the epistles, it is very commonly the *differences* between the Old and the New, rather than the *agreements*, that are pressed on our notice. A necessity for this arose from the abuse to which the Jews had turned the handwriting of ordinances delivered to them by Moses. In the carnality of their minds, they mistook the means for the end, embraced the shadow for the substance, and so converted what had been set up for the express purpose of leading them to Christ, into a mighty stumbling-block to obstruct the way of their approach to him. On this account it became necessary to bring prominently out the differences between the preparatory and the ultimate schemes of God, and to shew that what was perfectly suited to the one was quite unsuited to the other. But there were, at the same time, many real agreements of a most essential nature between them, and these also are often referred to in New Testament Scripture. Moses and Christ, when closely examined and viewed as to the more fundamental parts of their respective systems, are found to teach in perfect harmony with each other. The law and the prophets of the Old Testament, and the Gospels and Epistles of the New, exhibit but different phases of the same wondrous scheme of grace. The light varies from time to time in its clearness and intensity, but never as to the elements of which it is composed. And the very differences, which so broadly distinguish the Gospel dispensation from all that went before it, when taken in connection with the entire plan and purpose of God, afford evidence of an internal harmony, and a profound agreement.

The truth of what we say, if illustrated to its full extent, would require us to traverse almost the entire field of Scripture Typology. We shall, therefore, content ourselves here with selecting a single point, which, in its most obvious aspect, belongs rather to the differences than the arguments between the Old and the New dispensations. For in what do the two more apparently and widely differ from each other than in regard to the place occupied in them respectively by the doctrine of a future state? In the Scriptures of the New Testament the eternal world comes constantly into view; it meets us in every page, inspirits every religious character, mingles with every important truth and obligation, and gives an ethereal tone and an ennobling impress to the whole genius and framework of Christianity. Nothing of this, however, is to be found in the earlier portions of the Word of God. That these contain no reference of any kind to a future state of rewards and punishments, we are far from believing, as will abundantly appear in the sequel. But still the doctrine of such a state is nowhere broadly announced, as an essential article of faith, in the revelations of Old Testament Scripture; it has no distinct and easily-recognized place either in the patriarchal or the Levitical dispensations; it is never set forth as a formal ground of action, and is implied, rather than distinctly affirmed, or avowedly acted on, excepting when it occasionally appears among the confessions of pious individuals, or in the later declarations of prophecy; so that, though itself one of the first principles of all true religion, there yet was maintained respecting it a studied caution and reserve in the revelations of God to men up to the time when He came who was to "bring life and immortality to light."[1]

This obvious difference between the Old and the New Testament revelations, in respect to a future state, has been deemed such a palpable incongruity, that sometimes the most forced interpretations have been resorted to with the view of getting rid of the fact, while, at other times, extravagant theories have been proposed to account for it. But we have no need to travel farther than to the typical character of God's earlier dispensations for a satisfactory explanation of the difficulty—and we shall find it in nothing else. For, leave this out of view—suppose that God's method of teaching and training the Old Testament Church was not *necessarily formed* on the plan of unfolding Gospel ideas and principles by means of earthly relations and fleshly symbols, then we see not how it could have consisted with divine wisdom to keep such a veil hanging for so many ages over the realities of a coming eternity. But let the typical element be duly taken into account, let it be understood that inferior and earthly things were systematically employed of old to image and represent those which are heavenly and divine; and then we can as little see how it could have consisted with divine wisdom to have disclosed the doctrine of a future state, otherwise than under the figures and shadows of what is seen and temporal. For this doctrine, in its naked form, stands inseparably connected with the facts of Christ's death and resurrection, on which it is entirely based as a ground of consolation and an object of hope to the believer. And if the one had been openly disclosed, while the other still remained under the

---

[1] A clear proof in a single instance of what is here said of the Old Testament in respect to an eternal world, may be found in what is written of Enoch, "He was not, for God took him," and this *because* he had walked with God. A causal connection plainly existed between his walk on earth and his removal to God's presence; and yet this is so indicated as clearly to shew that it was the divine purpose to spread a veil of secrecy over the future world, as if the distinct knowledge of it depended on conditions that could not then be formally brought out.

veil of typical shadows, utter confusion must necessarily have been introduced into the dispensations of God; the old covenant, with ordinances suited only to an inferior and preparatory course of training, should have possessed a portion of the light properly belonging to a complete and finished revelation. The ancient Church, with her faith in that case *professedly* directed on the eternal world, must have lost her symbolical relation to the present; her experiences must have been as spiritual, her life as hidden, her conflict with temptation, and victory over the world, as inward as those of believers under the Gospel. But then the Church of the Old Testament, being without the clear knowledge of Christ and his salvation, still wanted the true foundation for so much of a spiritual, inward, and hidden nature; and it must have been next to impossible to prevent false confidences from mingling with her expectations of the future, since she had only the shadowy and carnal in worship with which to connect the real and eternal in blessing.

Is this not what actually happened in the case of the later Jews? In the course of that preparatory training through which they were conducted, an increasing degree of light was at length imparted, among other things, in respect to a future state of reward and punishment; the later Scriptures contained not a few quite explicit intimations on the subject (as in Hos. xiii. 14, Dan. xii. 2, Isaiah xxvi. 19); and by the time of Christ's appearing, the doctrine of a resurrection from the dead to a world of endless happiness or misery, formed nearly as distinct and prominent an article in the Jewish faith as it does now in the Christian. (Acts xxiii. 6; xxvi. 6-8; Matt. v. 29; x. 28, &c.) Now, this had been well, and should have only disposed the Jews to give to Jesus a more enlightened and hearty reception had they been careful to couple with the clearer view thus obtained, and the more direct introduction of a future world, the intimations that accompanied it of a higher and better dispensation—of the old things, under which they lived, being to be done away, that others of a nobler description might take their place. But this was what the later Jews, as a class, failed to do. Partial in their knowledge of Scripture, and confounding together the things that differed, they took the prospect of immortality as if it had been directly unfolded, and ostensibly provided for in the shadowy dispensation itself.

The result necessarily was, that that dispensation ceased in their view to *be* shadowy; it contained in itself, they imagined, the full apparatus required for sinful men, to redeem them from the curse of sin, and bring them to eternal life; and whatever purposes the Messiah might come to accomplish, that he should supplant its carnal observances by something of a higher nature, and more immediately bearing on the immortal interests of man, formed no part of their expectations concerning him. Thus, by coming to regard the doctrine of a future state of happiness and glory as, in its naked or direct form, an integral part of the revelations of the old covenant, they naturally fell into two most serious mistakes. They first overlooked the shadowy nature of their religion, and exalted it to an undue rank by looking to it for blessings which it was never intended, unless typically, to impart—and then, when the Messiah came, they entirely misapprehended the great object of his mission, and lost all inheritance in his kingdom.

So much, then, for the palpable difference in this respect between the Old and the New. There was a necessity in the case, arising from the very nature of the divine plan. So long as the church was under symbolical ordinances and typical relations, the future world must fall into the background; the things concerning it could only appear imaged in the seen and present. But that they did appear so imaged—in this, with all the outward diversity that prevailed, there still lay an essential agreement between the Old dispensation and the New. The minds of believers under the former neither were nor could be an entire blank in regard to a future state of being. From the very first—as we shall see afterwards, when we come to trace out the elements of the primeval religion—there was in God's dealings and revelations toward them, what in a manner compelled them to look beyond a present world; it was so manifestly impossible to realise here, with any degree of completeness, the objects he seemed to have in view. And the under-current of thought and expectation thus silently awakened toward the future, was continually fed by everything being arranged and ordered in the present, so as to establish in their minds a profound conviction of a divine retribution. The things connected with their relation to a worldly sanctuary, and an earthly inheritance of blessing, were one continued illustration of the principle so firmly expressed by Abraham, " that the Judge of all the earth must do right;" and, consequently, that in the final issues of things, "it must be well with the righteous, and ill with the wicked." The bringing distinctly out of this present recompense in the divine administration, and with infinite variety of light and vividness of colouring, impressing it on the consciences of God's people, was the peculiar service rendered by the ancient economy in respect to a coming eternity; and the peculiar service which, *as a preparatory economy, it required to render*. For the belief of a *present* retribution must, to a large extent, form the basis of a well-grounded belief in a *future* one. And for the believing Israelite himself, who lived under the operation of such strong temporal sanctions, and who was habituated to contemplate the unseen in the seen, the future in the past, there was everything in the visible movements of Providence around him, both to confirm in him the expectation of a coming state of reward and punishment, and to form him to the dispositions and conduct which might best prepare him for meeting it. His position so far differed from that of believers now, that he was not formally called to direct his views to the coming world, and he had comparatively slender means of information concerning its realities. But it agreed in this, that he too was a child of faith, believing in the retributive character of God's administration; and in him, as well as in us, only in a more outward and sensible manner, this faith had its trials and dangers, its discouragements, its warrings with the flesh and the world, its times of weakness and of strength, its blessed satisfactions and triumphant victories. In short, his light, so far as it went, was the same with ours; it was the same also in the nature of its influence on his heart and conduct; and if he but faithfully did his part amid the scenes and objects around him, he was equally prepared at its close to take his place in the mansions of a better inheritance,—though he might have to go to them as one not knowing whither he went.[1]

Thus it appears, on careful examination, that all was in its proper place. A mutual adaptation and internal harmony binds together the Old and the New dispensations, even under the striking diversity that characterizes the two in respect to a future world. And the further the investigation is pursued, the more will such

[1] See Appendix C.

be found to be the case generally. It will be found that the connection of the Old with the New is something more than typical, in the sense of foreshadowing, or prefigurative of what was to come; it is also inward and organic. Amid the ostensible differences, there is a pervading unity and agreement—one faith, one life, one hope, one destiny. And while the Old Testament church, in its outward condition and earthly relations, typically shadowed forth the spiritual and heavenly things of the New, it was also, in so far as it realized and felt the truth of God presented to it, the living root out of which the New ultimately sprang. The real beginnings were there, of all that exists in comparative perfection now.

III. Another advantage resulting from a correct knowledge and appreciation of the Typology of ancient Scripture, is *the increased value and importance with which it invests the earlier portions of Revelation*. This has respect more especially to the historical parts of Old Testament Scripture; yet not to these exclusively. For, the whole of the Old Testament will be found to rise in our esteem, in proportion as we understand and enter into its typological bearing. But the point may be more easily and distinctly illustrated by a reference to its records of history.

Many ends, undoubtedly, had to be served by these; and we must beware of making so much account of one, as if it were the whole. Even the least interesting and instructive parts of the historical records, the genealogies, are not without their use; for they supply some valuable materials both for the general knowledge of antiquity, and for our acquaintance, in particular, with that chosen line of Adam's posterity, which was to have its culmination in Christ. But the narratives in which these genealogies are imbedded, which record the lives of so many individuals, pourtray the manners and customs of such different ages and nations, and relate the dealings of God's providence, and the communications of his mind with so many of the earliest characters and tribes in the world's history—these, in themselves, and apart altogether from any prospective reference they may have to gospel-times, are on many accounts interesting and instructive. Nor can they be attentively perused, as simple records of the past, without being found "profitable for doctrine, for reproof, for correction, and for instruction in righteousness."

Yet when viewed only in that light, one-half their worth is still not understood; nor shall we be able altogether to avoid some feeling of strangeness occasionally at the kind of notices embraced in the inspired narrative. For, whatever interest and instruction may be connected with it, how trifling often are the incidents it records! how limited the range to which it chiefly draws our attention! and how easy might it seem, at various points, to have selected other histories, which would have led the mind through scenes more obviously important in themselves, and less closely, perhaps, interwoven with evil! Infidels have often given to such thoughts as these an obnoxious form, and have endeavoured by means of them to bring sacred Scripture into discredit. But in doing so, they have only displayed their own partiality and ignorance; they have looked at this portion of the word of God in a contracted light, and away from its proper connection with the entire plan of revelation. Let the notices of Old Testament history be viewed in their subservience to the scheme of grace unfolded in the Gospel—let the field which it traverses, however limited in extent, and the transactions it describes, however unimportant in a political respect, be regarded as that field, and those transactions, through which, as on a lower and common stage, the Lord sought to familiarize the minds of his people with the truths and principles, which were ultimately to appear in the highest affairs of his kingdom—let the notices of Old Testament history be viewed in this light, which is the one Scripture itself would have us to take, and then what dignity and importance is seen to attach to every one of them! The smallest movements on the earth's surface acquire a sort of greatness, when connected with the law of gravitation; since then even the fall of an apple from the tree stands related to the revolution of the planets in their courses. And, in like manner, the relation which the historical facts of ancient Scripture bear to the glorious work and kingdom of Christ, gives to the least of them such a character of importance, that they are brought within the circle of God's highest purposes, and are perceived to be in reality "the connecting links of that golden chain which unites heaven and earth."

This, however, is not all. While a proper understanding of the Typology of Scripture imparts an air of grandeur and importance to its smallest incidents, and makes the little relatively great, it does more. It warrants us to proceed a step farther, and to assert, that such personal narratives and comparatively little incidents as fill up a large portion of the history, not only *might*, without impropriety, have been admitted into the sacred record, but that they *must* to some extent have been found there, in order to adapt it properly to the end which it was intended to serve. It was precisely the limited and homely character of many of the things related, which rendered them such natural and easy stepping-stones to the discoveries of a higher dispensation. It is one thing, that an arrangement exists in nature, which comprehends under the same law the falling of an apple to the ground, and the vast movements of the heavenly bodies; but it is another thing, and also true, that the perception of that law, as manifested in the motion of the small and terrestrial body—because manifested there on a scale which man could bring fully within the grasp of his comprehension—was what enabled him to mount upwards and scan the similar, though incomparably grander phenomena of the distant universe. In this case, there was not only a connection in nature between the little and the great, but also such a connection in the order of man's acquaintance with both, that it was the knowledge of the one that conducted him to the knowledge of the other. The connection is much the same that exists between the facts of Old Testament history, and the all-important revelations of the Gospel—with this difference, indeed, that the laws and principles developed amid the familiar objects and comparatively humble scenes of the one, were not so properly designed to fit man for discovering, as for receiving when discovered, the sublime mysteries of the other. But to do this, it was not less necessary here, than in the case above referred to, that the earlier developements should have been made in connection with things of a diminutive nature, such as the occurrences of individual history, or the transactions of a limited kingdom. A series of events considerably more grand and majestic could not have accomplished the object in view. They would have been too far removed from the common course of things; and would have been more fitted to gratify the curiosity and dazzle the imagination of those who witnessed or read of them, than to indoctrinate their minds with the fundamental truths and principles of God's spiritual economy. This result could be best produced by such a series of transactions as we find actually recorded in the Scriptures of the Old Testament—transactions infinitely varied, yet always capable of being quite easily grasped and understood. And thus, what to a superficial consideration appears strange or even objectionable in the structure of the inspired record, becomes, on a more comprehensive view, an evidence of wise adaptation to the wants of our nature, and of supernatural foresight in adjusting one portion of the divine plan to another.

It will be readily understood, that what we have said of the purpose of God with reference more immediately to those who lived in Old Testament times, applies, without any material difference, to such as are placed under the Christian dispensation. For what the transactions required to be for the accomplishment of God's purpose in regard to the one, the record of these transactions required to be for the accomplishment of his purpose in regard to the other. Whatever confirmation such things may lend to our faith in the mysteries of God—whatever force or clearness to our perceptions of the truth—whatever encouragement to our hopes or direction to our walk in the life of holiness and virtue, it may all be said to depend upon the history being composed of facts, so homely in their character and so circumscribed in their range, that the mind can without difficulty both realize their existence and enter into their spirit.

IV. Another service, the last we shall mention, which a truly scriptural typology is fitted to render to the cause of divine knowledge and practice, is the *aid it furnishes to help out spiritual ideas, in our minds, and enable us to realize them with sufficient clearness and certainty.* This follows very closely on the last-named benefit, and may be regarded rather as a further application of the truth contained in it, than the advancement of something altogether new. But we wish to draw attention to an important advantage, not yet distinctly noticed, connected with the typical element in Old Testament Scripture, and on which to a considerable extent the people of God are still dependent for the strength and liveliness of their faith.

It is true, they have now the privilege of a full revelation of the mind of God respecting the truths of salvation; and this elevates their condition as to spiritual things far above that of the Old Testament believers. But it does not thence follow, that they can in all respects so distinctly apprehend the truth in its naked spirituality, as to be totally independent of some outward exhibition of it. We are still in a state of imperfection, and are so much creatures of sense, that our ideas of abstract truth, even in natural science, often require to be aided by visible forms and representations. But things strictly spiritual and divine are yet more difficult to be brought distinctly within the reach and comprehension of the mind.—It was a relative advantage possessed by the Old Testament worshipper, in connection with his worldly sanctuary, and the more fleshly dispensation under which he lived, that spiritual and divine things, so far as they were revealed to him, acquired a sort of local habitation to his view, and assumed the appearance of a life-like freshness and reality. Hence chiefly arose that " impression of passionate individual attachment," as it has been called, which, in the authors of the Old Testament Scriptures, appears mingling with and vivifying their faith in the Invisible, and which breathes in them like a breath of supernatural life. What Hengstenberg has said in this respect of the Book of Psalms, may be extended to Old Testament Scripture generally: " It has contributed vast materials for developing the consciousness of mankind, and the Christian church is more dependent on it for its apprehensions of God than might at first sight be supposed. It presents God so clearly and vividly before men's eyes, that they see him, in a manner, with their bodily sight, and thus find the sting taken out of their pains. In this, too, lies one great element of its importance for the present times. What men now most of all need, is to have the blanched image of God again freshened up in them. And the more closely we connect ourselves with these sacred writings, the more will God cease to be to us a shadowy form, which can neither hear, nor help, nor judge us, and to which we can present no supplication."[1]

Besides, there are portions of revealed truth which relate to events still future, and do not at all come within the range of our present observation and experience, though very important as objects of faith and hope to the church. It might materially facilitate our conception of these, and strengthen our belief in the certainty of their coming existence, if we could look back to some corresponding exemplar of things, either in the symbolical handwriting of ordinances, or in the typical transactions of an earthly and temporal kingdom. But this also has been prepared to our hand by God in the Scriptures of the Old Testament. And to shew how much may be derived from a right acquaintance, both in this and in the other respect mentioned, with the typical matter of these Scriptures, we shall give here a twofold illustration of the subject—the one referring to truths affecting the present state and condition of believers, and the other to such as respect the still distant future.

1. For our first illustration we shall select a topic, that will enable us, at the same time, to explain a commonly misunderstood passage of Scripture. The passage is 1 Pet. i. 2, where, speaking of the elevated condition of believers, the apostle describes them as " elect according to the foreknowledge of God the Father, through sanctification of the Spirit, unto obedience and sprinkling of the blood of Jesus Christ." The peculiar part of the description is the last—" sprinkling with the blood of Jesus Christ" —which, being represented along with obedience as the end, to which believers are both elected of the Father and sanctified of the Spirit, seems at first sight to be out of its proper place. The application of the blood of Christ is usually thought of in reference to the pardon of sin, or its efficacy in the matter of the soul's justification before God; when, of course, its place stands between the election of the Father and the sanctification of the Spirit. Nor, in that most common reference to the effect of Christ's blood, is it of small advantage for the attainment of a clear and realizing faith, that we have in many of the Levitical services, and especially

[1] Supplem. Treatises on Psalms, § vii.

in those of the great day of yearly atonement, an outward form and pattern of things by which more distinctly to picture out the sublime spiritual reality.

It is plain, however, that the sprinkling of Christ's blood, mentioned by St Peter, is not that which has for its effect the sinner's pardon and acceptance (although Leighton and most commentators have so understood it); for it is not only coupled with a personal obedience, as being somewhat of the same nature, but the two together are set forth as the result of the electing and sanctifying grace of God upon the soul. The good here intended must be something inward and personal; something not wrought for us, but wrought upon us and in us; implying our justification, as a gift already received, but itself belonging to a higher and more advanced stage of our experience—to the very top and climax of our sanctification. What, then, is it? Nothing new, certainly, or of rare occurrence in the word of God, but often described in the most explicit terms; while yet the idea involved in it is so spiritual and elevated, that we greatly need the aid of the Old Testament types to give strength and vividness to our conceptions of it. "The blood of the yearly sacrifice," says Steiger on the passage, "was divided (as previously at the altar in the wilderness, Ex. xxiv. 6-8) into two parts, of which the first served for sprinkling the tabernacle before and behind the veil, and especially the mercy-seat; the other for afterwards sprinkling the people (Lev. xvi. 14-19). Now, if we represent to ourselves the whole work of redemption, in allusion to this rite, it will be as follows:—The expiation of one and of all sin, the propitiation, was accomplished when Christ offered his blood to God on the altar of the accursed tree. That done, he went with his blood into the most Holy Place. Whosoever looks in faith to His blood, has part in the atonement (Rom. iii. 25); that is, he is justified on account of it, receiving the full pardon of all his sins (Rom. v. 9). Thenceforth he can appear with the whole community of believers (1 John i. 7), full of boldness and confidence before the throne of grace (Heb. iv. 16), in order that he may be purified by Christ, as high-priest, from every evil lust." It is this personal purifying from every evil lust, which the apostle describes in ritual language as " the sprinkling of the blood of

Jesus Christ," and which is also described in the epistle to the Hebrews, with a similar reference to the blood of Christ, by having " the heart sprinkled from an evil conscience," and again, " by having the conscience purged from dead works to serve the living God." The sprinkling or purging spoken of in these several passages, is manifestly the cleansing of the soul from all internal defilement, so as to dispose and fit it for whatever is pure and good, and the purifying effect is produced by the sprinkling of the blood of Jesus, or its spiritual application to the conscience of believers, because the blessed result is attained through the holy and divine life, represented by that blood becoming truly and personally theirs.

Now, this great truth is certainly taught with the utmost plainness in many passages of Scripture. As, when it is written of believers, that " their hearts are purified by faith ;" that they " purify themselves even as Christ is pure." Or, when it is said, that " Christ lives in them," that " their life is hid with him in God," that " they are in him that is true, and cannot sin because their seed (the seed of that new, spiritual nature, to which they have been quickened by fellowship with the life of Jesus) remains in them;" and, in short, in every passage which connects with the pure and spotless life-blood of Jesus an impartation of life-giving grace and holiness to his people. I can understand the truth, even when thus spiritually, and, if I may so say, nakedly expressed. But I feel that I can obtain a more clear and comforting impression of it, when I keep my eye upon the simple and striking exhibition given of it in the visible type. For, with what effect was the blood of atonement sprinkled upon the true worshippers of the old covenant? With the effect of making whatever sacredness, whatever virtue (symbolically) was in that blood, pass over upon them; the life, which in it had flowed out in holy offering to God, was given to be theirs, and to be by them laid out in all pure and faithful ministrations of righteousness. Such precisely is the effect of Christ's blood sprinkled on the soul; it is to have his life made our life, or to become one with him in the stainless purity and perfection which expressed itself in his sacrifice of sweet-smelling savour to the Father. What a sublime and elevating thought! It is much, assuredly, for me to know, that, by faith in his blood, the crimson guilt of my sins is blotted out, heaven itself reconciled, and the way into the holiest of all laid freely open for my approach. But it is much more still to know, that by faith in the same blood, realized and experienced through the power of the Holy Spirit, I am made a partaker of its sanctifying virtue; the very holiness of the Holy One of Israel passes into me; his life-blood becomes in my soul the well-spring of a new and deathless existence. So that to be sealed up to this fountain of life, is to be raised above the defilement of nature, to dwell in the light of God, and sit as in heavenly places with Christ Jesus. And, amid the imperfections of our personal experience, and the clouds ever and anon raised in the soul by remaining sin, it should unquestionably be to us a matter of unfeigned thankfulness, that we can repair to such a lively image of the truth as is presented in the Old Testament service, in which, as in a mirror, we can see how high in this respect is the hope of our calling, and how much it is God's purpose we should enter into the blessing.

2. There are revelations in the Gospel, however, which point to events still future in the Messiah's kingdom; and in respect to these, also, the typical arrangements of former times are capable of rendering important service. A service, too, which is the more needed, as the things indicated, in regard to these future developements of the kingdom, are not only remote from present observation, but also in many respects different from what the ordinary course of events might lead us to expect. We do not refer to the last issues of the Gospel dispensation, when the concerns of time shall have become finally merged in the unalterable results of eternity; but to events, of which this earth itself is still to be the theatre, in the closing periods of Messiah's reign. This prospective ground is in many points overlaid with controversy, and much concerning it must be regarded as matter of doubtful disputation. Yet, there are certain great landmarks, which intelligent and sober-minded Christians can scarcely fail to consider as fixed. It is not, for example, a more certain mark of the Messiah, who was to come, that he should be a despised and rejected man, should pass through the deepest humiliation, and, after a mighty struggle with evil, attain to the seat of empire, than it is of the Messiah,

who has thus personally fought and conquered, that he shall totally subdue all the adversaries of his church and kingdom, make his church co-extensive with the boundaries of the habitable globe, and exalt her members to the highest position of honour and blessing. For my own part, I should as soon doubt that the first series of events were the just object of expectation before, as the other have become since, the personal appearing of Christ; and for breadth and prominence of place in the prophetical portions, especially of New Testament Scripture, this has all that could be desired in its behalf. But how far still is the object from being realized? How unlikely, even, that it should ever be so, if we had nothing more to found upon than calculations of reason, and the common agencies of providence?

That the progress of society in knowledge and virtue should gradually lead, at however distant a period, to the extirpation of idolatry, the abolition of the grosser forms of superstition, and a general refinement and civilization of manners, requires no great stretch of faith to believe. Such a result evidently lies within the bounds of natural probability, if only sufficient time were given to accomplish it. But, suppose it already done, how much would still remain to be achieved, ere the glorious King of Zion should have his promised ascendant in the affairs of men, and the spiritual ends for which he especially reigns should be adequately secured! This happy consummation might still be found at an unapproachable distance, even when the other had passed into a reality; nor are there wanting signs in the present condition of the world to awaken our fears, lest such may actually be the case. For in those countries, where the light of divine truth and the arts of civilization have become more widely diffused, we see many things prevailing that are utterly at variance with the purity and peace of the Gospel—numberless heresies in doctrine, disorders that seem to admit of no healing, and practical corruptions which set at defiance all authority and rule. In the very presence of the light of heaven, and amid the full play of Christian influences, the god of this world still holds possession of by far the larger portion of mankind; and innumerable obstacles present themselves on every side against the universal diffusion and the complete ascendancy of the pure principles of the Gospel of Christ. When such things are taken into account, how hopeless seems the prospect of a triumphant church, and a regenerated world! of a Saviour holding the undivided empire of all lands! of a kingdom, in which there is no longer any thing to offend, and all shall be replenished with life and blessing! The partial triumphs which Christianity is still gaining in single individuals and particular districts, can go but a little way to assure us of so magnificent a result. And it may well seem as if other influences, than such as are now in operation, would require to be put forth before the expected good can be realized.

Something, no doubt, may be done to reassure the mind, by looking back on the past history of Christianity, and contrasting its present condition with the point from which it started. The small mustard-seed has certainly sprung into a lofty tree, stretching its luxuriant branches over many of the best regions of the earth. See Christianity as it appeared in its divine Author, when he wandered about as a despised and helpless individual, attended only by a little band of followers as despised and helpless as himself,—or again, when he was hanging on a malefactor's cross, his very friends ashamed or terrified to avow their connection with him,—or even at another and more advanced stage of its earthly history, when its still small, and now resolute company of adherents, unfurled the banner of salvation, with the fearful odds everywhere against them of hostile kings and rulers, an ignorant and debased populace, a powerful and interested priesthood, and a mighty host of superstitions, which had struck their roots through the entire framework of society, and had become venerable, as well as strong, by their antiquity. See Christianity as it appeared then, and see it now standing erect upon the ruins of the hierarchies and superstitions which once threatened to extinguish it—planted with honour in the regions, where for a time it was scarcely suffered to exist—the recognized religion of the most enlightened nations of the earth, the delight and solace of the good, the study of the wise and learned, at once the source and the bulwark of all that is most pure, generous, free, and happy in modern civilization. Comparing thus the present with the past—looking down from the altitude that has been reached upon the low and unpromising condition out of which Christianity at first arose, we are not without considerable materials in the history of the Gospel itself, for confirming our faith in the prospects which still wait for their fulfilment. On this ground alone it may scarcely seem more, that Christianity should proceed from the elevation it has already won to the greatly more commanding attitude it is yet destined to attain, than to have risen from such small beginnings, and in the face of obstacles so many and so powerful, to its present influential and honourable position.

But why not revert to a still earlier period in the Church's history? Why withhold from our wavering hearts the benefit which they might derive from the form and pattern of divine things, formerly exhibited in the parallel affairs of a typical and earthly kingdom? It was the divine appointment concerning Christ, that he should sit upon the throne of David, to order and to establish it. In the higher sphere of God's administration, and for the world at large, he was to do what had been done through David in the lower, and on the limited territory of an earthly kingdom. The history of the one, therefore, may justly be regarded as the shadow of the other. But it is still only the earlier part of the history of David's kingdom which has found its counterpart in the events of gospel-times. The Shepherd of Israel has been anointed king over the heritage of the Lord, and the impious efforts of his adversaries to disannul the appointment have entirely miscarried. The formidable train of evils which obstructed his way to the throne of government, and which were directed with the profoundest cunning and malice by him, who on account of sin, had been permitted to become the prince of this world, have been all met and overcome—with no other effect than to render manifest the Son's indefeasible right to hold the sceptre of universal empire over the affairs of men. Now, therefore, He reigns in the midst of his enemies; but He must also reign till these enemies themselves are put down—till the inheritance has been redeemed from all evil, and universal peace, order, and blessing, have been established.

Is not this also what the subsequent history of the earthly kingdom fully warrants us to expect? It was long after David's appointment to the throne, before his divine right to reign was generally acknowledged; and still longer before the overthrow of the last combination of adversaries and the termination of the last train of evils, admitted of the kingdom entering on its ultimate stage of settled peace and glory. The affairs of David himself never wore a more discouraging and desperate aspect, than immediately before his great adversary received the mortal blow which laid him in the dust. After this, years had to elapse before the adverse parties in Israel were even externally subdued, and brought to render a formal acknowledgment to the Lord's anointed. When this point again had been reached, what internal evils festered in the kingdom, and what smouldering fires of enmity still burned! Notwithstanding the vigorous efforts made to subdue these, we see them at last bursting forth in the dreadful and unnatural outbreak of Absalom's rebellion, which threatened for a time to involve all in hopeless ruin and confusion. And with these internal evils and insurrections, how many hostile encounters had to be met from without! some of which were so terrible, that the very earth was felt, in a manner, to shake under the stroke (Ps. lx.). Yet all at length yielded; and partly by the prowess of faith, partly by the remarkable turns given to events in providence, the kingdom did reach a position of unexampled prosperity, peace and blessing. But in all this we have the developement of a typical dispensation, bringing the assurance, that the same position shall in due time be reached in the higher sphere and nobler concerns of Messiah's kingdom. The same determinate counsel and foreknowledge, the same living energy, the same overruling providence, is equally competent now, as it is alike pledged, to secure a corresponding result. And if the people of God have but discernment to read aright the history of the past, and faith and patience to fulfil their appointed task, they will find that they have no need to despair of a successful issue, but every reason to hope that judgment shall at length be brought forth into victory.

This one illustration may meanwhile be sufficient to show, (others will afterwards present themselves), how valuable an handmaid to the unfulfilled prophecies of Scripture may be found in a correct acquaintance with its Typology. Its province does not, indeed, consist in definitely marking out beforehand the particular agents and transactions that are to fill up the page of the eventful future. It fulfils the whole that in this respect it is fitted to accomplish, when it enables us to obtain some insight—not into the *what*, or the *when*, or the *instruments by which*—but rather into the *how* and the *wherefore* of the future:—when it instructs us respecting the nature of the principles that must prevail, and the general lines of dealing that shall be adopted, in conducting the affairs of Messiah's kingdom to its destined results. The future here is mirrored in the past; and the thing that hath been, is, in all its essential features, the same that shall be.

BOOK SECOND.

THE DISPENSATION OF PRIMEVAL AND PATRIARCHAL TIMES.

PRELIMINARY REMARKS.

HITHERTO we have been occupied chiefly with an investigation of principles. It was necessary, in the first instance, to have these ascertained and settled, before we could apply, with any prospect of success, to the particular consideration of the typical materials of Old Testament Scripture. And in now entering on this, the more practical, as it is also the more varied and extensive, branch of our subject, it is proper to indicate at the outset the general features of the arrangement we propose to adopt, and notice certain landmarks of a more prominent kind that ought to guide the course of our inquiries.

1. As all that was really typical formed part of an existing dispensation, and stood related to a religious worship, our primary divisions must connect themselves with the divine dispensations. These dispensations were undoubtedly based on the same fundamental truths and principles. But they were also marked by certain characteristic differences, adapting them to the precise circumstances of the church and the world, at the time of their introduction. It is from these, therefore, we must take our starting-points; and in these also should find the natural order and succession of the topics which must pass under our consideration. In doing so we shall naturally look, first, to the fundamental facts on which the dispensation is based; then to the religious symbols in which its lessons and hopes were embodied; and finally, to the future and subsidiary transactions which afterwards carried forward and matured the instruction.

2. In the whole compass of sacred history we find only three grand eras, that can properly be regarded as the formative epochs

of distinct religious dispensations. They are those of the fall, of the redemption from Egypt, and of the appearance and work of Christ, as they are usually designated; though they might be more fitly described, the first as the entrance of faith and hope for fallen man, the second as the giving of the law, and the third as the revelation of the Gospel. For, it was not properly the fall, but the new state and constitution of things brought in after it, that, in a religious point of view, forms the first commencement of the world's history. Neither is it the redemption from Egypt, considered by itself, but this in connection with the giving of the law, which was its immediate aim and object, that forms the great characteristic of the second stage, as the coming of grace and truth by Jesus Christ does of the third. Between the first and second of these eras two very important events intervened—the deluge and the call of Abraham—both alike forming prominent breaks in the history of the period. Hence, not unfrequently, the antediluvian is distinguished from the patriarchal church, and the church, as it existed before, from the church as it stood after, the call of Abraham. But important as these events were, in the order of God's providential arrangements, they mark no material alteration in the constitutional basis, or even formal aspect of the religion then established. As regards the institutions of worship, properly so called, Abraham and his descendants appear to have been much on a footing with those who lived before the flood; and therefore, not primary and fundamental, but only subsidiary elements of instruction could be evolved by means of the events referred to. The same may also be said of another great event, which formed a similar break during the currency of the second period—the Babylonish exile and return. This occupies a very prominent place in Scripture, whether we look to the historical record of the event, or to the announcements made beforehand concerning it in prophecy. Yet it introduced no essential change into the spiritual relations of the church, nor altered in any respect the institutions of her symbolical worship. The restored temple was built at once on the site, and after the pattern of that which had been laid in ruins by the Chaldeans; and nothing more was aimed at by the immediate agents in the work of restoration, than the re-establishment of the rites and services enjoined by Moses. Omitting, therefore, the gospel dispensation, as the antitypical, there only remain for the commencement of the earlier dispensations, in which the typical is to be sought, the two epochs already mentioned—those of Adam and Moses.

3. It is not simply the fact, however, of these successive dispensations which is of importance for our present inquiry. Still more depends for a well-grounded and satisfactory exhibition of divine truth as connected with them, upon a correct view of their mutual and interdependent relation to each other; the relation not merely of the Mosaic to the Christian, but also of the Patriarchal to the Mosaic. For as the revelation of law laid the foundation of a religious state, which, under the moulding influence of providential arrangements and prophetic gifts, developed and grew till it had assumed many of the characteristic features of the Gospel; so the original constitution of grace settled with Adam after the fall, comparatively vague and indistinct at first, gradually became more definite and exact, and, in the form of heaven-derived or time-honoured institutions, exhibited the germ of much that was afterwards established as law. In the primeval period nothing wears a properly legal aspect; and it has been one of the capital mistakes of theological writers, especially in this country—a source of endless controversy and arbitrary explanations—to seek there for law in the *direct and obtrusive*, when, as yet, the order of the divine plan admitted of its existing only in the *latent* form. We read of promise and threatening, of acts and dealings of God, pregnant with spiritual light and moral obligation, meeting from the very first the wants and circumstances of fallen man; but of express and positive enactments there is no trace. Some of the grounds and reasons of this will be adverted to in the immediately following chapters. At present, we simply notice the fact, as one of the points necessary to be kept in view for giving a right direction to the course of inquiry before us. Yet, on the other hand, while in the commencing period of the Church's history, we find nothing that bears the rigid and authoritative form of law, we find on every hand the foundations of law; and these gradually enlarging and widening, and sometimes even assuming a distinctly legal aspect, before the patriarchal dispensation closed. So that when the properly legal period came, the materials, to a considerable extent, were already in existence,

and only needed to be woven and consolidated into a compact system of truth and duty. It is enough to instance, in proof of what has been stated, the case of the Sabbath—not formally imposed, though divinely instituted from the first—the rite of piacular sacrifice, very similar (as we shall shew) as to its original institution—the division of animals into clean and unclean—the consecration of the tenth to God—the sacredness of blood—the Levirate usage—the ordinance of circumcision. The whole of these had their foundations laid, partly in the procedure of God, partly in the consciences of men, before the law entered; and in regard to some of them the law's prescriptions might be said to be anticipated, while still the patriarchal age was in progress. As the period of law approached, there was also a visible approach to its distinctive characteristics. And, without regard had to the formal difference, yet gradual approximation of the two periods, we can as little hope to present a solid and satisfactory view of the progressive developement of the divine plan, as if we should overlook either their fundamental agreement with each other, or their common relation to the full manifestation of grace and truth in the kingdom of Christ. We must hold it fast, that the Law—the intermediate point between the fall and redemption—had its preparation as well as the Gospel.

4. In regard to the mode of investigation to be pursued respecting particular types, as the first place is due to those which belonged to the institutions of religion, so our first care must be, according to the principles already established, to ascertain the views and impressions which, as parts of an existing religion, they were fitted to awaken in the ancient worshipper. It may, of course, be impossible to say, in any particular case, that such views and impressions were actually derived from them, with as much precision and definiteness as may appear in our description; for we cannot be sure that the requisite amount of thought and consideration was actually addressed to the subject. But due care should be taken in this respect, not to make the typical symbols and transactions indicative of more than what *may*, with ordinary degrees of light and grace, have been learned from them by men of faith in Old Testament Scripture. It is not, however, to be forgotten that, in their peculiar circumstances, much greater insight was attainable through such a medium, than it is quite easy for

us now to realize. At first, believers were largely dependent upon it for their knowledge of divine truth; it was their chief talent, and would hence be cultivated with especial care. Even afterwards, when the sources of information were somewhat increased, the disposition and capacity to learn by means of symbolical acts and institutions, would be materially aided by that mode of contemplation which has been wont to distinguish the inhabitants of the East. This proceeds (to use the language of Bähr) "on the ground of an inseparable connection subsisting between the spiritual and the bodily, the ideal and the real, the seen and the unseen. According to it, the whole actual world is nothing but the manifestation of the ideal one; the entire creation is not only a production, but, at the same time, also an evidence and a revelation of Godhead. Nothing real is merely dead matter, but is the form and body of something ideal; so that the whole world, even to its very stones, appears instinct with life, and on that account especially becomes a revelation of Deity, whose distinguishing characteristic it is to have life in himself. Such a mode of viewing things in nature may be called emphatically the religious one; for it contemplates the world as a great sanctuary, the individual parts of which are so many marks, words, and letters of a grand revelation-book of Godhead, in which God speaks and imparts information respecting himself. If, therefore, that which is seen and felt was generally regarded by men as the immediate impression of that which is unseen, a speech and revelation of the invisible Godhead to them, it necessarily follows, that if they were to have unfolded to them a conception of His nature, and to have a representation given them of what His worship properly consists in, the same language would require to be used which God spake with them; the same means of representation would need to be employed which God himself had sanctioned—the sensible, the visible, the external."[1]

The conclusion drawn here goes somewhat farther than the premises fairly warrant. If the learned author had merely said that there was a propriety or fitness in employing the same means of outward representation, as they fell in with the prevailing cast of thought in those among whom they were instituted, and were

[1] Bähr's Symbolik, B. I. p. 24.

thus wisely adapted to the end in view, we would have entirely concurred in the statement. But that such persons absolutely required to be addressed by means of a symbolical language in matters of religion could scarcely be admitted, without conceding that they were incapable of handling another and more spiritual one, and that consequently a religion of symbols must have held perpetual ascendency in the East. Besides, it may well be questioned, whether this "peculiarly religious mode of viewing things," as it is called, was not, to a considerable extent, the result of a symbolical religion already established, rather than the originating cause of such a religion. At all events, the *real* necessity for the preponderating carnality and outwardness of the earlier dispensations was of a different kind. It arose from the very nature of the institutions belonging to them, as temporary substitutes for the better and the more spiritual things of the Gospel; rendering it necessary that symbols should then hold the place of the coming reality. It is the capital error of Bähr's system to give to the symbolical in religion a place that does not properly belong to it; and so to assimilate too nearly the Old and the New—to represent the symbolical religion of the Old Testament as less imperfect than it really was, and inversely to convert the greatest reality of the New Testament—the atoning death of Christ—into a merely symbolical representation of the placability of heaven to the penitent.

But with this partial exception to the sentiments expressed in the quotation above given, there can be no doubt that the mode of contemplation and insight there described has remarkably distinguished the inhabitants of the East, and that it must have peculiarly fitted them for the intelligent use of a symbolical worship. They could give life and significance, in a manner *we* can but imperfectly understand, to the outward and corporeal emblems through which their converse with God was chiefly carried on. To reason from our own case to theirs would be to judge by a very false criterion. Accustomed from our earliest years to oral and written discourse, as the medium through which we receive our knowledge of divine truth, and express the feelings it awakens in our bosom, we have some difficulty in conceiving how any definite ideas could be conveyed on the one side or the other, where that was so sparingly employed as the means of communication

But the "grey fathers of the world" were placed in other circumstances, having from their childhood been trained to the use of symbolical institutions as the most expressive and appropriate channels of divine communion. So that the native tendency first, and then the habitual use strengthening and improving the tendency, must have rendered them adepts, as compared with Christian communities now, in perceiving the significance, and employing the instrumentality of religious symbols.

5. When the symbolical institutions and services of former times shall have been explained in the manner now indicated, the next step will be to consider in detail the import and bearing of the typical transactions which took place during the continuance of each dispensation. In doing this, care will require, in the first instance, to be taken, that the proper place be assigned them as intended only to exhibit ideas subsidiary to those embodied in the religion itself. And as in reading the typical symbols, so in reading the typical transactions connected with them, we must make the views and impressions they were fitted to convey to those whom they immediately respected concerning the character and purposes of God, the ground and measure of that higher bearing which they carried to the coming events of the Gospel. Nor are we here again to overlook that religious tendency and habit of mind which has been noticed as a general characteristic of the inhabitants of the East; for they would certainly be disposed to do with the acts of providence as with the works of creation—would contemplate them as manifestations of Godhead, or revelations in the world of sense of what was thought and felt in the higher world of spirit. Besides, it is to be borne in mind, that the historical transactions referred to were all *special* acts of providence. While they formed part of the current events of history, they were, at the same time, so singularly planned and adjusted, that the persons immediately concerned in them could scarcely overlook either their direct appointment by God, or their intimate connection with his plans and purposes of grace. It is the hand of God himself that ever appears to be directing the transactions of Old Testament history. And the acts in which He more peculiarly discovers himself, being the operations of One, whose grand object, from the period of the fall, was the foiling of the tempter, and the raising up of a seed of blessing, they could

scarcely fail to be regarded by intelligent and pious minds as standing in a certain relation to this centre-point of the divine economy. In proportion as the people of God had faith to "wait for the consolation of Israel," they would also have discernment to read, with a view to the better things to come, the disclosures of His mind and will, which were interwoven with the history of His operations.

It is in this way we are chiefly to account for God's frequent appearance on the stage of patriarchal history, and His more direct personal agency in the affairs of the ancient church. The things that happened to it could not otherwise have accomplished the great ends of their appointment. For, through these God was continually making revelation of himself to the church, and imparting what it was needful for her to know of Him as the God of salvation. It was, therefore, of essential moment to the object in view, that His people should be able, without hesitation, to regard them as indications of His mind; that they should not merely consider them as His, in the general sense in which it may be said, that "God is in history;" but His also in the more definite and peculiar sense of conveying specific and progressive discoveries of the divine administration. How could they have been recognised as such, unless the finger of God had, in some form, laid its distinctive impress upon them? Taking into account, therefore, all the peculiarities belonging to the typical facts of Old Testament history—the close relation in which they commonly stood to the rites and institutions of a religion of hope—the evident manner in which many of them bore upon them the interposition of God—and the place occupied by others in the announcements of prophecy—they had quite enough to distinguish them from the more general events of Providence, and were perfectly capable of ministering to the faith and the just expectations of the people of God.

6. We simply note farther, that when passing under review acts and institutions of God, which stretch through successive ages and dispensations, there will necessarily recur, under somewhat different forms, substantially the same exhibitions of divine truth. It was unavoidable, but that all the more fundamental ideas of religion, and the greater obligations connected with it, should be the subject of many an ordinance in worship, and many a transaction in Providence. The briefest mode of treatment, as

it would naturally involve fewest repetitions, would be to classify, first the primary heads of doctrine and duty, and then arrange under them the successive exhibitions given of each in the future enactments and dealings of God, without adhering rigidly to the period of their appearance. This plan was partially followed in our first edition, but was found impracticable as a whole. We deem it necessary to keep by the historical order, though it may be occasionally attended with the disadvantage of having the same truths brought anew before us. For, thus alone can we mark aright the course of developement, which, in a work of this nature, is too important an element to be sacrificed to the fear of at times trenching on ground, that may have been partially trodden before.

CHAPTER FIRST.

THE DIVINE TRUTHS EMBODIED IN THE HISTORICAL TRANSACTIONS CONNECTED WITH THE FALL, BEING THOSE ON WHICH THE FIRST SYMBOLICAL RELIGION WAS BASED.

THE religion of man, as it falls under our consideration at present, must be viewed as taking its commencement at the fall. What knowledge Adam possessed of the character and ways of God, before he fell; or with what forms of worship he gave expression to the thoughts and feelings which were called forth by his relation to God, and the circumstances of his condition, it is not possible for us now exactly to determine. Nor does it much concern us to know. Our interest in his religious views and prospects properly begins with the new aspect and constitution of things which arose with the entrance of sin. Then, too, for the first time, did an occasion arise for the introduction of typical acts and institutions, which otherwise should have had no proper foundation to rest on. From their very nature and object, they bear respect to another and better state of things preparing to be introduced; and hence necessarily imply, that man's existing condition already partook of evils and dangers which required to be met by the provisions of divine grace and benevolence, as necessary to prepare the way for a state of ultimate rest and satisfaction.

The opinion certainly began to be broached at an early period in the Christian church, and has often been formally propounded since, "That Paradise was to Adam a type of heaven; and that the never-ending life of happiness promised to our first parents, if they had continued obedient, and grown up to perfection under that economy wherein they were placed, should not have continued in the earthly paradise, but only have commenced there, and been perpetuated in a higher state."[1] It is possible, indeed, that such might have been the destination of man in the case supposed; but it is a point upon which Scripture is altogether silent, and in its original form too plainly bore the impress of the Eastern philosophy, which associated with matter in every form imperfection and evil. Those who were tinctured with this philosophy could not imagine, that Adam should feel himself to be in a state of proper satisfaction, so long as he was clothed upon with a body formed of the dust of earth, and dependent upon earthly productions for its support; and that he must, from the outset, have had his eye directed toward a higher and more ethereal state of being, of which the enjoyments he actually possessed could present him with nothing more than an image and a foretaste. Whatever elements of truth there might be in such ideas, they belong entirely to the region of speculation, and are so far at variance with the representations of Scripture, as there the original frame and constitution of things appears as the relatively perfect, and what is to be hereafter as the recovery of what has been lost—the restoration of what was at the beginning. It will, no doubt, be more than this; but its being so, is the incidental result of the way in which the good has been achieved, rather than its direct and professed object.

It was from an entirely different tendency—from a disposition to multiply typical meanings without rule or limit—that most writers of the Cocceian school were led to give a typical interpretation to many things in the primeval world—such as the mode of Adam's creation, the formation of Eve from his side while he slept, his relation to the trees in the midst of the garden. An eminent writer of that school, however, has justly remarked, that " in the state of innocence there were no typical rites adumbrating Christ and his merits, whereof there was then neither know-

[1] This proposition, with the Patristic authorities that support it, may be found in the discourses of Bishop Bull. His proofs from the earlier Fathers—Justin Martyr, Tatian, Irenæus, are very general. The first explicit proof is from Theophilus of Antioch, who speaks of Adam being " at length canonized or consecrated, and ascending to heaven," if he had gone on to perfection. The testimony becomes more full, as the speculative influence of the Greek philosophy gains strength in the Church. And Clement of Alexandria expressly says in his Liturgy, that " if Adam had kept the commandments, he would have received immortality as the reward of his obedience"—that is, immortality in heaven.

ledge nor need; as the very word *creation* imports, which has nothing to do with a restoration or a restorer. All typical ceremonies were subsequent to the fall, and the promise of grace in Christ."[1] This was said by Alting with immediate reference to the Sabbath, and for the purpose of proving the Sabbath, in respect to its typical foreshadowing of the final rest of the redeemed, to have been instituted after the fall. In which case, the whole series of transactions connected with the formation of Eve, her presentation to Adam, and their joint participation of the forbidden fruit, must have taken place on the very day on which Adam himself was created. This is altogether an improbable opinion; although it appears to have obtained some prevalence in Alting's age, and the times immediately succeeding. A typical employment of the Sabbath with reference to better things to come, by no means inferred its original and primary establishment for such a purpose. It may only have inferred, that the institution was now invested with a new meaning and importance, and brought within the circle of God's purposes of grace; precisely as in later times was done with articles of food and circumcision, and other things taken from the field of nature or of history, and associated with the hopes of salvation. Still, the general principle announced by Alting is undoubtedly correct. Nothing belonging to the garden of Eden could possess, in the theological sense, a typical character, till it had ceased to be the abode of man, and his relation to it had undergone an essential change. Till then the physical and moral constitution of this world must be regarded as in itself good, without any evil existing in it to call for the intervention of a Mediator, and consequently without any reference appearing to the work or benefits of redemption. Yet this by no means hinders, that all may have been so planned and arranged by the foreseeing eye of God, as to have readily admitted of various typical applications to the interests of redemption, after the entrance of sin required the things of redemption to be provided for. Nay, as the work of redemption is itself a creation—a new work of God fashioning after a higher ideal the materials of the old—we may reasonably expect that much in the second

[1] Altingi Opera, tom. v. p. 327.

should be made to assume the form and image of what had originally appeared in the first. It is on this ground, indeed, that the argument from analogy is based.

But this is not our present theme. We have to do simply with man as fallen—man as standing in need of redemption. And contemplating from this point of view his religious condition and prospects, we have first of all to take into account what has ever been, and what must necessarily be, a fundamental characteristic of the true religion—the historical nature of its origin. It does not come forth with a kind of independent and theoretical completeness, but grows, by successive stages, out of the actual manifestations God gives of himself, and the circumstances in which his creatures are placed. Its primary elements of truth and duty are but deductions—such as naturally force themselves on reflective minds—from facts already known, and relations actually established in the course of providence. It is by no means necessary, therefore, that they should appear in the shape of formal enunciations or authoritative precepts, to give them a claim on the heart and conscience. That claim may both exist, and be distinctly recognised and felt, where it has not been legislatively imposed. Indeed, direct and explicit enactments are rather a mark of imperfection than otherwise—of imperfection either in the objective grounds of religious instruction, or in the spiritual capacity and disposition to make an adequate use of those that exist. And hence it is that, as compared with Old Testament times, they are not to be found in the New. Believers in Christ are not under the law, but under grace. And yet, so far from being thereby released from the obligations of duty, they are placed in that respect on a higher level, and called to a more spiritual life. The law in its very form is an evidence of abounding iniquity. It contemplates a state of ignorance and depravity which it seeks to regulate and restrain by specific directions that presuppose an utter inability to discover the right, and a prevailing tendency to depart from it.

This, however, required time and opportunity for developement; and the world was at first no more prepared for the introduction of the Law than for the introduction of the Gospel. Man had fallen, indeed, from his original rectitude; but he had not therefore sunk into total blindness and corruption. Nor was he, in fact, treated as in such a condition by God. On the contrary, he was still regarded as possessing somewhat of that nobility of nature, that divine image, in the likeness of which he was so recently created—as not needing, and, therefore, not receiving, any formal enactments to prescribe to him the path of duty, but capable himself of discerning these in God's manifested character and dealings, and in the facts connected with his own altered position. In these he was furnished with the materials of light and the grounds of obligation, such as, if rightly used, were perfectly sufficient to direct his course, and yet such as to allow ample scope for the display of the native tendencies of the heart. And only when these tendencies had proved to be so strong on the side of evil, that men were manifestly incapable of either knowing or doing what was right in the deteriorated condition of the world—then only did it become necessary to present them with positive enactments, and hedge them round with stringent rules and prohibitions. The history of mankind as a whole, viewed in connection with the divine dispensations, bears an exact analogy to the history of each individual man. First, he appears as a child, weak, indeed, and prone to err, yet bearing the paternal image, and capable of learning from, and copying after the paternal example. This is at once the safe and the dutiful course for him. By and bye, however, as youth advances, the lawless desires and irregular passions of nature break forth, and he must be restrained and checked on every side by the bonds of law. Farther on, again, when these have served their end—when the youth has sprung to manhood, and the paternal mind has become the mind also of the son, the age of law passes away; there is the liberty of the spirit, the freedom of full-grown man.

It will be understood, then, that we are not now to look for explicit statements of doctrines and authoritative commands, but, in the intentional absence of these, to consider what might be learned of divine truth and duty by the earliest race of worshippers, first, from the palpable facts of history and experience, and then from the symbolical acts and institutions, in connection with which their faith was to be maintained and exercised.

1. What, in such an enumeration, is obviously entitled to rank first, is the *doctrine of human guilt and corruption*.

From the moment of their transgression, our first parents knew that their relation to God had become sadly altered. The calm of their once peaceful bosoms was instantly agitated and disturbed by tormenting fears of judgment. Nor did these prove to be groundless alarms; they were the forerunners of a curse, which was soon thundered in their ears by the voice of God, and written out in their exiled and blighted condition. It was impossible for them to escape the conviction, that they were no longer in the sight of God very good. And as their posterity grew, and one generation sprung up after another, the story of the lost heritage of blessing (no doubt perpetually repeated), and the still continued exclusion from the hallowed region of life, must have served to keep up the impression that sin had corrupted the nature, and marred the inheritance of man.

Evidences were not long wanting to shew, that sin in the first pair was evil in the root, which must, more or less, communicate itself to every branch of the human family. In the first-born of the family it sprung at once into an ill-omened maturity, as if to give warning of the disastrous results that might be expected in the future history of mankind. And constantly as the well-spring of life flowed on, the stream of human depravity swelled into a deeper and broader flood. There were things in God's earlier procedure that were naturally fitted to check its working, and repress its growth—especially the mild forbearance and paternal kindness with which He treated the first race of transgressors—the wonderful longevity granted to them—the space left for repentance even to the greatest sinners, while still sufficient means were employed to convince them of their guilt and danger—all seeming to betoken the tender solicitude of a father yearning over his infant offspring, and restraining for a season the curse that now rested on their condition, if so be they might be won to His love and service. But it was the evil, not the good in man's nature, which took advantage of this benign treatment on the part of God, to ripen into strength and fruitfulness. And, ere long, the very goodness of God found it needful to interpose, and relieve the earth of the mass of violence and corruption which, as in designed contrast to the benignity of heaven, had come to usurp possession of the world. So that, looking simply to the broad facts of history, the doctrine of human guilt and depravity stands forth with a melancholy prominence and particularity which could leave no doubt concerning it upon thoughful minds.

2. Another doctrine, which the facts of primeval history rendered it equally impossible for thoughtful minds to gainsay or overlook, is the *righteousness of God's character and government.*

For, that mankind should have been expelled from the region of life, and made subject to a curse which doomed them to sorrow and trouble, disease and death, in consequence of their violation of a single command of Heaven, was a proof patent to all, and memorable in the annals of the world, that everything in the divine government is subordinate to the principles of rectitude. " There was in it," as was said by Irving in one of his best moods, "a most sublime act of holiness. God, after making Adam a creature for an image and likeness of himself, did resolve him into vile dust through viler corruption, when once he had sinned; proving that one act of sin was, in God's sight, of far more account than a whole world teeming with beautiful and blessed life, which He would rather send headlong into death than suffer one sin of His creature to go unpunished. And though creation's teeming fountain might flow on ever so long, still the flowing waters of created life must ever empty themselves into the gulph of death. This is a most sublime exaltation of the moral above the material, shewing that all material beauty and blessedness of life is but, as it were, the clothing of one good thought, which, if it become evil, straightway all departs like the shadow of a dream." Who could seriously reflect on this—on the good that was lost, and the inheritance of evil that came in its place—without being solemnly impressed with the conviction, that the sceptre of God's government is a sceptre of righteousness, and that blessing might be expected under it only by such as love righteousness and hate iniquity?

3. But if nothing more had been manifested of God in the facts of primeval history than this—had He appeared only as a righteous judge executing deserved condemnation on the guilty, Adam and his fallen offspring might have been appalled and terrified before Him, but they could not have ventured to approach Him with acts of worship. We notice, therefore, as another truth brought out in connection with the circumstances of the fall, and an essentially new feature in the divine character, the *exhibition*

of grace which was then given on the part of God to the fallen. That everything was not subjected to instantaneous and overwhelming destruction, was itself a proof of the introduction of a principle of grace into the divine administration. The mere respite of the sentence of death (which, if justice alone had prevailed, must have been executed on the very day of transgression), and the establishment of an order of things which still contained many tokens of divine goodness, gave evidence of thoughts of mercy and loving-kindness in God toward man. But as no vague intimations, or even probable conclusions of reason, from the general course of providence, could be sufficient to re-assure the heart on such a matter as this, an explicit assurance was given, that " the seed of the woman should bruise the head of the serpent,"—which, however dimly understood at first, could not fail even then to light up the conviction in the sinful heart, that it was the purpose of God to aid man in obtaining a recovery from the ruin of the fall. The serpent had been the ostensible occasion and instrument of the fall,—the visible and living incarnation of the evil power which betrayed man to sell his birthright of life and blessing. And that this power should be destined to be not only successfully withstood, but bruised in the very head by the offspring of her over whom he had so easily prevailed, clearly bespoke the intention of God to defeat the malice of the tempter, and secure the final triumph of the lost.

But this, if done at all, must evidently be done in a way of grace. All natural good had been forfeited by the fall, and death—the utter destruction of life and blessing—had become the common doom of humanity. Whatever inheritance, therefore, of good, or whatever opportunity of acquiring it, might be again presented, could be traced to no other source than the divine beneficence freely granting what could never have been claimed on the ground of merit. And as the recovery promised necessarily implied a victory over the might and malice of the tempter, to be won by the very victims of his artifice, how otherwise could this be achieved than through the special interposition and grace of the Most High? Manhood in Adam and Eve, with every advantage on its side of a natural kind, had proved unable to stand before the enemy, to the extent of keeping the easiest possible command, and retaining possession of an inheritance already conferred. How greatly more unable must it have felt itself, if left unaided and alone, to work up against the evil, and destroy the destroyer? In such a case, hope could have found no solid footing to rest upon for the fulfilment of the promise, excepting what it descried in the gracious intentions and implied aid of the promiser. And when it appeared, as the history of the world advanced, how the evil continued to take root and grow, so as even for a time to threaten the extermination of the good, the impression must have deepened in the minds of the better portion of mankind, that the promised restoration must come through the intervention of divine power and goodness,—that the saved must owe their salvation to the grace of God.

4. Thus far the earliest inhabitants of the world might readily go in learning the truth of God, by simply looking to the broad and palpable facts of history. And without supposing them to have possessed any extraordinary reach of discernment, they might surely be conceived capable of taking one step more respecting the accomplishment of that salvation or recovery which was now the object of their desire and expectation. Adam saw—and it must have been one of the most painful reflections which forced itself on his mind, and one, too, which subsequent events came, not to relieve, but rather to imbitter and aggravate—he saw how his fall carried in its bosom the fall of humanity; and the nature, which in him had become stricken with pollution and death, went down thus degenerate and corrupt to all his posterity. It was plain, therefore, that the original constitution of things was based on a *principle of headship*, in virtue of which the condition of the entire race was made dependent on that of its common parent. And the thought was not far to seek, that the same constitution might somehow have place in connection with the work of recovery. Indeed, it seems impossible to understand how, excepting through such an idea, any distinct hope could be cherished of the attainment of salvation. By the one act of Adam's disobedience, he and his posterity together were banished from the region of pure and blessed life, and made subject to the law of sin and death. Whence, in such a case, could deliverance come? How could it so much as be conceived possible, to re-open the way of life, and place the restored inheritance of good on a secure and satisfactory footing, except through some second head of humanity

supernaturally qualified for the undertaking ? A fallen head could give birth only to a fallen offspring—so the righteousness of heaven had decreed ; and the prospect of rising again to the possession of immortal life and blessing, seemed, by its very announcement, to call for the institution of another head, unfallen and yet human, through whom the prospect might be realised. Thus only could the divine government retain its uniformity of principle in the altered circumstances that had occurred ; and thus only might it seem possible to have the end it proposed accomplished.

We do not suppose that the consideration of this principle of headship, as exhibited in the case of Adam and his posterity, could, of itself, have enabled those, who lived immediately subsequent to the fall, to obtain very clear or definite views in regard to the mode of its application in the working out of redemption. We merely suppose, that, in the circumstances of the case, there was enough to suggest to intelligent and discerning minds that it should in some way have a place. But the full understanding of the principle, and of the close harmony it establishes between the fall and redemption, as to the descending curse of the one, and the distributive grace and glory of the other, can be perceived only by *us*, whose privilege it is to look from the end of the world to its beginnings, and to trace the first dawn of the Gospel to the effulgence of its meridian glory. Even the Jewish Rabbins, who were far from occupying the vantage-ground we have reached, could yet discern some common ground between the heritage of evil derived from Adam, and the good to be effected by Messiah. " The secret of Adam," one of them remarks, " is the secret of the Messiah ;" and another, " As the first man was the one that sinned, so shall the Messiah be the one to do sin away."[1] They recognised in Adam and Christ the two heads of humanity, with whom all mankind must be associated for evil or for good. On surer grounds, however, than lay within the ken of their apprehension, we know that Adam was in this respect " the type of him that was to come" (Rom. v. 14.) But in this respect alone ; for in all other points we have to think of differences, not of resemblances. The principle, that belongs to them in common,

---

[1] See Tholuck Comm. on Rom. v. 12.

stands simply in the relation they alike hold, the one to a fallen, the other to a restored offspring. The natural seed of Adam are dealt with as one with himself, first in transgression, and then in death the wages of transgression. And, in like manner, the spiritual seed of Christ are dealt with as one with him, first in the consummate righteousness he brought in, and then in the eternal life, which is its appointed recompense of blessing. " As in Adam all die, so in Christ shall all be made alive"—all, namely, who stand connected with Christ in the economy of grace, as they do with Adam in the economy of nature. How could this be, but by the sin of Adam being regarded as the sin of humanity, and the righteousness of Christ as the property of those who by faith rest upon his name! Hence, in the fifth chapter of the epistle to the Romans, along with the facts which in the two cases attest the doctrine of headship, we find the parallel extended, so as to include also the respective grounds out of which they spring: " As by the *offence* of one, judgment came upon all men to condemnation; even so by the *righteousness* of one, the free gift came upon all men unto justification of life. For, as by one man's *disobedience* many were made sinners, so by the *obedience* of one, shall many be made righteous."

These statements of the Apostle are no more than an explanation of the facts of the case by connecting them with the moral government of God; and it is not in the power of human reason to give, either a satisfactory view of his meaning, or a rational account of the facts themselves, on any other ground than this principle of headship. It has also many analogies in the constitution of nature, and the history of providence to support it. And though, like every other peculiar doctrine of the Gospel, it will always prove a stone of stumbling to the natural man, it will never fail to impart peace and comfort to the child of faith. Some degree of this he will derive from it, even by contemplating it in its darkest side—by looking to the inheritance of evil which it has been the occasion of transmitting from Adam to the whole human race. For, humbling as is the light in which it presents the natural condition of man, it still serves to keep the soul possessed of just and elevated views of the goodness of God. That all are naturally smitten with the leprosy of a sore disease, is matter of painful experience, and cannot be denied without setting aside the plainest lessons of history. But how much deeper must have been the pain, which the thought of this awakened, and how unspeakably more pregnant should it have appeared with fear and anxiety for the future, if the evil could have been traced to the operation of God, and had existed as an original and inherent element in the state and constitution of man? It was a great relief to the wretched bosom of the prodigal, and was all, indeed, that remained to keep him from the blackness of despair, to know that it was not his father who sent him forth into the condition of a swine-herd, fain to feed himself with the husks with which they were fed; a comforting thing to know, that these husks and that wretchedness were not emblems of his father. And can it be less comforting for the thoughtful mind, when awakening to the sad heritage of sin and death, under which humanity lies burdened, to know, that this ascends no higher than the first parent of the human family, and that, as originally settled by God, the condition of mankind was in all respects " very good." The evil is thus seen to have been not essential, but incidental; a root of man's planting, not of God's; an intrusion into Heaven's workmanship, which Heaven may again drive out.

But a much stronger consolation is yielded by the consideration of this principle of headship, when it is viewed in connection with the second Adam; since it then assumes the happier aspect of the ground-floor of redemption—the actual, and, as far as we can perceive, the only possible foundation, on which a plan of complete recovery could have been reared. Excepting in connection with this principle, we cannot imagine how a remedial scheme could have been devised, that should have been in any measure adequate to the necessities of the case. Taken individually and apart, no man could have redeemed either his own soul, or the soul of a brother; he could not in a single case have recovered the lost good, far less have kept it in perpetuity if it had been recovered: and either divine justice must have foregone its claims, or each transgressor must have sunk under the weight of his own guilt and helplessness. But by means of the principle, which admits of an entire offspring having the root of its condition and the ground of its destiny in a common head, a door stood open in the divine administration for a plan of recovery co-extensive (it might be) with the work of ruin. And unless we could have assured ourselves of an absolute and continued freedom from sin (which even angelic natures could not do), we may well reconcile ourselves to such a principle in the divine government, as for one man's transgression has made us partakers of a *fallen* condition, since in that very principle we perceive the one channel through which access could be found for those who have fallen, to the peace and safety of a *restored* condition.

He must know nothing aright of sin or salvation, who is incapable of finding comfort in this view of the subject. And yet there is a ground of comfort higher still, arising from the prospect it secures for believers of a condition better and safer than what was originally possessed by man before the fall. For, the second Adam, who, as the new head of humanity, gives the tone and character to all that belongs to the kingdom of God, is incomparably greater than the first, and has received for himself and his redeemed an inheritance corresponding to his personal worth and dignity. So that if the principle, of which we speak, appears in the first instance like a depressing load weighing humanity down to the very brink of perdition, it becomes at length a divine lever to raise it to a height far beyond what it originally occupied, or could otherwise have had any prospect of reaching. As the Apostle graphically describes in his first epistle to the Corinthians, "The first man is of the earth, earthy; the second man is the Lord from heaven. As is the earthy, such are they also that are earthy; and as is the heavenly, such are they also that are heavenly. And as we have borne the image of the earthy, we shall also bear the image of the heavenly." Elevating thought! destined to be conformed to the image of the Son of God, and therefore to share with him in the life, the blessedness, and the glory, which he inherits in the kingdom of the Father! Coupling, then, the end of the divine plan with the beginning, and entering with childlike simplicity into its arrangements, we find, that the principle of headship on which the whole hinges for evil and for good, is really fraught with the richest beneficence, and should call forth our admiration of the manifold wisdom and goodness of God. For, through this an avenue has been laid open for us into the realms above, and our natures have become linked in fellowship of good with what is best and highest in the universe.

It thus appears, that there were four fundamental principles or ideas, which the historical transactions connected with the fall served strikingly to exhibit, and which must have been incorporated as primary elements with the religion then introduced. 1. The doctrine of human guilt and depravity; 2. of the righteousness of God's character and government; 3. of grace in God as necessary to open, and actually opening the door of hope for the fallen; 4. and, finally, of a principle of headship, by which the offspring of a common parent were associated in a common ruin, and by which again, under a new and better constitution, the heirs of blessing might be associated in a common restoration. In these elementary principles, however, we have rather the basis of the patriarchal religion, than the religion itself. For this, we must look to the symbols and institutions of worship. And, as far as appears from the records of that early time, the materials out of which these had at first to be fashioned were: The position assigned to man in respect to the tree of life, the placing before him of the cherubim and the flaming sword at the East of Eden, the covering of his guilt by the sacrifice of animal life, and his still subsisting relation to the day of rest originally hallowed and blessed by God. To these we now proceed, in succession, to direct our inquiries.

CHAPTER SECOND.

THE TREE OF LIFE.

THE first mention made of the tree of life has respect to its place and use, as part of the original constitution of things, in which all presented the aspect of relative perfection and completeness. "Out of the ground," it is said, "made the Lord God to grow every tree that is pleasant to the sight, and good for food; the tree of life also in the midst of the garden, and the tree of the knowledge of good and evil." The special notice taken of these two trees plainly indicates their singular and preeminent importance in the economy of the primeval world; but in different respects. The design of the tree of knowledge was entirely moral; it was set there as the test and instrument of probation; and its disuse, if we may so speak, was its only allowable use. The tree of life, however, had its natural use, like the other trees of the garden; and both from its name, and from its position in the centre of the garden, we may infer that the effect of its fruit upon the human frame was designed to be altogether peculiar. But this comes out more distinctly in the next notice we have of it—when, from being simply an ordinance of nature, it passed into a symbol of grace. "And the Lord God said, Behold the man is become as one of us, to know good and evil; and now lest he put forth his hand, and take also of the tree of life, and eat, and live for ever; therefore the Lord God sent him forth from the garden of Eden, to till the ground, from whence he was taken. So he drove out the man; and he placed at the east of the garden of Eden the cherubim, and a flaming sword, which turned every way, to keep the way of the tree of life."

These words put it beyond a doubt, that the tree of life was originally intended for the food of man; that the fruit it yielded was the divinely appointed medium of maintaining in him the power of an endless life ; and that now, since he had sinned against God, and had lost all right to the possession of such a power, he was debarred from access to the natural means of sustaining it, by being himself rigorously excluded from the garden of Eden. What might be the peculiar properties of that tree—whether in its own nature it differed essentially from the other trees of the garden, or differed only by a kind of sacramental efficacy attached to it—we are left without any specific information. But in its relation to man's frame, there plainly was this difference between it and the other trees, that while they might contribute to his daily support, it alone could preserve in undecaying vigour a being to be supported. In accordance with its position in the centre of the garden, it possessed the singular virtue of ministering to human life in the fountainhead—of upholding that life in its root and principle, while the other trees could only furnish what was needed for the exercise of its existing functions. *They* might have kept nature alive for a time, as the fruits of the earth do still ; but to *it* belonged the property of fortifying the vital powers of nature against the injuries of disease and the dissolution of death.

This was undoubtedly well known to Adam, as it was an essential part of the constitution of things around him. And if he had remained stedfast in his allegiance to God, ever restraining his desire from the tree of knowledge, and partaking only of the tree of life, he would have continued to possess life, in incorrupt purity and blessedness, as he received it from the hand of God. But choosing the perilous course of transgression, he forfeited his inheritance of life, and became subject to the threatened doom of death. The tree of life, however, did not lose its life-sustaining virtue, because the condition, on which man's right to partake of it, had been violated. It remained what God originally made it. And though effectual precautions must now be taken to guard its sacred treasure from the touch of polluted hands, yet there it stood in the centre of the garden still, the object of fond aspirations as well as hallowed recollections—though enshrined in a sacredness which rendered it for the present inaccessible to fallen man. Why should its place have been so carefully preserved ? and the symbols of worship, the emblems of fear and hope, planted in the very way that led to it ? if not to intimate, that the privilege of partaking of its immortal fruit was only for a season withheld, not finally withdrawn—waiting till a righteousness should be brought in, which might again open the way to its blessed provisions. For, as the loss of righteousness had shut up the way, it was manifest the re-possession of righteousness alone could re-open it. And hence it became, as we shall see, one of the leading objects of God's administration, to disclose the necessity, and unfold the nature and conditions of such a work of righteousness, as might be adequate to so important an end. The relation man now occupied to the tree of life could of itself furnish no information on this point. It could only indicate, that the inheritance of immortal life was still reserved for him, on the supposition of a true and proper righteousness being attained. So that in this primary symbolical ordinance, the hope, which had been awakened in his bosom by the first promise, assumed the pleasing aspect of a return to the enjoyment of that immortal life, from which, on account of sin, he was appointed to suffer a temporary exclusion.

But, coupled as this hope was with the present existence of a fallen condition, and the certainty of a speedy return for the body to the dust of death, it of necessity carried along with it the expectation of a future state of being, and of a resurrection from the dead. The prospect of a deliverance from evil, and of a restored immortality of life and blessing, was not to be immediately realized. The now forbidden tree of life was still to be forbidden, so long as men bore about with them the body of sin and death. They could find the way of life only through the charnel-house of the grave. And it had been a mocking of their best feelings and aspirations, to have held out to them the promise of a victory over the tempter, or to have embodied that promise in a new direction of their hopes toward the tree of life, if there had not been couched under it the assured prospect of a life after death, and out of it. In truth, religious faith and hope could not have taken form and being in the bosom of fallen men, excepting on the ground of such an anticipated futurity. Nor were there long wanting events in the history of divine providence which would naturally tend to strengthen, in thoughtful and considerate minds, this hopeful regard to a future world. The untimely death of Abel and the translation of Enoch in the mid-time of his days, must especially have wrought in this direction ; as, viewed in connection with the whole circumstances of the time, they could scarcely fail to produce the impression, that not only was the real inheritance of blessing to be looked for in a scene of existence beyond the present, but that the clearest title to this might be conjoined with a comparatively brief and contracted portion of good on earth. Such facts, read in the light of the promise, that the destroyer was yet to be destroyed, and a pathway opened to the lost for partaking anew of the food of immortality, could lead to but one conclusion—that the good to be inherited by the heirs of promise necessarily involved a state of life and blessing after this. We find the later Jews—notwithstanding their false views respecting the Messiah—indicating in their comments some knowledge of the truth thus signified to the first race of worshippers by their relation to the tree of life. For, of the seven things which they imagined the Messiah should shew to Israel, two were, the garden of Eden and the tree of life ; and again, " There are also that say of the tree of life, that it was not created in vain, but the men of the resurrection shall eat thereof, and life for ever."[1] These were but the glimmerings of light obtained by men, who had to grope their way amid judicial blindness and the misguiding influence of hereditary delusions. Adam and his immediate offspring were in happier circumstances for the discernment of the truth now under consideration. And unless the promise of recovery remained absolutely a dead letter to them, and nothing was learned from their symbolical and worshipful position in respect to the tree of life (a thing impossible in the circumstances), there must have been cherished in their minds the conviction of a life after death, and the hope of a deliverance from its corruption. Religion at the very first rooted itself in the belief of immortality.

So much for what the things connected with the tree of life imported to those whom they more immediately respected. Let us glance for a little to the fuller insight afforded into them for such as possess the later revelations of Scripture. " To-day," said Jesus on the cross to the penitent malefactor, "to-day shalt thou be with me in Paradise"—shewing how confidently he regarded

[1] R. Elias ben Mosis, and R. Menahem, in Ainsworth on Gen. iii.

death as the way to victory, and how completely he was going to bruise the head of the tempter, since he was now to make good for himself and his people a return to the region of bliss, which that tempter had been the occasion of alienating. " To him that overcometh," says the same Jesus, after having entered on his glory, " will I give to eat of the tree of life, that is in the midst of the paradise of God." And again, " Blessed are they that do his commandments, that they may have right to the tree of life, and may enter in through the gates into the city" (Rev. ii. 7 ; xxii. 14). The least we can gather from such declarations is, that every thing which was lost in Adam, shall be again recovered in Christ for the heirs of his salvation. The far distant ends of revelation are seen embracing each other; and the last look we obtain into the workmanship of God corresponds with the first, as face answers to face. In both alike there is seen a paradise of delight, with the river of life flowing through it, and the tree of life in the midst, bearing its immortal fruit. The same God of love and beneficence who was the beginning, proves himself to be also the ending. It is the intermediate portion alone which seems less properly to hold of him—being in so many respects marred with evil, and chequered with adversity to the members of his family. *There*, indeed, we see much that is unlike God— his once beautiful workmanship defaced—the comely order of his government disturbed—the world he had destined for " the house of the glory of his kingdom" rendered the theatre of a fierce and incessant warfare between the elements of good and evil, in which the better part is too often put to the worse—and humanity, which he had made to be an image of himself, smitten in all its members with the wound of a sore disease, beset when living with numberless calamities, and becoming, when dead, the prey of its most vile and loathsome adversaries. How cheering to know that this ungod-like state of disorder and confusion is not to be perpetual—that it occupies but the mid-region of time—and is destined to be supplanted in the final issues of providence by the restitution of all things to their original harmony and blessedness of life ! The tempter has prevailed long, but, God be thanked, he is not to prevail for ever. There is yet to come forth from the world, which he has filled with his works of evil, new heavens and a new earth, where righteousness shall dwell—another paradise with its tree of life—and a ransomed people created anew after the image of God, and fitted for the high destiny of manifesting his glory before the universe. How blessed to be indeed the heirs of such a destiny!

But great as this is, it is not the whole. The antitype is always higher than the type; and the work of grace transcends in excellence and glory the work of nature. When, therefore, we are told of a new creation, with its tree of life, and its paradisiacal delights yet to be enjoyed by the people of God, much more is actually promised than the simple recovery of what was lost by sin. There will be a sphere and condition of being similar in kind, but, in the nature of the things belonging to it, immensely higher and better than what was originally set up by the hand of God. All things proceeding from him are beautiful in their place and season. And it is true of the paradise which has been lost, that its means of life and enjoyment were in every respect wisely adapted to the frames of those who were made for occupying it. But of these it is written, that they were " of the earth, earthy"—only relatively, not absolutely good—in themselves lumpish and infirm tenements of clay, and as such necessarily imperfect in their tastes, their faculties of action and enjoyment, as compared with what is found in the higher regions of existence.

But, undoubtedly, the same adaptation that existed in the old creation between the nature of the region and the frames of its inhabitants shall exist also in the new. And as the occupants here shall be the second Adam and his seed—the Lord from heaven, in whom humanity has been raised to peerless majesty and splendour—there must also be a corresponding rise in the nature of the things to be occupied. A higher sphere of action and enjoyment shall be brought in, because there is a higher style of being to possess it. There shall not be the laying anew of earth's old foundations, but rather the raising of these aloft to a nobler elevation—not nature revived merely, but nature glorified —humanity, no longer as it was in the earthy and natural man, but as it is and ever shall be in the spiritual and heavenly, and that placed in a theatre of life and blessing every way suitable to its exalted condition.

Such being the case, it will readily be understood, that the promise, symbolically exhibited in the Old, and distinctly expressed in New Testament Scripture, of a return to paradise and its tree of life, is not to be taken literally. The dim shadow only, not the very image of the good to be possessed, is presented under this imperfect form. And we are no more to think of an actual tree, such as that which originally stood in the centre of Eden, than of actual manna, or of a material crown, which are, in like manner, promised to the faithful. These, and many similar expressions employed respecting the world to come, are but a figurative employment of the best in the past or present state of things, to aid the mind in conceiving of the future ; as thus alone can it attain to any distinct conception of them whatever. Yet, while all are figurative, they have still a definite and intelligible meaning. And when the assurance is given to sincere believers, not only of a paradise for their abode, but also of a tree of life for their participation, they are thereby certified of all that may be needed for the perpetual refreshment and support of their glorified natures. These shall certainly require no such carnal sustenance as was provided for Adam in Eden ; they shall be cast in another mould. But, as they shall still be material frameworks, they must have a certain dependence on the material elements around them for the possession of a healthful and blessed existence. The internal and the external, the personal and the relative, shall be in harmonious and fitting adjustment to each other. All hunger shall be satisfied, and all thirst for ever quenched. The inhabitant shall never say, " I am sick." And like the river itself, which flows in perennial fulness from the throne of God, the well-spring of life in the redeemed shall never know interruption or decay. Blessed, then, truly are those who do the commandments of God, that they may have right to the tree of life, and may enter in through the gates into the city. What can a sinful and perishing world afford in comparison of such a prospect !

CHAPTER THIRD.

THE CHERUBIM (AND THE FLAMING SWORD).

THE truths symbolized by man's new relation to the tree of life have still to be viewed in connection with the means appointed by God to fence the way of approach to it, and the creaturely forms that were now planted on its borders. "And the Lord God," it is said, "placed at the east of the garden of Eden cherubim, and a flaming sword, which turned every way, to keep the way of the tree of life." We can easily imagine that the sword, with its flaming brightness and revolving movements, might be suspended there simply as the emblem of God's avenging justice, and as the instrument of man's exclusion from the region of life. In that one service the end of its appointment might be fulfilled, and its symbolical meaning exhausted. Such, indeed, appears to have been the case. But the cherubim, which also had a place assigned them toward the east of the garden, must have had some farther use, as the sword alone would have been sufficient to prevent access to the forbidden region. The cherubim must have been added for the purpose of rendering more complete the instruction intended to be conveyed to man by means of the symbolical apparatus here presented to his contemplation. And as these cherubic figures hold an important place also in subsequent revelations, we shall here enter into a somewhat minute and careful investigation of the subject. The view we mean to exhibit cannot be said to differ radically from that presented in our former edition; but it will certainly differ considerably in the mode of investigation pursued, and in some also of the results obtained. We leant formerly too much upon the representations of Bähr, which we now perceive to be in themselves, as well as in the purpose to which they are applied, of a more fanciful and objectionable nature than they at first appeared.

There is nothing to be expected here from etymological researches. Many derivations and meanings have been ascribed to the term *cherub*; but nothing certain has been established regarding it; and it may now be confidently assigned to that class of words, whose original import is involved in hopeless obscurity.[1] In the passage of Genesis above cited, where the word first occurs, not only is no clue given in regard to the meaning of the name, but there is not even any description presented of the objects it denoted; they are spoken of as definite forms or existences, of which the name alone afforded sufficient indication. This will appear more clearly if we adhere to the exact rendering: " And he placed (or, made to dwell) at the east of the garden of Eden *the cherubim*"—not certain unknown figures or imaginary existences, but the specific forms of being, familiarly designated by that name.

In other parts of Scripture, however, the defect is in great measure supplied; and by comparing the different statements there contained with each other, and putting the whole together, we may at least approximate, if not absolutely arrive at, a full and satisfactory knowledge of the symbol.

But in ascertaining the sense of Scripture on the subject, there are two considerations which ought to be borne in mind, as a necessary check on extreme or fanciful deductions. The first is, that in this, as well as in other religious symbols (those, for example, connected with food and sacrifice), there may have been, and most probably was, a progression in the use made of it from time to time. In that case, the representations employed at one period must have been so constructed as to convey a fuller meaning than those employed at another. Whatever aspects of divine truth, therefore, may be discovered in the later passages which

---

[1] Hofmann has lately revived the notion, that כְּרוּב (cherub), is simply רְכוּב (chariot), with a not unusual transposition of letters; and conceives the name to have been given to the cherubim on account of their being employed as the chariot or throne of Jehovah (Weissagung und Erfullung, i. p. 80). Delitzsch, too, is not disinclined to this derivation and meaning, though he would rather derive the term from כָּרַב to lay hold of, and understands it of the cherubim as laying hold of and bearing away the throne of Jehovah (Die Genesis Ausgelegt, p. 46). Thenius in his Comm. on Kings also adopts this derivation, but applies it differently. Both derivations, and the ideas respecting the cherubim they are intended to support, are quite unsupported.

treat of the cherubim, should not, as a matter of course, be ascribed in all their entireness to the earlier. Respect must always be had to the relative differences of place and time. Another consideration is, that whatever room there may be for diversity in the way now specified, we must not allow any representation that may be given in one place—a specific representation—to impose a generic meaning on the symbol, which is not borne out, but possibly contradicted by representations in others. Progressive differences can only affect what is circumstantial, not what is essential to the subject; and all that is properly fundamental in the cherubic imagery, must be found in accordance, not with a partial, but with the complete testimony of Scripture respecting it.

With these guiding principles in our eye, we proceed to exhibit what may be collected from the different notices of Scripture on the subject—ranging our remarks under the following natural divisions: the descriptions given of the cherubim as to form and appearance, the designations applied to them, the positions assigned them, and the kinds of agency with which they are associated.

1. In regard to the first of these points—the descriptions given of the cherubim as to form and appearance—there is nothing very definite in the earlier Scriptures, nor are the accounts in the later perfectly uniform. Even in the detailed narrative of Exodus respecting the furniture of the tabernacle, it is still taken for granted, that the forms of the cherubim were familiarly known; and we are told nothing concerning their structure, besides its being incidentally stated, that they had faces and wings (Ex. xxv. xxxvii.) It would seem, however, that while certain elements were always understood to enter into the composition of the cherub, the form given to it was not absolutely fixed, but admitted of certain variations. The cherubim seen by Ezekiel beneath the throne of God, are represented as having each four faces and four wings (ch. i. 6), while in the description subsequently given by him of the cherubic representations on the walls of his visionary temple (ch. xli. 18, 19), mention is made of only two faces appearing in each. In Revelation, again, (ch. iv. 7, 8) while four composite forms, as in Ezekiel, are adhered to throughout, the creatures are represented as not having each four faces, but having each their several face different; and the number of wings belonging to each is also

different—not four but six.[1] In the Apocalyptic vision the creatures themselves appear full of eyes, before and behind, as they do also in Ezek. x. 12, where "their whole flesh, and their backs, and their hands, and their wings," are said to have been full of eyes; but in Ezekiel's first vision, the eyes were confined only to the wheels connected with the cherubim (ch. i. 18.) It is impossible, therefore, without doing violence to the accounts given in the several delineations, to avoid the conviction, that a certain latitude was allowed in regard to the particular forms; and that, as exhibited in vision at least, they were not altogether uniform in appearance. They *were* uniform, however, in two leading respects, which may hence be regarded as the more important elements in the cherubic form. They had, first, the predominating appearance of a man—a man's body and gesture—as is evident, first, from their erect posture; then from Ezek. i. 5, "they had the appearance of a man;" and also, from the peculiar expression in Rev. iv. 7, where it is said of the third, "that it had a face as a man"—which is best understood to mean, that while the other creatures were unlike man in the face, though like in the body, this was like in the face too. The same inference is still further deducible from the part taken by the cherubim in the Apocalypse, along with the elders and the redeemed generally, in celebrating the praise of God. The other point of agreement is, that in all the descriptions actually given, the cherubim have a composite appearance—with the form of a man, indeed, predominating, but with other animal forms combined—those, namely, of the lion, the ox, and the eagle.

Now, there can be no doubt that these three creatures, along with man, make up together, according to the estimation of a remote antiquity, the most perfect forms of animal existence. They belong to those departments of the visible creation which constitute the first in rank and importance of its three kingdoms—the kingdom of organic life. And in that kingdom they belong to the highest class—to that which possesses warm blood and phy-

---

[1] Vitringa justly remarks as to the difference between St John's representation and Ezekiel's respecting the faces, that "it is not of essential moment; for the beasts most intimately connected together form, as it were, one beast-existence, and it is a matter of indifference whether all the properties are represented as belonging to each of the four, or singly to each."

sical life in its fullest developement. Nay, in that highest class they are again the highest ; for the ox in ancient times was placed above the horse, on account of the useful purposes in husbandry which he was made to serve. And hence the old Jewish proverb, " Four are the highest in the world—the lion among wild beasts, the ox among tame cattle, the eagle among birds, man among all (creatures) ; but God is supreme over all." The meaning is, that in these four kinds are exhibited the highest forms of creature-life on earth, but that God is still infinitely exalted above these ; since all creature-life springs out of his fulness, and is dependent on his hand. So that a creature compounded of all these—bearing in its general shape and structure the lineaments of a man, but associating with the human the appearance and properties also of the three next highest orders of animal existence—might seem a kind of concrete manifestation of created life on earth—a sort of personified creaturehood.

But the thought naturally occurs, why thus strangely amalgamated and combined ? If the object had been simply to afford a representation of creaturely existence in general by means of its higher forms, we would naturally have expected them to stand apart as they actually appear in nature. But instead of this they are thrown into one representation ; and so, indeed, that however the representation may vary, still the inferior forms of animal life constantly appear as grafted upon, and clustering around, the organism of man. There is thus a striking unity in the diversity —a human ground and body, so to speak—in the grouped figures of the representation, which could not fail to attract the notice of a contemplative mind, and must have been designed to form an essential element in the symbolical instruction. It is an ideal combination ; no such composite creature as the cherub exists in the actual world ; and we can think of no reason why the singular combination it presents of animal forms, should have been set upon that of man as the trunk and centre of the whole, unless it were to exhibit the higher elements of humanity in some kind of organic connection with certain distinctive properties of the inferior creation. The nature of man is immensely the highest upon earth, and towers loftily above all the rest by powers peculiar to itself. And yet we can easily conceive how this very nature of man might be greatly raised and ennobled by having superadded to its own inherent qualities, those of which the other animal forms now before us stand as the appropriate types.

Thus, the lion among ancient nations generally, and in particular among the Hebrews, was the representative of king-like majesty and peerless strength. All the beasts of the field stand in awe of him, none being able to cope with him in might; and his roar strikes terror wherever it is heard. Hence the lion is naturally regarded as the king of the forest, where might is the sole ground of authority and rule. And hence, also, lions were placed both at the right and left of Solomon's throne, as symbols of royal majesty and supreme power.—As the lion among quadrupeds, so the *eagle* is king among birds, and stands pre-eminent in the two properties that more peculiarly distinguish the winged creation—those of sight and flight. The term *eagle-eyed* has been quite proverbial in every age. The eagle perceives his prey from the loftiest elevation, where he himself appears scarcely discernible; and it has even been believed, that he can descry the smallest fish in the sea, and look with undazzled gaze upon the sun. His power of wing, however, is still more remarkable: no bird can fly either so high or so far. Moving with king-like freedom and velocity through the loftiest regions and the most extended space, we naturally think of him as the fittest image of something like angelic nimbleness of action. It is this more especially, or, we should rather say, this exclusively, which is symbolically associated with the eagle in Scripture. No reference is made there to the eagle's powers of vision, but very frequent allusion to his extraordinary power of flight (Deut. xxviii. 49; Job ix. 26; Prov. xxiii. 5; Hab. i. 8, &c.) And hence, too, in Rev. iv. 7, the epithet flying is attached to the eagle, to indicate that this is the quality to be made account of.—Finally, the *ox* was among the ancients the common image of patient labour and productive energy. It naturally came to bear this signification from its early use in the operations of husbandry—in ploughing and harrowing the ground, then bearing home the sheaves, and at last treading out the corn. On this account the bovine form was so frequently chosen, especially in agricultural countries like Egypt, as the most appropriate symbol of Deity, in its inexhaustible productiveness. And if associated with man, the idea would instinctively suggest itself of patient labour and productive energy in working.

THE CHERUBIM. 227

Such, then, not by any conjectural hypothesis or strained interpretations, but by the simplest reading of the descriptions given in the Bible, appear to have been the generic form and idea of the cherubim. It is absolutely necessary, that we should apply the light furnished by those passages, in which they *are* described, to those also in which they are not, and that what are expressly named and described as the cherubim, when seen in prophetic vision, must be regarded as substantially agreeing with those which had a visible appearance, and a local habitation on earth—for, otherwise, the subject would be involved in inextricable confusion by Scripture itself. Assuming these points, we are warranted to think of the cherubim, wherever they are mentioned, as presenting in their composite structure, and having, as the very basis of that structure, the form of man—the only being on earth that is possessed of a rational and moral nature; yet combining, along with this, and organically uniting to it, the animal representatives of majesty and strength, winged velocity, patient and productive labour. Why united and combined thus, the mere descriptions of the cherubic appearances give no intimation; we must search for information concerning it in the other points that remain to be considered. So far, we have been simply putting together the different features of the descriptions, and viewing the cherubic figures in their individual characteristics and relative bearing.[1]

---

[1] Hengstenberg, in his remarks on Rev. iv. 7, regarding the cherubim as simple representations of the animal creation on earth, objects to any symbolical meaning being attached to the separate animal forms, on the special ground that in that passage of Revelation it is the *calf*, not the *ox*, which is mentioned in the description—as it is also found once in the description of Ezekiel, ch. i. 7. He thinks this cannot be accidental, but must have been designed to prevent our attributing to it the symbolical meaning of productiveness, or such like; as no one would think of associating that idea with a calf. We are surprised at so weak an objection from such a quarter. There can be no doubt—and it is not only admitted but contended for by Hengstenberg himself in his Beiträge, i. p. 161, sq.—that in connection with that symbolical meaning the ox-worship of Egypt was erected, and from Egypt was introduced among the Israelites at Sinai, and again by Jeroboam at a later period. Yet in Scripture it is always spoken of, not as ox, or bull, or cow, but as calf-worship. This conclusively shews that, symbolically viewed, no distinction was made between ox and calf. And in the description of such figures as the cherubim, calf might very naturally be substituted for ox, simply on account of the smaller and more delicate outline which the form would present. It is possible the same appearance may partly have contributed to the idols at Bethel and Dan being designated calves rather than oxen.

2. We named, as our second point of inquiry, the designations applied to the cherubim in Scripture. The term cherubim itself being the more common and specific of these, would naturally call for consideration first—if any certain key could be found to its correct import. But this we have already assigned to the class of things over which a hopeless obscurity may be said to hang. There is another designation, however, originally applied to them by Ezekiel, and the sole designation given to them in the Apocalypse, from which some additional light may be derived. This expression is in the original חיות, animantia, living ones, or living creatures. The Septuagint uses the quite synonymous term $\zeta\tilde{\omega}\alpha$; and this, again, is the word uniformly employed by St John, when speaking of the cherubim. It has been unhappily rendered by our translators *beasts* in the Revelation; thus incongruously associating with the immediate presence and throne of God mere bestial existences, and identifying in name the most exalted creaturely forms of being in the heavenly places, with the grovelling symbolical head of the antichristian and ungodly elements of the world. This is what bears, in the Apocalypse the distinctive name of the *beast* ($\vartheta\eta\rho\iota\sigma\nu$); and the name should never have been applied to the ideal existences, which derive *their* distinctive appellation from the fulness of life belonging to them—the *living ones*. The frequency with which this name is used of the cherubim is remarkable. In Ezekiel and the Apocalypse together it occurs nearly thirty times; and may consequently be regarded as peculiarly expressive of the symbolical character of the cherubim. It presents them to our view as exhibiting the property of life in its highest state of power and activity; therefore, as creatures altogether instinct with life. And the idea thus conveyed by the name is further substantiated by one or two traits associated with them in Ezekiel and the Apocalypse. Such, especially, is the very singular multiplicity of eyes attached to them, appearing first in the mystic wheels that regulated their movements, and afterwards in the cherubic forms themselves. For, the eye is the symbol of intelligent life; the living spirit's most peculiar organ and index. And to represent the cherubim as so strangely replenished with eyes, could only be intended to make them known to us as wholly inspirited. Accordingly, in the first vision of Ezekiel, in which the eyes belonged immediately to the wheels, " the *spirit* of the

living creatures" is said to have been in the wheels (ch. i. 20)—where the eye was, there was the intelligent, thinking, directive spirit of life. Another, and quite similar trait, is the quick and restless activity ascribed to them by both writers—by Ezekiel, when he represents them as "running and returning" with lightning speed; and by St John, when he describes them as "resting not day or night." Incessant motion is one of the most obvious symptoms of a plenitude of life. We instinctively associate the property of life even with the inanimate things that exhibit motion—such as fountains and running streams, which are called living, in contradistinction to stagnant pools, that seem comparatively dead. And in the Hebrew tongue, these two symbols of life—eyes and fountains—have their common symbolical meaning marked by the employment of the same term to denote them both (עין). So that creatures which appeared to be all eyes and all motion, are, in plain terms, those in which the powers and properties of life were quite peculiarly displayed.

We believe there is a still further designation applied to the same objects in Scripture—the seraphim of Isaiah (ch. vi.) It is in the highest degree improbable, that the prophet should by that name, so abruptly introduced, have pointed to an order of existences, or a form of being, nowhere else mentioned in Scripture; but quite natural that he should have referred to the cherubim in the sanctuary, as the scene of the vision lay there; and the more especially, as three characteristics—the possession by each of six wings, the position of immediate proximity to the throne of God, and the threefold proclamation of Jehovah's holiness—are those also which re-appear again, at the very outset, in St John's description of the cherubim. That they should have been called by the name of seraphim (burning ones) is no way inconsistent with this idea, for it merely embodies in a designation the thought symbolized in the vision of Ezekiel under the appearance of fire, giving forth flashes of lightning, which the cherubim presented (ch. i. 13). In both alike the fire, whether connected with the name or the appearance, denoted the wrath, which was the most prominent feature in the divine manifestation at the time. But as, in thus identifying the cherubim with the seraphim, we tread on somewhat doubtful ground, we shall make no further use of the thoughts suggested by it.

It is right to notice, however, that the designation we have more particularly considered, and the emblematic representations illustrative of it, belong to the later portions of Scripture, which treat of the cherubim; and while we cannot but regard the idea thus exhibited, as essentially connected with the cherubic form of being, a fundamental element in its meaning, it certainly could not be by any means so vividly displayed in the cherubim of the tabernacle, which were stationary figures. Nor can we tell distinctly how it stood in this respect with the cherubim of Eden; we know not what precise form and attitude were borne by them. But not only the representations we have been considering—the analogy also of the cherubim in the tabernacle, with their outstretched wings, as in the act of flying, and their eyes intently directed toward the mercy-seat, as if they were actually beholding and pondering what was there exhibited, may justly lead us to infer, that in some way or another a life-like appearance was also presented by the cherubim of Eden. Absolutely motionless or dead-like forms would have been peculiarly out of place in the way to the tree of life. Yet of what sort this fulness of life might be, which was exhibited in the cherubim, we have still had no clear indication. From various things that have pressed themselves on our notice, it might not doubtfully have been inferred to be life in the highest sense—spiritual and divine. But this comes out more prominently in connection with the other aspects of the subject which remain to be contemplated.

3. We proceed, therefore, to the point next in order—the positions assigned to the cherubim in Scripture. These are properly but two, and, by having regard only to what is essential in the matter, might possibly be reduced to one. But as they ostensibly and locally differ, we shall treat them apart. They are the garden of Eden, and the dwelling-place, or throne of God.

The first local residence in which the cherubim appear, was the garden of Eden—the earthly paradise. What, however, was this, but the proper home and habitation of life? of life generally, but emphatically of the divine life? Every thing there seemed to breathe the air, and to exhibit the fresh and blooming aspect of life. Streams of water ran through it to supply all its productions with nourishment, and keep them in perpetual healthfulness; multitudes of living creatures roamed amid its bowers, and the tree of life, at once the emblem and the seal of immortality, rose in the centre, as if to shed a vivifying influence over the entire domain. Most fitly was it called by the Rabbins " the land of life." But it was life, we soon perceive, in the higher sense—life, not merely as opposed to bodily decay and dissolution, but as opposed also to sin, which is the soul's death. Eden was the garden of delight, which God gave to man as the image of himself, the possessor of that spiritual and holy life which has its fountainhead in God. And the moment man renounced his part in this divine property of life, and yielded himself as an instrument of unrighteousness, he lost his heritage of blessing, and was driven forth as a child of mortality and corruption from the hallowed region of life. When, therefore, the cherubim were set in the garden to occupy the place which man had forfeited by his transgression, it was impossible but that they should be regarded as the representatives, not of life merely, but of the life that is in God, and in connection with which evil cannot dwell. This they were by their very position within the sacred territory—whatever other ideas may have been symbolized by their peculiar structure, and more special relations.

The other and more common position assigned to the cherubim is in immediate connection with the dwelling-place and throne of God. This connection comes first into view when the instructions were given to Moses regarding the construction of the tabernacle in the wilderness. As the tabernacle was to be, in a manner, the habitation of God, where he was to dwell and manifest himself to his people, the whole of the curtains forming the interior of the tent were commanded to be inwoven with cherubic figures. But as the inner sanctuary was more especially the habitation of God, where he fixed his throne of grace, Moses was commanded, for the erection of this throne, to make two cherubims, one at each end of the ark of the covenant, and to place them so, that they should stand with outstretched wings, their faces toward each other, and toward the mercy-seat, the lid of the ark, which lay between them. That mercy-seat, or the space immediately above it, bounded on either side by the cherubim, and covered by their wings (Ex. xxv. 20), was the throne of God, as the God of the old covenant, the ideal seat of the divine commonwealth in Israel. "*There*," said God to Moses, " will I meet with thee, and I will commune with thee from above the mercy-seat, from between the two cherubim which are upon the ark of the testimony, of all things which I will give thee in commandment to the children of Israel" (Ex. xxv. 22.) This is the fundamental passage regarding the connection of the cherubim with the throne of God; and it is carefully to be noted, that while the seat of the divine presence and glory is said to be *above* the mercy-seat, it is also said to be *between* the cherubim. And the same form of expression is used in another passage in the Pentateuch, which may also be called a fundamental one, Numb. vii. 89, "And when Moses was gone into the tabernacle of the congregation (more properly, the tent of meeting) to speak with him, then he heard the voice of one speaking unto him from off the mercy-seat, that was upon the ark of testimony, from between the two cherubim." Hence the Lord was spoken of as the God "who dwelleth between the cherubims," according to our version, and correctly as to the sense; though as the verb is used without a preposition in the original, the more exact rendering would be, the God who dwelleth-in (inhabitest, ישׁב), or occupies (ישׁב viz. as a throne or seat) the cherubim. These two verbs are interchanged in the form of expression, which is used with considerable frequency (for example, 1 Sam. iv. 4; 2 Sam. vi. 2; Ps. lxxx. 1; xcix. 1, &c.); and it is from the use of the first of them that the Jewish term Shekinah (the indwelling), in reference to the symbol of the divine presence, is derived. The space above the mercy-seat, enclosed by the two cherubim with their outstretched wings, bending and looking toward each other, was regarded as the precise local habitation which God possessed as a dwelling-place, or occupied as a throne in Israel. And it is entirely arbitrary, and against the plain import of the two fundamental passages, to insert *above*, as is still very often done by interpreters ("dwelleth," or "sitteth enthroned above the cherubim"), still more so to make anything depend, as to the radical meaning of the symbol, on the seat of God being considered above, rather than between the cherubim.

Hengstenberg is guilty of this error, when he represents the proper place of the cherubim as being *under* the throne of God, and holds that to be their first business—though he disallows the propriety of regarding them as material supports to the throne

(Comm. on Rev. iv. 6). The meaning he adopts of the symbol absolutely required them to be in this position; since only by their being beneath the throne of God, could they with any fitness be regarded as imaging the living creation below, as subject to the overruling power and sovereignty of God. Hofmann and Delitzsch go still farther in this direction; and, adopting the notion repudiated by Hengstenberg, consider the cherubim as the formal bearers of Jehovah's throne. Delitzsch even affirms, in defiance (we think) of the plainest language, that wherever the part of the cherubim is distinctly mentioned in Old Testament Scripture, they appear as the bearers of Jehovah and his throne, and that he sat enthroned upon the cherubim in the midst of the worldly sanctuary (Die Genesis Ausgelegt, p. 145). There are in fact only two representations of the kind specified. One is in Ps. xviii. 10, where the Lord is described as coming down for judgment upon David's enemies, and in doing so, "riding upon a cherub, and flying upon the wings of the wind"—obviously a poetical delineation, in which it would be as improper to press closely what is said of the position of the cherub, as what is said of the wings of the wind. The one image was probably introduced with the view merely of stamping the divine manifestation with a distinctively covenant aspect, as the other for the purpose of exhibiting the resistless speed of its movements. But if the allusion is to be taken less ideally, it must be borne in mind, that the manifestation described is primarily and pre-eminently for judgment, not as in the temple, for mercy; and this may explain the higher elevation given to the seat of divine Majesty. The same holds good also of the other representation, in which the throne or glory of the Lord appears above the cherubim. It is in Ezekiel, where, in two several places (ch. i. 26, x. 1), there is first said to have been a firmament upon the heads of the living creatures, and then above the firmament the likeness of a throne. The description is so palpably different from that given of the Sanctuary, that it would be absurd to make the one rule the other. We must rather hold, that in the special and immediate object of the theophany exhibited to Ezekiel, there was a reason for giving such a position to the throne of God—one so much apart from the cherubim, and elevated so distinctly above them. And we believe that reason may be found, in its being predominantly a manifestation for judgment, in which the seat of the divine glory naturally appeared to rise to a loftier and more imposing elevation, than it was wont to occupy in the Holiest. This seems to be clearly indicated in ch. x. 4, where, in proceeding to the work of judgment, the glory of the Lord is represented as *going up from the cherub*, and standing over the threshold of the house; immediately after which the house was filled with the cloud—the symbol of divine wrath and retribution. We may add, that the statement in Rev. iv. 6, where the cherubic forms are said to have appeared " in the midst of the throne, and round about the throne," is plainly at variance with the idea of their acting as supports to the throne. The throne itself is described in v. 2, as being *laid* ($\mathit{\check{\varepsilon}\kappa\varepsilon\tilde{\iota}\tau o}$) in heaven, which excludes the supposition of any instruments being employed to bear it aloft. And from the living creatures being represented as at once in the midst of the throne, and round about it, nothing further or more certain can be inferred beyond their appearing in a position of immediate nearness to it. The elders sat round about the throne; but the cherubim appeared in it, as well as around it—implying that theirs was the place of closest proximity to the divine Being, who sat on it.

The result, then, which arises, we may almost say, with conclusive certainty from the preceding investigation, is, that the kind of life which was symbolized by the cherubim, was life most nearly and essentially connected with God—life as it is, or shall be held, by those who dwell in his immediate presence, and form, in a manner, the very inclosure and covering of his throne;—pre-eminently, therefore, spiritual and holy life. Holiness becomes God's house, in general; and of necessity it rises to its highest creaturely representation in those who are regarded as compassing about the most select and glorious portion of the house—the seat of the living God himself. Whether His peculiar dwelling were in the garden of Eden, or in the recesses of a habitation made by men's hands, the presence of the cherubim alike proclaimed him to be One, who indispensably requires of such as are to be round about Him, the property of life, and in connection with that with the beauty of holiness, which is, in a sense, the life of life, as possessed and exercised by his intelligent offspring.

4. Our last point of scriptural inquiry, was to be respecting the kinds of agency attributed to the cherubim.

We naturally revert, first again, to what is said of them in connection with the garden of Eden, though our information there is the scantiest. It is merely said, that the cherubim were made to dwell at the east of the garden, and a flaming sword, turning every way, to keep the way to the tree of life. The two instruments—the cherubim and the sword—are associated together, in regard to this keeping; and, as the text draws no distinction between them, it is quite arbitrary to say, with Bähr, that the cherubim alone had to do with it, and to do with it precisely as Adam had. It is said of Adam, that "God put him into the garden to dress it and to keep it" (Gen. ii. 15)—not the one simply, but both together. He had to do a twofold office in respect to the garden—to attend to its cultivation, as far as might then be needful, and to keep or preserve it, namely, from the disturbing and desolating influence of evil. The charge to keep plainly implied some danger of losing. And it became still plainer, when the tenure of possession was immediately suspended on a condition, the violation of which was to involve the penalty of death. The keeping was to be made good against a possible contingence, which might subvert the order of God, and change the region of life into a charnel-house of death. Now, it is the same word that is used in regard to the cherubim and the flaming sword: These now were to keep—not, however, like Adam, the entire garden, but simply the way to the tree of life; to maintain in respect to this one point the settled order of Heaven, and that more especially by rendering the way inaccessible to fallen man. There is here also, no doubt, a present occupancy—but the occupancy of only a limited portion, a mere path-way, and for the definite purpose of defending it from unhallowed intrusion.

Still, not simply for defence; for occupancy as well as defence. And the most natural thought is, that as in the keeping there was a twofold idea, so a twofold representation was given to it; that the occupancy was more immediately connected with the cherubim, and the defence against intrusion with the flaming sword. One does not see otherwise, what need there could have been for both. Nor is it possible to conceive how the ends in view could otherwise have been served. It was, beyond all doubt, for man's spiritual instruction, that such peculiar instruments were employed at the east of the garden of Eden, to awaken and preserve in his bosom right thoughts of the God with whom he had to do. But an image of terror and repulsion was not alone sufficient for this. There was needed along with it an image of mercy and hope. And in what was actually exhibited man had both. When his eye looked to the sword, with its burnished and fiery aspect, he could not but be struck with awe at the thought of God's severe and retributive justice. But when he saw, at the same time, in near and friendly connection with that emblem of Jehovah's righteousness, living or life-like forms of being, cast pre-eminently in his own mould, but bearing along with his the likeness also of the choicest species of the animal creation around him—when he saw this, what could he think, but that still for creatures of earthly rank, and for himself most of all, an interest was reserved by the mercy of God in the things that pertained to the blessed region of life? That region could not now, by reason of sin, be actually held by him; but it was ideally held—by composite forms of creature-life, in which his nature appeared as the predominating element. And for what end? if not to teach, that when that nature of his should have nothing to fear from the avenging justice of God, it should regain its place in the holy and blissful haunts from which it had meanwhile been excluded? So that, standing before the eastern approach to Eden, and scanning with intelligence the appearances that there presented themselves to his view, the child of faith might say to himself, That region of life is not finally lost to me. It has neither been blotted from the face of creation, nor entrusted to natures of another sphere. Earthly forms still hold possession of it. The very natures that have lost the privilege continue to have their representation in the new and unreal-like occupants that are meanwhile appointed to keep it. Better things, then, are doubtless in reserve for them; and *my* nature, which stands out so conspicuously above them all, fallen though it be at present, is assuredly destined to rise again, and enjoy in the reality what is there representatively assigned to it.

There is nothing surely unnatural or far-fetched in such a line of reflection. It manifestly lay within the reach of the very earliest members of a believing seed; especially, since the light it is supposed to have conveyed, did not stand alone, but was only supplementary to that embodied in the first grand promise to the fallen, that the seed of the woman should bruise the head of the serpent. The supernatural machinery at the east of the garden merely shewed how this bruising was to proceed, and in what result it might be expected to issue. It was to proceed, not by placing in abeyance the manifestation of divine righteousness, but by providing for its being exercised without the fallen creature being destroyed. Nor should it issue in a partial, but in a complete recovery—nay, in the possession of a state higher than before. For, the creaturehood of earth, it would seem, was yet to stand in a closer relation to the manifested glory of God, and was to become capable of enduring sights and performing ministrations, which were not known in the original constitution of things on earth.

It might not be possible, perhaps, for the primeval race of worshippers to go farther, or to get a more definite insight into the purposes of God, by contemplating the cherubim. We scarcely think it could. But we can easily conceive, how the light and hope therewith connected would be felt to grow, when this embodied creaturehood—or, if we rather choose so to regard it, this ideal manhood—was placed in the sanctuary of God's presence and glory, and so as to form the immediate boundary and covering of his throne. A relation of greater nearness to the divine was there evidently won for the human and earthly. And not that only, but a step also in advance toward the actual enjoyment of what was ideally exhibited. For, while at first men in flesh and blood were not permitted to enter into the region of holy life occupied by the cherubim, but only to look at it from without, now the way was at length partially laid open, and in the person of the high-priest, through the blood of atonement, they could make an approach, though still only at stated times, to the very feet of the cherubim of glory. The blessed and hopeful relation of believing men to these singular attendants of the divine majesty, rose thus more distinctly into view, and in more obvious connection also with the means, through which the ultimate realization was to be attained. But the information in this line, and by means of these materials, reaches its farthest limit, when, in the Apocalyptic vision of a triumphant church, the four and twenty elders, who represent her, are seen sitting in royal state and crowned majesty close beside the throne, with the cherubic forms in and around it. *There*, at last, the ideal and the actual freely meet together—the merely symbolical representatives of the life of God, and its real possessors, the members of a redeemed and glorified church. And the inspiring element of the whole, that which at once explains all and connects all harmoniously together, is the central object appearing there of " a Lamb, as if it had been slain, in the midst of the throne, and of the four living creatures, and in the midst of the elders." Here the mystery resolves itself; in this consummate wonder all other wonders cease, all difficulties vanish. The Lamb of God, uniting together heaven and earth, human guilt and divine mercy, man's nature and God's perfections, has opened a pathway for the fallen to the very height and pinnacle of created being. With him in the midst, as a sun and shield, there is ground for the most secure standing, and the closest fellowship with God.

We must glance, however, at the other kinds of agency connected with the cherubim. In the first vision of Ezekiel, it is by their appearance, which we have already noticed, not by their agency, properly speaking, that they convey instruction regarding the character of the manifestations of himself, which the Lord was going to give through the prophet. But at ch. x. 7, where the approaching judgment upon Jerusalem is symbolically exhibited by the scattering of coals of fire over the city, the fire is represented as being taken from between the cherubim, and by the hand of one of them given to the ministering angel to be cast forth upon the city. It was thus indicated—so far we can easily understand the vision—that the coming execution of judgment was not only to be of God, but of him in connection with the full consent and obedient service of the holy powers and agencies around him. And the still more specific indication might be intended to be given, that as the best interests of humanity required the work of judgment to be executed, so a fitting human instrument should be found for the purpose. The wrath of God, represented by the coals of fire, should be put in force by an earthly agency, represented by the cherub's hand that ministered them.

An entirely similar action, differing only in the form it assumes, is connected with the cherubim in ch. xv. of Revelation, where one of the living creatures is represented as giving into the hands of the angels the seven last vials of the wrath of God. The rational and living creaturehood of earth, in its state of alliance and fellowship with God, thus appeared to go along with the concluding judgments, which were necessary to bring the evil in the world to a perpetual end. Nor is the earlier and more prominent action ascribed to them materially different—that connected with the seven-sealed Book. This book, viewed generally, unquestionably represents the progress and triumph of Christ's kingdom upon earth over all that was there naturally opposed to it. The first seal, when opened, presents the divine king riding forth in conquering power and majesty; the last exhibits all prostrate and silent before him. The different seals, therefore, unfold the different stages of this mighty achievement; and as they successively open, the living creatures successively proclaim, Come and see. The work, in its fundamental character, was the going forth of the energetic and judicial agency of God upon the sinfulness of the world, for the purpose of subduing it to himself, of establishing righteousness and truth among men, and bringing the actual state of things on earth into conformity with what is ideally right and good. Who, then, should announce and herald such a work, if not the ideal creatures, in which earthly forms of being appeared replete with the life of God, and in closest contact with his throne ? Such might be said to be *their* special interest and business. And hence, though there were only four of them in the vision, (with some reference, perhaps, to the four corners of the earth),[1] and so one for but the first four seals of the book ; yet rather than introduce any less fitting agency, it was

---

[1] We say only *perhaps;* for though Hengstenberg and others lay much stress upon the number *four*, as the signature of the earth, yet there being only two in the tabernacle, would seem to indicate that nothing material depends on the number. We think, that the increase from the original two to four may, with more probability of truth, be accounted for historically. When the temple was built, two cherubim of immense proportions were put into the most Holy Place, and under these were placed the ark with its old and smaller cherubim: So that there were henceforth actually four cherubim over the ark. And as the form of Ezekiel's vision, in its leading elements, was evidently taken from the temple, and John's again from that, it seems quite natural to account for the four in this way.

deemed better to leave the three remaining seals without any separate heralding of their own.

We can discern the same leading characteristics in the further use made of the cherubic imagery in the Apocalypse. They are represented as ceaselessly proclaiming, "Holy, holy, holy, Lord God Almighty, which was and is, and is to come," thereby shewing it to be their calling to make known the absolute holiness of God, as infinitely removed, not merely from the natural, but also, and still more, from the moral imperfections and evils of creation. In their ascriptions of praise, too, they are represented not only as giving honour and glory, but also thanks to Him that sitteth on the throne, and as joining with the elders in the new song that was sung to the Lamb for the benefits of his salvation (Rev. iv. 9 ; v. 8). So that they plainly stand related to the redemptive as well as the creative work of God. And yet in all, from first to last, only ideal representatives of what pertains to God's kingdom on earth, not as substantive existences themselves possessing it. They belong to the imagery of faith, not to her abiding realities. And so, when the ultimate things of redemption come, their place is no more found. They hold out the lamp of hope to fallen man through the wilderness of life, pointing his expectations to the better country. But when this country breaks upon our view—when the new heavens and the new earth supplant the old, then also the ideal gives way to the real. We see another paradise, with its river and tree of life, and a present God, and a presiding Saviour, and holy angels, and a countless multitude of redeemed spirits rejoicing in the fulness of blessing and glory provided for them ;—but no sight is anywhere to be seen of the cherubim of glory. They have fulfilled the end of their temporary existence ; and when no longer needed, vanish like the guiding stars of night before the bright sunshine of eternal day.

To sum up, then : The cherubim were in their very nature and design artificial and temporary forms of being—uniting in their composite structure the distinctive features of the highest kinds of creaturely existence on earth—man's first and chiefly. They were set up for representations to the eye of faith of earth's living creaturehood, and more especially of its rational and immortal, though fallen head, with reference to the better hopes and destiny in prospect. From the very first they gave promise of a restored condition to the fallen ; and by the use afterwards made of them, the light became clearer and more distinct. By their designations, the positions assigned them, the actions from time to time ascribed to them, as well as their own peculiar structure, it was intimated, that the good in prospect should be secured, not at the expense of, but in perfect consistence with the claims of God's righteousness,— that restoration to the holiness must precede restoration to the blessedness of life ; and that only by being made capable of dwelling beside the presence of the only Wise and Good, could man hope to have his portion of felicity recovered. But all this, they further betokened, it was in God's purpose to have accomplished, and in the process to raise humanity to a higher than its original destination ; in its standing nearer to God, and greatly ennobled in its powers of life and capacities of working.

Before passing from the subject of the cherubim, we must briefly notice some of the leading views that have been entertained by others respecting them. These will be found to rest upon a part merely of the representations of Scripture to the exclusion of others, and most commonly to a neglect of what we hold it to be of especial moment to keep prominently in view—the historical use of the cherubim in Scripture. That such must be the case with an opinion once very prevalent both among Jews and Christians, and not without its occasional advocates still,[1] which held them to be celestial existences, or more specifically angels, is obvious at first sight. For, the component parts of the cherubic appearance being all derived from the forms of being which have their local habitation on earth, it is terrestrial, as contradistinguished from celestial objects, which we are necessitated to think of. And their original position at the east of Eden would have been inexplicable, as connected with a religion of hope, if celestial and not earthly natures had been represented in them. The natural conclusion in that case must have been, that the way of life was finally lost for man. In the Apocalypse, too, they are expressly distinguished from the angels ; and in ch. v. the living creatures and the elders form one distinct chorus (v. 8), while the angels form another (v.

---

[1] Elliott's Horæ Apoc. Introd.—partially adopted also, and especially in regard to the cherubim of Eden, by Mr Mills in his recent work on Sacred Symbology, p. 136.

11). There is more of verisimilitude in another, and at present more prevalent opinion, that the cherubim represent the church of the redeemed. This opinion has often been propounded, and quite recently has been set forth in a separate work on the cherubim.[1] It evidently fails, however, to account satisfactorily for their peculiar structure, and is of a too concrete and specific character to have been represented by such ideal and shifting formations as the cherubim of Scripture. These are more naturally conceived to have had to do with natures than with persons. Besides, it is plainly inconsistent with the place occupied by the cherubim in the Apocalyptic vision, where the four-and-twenty crowned elders obviously represent the church of the redeemed. To ascribe the same office to the cherubim would be to suppose a double and essentially different representation of the same object. To avoid this objection, Vitringa (Obs. Sac. i. 846) modified the idea so as to make the cherubim in the Revelation (for he supposed those mentioned in Gen. iii. 24, to have been angels) the representatives of such as hold stations of eminence in the church, evangelists and ministers, as the elders were of the general body of believers. But it is an entirely arbitrary notion, and destitute of support in the general representations of Scripture; as indeed is virtually admitted by the learned author, in so peculiarly connecting it with the vision of St John. An opinion which finds some colour of support only in a single passage, and loses all appearance of probability when applied to others, is self-confuted.

It was the opinion of Michaelis, an opinion bearing a vivid impress of the general character of his mind, that the cherubim were a sort of "thunder-horses" of Jehovah, somewhat similar to the horses of Jupiter among the Greeks. This idea has so much of a heathen aspect, and so little to give it even an apparent countenance in Scripture, that no further notice need be taken of it. More acceptance on the continent has been found for the view of Herder, who regards the cherubim as originally feigned monsters, like the dragons or griphins, which were the fabled guardians among the ancients of certain precious treasures. Hence, he thinks, the cherubim are represented as first of all appointed to keep watch at the closed gates of paradise; and for the same rea-

---

[1] Doctrine of the Cherubim, by George Smith, F.A.S.

son were afterwards placed by Moses in the presence-chamber of God, which the people generally were not permitted to enter. Latterly, however, he admits they were differently employed, but more after a poetical fashion, and as creatures of the imagination. This admission obviously implies, that the view will not stand an examination with all the passages of Scripture bearing on the subject. Indeed, we shall not violate the truth if we say, that it can stand an examination with none of them. The cherubim were not set up even in Eden as formidable monsters to fray sinful man from approaching it. They were not needed for such a purpose, as this was sufficiently effected by the flaming sword. Nor were they placed at the door, or about the threshold of the sanctuary, to guard its sanctity, as on that hypothesis they should have been, but formed a part of the furniture of its innermost region. And the later notices of the cherubim in Scripture, which confessedly present them in a different light, are not by any means independent and arbitrary representations; they have a close affinity, as we have seen, with the earlier statements; and we cannot doubt that the same fundamental character is to be found in all the representations.

Spencer's idea of the cherubim was of a piece with his views generally of the institutions of Moses: they were of Egyptian origin, and were formed in imitation of those monstrous compounds which played so prominent a part in the sensuous worship of that cradle of superstition and idolatry. Such composite forms, however, were by no means so peculiar to Egypt as Spencer represents. They were common to heathen antiquity, and are even understood to have been more frequently used in the East than in Egypt. Nor is it unworthy of notice, that of all the monstrous combinations which are mentioned in ancient writings, and which the more successful investigations of later times have brought to light from the remains of Egyptian idolatry, not one has an exact resemblance to the cherub; the four creature-forms combined in it seem never to have been so combined in Egypt; and the only thing approaching to it yet discovered, is to be found in India. It is quite gratuitous, therefore, to assert that the cherubim were of Egyptian origin. But even if similar forms had been found there, it would not have settled the question, either as to the proper origin, or the real nature of the cherubim. If they were placed in Eden after the fall, they had a known character and habitation in the world many centuries before Egypt had a being. And then, whatever composite images might be found in Egypt, or other idolatrous nations, these, in accordance with the whole character of heathen idolatry, which was essentially the deification of nature, must have been representations of the Godhead itself, as symbolized by the objects of nature, while the cherubim are uniformly represented as separate from God, and as ministers of righteousness before him. So well was this understood among the Israelites, that even in the most idolatrous periods of their history, the cherubim never appear among the instruments of their false worship. This separate and creaturely character of the cherubim is also fatal to the opinion of those who regard them as "emblematical of the ever-blessed Trinity in covenant to redeem man," which is, besides, utterly at variance with the position of the cherubim in the temple—for how could God be said to dwell between the ever-blessed Trinity?[1] And the same objections apply to another opinion, closely related to this, according to which the cherubim represent, not the Godhead personally, but the attributes and perfections of God; are held to be symbolical personifications of these as manifested in God's works and ways. This view has been adopted with various modifications by persons of great name, and of very different tendencies—such as Philo, Grotius, Bochart, Rosenmüller, De Wette; but it is not supported, either by the fundamental nature of the cherubim, or by their historical use. We cannot perceive, indeed, how the cherubim could really have been regarded as symbols of the divine perfections, or personifications of the divine attributes, without falling under the ban of the second commandment. It would surely have been an incongruity to have forbidden, in the strongest terms and with the severest penalties, the making of any likeness of God, and, at the same time, to have set up certain symbolical images of his perfections in the very region of his pre-

---

[1] It is Parkhurst, and the Hutchinsonian school, who are the patrons of this ridiculous notion. Horsley makes a most edifying improvement upon it, with reference to modern times: "The cherub was a compound figure, the calf (of Jeroboam) single. Jeroboam, therefore, and his subjects were Unitarians!"—(Works, vol. viii. 241). He forgot, apparently, that there were four parts in the cherub; so that not a trinity, but a quaternity, would have been the proper co-relative under the Gospel.

sence, and in immediate contact with his throne. No corporeal representation could consistently be admitted there of any thing but what directly pointed to creaturely existences, and their relations and interests. And the nearest possible connection with God, which we can conceive the cherubim to have been intended to hold, was that of shadowing forth how the creatures of his hand, and (originally) the bearers of his image on earth, might become so replenished with his spirit of holiness as to be, in a manner, the shrines of his indwelling and gracious presence.

Bähr, in his Symbolik, approaches more nearly to this view than any of the preceding ones, and theoretically avoids the more special objection we have urged against it; but it is by a philosophical refinement too delicate, especially without some accompanying explanation, to catch the apprehension of a comparatively unlearned and sensuous people. The cherubim, he conceives, were images of the creation in its highest parts—combining, in a concentrated shape, the most perfect forms of creature-life on earth—and, as such, serving as representatives of all creation. But the powers of life in creation are the signs and witnesses of those which, without limit or imperfection, are in God; and so, the relative perfection of life exhibited in the cherubim symbolized the absolute perfection of life that is in God—his omniscience, his peerless majesty, his creative power, his unerring wisdom. The cherub was not an image of the Creator, but it was an image of the Creator's manifested glory. We say, this is far too refined and shadowy a distinction to lie at the base of a popular religion, and to serve for instruction to a people surrounded on every hand by the gross forms and dense atmosphere of idolatry. It could scarcely have failed, in the circumstances, to lead to the worship of the cherubim, as, reflectively at least, the worthiest representations of God which could be conceived by men on earth. But, if this evil could have been obviated, which we can only think of as an inseparable consequence, there is another and still stronger attaching to the view, which we may call an inseparable ingredient. For, if the cherubim were representatives of created life, and thence factitious witnesses of the Creator's glory—if such were the sum and substance of what was represented in them, then it was, after all, but a symbol of things in nature; and, unlike all the other symbols in the religion of the Old Testament, it would have borne no respect to God's work, and character, and purposes of grace. That religion was one essentially adapted to the condition, the necessities, and desires of fallen man; and the symbolical forms and institutions belonging to it bear respect to God's nature and dealings, not so much in connection with the gifts and properties of creation, as with the principles of righteousness and the hopes of salvation. If the cherubim are held to be symbolical only of what is seen of God in nature, they stand apart from this properly religious province; they have no real adaptation to the circumstances of a fallen world; they have to do simply with creative, not with redemptive manifestations of God; and, so far as *they* are concerned, the religion of the Old Testament would after all have been, like the different forms of heathenism, a mere nature-religion. No further proof, surely, is needed of the falseness of the view in question; for, in a scheme of worship so wonderfully compact, and skilfully arranged toward a particular end, the supposition of a heterogeneous element at the centre necessarily carries its own refutation along with it.

We have already referred to the view of Hengstenberg, and shewn its incompatibility to some extent with the scriptural representations. His opinions upon this subject, indeed, appear to have been somewhat fluctuating. In one of his earlier productions, his work on the Pentateuch, he expresses his concurrence with Bähr, and even goes so far as to say, that he regarded Bähr's treatment of the cherubim as the most successful part of the *Symbolik*. Then in his Egypt and the Books of Moses, he gave utterance to an opinion, at variance with the radical idea of Bähr, that the cherubim had a connection, both in nature and origin, with the sphinxes of Egypt. And in his work on the Revelation, he expressly opposes Bähr's view, and holds that the living forms in the cherubim were merely the representation of all that is living on the earth. But representing the higher things on earth, they also naturally serve as representations of the earth itself; and God's appearing enthroned above the cherubim symbolized the truth, that he is the God of the whole earth, and has every thing belonging to it, matter and mind, subject to his control. As mentioned before, this view, if correct, would have required the position of the cherubim to be always very distinctly and manifestly below the throne of God—which, however, it does not appear to have been, except when the manifestation described was primarily for judgment. It leaves unexplained also the prominence given in the cherubic delineations to the form and likeness of man, and the circumstance that the cherubim should, in the Revelation, be nearer to the throne than the elders—placing, according to that view, the creation merely as such, nearer than the church. But the representation errs, rather as giving a partial and limited view of the truth, than maintaining what is absolutely contrary to it. It approaches, in our judgment, much nearer to the right view than that more recently set forth by Delitzsch, who considers the cherubim as simply the bearers of Jehovah's chariot, and as having been placed originally at the eastern gate of Paradise, as if to carry him aloft to heaven for the execution of judgment, should mankind proceed farther in the course of iniquity. A poetical notion certainly! but leaving rather too much to the imagination for so early an age, and scarcely taking the form best fitted for working either on men's fears or hopes! What Adam dreaded when he sinned, was not God's going to heaven to inflict punishment, but his coming down from heaven to reckon with him for his guilt. And though, in later times, the cherubim are represented as leaving the temple, preparatory to the execution of judgment, yet this was only to indicate that the temple had now become a common place—a doomed, because a corrupt habitation; and so abandoned to the destroying influences that were ready to alight on it. But the view seems altogether of an arbitrary and fanciful character, and it is unnecessary to enter more minutely into its refutation.

CHAPTER FOURTH.

SACRIFICIAL WORSHIP.

The symbols, to which our attention has hitherto been directed, were simply ordinances of teaching. They spake in language not to be mistaken of the righteous character of God, of the evil of sin, of the moral and physical ruin it had brought upon the world, of a purpose of grace and a prospect of recovery—but they did no more. There were no rites of service associated with them; nor of themselves did they call men to embody in any outward action the knowledge and principles they were the means of imparting. But religion must have its active services as well as its teaching ordinances. The one furnish light and direction, only that the other may be intelligently performed. And a symbolical religion, if it could ever be said to exist, could certainly not have perpetuated itself, or kept alive the knowledge of divine truth in the world, without the regular employment of one or more symbolical institutions, fitted for the suitable expression of religious ideas and feelings. Now, the only thing of this description which makes its appearance in the earlier periods of the world's history, and which continued to hold, through all the after stages of symbolical worship, the paramount place, is the rite of sacrifice.

We are not told, however, of the actual institution of this rite in immediate connection with the fall; and the silence of inspired history regarding it till Cain and Abel had reached the season of manhood, and the mention of it then simply as a matter of fact in the narrative of their lives, has given rise to much disputation concerning the origin of sacrifice—whether it was of divine appointment, or of human invention? And if the latter, to what circumstances in man's condition, or to what views and feelings naturally arising in his mind, might it owe its existence? In the investigation of these questions, a line of inquiry has not unfrequently been pursued by theologians, more befitting the position of philosophical reasoners, than of Christian divines. The solution has been sought for chiefly in the general attributes of human nature, and the practices of a remote and semi-barbarous heathenism, as if Scripture were entirely silent upon the subject till we come far down the stream of time. Discarding such a mode of conducting the investigation, and looking to the notices of Scripture for our only certain light upon the subject, we hope, without material difficulty, to find our way to conclusions on the leading points connected with it, which may be generally acquiesced in as legitimately drawn and firmly established.

1. In regard, first of all, to the divine authority and acceptable nature of worship by sacrifice—which is often mixed up with the consideration of its origin—Scripture leaves very little room for controversy. The only debateable ground, as concerns this aspect of the matter, respects that very limited period of time, which stretches from the fall of Adam to the offerings of Cain and Abel. From this latter period, verging too on the very commencement of the world's history, we are expressly informed that sacrifice of one kind had a recognised place in the worship of God, and met with his acceptance. Not only did Abel appear before God with a sacrificial offering, but by a visible token of approval—conveyed in all probability through some action of the cherubim or the flaming sword, near which, as the seat of the manifested presence of God, the service would naturally be performed—the seal was given of the divine acceptance and blessing. Thenceforth, at least, sacrifice presented after the manner of Abel's might be regarded as of divine authority. It bore distinctly impressed upon it the warrant and approbation of heaven; and whatever uncertainty might hang around it during the brief space which intervened between the fall and the time of Abel's accepted offering, it was from that time determined to be a mode of worship, with which God was well pleased. We might rather say *the* mode of worship; for sacrifice, accompanied, it is probable, with some words of prayer, is the only stated act of worship, by which believers in the earlier ages appear to have given more formal expression to their faith and hope in God. When it is said of the

times of Enos, the grandson of Adam in the pious line of Seth, that " then men began to call upon the name of the Lord," there can be little doubt that they did so after the example of Abel, by the presentation of sacrifice—only, as profiting by the fatal result of his personal dispute with Cain, in a more public and regularly concerted manner. It appears to have been then agreed among the worshippers of Jehovah, what offerings to present, and how to do so; as, in later times, it is frequently reported of Abraham and his family, in connection with their having built an altar, that they then "called upon the name of the Lord" (Gen. xii. 8; xiii. 4; xxvi. 25). That sacrifice held the same place in the instituted worship of God after the deluge, which it had done before, we learn, first of all, from the case of Noah—the connecting link between the old and new worlds—who no sooner left the ark than he built an altar to the Lord, and offered burnt-offerings of every clean beast and fowl, from which the Lord is said to have smelled a sweet savour. In the delineation given of the earlier patriarchal times in the Book of Job, we find him, not only spoken of as exhibiting his piety in the stated presentation of burnt-offerings, but also as expressly required by God to make sacrifice for the atonement of his friends, who had sinned with their lips in speaking what was not right. And as we have undoubted testimonies respecting the acceptable character of the worship performed by Abraham and his chosen seed, so we learn, that in this worship sacrificial offerings played the principal part, and were even sometimes directly enjoined by God (Gen. xv. 9, 10, 17; xxii. 2, 13; xxxv. 1, &c.)

The very latest of these notices in sacred history carry us up to a period far beyond that to which the authentic annals of any heathen kingdom reach, while the earliest refer to what occurred only a few years subsequent to the fall. From the time of Abel, then, downwards through the whole course of antediluvian and patriarchal history, it appears that the regular and formal worship of God mainly consisted in the offering of sacrifice, and that this was not rendered by a sort of religious venture on the part of the worshippers, but with the known sanction and virtual, if not explicit, appointment of God. As regards the right of men to draw near to God with such offerings, and their hope of acceptance at his hands, no shadow of doubt can fairly be said to rest upon any portion of the field of inquiry, except what may relate to the worship of the parents themselves of the human family.

2. It is well to keep in view the clear and satisfactory deliverance we obtain on this branch of the subject. And if we could ascertain definitely what were the views and feelings expressed by the worshippers in the kind of sacrifice which *was* accepted by God, the question of its precise origin would be of little moment; since, so recently after the institution of the rite, we have unequivocal evidence of its being divinely owned and approved, as actually offered. But it is here that the main difficulty presents itself, as it is only indirectly we can gather the precise objects for which the primitive race of worshippers came before God with sacrificial offerings. The question of their origin still is of moment for ascertaining this, and, at the same time, for determining the virtue possessed by the offerings in the sight of God. If they arose simply in the devout feelings of the worshipper, they might have been accepted by God as a natural and proper form for the expression of these feelings; but they could not have borne any typical respect to the higher sacrifice of Christ, as, in the things of redemption, type and antitype must be alike of God. And on this point we now proceed to remark negatively, that the facts already noticed concerning the first appearance and early history of sacrifice, present insuperable objections to all the theories which have sought on simply natural grounds to account for its *human* origin.

The theory, for example, which has received the suffrage of many learned men, both in this country and on the continent,[1] and which attempts to explain the rise of sacrifice by a reference to the feelings of men when they were in a kind of bestial roughness, capable of entertaining only the most gross and carnal ideas of God, and consequently disposed to deal with him much as they would have done with a fellow-creature, whose favour they desired to win by means of gifts,—this theory is utterly at variance with the earlier notices of sacrificial worship. It is founded upon a sense of the value of property, and of the effect wont to be produced by gifts of property between man and man, which could

---

[1] Spencer de Leg. Heb. L. iii. c. 9. So also substantially, Priestly, H. Taylor, Michaelis, Rosenmüller, &c.

not have been acquired at a period when society as yet consisted only of a few individuals, and these the members of a single family. And whether the gift were viewed in the light of a fine, a bribe, or a feast (for each in different hands has had its share in giving a particular shape to the theory), no sacrifice offered with such a view could have met with the divine favour and acceptance. The feeling that prompted it must in that case have been degrading to God, indeed essentially idolatrous ; and the whole history of patriarchal worship, in which God always appears to look so benignly on the offerings of believing worshippers, reclaims against the idea.

Of late, however, it has been more commonly sought to account for the origin of sacrifice, by viewing it as a symbolical act, such as might not unnaturally have suggested itself to men, in any period of society, from the feelings or practices with which their personal experience, or the common intercourse of life, made them familiar. But very different modes of explaining the symbol have been resorted to by those who concur in the same general view of its origination. Omitting the minor shades of difference which have arisen from an undue regard being had to distinctively Mosaic elements, Sykes, in his Essay on Sacrifice, raised his explanation on the ground, that " eating and drinking together were the known ordinary symbols of friendship, and were the usual rites of engaging in covenants and leagues." And in this way some plausible things may doubtless be said of sacrifice, as it appeared often in the later ages of heathenism, and also on some special occasions among the covenant people. But nothing that can seem even a probable account is thereby given of the offerings presented by believers in the first ages of the world. For it is against all reason to suppose that such a symbol of friendship should then have been in current use,—not to mention that the offerings of that period seem to have been precisely of the class in which no part was eaten by the worshippers—*holocausts*. Warburton laid the ground more deeply, and with greater show of probability, when he endeavoured to trace the origin of sacrifice to the ancient mode of converse by action, to aid the defects and imperfections of early language,—this being, in his opinion, sufficient to account for men being led to adopt such a mode of worship, whether the sacrifice might be eucharistical, propitiatory, or expiatory. Gratitude for good bestowed, he conceives, would lead the worshipper to present, by an expressive action, the first-fruits of agriculture or pasturage—the *eucharistical* offering. The desire of the divine favour or protection in the business of life would, in like manner, dispose him to dedicate a portion of what was to be sown or propagated—the *propitiatory*. And for sacrifices of an *expiatory* kind, the sense of sin would prompt him to take some chosen animal, precious to the repenting criminal who deprecated, or supposed to be obnoxious to the Deity who was to be appeased, and slay it at the altar, in an action which, in all languages when translated into words, speaks to this purpose: " I confess my transgressions at thy footstool, O my God; and with the deepest contrition implore thy pardon, confessing that I deserve the death which I inflict on this animal."[1] If for the infliction of death, which Warburton here represents as the chief feature in the action of expiatory sacrifice, we substitute the pouring out of the blood, or simply the giving away of the life to God, there is no material difference between his view of the origin of such sacrifices, and that recently propounded by Bähr. This ingenious and learned writer rejects the idea of sacrifice having come from any supernatural teaching or special appointment of God, as this would imply that man needed extraneous help to direct him, whether he was to sacrifice, or how he was to do it. He maintains, that " as the idea of God, and its necessary expression, was not something that came upon humanity from without, nothing taught it, but something immediate, an original fact; so also is sacrifice the form of that expression. From the point of view at which *we* are wont to contemplate things, separating the divine from the natural, the spiritual from the corporeal, this form must indeed always present a strange appearance. But if we throw ourselves back on that

---

[1] Warburton's Div. Legation, B. vii. c. 2. Davison substantially adopts this view, with no other difference than that he conceives it unnecessary to make any account of the defects and imperfections of early language in explaining the origin of sacrifice; but, regarding " representation by action as gratifying to men who have every gift of eloquence," and " as singularly suited to great purposes of solemnity and impression," he thinks "not simple adoration, not the naked and unadorned oblations of the tongue, but adoration invested in some striking and significative form, and conveyed by the instrumentality of material tokens, would be most in accordance with the strong energies of feeling, and the insulated condition of the primitive race." (Inquiry into the Origin and Intent of Sacrifice, p. 19, 20.)

mode of contemplation, which views the divine and spiritual as inseparable from the natural and corporeal, we shall find nothing so far out of the way in man's feeling himself constrained to represent the internal act of the giving up of his whole life and being to the Godhead—and in that all religion lives and moves—through the external giving away of an animal, perhaps, which he loved as himself, or on which he himself lived, and which stood in the closest connection with his own existence."[1] Something of a like nature (though exhibited in a form decidedly more objectionable) has also received the sanction of Tholuck, who, in the Dissertation on Sacrifices, appended to his Commentary on Hebrews, affirms, that " an offering was originally a gift to the Deity —a gift by which man strives to make up the deficiency of the always imperfect surrender of himself to God." And in regard especially to burnt-offerings, he says: "Both objects, that of thanksgiving and of propitiation, were connected with them; on the one hand, gratitude required man to surrender what was external as well as internal, to God; and, on the other hand, the surrender of an outward good was considered as a substitution, a propitiation for that which was still deficient in the internal surrender."[2] A salvation, it would seem, by works so far, and only where these failed, a calling in of extraneous and supplementary resources!

These different modes of explanation are obviously one in principle, and are but varying aspects of the same fundamental view. In each form it lies open to three serious objections, which together appear to us quite conclusive against it. 1. First, the analogy of God's method of dealing with his church in the matter of divine worship, at other periods in her history, is opposed to the simply human theory in any of its forms. Certainly at no other era did God leave his people altogether to their own inventions for the discovery of an acceptable mode of approaching him, and of giving expression to their religious feelings. Some indications he has always given of what in this respect might be accordant with his mind, and suitable to the position in which his worshippers stand towards him. The extent to which this directing influence was carried, formed one of the leading characteristics of the dispensation brought in by Moses; the whole

---

[1] Bähr's Symbolik, B. ii. p. 272. [2] Biblical Cabinet, vol. xxxix. p. 252

field of religious worship was laid under divine prescription, and the inventions of men solemnly interdicted. But even in the dispensation of the Gospel, which is distinguished for the spirituality of its nature, and its comparative freedom from legal enactments and independence of outward forms, the leading ordinances of divine worship are indicated with sufficient plainness, and what has no foundation in the revealed word is expressly denounced as "will-worship." And if the church of the New Testament, with all her advantages of a completed revelation, a son-like freedom, and an unction from the Holy One, that is said to "teach her all things," was not without some direction and control in regard to the proper celebration of God's service, is it conceivable that all should have been left utterly loose and indeterminate, when men were still in the very infancy of a fallen condition, and their views of spiritual truth and duty only in the forming? Where, in that case, would have been God's jealousy for the purity of his church? And where, we may also ask, his compassion toward men? He had disclosed to them purposes of grace, and awakened in their bosoms the hope of a recovery from the ruin they had incurred; but to set them adrift without even pointing to any ordinance fitted to meet their sense of sin, and re-assure their hearts before God, would have been to leave the exhibition of mercy strangely defective and incomplete. For, while they knew they had to do with a God of grace and forgiveness, they should still have been in painful uncertainty how to worship and serve him, so as to get personal experience of his blessing, and how, especially when conscience of sin troubled them anew, they might get the uneasiness allayed. Never surely was the tenderness of God more needed to point the way to what was acceptable and right, than in such a day of small things to the children of hope. And if it had not been shewn, the withholding of it could scarcely seem otherwise than an exception to the general analogy of God's dealings with men. 2. But, secondly, the simply human theory of the origin of sacrifice is met by an unresolved, and, we are persuaded, on that supposition an unresolvable difficulty in respect to the nature of ancient sacrifice. For, as the earliest, and indeed the *only* recorded mode of sacrifice in primitive times, among acceptable worshippers of God, consisted in the offering of slain victims, it seems impossible that this particular form of sacrifice should have been fallen upon at first, without some special direction from above. Let the symbolical action be viewed in either of the shades of meaning formerly described—as expressive of the offerer's deserved death, or of the surrender of his life to God, or as a propitiatory substitution to compensate for the conscious defect of such surrender—either way, how could he have imagined, that the devoting to death of a living creature of God should have been the appropriate mode of expressing the idea ? Death is so familiar to *us*, as regards the inferior creation, and so much associated with the means of our support and comfort, that it might seem a light thing to put an animal to death for any purpose connected with the wants or even the convenience of men. But the first members of the human family were in different circumstances. They must have shrunk—unless divinely authorised—from inflicting death on any, and especially on the higher forms of the animal creation ; since death, in so far as they had themselves to do with it, was the peculiar expression of God's displeasure on account of sin. All, indeed, belonging to that creation were to be subject to them. Their appointment from the very first was to subdue the earth, and render everything in it subservient to their legitimate use. But this use did not originally include a right to deprive animals of their life for the sake of food ; the grant of flesh for that end was only given at the deluge. And that they should yet have thought it proper and becoming to shed the blood of animals merely to express a religious idea, nay, should have regarded that as so emphatically the appropriate way of worshipping God, that for ages it seems to have formed the more peculiar medium of approach to him, can never be rationally accounted for without something on the part of God directing them to such a course. 3. Finally, the theories now under consideration are still farther objectionable, in that they are confronted by a specific fact, which was evidently recorded for the express purpose of throwing light on the original worship of fallen man, and with which their advocates have never been able to reconcile them —the fact of Abel's accepted offering from the flock, as contrasted with the rejection of Cain's from the produce of the field (Gen. iv. ; Heb. xi. 4). The offerings of the two brothers differed, we are told in the epistle to the Hebrews, and the account in Genesis implies as much, not only in regard to the outward oblation—the one being a creature with life, the other without it—but also in the principle which moved the two brothers respectively to present them. That principle in Abel was faith ; not this, therefore, but something else in Cain. And as it was faith which both rendered Abel's sacrifice in itself more excellent than Cain's, and drew down upon it the seal of Heaven's approval, the kind of faith meant must obviously have been something more than a general belief merely in the being of God, or his readiness to accept an offering of service from the hands of men. Faith in that sense must have been possessed by him who offered amiss, as well as by him who offered with acceptance. It must have been a more special exercise of faith which procured the acceptance of Abel—faith having respect not simply to the obligation of approaching God with some kind of offering, but to the duty of doing so with a sacrifice like that actually rendered, of the flock or the herd. But whence could such faith have come, if there had not been a testimony or manifestation of God for it to rest upon, which the one brother believingly apprehended, and the other scornfully slighted ? We see no way of evading this conclusion, without misinterpreting and doing violence to the plain import of the account of Scripture on the subject. Taking this in its obvious and natural meaning, Cain is presented to our view as a child of nature, not of grace—as one obeying the impulse and direction only of reason, and rejecting the more explicit light of faith as to the kind of service he presented to his Maker. His oblation is an undoubted specimen of what man could do in his fallen state to originate proper ideas of God, and give fitting expression to these in outward acts of worship. But unhappily for the advocates of nature's sufficiency in the matter, it stands condemned in the inspired record as a presumptuous and disallowed act of will-worship. Abel, on the other hand, appears as one who through grace had become a child of faith, and by faith first spiritually discerning the mind of God, then reverently following the course it dictated, by presenting that more excellent sacrifice ($\pi\lambda\varepsilon\acute{\iota}o\nu\alpha$ $\vartheta v\sigma\acute{\iota}\alpha\nu$) of the firstlings of the flock, with which God was well pleased.

On every account, therefore, the conclusion seems inevitable, that the institution of sacrifice must have been essentially of divine origin ; for though we cannot appeal to any record of its direct appointment by God, yet there are notices concerning sacrificial worship which cannot be satisfactorily explained on the supposition, in any form, of its merely human origin. There is a recorded fact, however, which touches the very borders of the subject, and which, we may readily perceive, furnished a divine foundation on which a sacrificial worship, such as is mentioned in Scripture, might be built. It is the fact noticed at the close of God's interview with our parents after the fall—" And unto Adam also and to his wife did the Lord God make coats of skin, and clothed them." The painful sense of nakedness that oppressed them after their transgression, was the natural offspring of a consciousness of sin—an instinctive fear lest the unveiled body should give indication of the evil thoughts and dispositions which now lodged within. Hence, to get relief to this uneasy feeling, they made coverings for themselves of such things as seemed best adapted to the purpose, out of that vegetable world which had been freely granted for their use. They girded themselves about with fig-leaves. But they soon found that this covering proved of little avail to hide their shame, where most of all they needed to have it hidden; it left them miserably exposed to the piercing glance of their offended God. If a real and valid covering should be obtained, sufficient to relieve them of all uneasiness, God himself must provide it. And so he actually did. As soon as the promise of mercy had been disclosed to the offenders, and the constitution of mingled goodness and severity brought in, he made coats to clothe them with, and these coats of skins. But clothing so obtained argued the sacrifice of life in the animal that furnished them; and thus, through the death of an inferior yet innocent living creature, was the needed relief brought to their disquieted and fearful bosoms. The outward and corporeal here manifestly had respect to the inward and spiritual. The covering of their nakedness was a gracious token from the hand of God, that the sin which had alienated them from him, and made them conscious of uneasiness, was henceforth to be in his sight as if it were not; so that in covering their flesh, he at the same time covered their consciences. If viewed apart from this higher symbolical aim, the outward act will naturally appear small and unworthy of God; but so to view it were to dissever it from the very reason of its performance. It was done purposely to denote the covering of guilt from the presence of God—an act which God alone *could* have done. But he did it, as we have seen, by a medium of death, by a sacrifice of life in those creatures which men were not yet permitted to kill for purposes of food, and in connection with a constitution of grace, which laid open the prospect of recovered life and blessing to the fallen. Surely it is not attributing to the venerable heads of the human family, persons who had so recently walked with God in paradise, an incredible power of spiritual discernment; or supposing them to stretch unduly the spiritual import of this particular action of God, if we should conceive them turning the divine act into a ground of obligation and privilege for themselves, and saying, Here is heaven's own finger pointing out the way for obtaining relief to our guilty consciences; the covering of our shame is to be found by means of the skins of irrational creatures, slain in our behalf; their life for our lives, their clothing of innocence for our shame; and we cannot err, we shall but shew our faith in the mercy and forgiveness we have experienced, if, as often as the sense of shame and guilt returns upon our consciences, we follow the footsteps of the Lord, and, by a renewed sacrifice of life, clothe ourselves anew with his own appointed badge of acquittal and acceptance.

We are not to be understood as positively affirming that our first parents, and their believing posterity reasoned thus, or that they actually had no more of instruction to guide them. We merely say, that they may quite naturally have so reasoned, and that we have no authority from the inspired record to suppose that any further instruction was communicated. Indeed, nothing more seems strictly necessary for the first beginnings of a sacrificial worship. And it was still but the age for beginnings; in what was taught and done, we should expect to find only the simplest forms of truth and duty. The Gospel, in its clearer announcements, even the law with its specific enactments, would then have been out of place. All that was absolutely required, and all that might be fairly expected, was some natural and expressive act of God toward men, laying, when thoughtfully considered, the foundation of a religious service toward him. The claims of the Sabbatical institution, and of the marriage-union, had a precisely similar foundation—the one in God's personal resting on the seventh day, hallowing and blessing it, the other in his formation of the first wife out of the first husband. It was simply the divine procedure in these cases which formed the ground of man's obligations—because that procedure was essentially a revelation of the mind and will of Godhead for the guidance of the rational beings who, being made in God's image, were to find their glory and their wellbeing in appropriating his acts, and copying after his example. So here, God's fundamental act in removing and covering out of sight the shame of conscious guilt in the first offenders, would both naturally and rightfully be viewed, as a revelation of God, teaching them, how, in henceforth dealing with him, they were to proceed in effecting the removal of guilt, and appearing, notwithstanding it, in the presence of God. They found, in this divine act, the key to a justified condition, and an acceptable intercourse with heaven. Had they not done so, it would have been incapable of rational explanation, how a believing Abel should so soon have appeared in possession of it. Yet, it could not have been rendered so palpable, as to obtrude itself on the carnal and unbelieving—otherwise, it would scarcely be less capable of explanation, how a self-willed Cain should so soon have ventured to disregard it. The ground of dissension between the two brothers must have been of a somewhat narrower and more debateable character, than if an explicit and formal direction had been given. And in the divine act referred to—viewed in its proper light, and taken in connection with the whole circumstances of the time—there was precisely what might have tended to originate both results; enough of light to instruct the humble heart of faith, mainly intent on having pardon of sin and peace with God, and yet not too much to leave proud and unsanctified nature without an excuse for following a course more agreeable to its own inclinations.[1]

---

[1] Substantially the correct view was presented of this subject in a work of Dr Croly, though, like several other things in the same volume, attended with the twofold disadvantage, of not being properly grounded, and of being encumbered with some untenable positions. "God alone is described as in act, and his only act is that of clothing the two criminals. The whole passage is but one of many, in which a rigid adherence to the text is the way of safety. The literal meaning at once exalts the rite, and illustrates its purposes. . . . Adam in Paradise has no protection from the divine wrath, but he needs none; he is pure. In his hour of crime, he finds the fatal difference between good and evil, feels that he requires protection from the eye of justice, and makes an ineffectual effort to supply that protection by his own means. But the expedient, which

3. We thus hold sacrifice—sacrifice in the higher sense, not as expressive of dependence and thankfulness merely, but as connected with sin and forgiveness, expiatory sacrifice—to have been, as to its foundation, of divine origin. It had its rise in an act of God, done for the express purpose of relieving guilty consciences of their sense of shame and confusion; and from the earliest periods of recorded worship it stands forth to our view as the religious solemnity, in which faith had its most peculiar exercise, and for which God bestowed the tokens of his acceptance and blessing. For the discussion of some collateral points belonging to the subject, and the disposal of a few objections, we refer to the Appendix.[1] And we now proceed here briefly to inquire what sacrifice as thus originating, and thus presented, symbolically expressed? What feelings on the part of the worshipper, what truths on the part of God, did it embody?

Partly, indeed, the inquiry has been answered already. It was impossible to conduct the discussion thus far without indicating the leading ideas involved in primitive sacrifice. It must be remembered, however, that we are still dealing with sacrifice in its simplest and most elementary form—radically, no doubt, the same as it was under the more complex and detailed arrangements of the Mosaic ritual, but in comparison of that wanting much in fulness and variety. As employed by the first race of believing worshippers, a few leading points are all that it can properly be regarded as embracing.

(1.) Both from the manner of its origin, and its own essential nature, as involving in every act of worship the sacrifice of a creature's life, it bore impressive testimony to the sinfulness of the offerer's condition. Those, who presented it, could not but know,

---

cannot be supplied by man, is finally supplied by the divine interposition. God clothes him, and his nakedness is the source of anguish and terror no more. The contrast of the materials of his imperfect and perfect clothing is equally impressive. Adam, in his first consciousness of having provoked the divine displeasure, covers himself with the frail produce of the ground, the branch and leaf; but from the period of forgiveness, he is clothed with the substantial product of the flock, the skin of the slain animal. If circumstances apparently so trivial, as the clothing of our original parents, are stated, what other reason can be assigned, than that they were *not trivial*, that they formed a marked feature of the divine dispensation, and that they were important to be recorded for the spiritual guidance of man?"—(Divine Providence, p. 194-196.)

[1] Appendix D.

that God was far from delighting in blood, and that death, either in man or beast, was not a thing in which he could be supposed to take pleasure. The explicit connection of death, also, with the first transgression, as the proper penalty of sin, was peculiarly fitted to suggest painful and humiliating thoughts in the minds of those who stood so near to the awful moment of the fall. And when death, under God's own directing agency, was brought so prominently into the divine service, and every act of worship, of the more solemn kind, carried in its bosom the life-blood of an innocent creature, what more striking memorial could they have had of the evil wrought in their condition by sin? With such an element of blood perpetually mingling in their services, they could not forget that they stood upon the floor of a broken covenant, and were themselves ever incurring anew the just desert of sin.

(2.) Then, looking more particularly to the sanction and encouragement of God, given to such a mode of worshipping him, it bespoke their believing conviction of his reconcileable and gracious disposition toward them, notwithstanding their sinfulness. They gave here distinct and formal expression to their faith, that as they needed mercy, so they recognised God as ready to dispense it to those who humbly sought him through this channel of communion. Such a faith, indeed, had been presumption, the groundless conceit of nature's arrogancy or ignorance, if it had not had a divine foundation to rest upon, and tokens of divine acceptance in the acts of service it rendered. But these, as we have seen, it plainly had. So that a sacrificial worship thus performed bore evidence as well to the just expectations of mercy and forgiveness on the part of those who presented it, as to their uneasy sense of guilt and shame, prompting them to do so.

(3.) But, looking again to the original ground and authority of this sacrificial worship,—the act of God in graciously covering the shame and guilt of sin,—and to the seal of acceptance afterwards set so peculiarly and emphatically on it, the great truth was expressed by it, on the part of God, that the taking away of life stood essentially connected with the taking away of sin—or, as expressed in later Scripture, that "without shedding of blood there is no remission of sins." In accordance with the general character of the primeval constitution of things, this truth comes out, not as a formal enunciation of principle, or an authoritative enactment of Heaven, but as an embodied fact; a fact, in the first instance, of God's hand, significantly indicating his mind and will, and then believingly contemplated, acted upon, substantially re-enacted by his sincere worshippers, with his clearly marked approval. The form may be regarded as peculiar, but not so the truth enshrined in it. This is common to all times, and, after holding a primary place in every phase of a preparatory religion, it rose at last to a position of transcendent importance in the work and kingdom of Christ. How far Adam and his immediate descendants might be able to descry, under their imperfect forms of worship, and the accompanying intimations of recovery, the ultimate ground in this respect of faith and hope for sinful men, can be to us only matter of vague conjecture, or doubtful speculation. Their views would, perhaps, considerably differ, according as their faith was more or less clear in its discernment, and lively in its perceptions of the truth couched under the symbolical acts and revelations of God. But unless more specific information was given them than is found in the sacred record (and it is mere conjecture to suppose there was more), the anticipations formed even by the most enlightened of those primitive believers, regarding the way and manner in which the blood of sacrifice was ultimately to enter into the plan of God, must have been comparatively vague and indefinite.

(4.) For us, however, who can read the symbol before us by the clear light of the Gospel, and from the high vantage-ground of a finished redemption can look back upon the temporary institutions that foreshadowed it, there is neither darkness nor uncertainty respecting the prophetic import of the primeval rite of sacrifice. We perceive there in the germ the fundamental truth of that scheme of grace which was to provide for the complete and final restoration of a seed of blessing—the truth of a suffering Mediator, giving his life a ransom for many. Here again we behold the ends of revelation mutually embracing and contributing to throw light on each other. And as amid the perfected glories of Messiah's kingdom all appears clustering around the Lamb that was slain, and doing homage to him for his matchless humiliation and triumphant victory, so the earliest worship of a believing church points to his coming sacrifice, as the one ground of hope and security to the fallen. At a subsequent period, when the church was furnished with a fuller revelation and a more complicated worship, symbolical representations were given of many other and subordinate parts of the work of redemption. But when that worship existed in its simplest form, and embodied only the first elements of the truth, it was meet that what was ultimately to form the groundwork of the whole, should have been alone distinctly represented. And *we* shall not profit, as we should, by the contemplation of that one rite, which stands so prominently out in the original worship of the believing portion of mankind, if it does not tend to deepen upon our minds the peerless worth and importance of a crucified Redeemer, as *the* wisdom and power of God unto salvation.

CHAPTER FIFTH.

THE SABBATICAL INSTITUTION.

The only remaining fact belonging to primeval history, which might present materials for the construction of a symbolical religion, is that of the day of sacred rest held by God at the close of creation: " And on the seventh day God ended his work, which he had made; and he rested on the seventh day from all his work, which he had made. And God blessed the seventh day and sanctified it; because that in it he had rested from all his work, which God created and made." (Gen. ii. 2, 3.) This act of God was done in such immediate connection with the work of creation, that the bearing it was intended to have on man must primarily have had respect to his original condition; and if designed to lay the foundation of a stated ordinance, the ordinance must have been one perfectly suited to the region of paradise itself. Yet, a slight reflection could scarcely fail to satisfy a reflective mind, that whatever significance the divine act might possess, and whatever obligation it might carry for man in his primeval state, he should still have found in it, and found increased rather than impaired, when he became involved in the troubles and calamities resulting from the fall.

Now, in the procedure of God, as recorded in the passage cited above, there may be noted a threefold stage, each carrying a separate and important meaning. First, the rest itself; " he rested on the seventh day from all his work;" and in Ex. xxxi. 17, the yet stronger expression is used of God *refreshing* himself on that day. Such expressions do not necessarily imply weariness or fatigue on account of the previous exertion, which, as regards God, is excluded by the infinitude of his perfections. " The Creator of the ends of the earth fainteth not, neither is weary" (Isa. xl. 28). They rather imply, that God's working in creation is of a reasonable kind; not an aimless activity, beginning and terminating in itself, but in acting toward a specific end, which on seeing accomplished, he withholds the outgoings of his creative energy, that he may rest in what he has done, and rejoice over the work of his hands. The end in this case was more particularly the creation of man with a living soul, bearing the rational and holy image of his Maker, and settled in a condition every way suited to his physical and moral nature. Throughout the whole of its stages the work was perceived to be good; but it was only when it reached this consummation—when the Creator saw his own image reflected in an intelligent and happy offspring, that he could regard the work as finished and could rest in his love. With the introduction of man into the world creation received its proper crown; and the Creator at length found among the works of his hands a spirit capable of discerning the manifestations of his glory, and returning love for love. It might be to give some intimation of this, of God's having found it then, and desiring to find it always, that the original seventh day is distinguished from the rest, not merely by the cessation of creative work, but also by the absence of any mention of a morning and an evening, at the beginning and the close; for the divine Sabbath, as has been remarked by Delitzsch, " has no close; it stretches over the entire future history of the world; and is ever seeking to raise this into a participation of the same character with itself." God's rest, no more than his work, is of an exclusive character. It looks benignly and graciously on the creatures, especially on man, who alone of earthly creatures can rise into the conscious apprehension of his Maker. And as God in him, so he again, in God, must find his satisfying and refreshing rest.

Thus, even the first stage of this divine act has respect to man, and still more the second, which points directly and exclusively to him: "And God blessed the seventh day." This blessing of the day is not to be confounded with the sanctifying of it, which immediately follows, as if the meaning were, God blessed it by sanctifying it. The blessing is distinct from the sanctification, and is, so to speak, the settling of a special dowry on it for every one, who should give due heed to its proper end and object. Let man—the divine act of blessing virtually said—only enter into God's mind, and tread in his footsteps, by resting every seventh day from his works, and he shall undoubtedly find it to his profit; the blessing, which is life for evermore, shall descend on him. What he may lose for the moment in productive employment, shall be amply compensated by the refreshment it will bring to his frame—by the enlargement and elevation of his soul—above all, by the spiritual fellowship and interest in God, which becomes the abiding portion of those who follow Him in their ways, and perpetually return to Him as the supreme rest of their souls.

Then, the last stage in the procedure of God on this occasion, indicates how the two earlier ones were to be secured: " He sanctified it," made it a day of sacredness. Having appointed it to a distinctive end, he conferred on it a distinctive character, that his creature, man, might from time to time be doing in *his* line of things what the Creator had already done in his own—might, after six successive days of work, take one to re-invigorate his frame, to reflect calmly on the past, and view the part he has taken and the relations he occupies on the outward and visible theatre of the world, in the light of the spiritual and the eternal. It was to be his calling and his destiny on earth, not simply to work, but to work as a reasonable and moral being, after the example of his Maker, for specific ends. And for this he needed seasons of quiet repose and thoughtful consideration, not less than time and opportunity for active labour; as, otherwise, he could neither properly enjoy the work of his hands, nor obtain for the higher part of his nature that nobler good which is required to satisfy it. God, therefore, when he had finished the work of creation by making man, sanctified the seventh day—*his own* seventh, but *man's* first; for man had not first to work and then to reap, but as God's vicegerent, nature's king and high-priest, could at once enter into his Maker's heritage of blessing. And henceforth, in the career that lay before him, ever and anon returning from the field of active labour assigned him in cultivating and subduing the earth, he must on the hallowed day of rest gather in his thoughts and desires from the world, and, retiring into God as his sanctuary, hold with him a sabbatism of peaceful and blessed rest.

The divine procedure, then, in every one of its stages, plainly points to man, and aims at his participation in the likeness and enjoyment of God. "With the Sabbath," says Sartorius happily, and we rejoice and hail it as a token for good, that such thoughts on the Sabbath are finding utterance in the high places of Germany—" with the Sabbath begins the sacred history of man—the day on which he stood forth to bless God, and, in company with Eve, entered on his divine calling upon earth. The creation without the creation-festival, the world's unrest without rest in God, is altogether vain and transitory. The sacred day appointed, blessed, consecrated by God, is that from which the blessing and sanctification of the world and time, of human life and human society, proceed. Nor is anything more needed than the recognition of its original appointment and sacred destination, for our receiving the full impression of its sanctity. How was it possible for the first man ever to forget it? From the very beginning was it written upon his heart, Remember the Sabbath-day to sanctify it."[1] There is nothing new in such views. Substantially the same interpretation, that we have given, is put on the original notice in Genesis, in the Epistle to the Hebrews (ch. iv.), where the record of God's rest at the close of creation is referred to as the first form of the promise made to man of entering into God's rest. The record, then, of what God in that respect did, was a revelation. It embodied a promise to man of high fellowship with the Creator in his peculiar felicity, and, consequently, inferred an obligation on man's part both to seek the end proposed, and to seek it in the method of God's appointment. But did the obligation cease when man fell? or was the promise cancelled? Assuredly not—not, at least, after the time that the introduction of an economy of grace laid open for the fallen the prospect of a new inheritance in God. So far from having lost its significance or its value, the Creator's Sabbatism then acquired fresh meaning and importance, and became so peculiarly adapted to the altered condition of the world, that we cannot but regard it as having from the first contemplated the physical and moral evils that were to issue from the fall. In the language of Hengstenberg, with whom we gladly concur on this branch of the subject, though on too many others we shall be constrained to differ from him,—" It pre-supposes work, and such work as has a tendency to draw us away from God. It is the remedy for the in-

---

[1] Sartorius über den alt und Neu Test. cultus, p. 17.

juries we are apt to incur through this work. If any thing is clear, it is the connection between the Sabbath and the fall. The work which needs intermission, lest the divine life should be imperilled by it, is not—[we would rather say, is not so much]—the cheerful and pleasant employment of which we read in Gen. ii. 15; it is [rather] the oppressive and degrading toil spoken of in Gen. iii. 19, work done in the sweat of the brow, upon a soil that brings forth thorns and thistles."[1] We would put the statement comparatively, rather than absolutely; for the rest of God being held on the first seventh day of the world's existence, and the day being immediately consecrated and blessed, it must have had respect to the place and occupation of man even in paradise. Why should work there be supposed to have differed in kind from work elsewhere and since? There could be room only for a difference in degree; and being work from its very nature that led the soul to aim at specific objects, and put forth continuous efforts *ad extra*, it required to be met by a stated periodical institution, that would recall the thoughts and feelings of the soul *ad intra*. Man's perfection in that original state was only a relative one. It needed certain correctives and stimulants to secure the continued enjoyment of the good belonging to it. It needed, in particular, perpetual access to the tree of life for the preservation of the bodily, and an ever-returning Sabbatism for that of the spiritual life. But if such a Sabbatism was required even for man's wellbeing in paradise, where the work was so light, and the order so beautiful, how could it be imagined that the Sabbatical institution might be either safely or lawfully disregarded in a world of sorrow, temptation, and hardship?

Was there really, however, *any* Sabbatical institution? There is no command respecting it in this portion of the inspired record. And may not the mention there made of God's keeping the Sabbath, and blessing and sanctifying the day, have been made simply with a prospective reference to the precept that was ultimately to be imposed on the Israelites? So it has been alleged with endless frequency by those who can find no revelation of the divine will, and no obligation of moral duty excepting what comes in the authoritative form of a command, and it is still substantially reiterated by

---

[1] Ueber den Tag des Herrn, p. 12.

Hengstenberg, who certainly cannot be charged with such a bluntness of spiritual discernment. We meet the allegation with the statement that has already been repeatedly urged—that it was not yet the time for the formal enactments of law, and that it was by other means man was to learn God's mind and his own duty. The ground of obligation lay in the divine act; the rule of duty was exhibited in the divine example; and these were disclosed to men from the first, not to gratify an idle curiosity, but for the express purpose of leading them to know and do what is agreeable to the will of God. If such means were not sufficient to speak with clearness and authority to men's consciences, then it may be affirmed that the first race of mankind were free from all authoritative direction and control whatever. They were not imperatively bound either to fear God, or to regard man; for excepting in the manner now stated, no general obligations of service were laid on them. But to suppose this; to suppose even in regard to what is written of the original Sabbatism of God, that it did not bear directly upon the privileges and duties of the very first members of the human family, is in truth to make void that portion of revelation—to treat it, where it stands, as a superfluity or a blemish. We cannot so regard it. We hold by the truthfulness and natural import of the divine record. And doing this, we are shut up to the conclusion, that it was at first designed and appointed by God, that mankind should sanctify every returning seventh day, as a season of comparative rest from worldly labour, of spiritual contemplation and religious employment, that so they might cease from their own works and enter into the rest of God.

But we shall not pursue the subject farther at present. We even leave unnoticed some of the objections that have been raised against the existence of a primeval Sabbath, as the subject must again return, and in a more controversial aspect, when we come to consider the place assigned to the law of the Sabbath in the revelation from Sinai. It is enough, at this stage of our inquiry, to have exhibited the foundation laid for the perpetual celebration of a seventh-day Sabbath, in the original act of God at the close of his creation-work. In that we have a foundation broad and large as the theatre of creation itself and the general interests of humanity, free from all local restrictions and national peculiarities. That in the infancy of the world, and during the ages of a remote antiquity, there would be much simplicity in the mode of its observance, may readily be supposed. Indeed, where all was so simple, both in the state of society and the institutions of worship, the symbolical act itself of resting from ordinary work, and in connection with that, the habit of recognising the authority of God, and realising the divine call to a participation in the blessed rest of the Creator, must have constituted no inconsiderable part of the practical observance of the day. And that this also in process of time should have fallen into general desuetude, is only what might have been expected from the fearful depravity and lawlessness which overspread the earth as a desolation. When men daringly cast off the fear of God himself, they would naturally make light of the privilege and duty set before them of entering into his rest. And considering the disadvantages, both personal and social, which were necessarily connected with a primeval Sabbath, it is not to be wondered at that, besides the original record of its divine origin and authoritative obligation, traces of its early existence should be found only in some occasional notices of history, and in the wide-spread sacredness of the number seven, which has left its impress on the religion and literature of nearly every nation of antiquity. But however neglected or despised, the original fact remains for the light and instruction of the world in all ages; and there perpetually comes forth from it a call to every one who has ears to hear, to sanctify a weekly rest unto the Lord, and rise to the enjoyment of his blessing.

CHAPTER SIXTH.

TYPICAL THINGS IN HISTORY DURING THE PROGRESS OF THE FIRST DISPENSATION.

HAVING now considered the typical bearing of the fundamental facts and symbolical institutions belonging to the first dispensation of grace, it remains that we endeavour to ascertain what there might afterwards be evolved of a typical nature during the progress of that dispensation, by means of the transactions and events that took place under it. These, it was already noted in our preliminary remarks, could only be employed to administer instruction of a subsidiary kind. In their remoter reference to gospel-times, as in their direct historical aspect, they can rank no higher than progressive developements—not laying a foundation, but proceeding on the foundation already laid, and giving to some of the points connected with it a more specific direction, or supplementing them with additional discoveries of the mind and will of God. It is impossible here, any more than in the subjects treated of in the preceding chapters, to isolate entirely the portions that have a typical bearing from others closely connected with them. And even in those which exhibit something of the typical element, it can scarcely be expected, at so early a period in the world's history, to possess much of a precise and definite character; for in type, as in prophecy, the progress must necessarily have been from the more general to the more particular. In tracing this progress, we shall naturally connect the successive developements with single persons or circumstances; yet without thereby meaning to indicate that these are in *every respect* to be accounted typical.

SECTION FIRST.

THE SEED OF PROMISE—ABEL, ENOCH.

The first distinct appearance of the typical in connection with the period subsequent to the fall, is to be found in the case of Abel; but in that quite generally. Abel was the first member of the promised seed; and through him supplementary knowledge was imparted more especially in one direction, viz. in regard to *the principle of election, which was to prevail in the actual fulfilment of the original promise.* That promise itself, when viewed in connection with the instituted symbols of religion, might be perceived—if very thoughtfully considered—to have implied something of an elective process; but the truth was not clearly expressed. And it was most natural, that the first parents of the human family should have overlooked what but obscurely intimated a limitation in the expected good. They would readily imagine, when a scheme of grace was introduced, which gave promise of a complete destruction of the adversary, with the infliction only of a partial injury on the woman's seed, that the whole of their offspring should attain to victory over the power of evil. This joyous anticipation affectingly discovers itself in the exclamation of Eve at the birth of her first-born son, " I have gotten a man from (or, as it should rather be, with) the Lord"—gratefully acknowledging the hand of God in giving her, as she thought, the commencement of that seed which was assured through divine grace of a final triumph. This she reckoned a real getting—gain in the proper sense—calling her child by a name that expressed this idea (Cain); and she evidently did so by regarding it as the precious gift of God, the beginning and the pledge of the ascendancy that was to be won over the malice of the tempter.[1] Never was mother destined to receive a sorer dis-

---

[1] I think it quite impossible, in the circumstances, that the faith of Eve should have gone farther than this; as the promise of recovery had as yet assumed only the most

appointment. She did not want faith in the divine word, but her faith was still without knowledge, and she must learn by painful experience how the plan of God for man's recovery was to be wrought out. A like ignorance, though tending now in the opposite direction, again discovers itself at the birth of Abel, whose name (breath, nothingness) seems, as Delitzsch has remarked, to have proceeded from her felt regard to the divine curse, as that given to Cain did from a like regard to the divine promise. It is possible that, between the births of the two brothers, what she had seen of the helpless and suffering condition of infancy in the first-born may have impressed the mind of Eve with such a sense of the evils entailed upon her offspring by the curse, as to have rendered her for the time forgetful of the better things disclosed in the promise. It is possible, also, that the corporeal frame and personal appearance of Abel may have been greatly less prepossessing than those of his brother. However it might be, the name imposed clearly indicates, that Eve associated with this second child her misgivings and fears respecting the future, as she had associated with the first her buoyant hopes and joyful anticipations. The result shewed how little the operations of grace were to pursue the course that might seem accordant with the views and feelings of nature. In particular, it shewed that, so far from the whole offspring of the woman being included, there was from the first to pervade the scheme a principle of election, in virtue of which a portion only, and that by no means the likeliest, according to the estimation of nature, were to inherit the blessing, while the rest should fall in with the designs of the tempter, and be reckoned to him for a seed of cursing. Abel, therefore, in his acceptance with God, in his faith respecting the divine purposes, and his presentation of offerings that drew down the divine favour, stands as the type of an elect seed of blessing—

general aspect; and though it might well have been understood to depend upon the grace and power of God for its accomplishment, yet who, from the revelations actually given, could have anticipated these to manifest themselves in the birth of Jehovah himself as a babe? The supposition of Baumgarten—who here revives the old explanation, "I have gotten a man, Jehovah," that Eve thought she saw in Cain "the redeeming and coming God," is arbitrary and incredible. The אֶת־יְהֹוָה should be taken as in ch. v. 24, vi. 9, *with, in fellowship with* the Lord; or as in Judg. viii. 7, *with, with the help of.*

a seed that was ultimately to have its root and its culmination in Him, who was to be peculiarly *the* child of promise. In Cain, on the other hand, the impersonation of nature's pride, waywardness, and depravity, there appeared a representative of that unhappy portion of mankind who should espouse the interest of the adversary, and seek by unhallowed means to establish it in the world.

The brief notices of antediluvian history are evidently framed for the purpose of exhibiting the contrary state and tendencies of these two seeds, and of rendering manifest the mighty difference, which God's work of grace was destined to make in the character and prospects of man. The name given by Eve to her third son (Seth, appointed), with the reason assigned for it, "For God, said she, hath appointed me another seed instead of Abel, whom Cain slew," bespoke the insight the common mother of mankind had now obtained into this mournful division in her offspring. Cain, she regards as having, in a manner, ceased to belong to her seed; he had become too plainly identified with that of the adversary. He seems now to her view to stand at the head of a God-opposing interest in the world—and, as in contrast to him, the destroyer of the true seed, God is seen mercifully providing another in its room.[1] So that there were again the two seeds in the world, each taking root, and bringing forth fruit after its kind. But how different! On the one hand appears the Cainite section, smitten with the curse of sin, yet proudly shunning the path of reconciliation—retiring to a distance from the emblems of God's manifested presence—building a city, as if to lighten, by the aid of human artifice and protection, the evils of a guilty conscience

---

[1] It is to be noted, however, that *both* the parents of the human family, Adam as well as Eve, are associated with this seed of blessing. It is a circumstance that has been too much overlooked; but for the very purpose of marking it, a fresh commencement is made at Gen. v. of the genealogical chain that links together Adam and Christ: "This is the book of the generations of Adam. In the day that God created man, in the likeness of God made he him. . . . And Adam lived an hundred and thirty years, and begat a son in his own likeness, after his image, and called his name Seth:"—as if his progeny before this were not to be reckoned—the child of grace had perished, and the other in a spiritual sense was not. Adam, therefore, is here distinctly placed at the head of a spiritual offspring—himself the first link in the grand chain of blessing. And the likeness, in which he begat this son—"his own image"—must not be limited, as it too often is, to the corruption that now marred the purity of his nature—as if *his* image stood simply in contrast to God's. It is as the parental head of the whole lineage of grace that he is represented, and such a contrast would here especially be out of place.

and a blighted condition—cultivating with success the varied elements of natural strength and worldly greatness, inventing instruments of music and weapons of war, trampling under foot, as seemed good to the flesh, the authority of heaven and the rights of men, and at last, by deeds of titanic prowess and violence, boldly attempting to bring heaven and earth alike under its sway (Gen. iv. 13–24; vi. 4–6).[1] On the other hand appears the woman's seed of promise, seeking to establish and propagate itself in the earth by the fear of God, and the more regular celebration of his worship (Gen. iv. 26)—trusting for its support in the grace and blessing of God, as the other did in the powers and achievements of corrupt nature—and so, continuing uninterrupted its line of godly descendants, yet against such fearful odds, and at last with such a perilous risk of utter extinction, that divine faithfulness and love required to meet violence with violence, and bring the conflict in its first form to a close by the sweeping desolation of the flood. It terminated, as every such conflict must do, on the side of those who stood in the promised grace and revealed testimony of God. These alone live for ever; and the triumph of all that is opposed to them can be but for a moment.

This seed of the woman, however,—the seed that she produces in faith upon the promise of God, and in which the grace of God

---

[1] It is in connection with this later developement of evil in the Cainites, that Lamech's song is introduced, and with special reference to that portion of his family, who were makers of instruments in brass and iron—instruments, no doubt, chiefly of a warlike kind. It is only by viewing the song in that connection, that we perceive its full meaning, and its proper place, as intended to indicate that the evil was approaching its final stage: "And Lamech said to his wives, Adah and Zillah, hear my voice; Ye wives of Lamech, hearken to my speech. For, men (the word is quite indefinite in the original, and may most fitly be rendered in the plural) I slay for my wound, and young men for my hurt. For, Cain is avenged seven times, and Lamech seventy times seven." He means apparently, that with such weapons as he now had at command, he could execute at will deeds of retaliation and revenge. So that his song may be regarded, to use the words of Drechsler, " as an ode of triumph on the invention of the sword. He stands at the top of the Cainite developement, from thence looks back upon the past, and exults at the height it has reached. How far has he got a-head of Cain! what another sort of ancestor he! No longer needing to look up in feebleness to God for protection, he can provide more amply for it himself than God did for Cain's; and he congratulates his wives on being the mothers of such sons. Thus the history of the Cainites began with a deed of murder, and here it ends with a song of murder."

takes vital effect—is found, not only as to its *existence*, to be associated with a principle of election, but also as to the *relative place* occupied by particular members in its line. All have by faith an interest in God, and in consequence triumph over the power of the adversary. But some have a larger interest than others, and attain to a higher victory. There was an election within the election. So it appeared especially in the case of Enoch, the seventh from Adam, and again in Noah, who, as they alone of the antediluvians were endowed with the spirit of prophecy, so they alone, also, are said to have "walked with God" (Gen. v. 22, vi. 9)—an expression never used of any who lived in later times, and denoting the nearest and most confidential intercourse, as if they had all but regained the old paradisiacal freedom of communion with Heaven. And as the divine seal upon this higher elevation of the life of God in their souls, they were both honoured with singular tokens of distinction—the one having been taken, without tasting of death, to still nearer fellowship with God, to abide in his immediate presence ("He was not, for God took him"), and the other became under God the saviour and father of a new world. Of the latter we shall have occasion to speak separately, as there were connected with his case other elements of a typical nature. But in regard to Enoch, as the short and pregnant notice of his life and of his removal out of it, plainly indicates something transcendently good and great, so, we cannot doubt, the contemporaries of the patriarch knew it to be such. They knew—at least they had within their reach the means of knowing—that in consideration of his eminent piety, and of the circumstances of the time in which he lived, he was taken direct to a higher sphere, without undergoing the common lot of mortality. That there should have been but one such case during the whole antediluvian period, could not but be regarded as indicating its exceptional character, and stamping it the more emphatically as a revelation from Heaven. Nor could the voice it uttered in the ears of reflecting men sound otherwise than as a proclamation, that God was assuredly with that portion of the woman's seed who served and honoured him—that he manifested himself to such, as a chosen people, in another manner than he did to the world, and made them sure of a complete and final victory over all the malice of the tempter and the evils of sin. If not usually without death, yet notwithstanding it, and through it, they should certainly attain to eternal life in the presence of God.

In this respect Enoch—as being the most distinguished member of the seed of blessing in its earlier division, and the most honoured heir of that life which comes through the righteousness of faith—is undoubtedly to be viewed as a type of Christ. Something he had in common with the line as a whole—he was a partaker of that electing grace and love of God, in virtue of which alone any could rise from the condemnation of sin to the inheritance of life in the divine kingdom. But apart from others in the same line, and above them, he passed to the inheritance by a more direct and triumphant path—a conqueror in the very mode of his transition from time to eternity. These characteristics, which in Enoch's case were broadly marked, though in themselves somewhat general, and incapable of being understood to have reference to a personal Messiah, till such a Messiah had been more distinctly announced, are yet pre-eminently the characteristics of Christ, and in the full and absolute sense could be found only in him. He is, as no other individual among men could be, the seed of the woman, considered as the seed of promise, destined by God's purpose of grace to bruise the head of the tempter, and reverse the process of nature's corruption. In him, as present from the first to the "determinate counsel and foreknowledge of God," was the ultimate root of such a seed to be found which should otherwise have had no existence in the world. He, therefore, beyond all others, was the chosen of God, "his elect in whom his soul delights." And though to the eye of a carnal and superficial world, which judges only by the appearance, he wanted what seemed necessary to justify his claim to such a position, yet in reality he possessed, and gave infallible proof of his divine connection with the Father, by a faith that never faltered in the hardest trials, a righteousness free from every stain of impurity, and a life that could only underlie for a moment the cloud of death, but even there could see no corruption, and presently rose, as to its proper home, in the regions of eternal light and glory.

With our eyes resting on this exalted object in the ends of time, we have no difficulty in perceiving, that what appeared of supernatural in such men as Abel and Enoch, only foreshadowed the higher and greater good that was to come. It did, however, foreshadow this—not indeed personally and formally, as if from the appearance of Abel and Enoch a personal Messiah could have been descried, or as if from the incidents in their respective lives, precisely similar ones might have been inferred as likely to happen in the eventful career of the man Christ Jesus. We could not descend thus to individual and personal marks of coincidence between the lives of those early patriarchs and the life of Messiah, without, in the first instance, anticipating the order of Providence, which had not yet directed the eye of the Church to a personal manifestation of Godhead, and then entangling ourselves in endless difficulties of practical adjustment—as in the case of Enoch's translation, who went to heaven without tasting death, while Christ could not enter into glory till he *had* tasted it. But let those patriarchs be contemplated as the earlier links of a chain, which, from its very nature, must have some higher and nobler termination; let them be viewed as characters that already bore upon them the lineaments, and possessed the beginnings of the new creation; what do they, then, appear but embodied prophecies of a more general kind in respect to " Him who was to come ?" They heralded his future redemptive work by exhibiting in part the signs and fruits of its prospective achievements. The beginning was prophetic of the end ; for if the one had not been in prospect, the other could not have come into existence. And in their selection by God from the general mass around them, their faith in God's Word, and their possession of God's favour and blessing, as outwardly displayed and manifested in their histories, we see struggling, as it were, into being the first elements of that new state and destiny, which were only to find their valid reason, and reach their proper elevation, in the person and kingdom of Messiah.

SECTION SECOND.

NOAH AND THE DELUGE.

The case of Noah, we have already stated, embodied some new elements of a typical kind, which gave to it the character of a distinct stage in the developement of God's work of grace in the world. It did so in connection with the deluge, which had a gracious, as well as a judicial aspect, and, by a striking combination of opposites, brought prominently out the principle, that *the accomplishment of salvation necessarily carries along with it a work of destruction.* This was not absolutely a new principle at the period of the deluge. It had a place in the original promise, and a certain exemplification in the lives of believers from the first. By giving to the prospect of recovery the peculiar form of a bruising of the tempter's head, the Lord plainly intimated, that somehow a work of destruction was to go along with the work of salvation, and was necessary to its accomplishment. No indication, however, was given of the way in which this twofold process was to proceed, or of the nature of the connection between the one part of it and the other. But light to a certain extent soon began to be thrown upon it by the consciousness in each man's bosom of a struggle between the evil and the good—a struggle, which so early as the time of Cain drew forth the divine warning, that either his better part must vindicate for itself the superiority, or it must itself fall down vanquished by the destroyer. Still farther light appeared, when the contending elements grew into two great contending parties, which by an ever-widening breach, and at length by most serious encroachments from the evil on the good, rendered a work of judgment from above necessary to the peace and safety of the believing portion of mankind. The conviction of some approaching crisis of this nature had become so deep in the time of Enoch, that it gave utterance to itself in the prophecy ascribed in the epistle of Jude to that patriarch: " Behold the Lord cometh with ten thousand of his saints to execute judgment upon all, and to convince all that are ungodly among them of all their ungodly deeds, which they have ungodly committed, and of all their hard speeches, which ungodly sinners have committed against him." The struggle, it was thus announced, should ere long end in a manifestation of God for judgment against the apostate faction, and, by implication, for deliverance to the children of faith and hope.

By the period of Noah's birth, however, the necessity of a divine interposition had become much greater, and it appeared manifest to the small remnant of believers, that the era of retribution, which they now identified with the era of deliverance, must be at hand. Indication was then given of the state of feeling by the name itself of Noah, with the reason assigned for imposing it, " This same shall comfort us concerning our work and toil of our hands, because of the ground, which the Lord hath cursed." The feeling is too generally expressed, to enable us to determine with accuracy, how the parents of this child might expect their troubles to be relieved through his instrumentality. But we hear, at least, in their words the groaning of the oppressed— the sighing of righteous souls, vexed on account of the evils which were thickening around them, from the unrestrained wickedness of those who had corrupted the earth; and, at the same time, not despairing, but looking up in faith, and even confident that in the lifetime of that child the God of righteousness and truth would somehow avenge the cause of his elect. Whether they had obtained any correct insight or not, into the way by which the object was to be accomplished, the event proved that the spirit of prophecy breathed in their anticipation. Their faith rested upon solid grounds, and in the hope, which it led them to cherish, they were not disappointed. Salvation *did* come in connection with the person of Noah, and it came in the way of an overwhelming visitation of wrath upon the adversaries.

When we look simply at the outward results produced by that remarkable visitation, they appear to have been twofold—on the one side preservation, on the other destruction. But when we look a little more closely, we perceive, that there was a necessary connection between the two results, and that there was properly but one object aimed at in the dispensation, though in accomplishing it there was required the operation of a double process. That object was, as stated by St Peter, " the saving of Noah and his house" (1 Pet. iii. 20)—saving them as the spiritual seed of God. But saving them from what ? Not surely from the violence and desolation of the waters ; for the watery element would then have acted as the preservative against itself, and instead of being saved *by* the water, according to the apostolic statement, the family of Noah would have been saved *from* it.[1] From what, then, were they saved ? Undoubtedly from that, which, before the coming of the deluge, formed the real element of danger—the corruption, enmity, and violence of ungodly men. It was this which wasted the church of God, and brought it to the verge of destruction. All was ready to perish. The cause of righteousness had at

---

[1] I am aware many eminent scholars give a different turn to this expression in the first epistle of Peter, and take the proper rendering to be " saved through (*i. e.* in the midst of) the water"—contemplating the water as the space or region through which the ark was required to bear Noah and his family in safety. So Beza, who says that " the water cannot be taken for the instrumental cause, as Noah was preserved from the water, not by it;" so also Tittmann, Bib. Cab. vol. xviii. p. 251; Steiger in his Comm. with only a minute shade of difference ; Robinson, in Lex., and many others. But this view is open to the following objections : 1. The water is here mentioned, not in respect to its several parts, or to the extent of its territory from one point to another, but simply as an instrumental agent. Had the former been meant, the expression would have been " saved through the waters," rather than saved by water. But as the case stood, it mattered nothing, whether the ark remained stationary at one point on the surface of the waters, or was borne from one place to another ; so that *through*, in the sense of *passing through*, or *through among*, gives a quite unsuitable meaning. That Noah needed to be saved from the water, rather than by it, is a superficial objection, proceeding on the supposition that the water had the same relation to Noah that it had to the world in general. For him, the water and the ark were essentially connected together ; it took both to make up the means of deliverance. In the same sense, and on the same account, we might say of the Red sea, that the Israelites were saved by it ; for, though in itself a source of danger, yet as regarded Israel's position, it was really the means of safety (1 Cor. x. 2). 2. The application made by the Apostle of Noah's preservation requires the agency of the water, as well as of the ark, to be taken into account. Indeed, according to the best authorities (which read ὅ καί), the reference in the antitype is specially to the water as the type. But apart from that, baptism is spoken as a *saving*, in consequence of its being a *purifying* ordinance, which implies, as in the deluge, that the salvation be accomplished through means of a destruction. This is virtually admitted by Steiger, who, though he adopts the rendering " through the water," yet in explaining the connection between the type and the antitype, is obliged to regard the water as also instrumental to salvation. " The flood was for Noah a baptism, and as such saved ; the same element, water, also saves us now—not, however, as mere water, but in the same quality as a baptism."

length but one efficient representative in the person of Noah; and he much " like a lodge in a garden of cucumbers, like a besieged city,"—the object of profane mockery and scorn, taunted, reviled, plied with every weapon fitted to overcome his constancy, and, if not in himself, at least in his family, in danger of suffering shipwreck amid the swelling waves of wickedness around him. It was to save him—and with him, the cause of God—from this source of imminent danger and perdition, that the flood was sent; and it could only do so, by effectually separating between him and the seed of evil-doers—engulphing *them* in ruin, and sustaining *him* uninjured in his temporary home. So that the deluge, considered as Noah's baptism, or the means of his salvation from an outward form of spiritual danger, was not less essentially connected with a work of judgment than with an act of mercy. It was by the one, that the other was accomplished; and the support of the ark on the bosom of the waters, was only a collateral object of the deluge. The direct and immediate object was the extermination of that wicked race, whose heaven-daring impiety and hopeless impenitence was the real danger that menaced the cause and people of God,—" the destroying of those (to use the language that evidently refers to it in Rev. xi. 18), who destroyed the earth."

This principle of salvation with destruction, which found such a striking exemplification in the deluge, has been continually appearing anew in the history of God's dealings among men. It appeared, for example, at the period of Israel's redemption from Egypt, when a way of escape was opened for the people of God by the overthrow of Pharaoh and his host; and again at the era of the return from Babylon, when the destruction of the enemy and the oppressor broke asunder the bands with which the children of the covenant were held captive. But it is in New Testament times, and in connection with the work of Christ, that the higher manifestation of the principle appears. Here alone perfection can be said to belong to it. Complete as the work in one respect was in the days of Noah, in another it soon gave unmistakeable evidence of its own imperfection. The immediate danger was averted by the destruction of the wicked in the waters of the deluge, and the safe preservation of Noah and his family as a better seed to replenish the depopulated earth. But it was soon found that the old leaven still lurked in the bosom of the preserved remnant itself; and another race of apostates and destroyers, though of a less ferocious spirit, and under more of restraint in regard to deeds of violence and bloodshed, rose up to prosecute anew the work of the adversary. In Christ, however, the very foundations of evil from the first were struck at, and nothing is left for a second beginning to the cause of iniquity. He came, as foretold by the prophet Isaiah (ch. lxi. 3), "to proclaim the acceptable year of the Lord, and the day of vengeance of our God," which was, at the same time, to be the "year of his redeemed." And, accordingly, by the work he accomplished on earth, "the prince of this world was judged and cast out" (John xii. 31); or, as it is again written, "principalities and powers were spoiled," and "he that had the power of death destroyed" (Col. ii. 14; Heb. ii. 14), thereby giving deliverance to those who were subject to sin and death. He did this once for all, when he fulfilled all righteousness, and suffered unto death for sin. The victory over the tempter then achieved by Christ, no more needs to be repeated than the atonement made for human guilt; it needs to be appropriated merely by his followers, and made vital in their experience. Satan has no longer any right to exercise lordship over men, and hold them in bondage to his usurped authority; the ground of his power and dominion is taken away, because the condemnation of sin, on which it stood, has been for ever abolished. Christ, therefore, at once destroys and saves—saves by destroying—casts the cruel oppressor down from his ill-gotten supremacy, and so relieves the poor, enthralled, devil-possessed nature of man, and sets it into the glorious liberty of God's children.

In the case of the Redeemer himself, this work is absolutely complete; the man Christ Jesus thoroughly bruised Satan under his feet, and won a position where in no respect whatever he could be any more subject to the power of evil. Theoretically, we may say, the work is also complete in behalf of his people; on *his* part, no imperfection cleaves to it. By virtue of the blood of Jesus, the house of our humanity, which naturally stood accursed of God, and was ready to be assailed by every form of evil, is placed on a new and better foundation. It is made holiness to the Lord. The handwriting of condemnation that was against us, is blotted out. The adversary has lost his bill of indictment; and nothing remains but that the members of the human family should, each for themselves, take up the position secured for them by the salvation of Christ, to render them wholly and for ever superior to the dominion of the adversary. But it is here that imperfection still comes in. Men will not lay hold of the advantage obtained for them by the all-prevailing might and energy of Jesus, or they will but partially receive into their experience the benefits it provides for them. Yet there is a measure of success also here, in the case of all genuine believers. And it is to this branch of the subject more immediately that the apostle Peter points, when he represents Christian baptism as the antitype of the deluge. In the personal experience of believers, as symbolized in that ordinance, there is a re-enacting substantially of what took place in the outward theatre of the world by means of the deluge. "The like figure whereunto (literally, the antitype to which, viz. Noah's salvation by water in the ark) even baptism doth also now save us; not the putting away of the filth of the flesh, but the answer of a good conscience toward God, by the resurrection of Jesus Christ" (1 Peter iii. 21). Like the apostle's delineations generally, the passage briefly indicates, rather than explicitly unfolds, the truths connected with the subject. Yet, on a slight consideration of it, we readily perceive, that with profound discernment, it elicits from the ordinance of baptism, as spiritually understood and applied, the same fundamental elements, discovers there the same twofold process, which appeared so strikingly in the case of Noah. Here also there is a salvation finding its accomplishment by means of a destruction—"not the putting away of the filth of the flesh"—not so superficial a riddance of evil, but one of a more important and vital character, bringing " the answer of a good conscience," or the deliverance of the soul from the guilt and power of iniquity. The water of baptism—let the subject be plunged in it ever so deep, or sprinkled ever so much—can no more of itself save him than the water of the deluge could have saved Noah, apart from the faith he possessed, and the preparation it led him to make in constructing and entering into the ark. It was because he held and exercised such faith, that the deluge brought salvation to Noah, while it overwhelmed others in destruction. So is it in baptism, when received in a spirit of faith. There is in this also the putting off of the old man of corruption—crucifying it together with Christ, and at the same time a rising through the resurrection of Christ to the new and heavenly life, which satisfies the demands of a pure and enlightened conscience. So that the really baptised soul is one in which there has been a killing and a making alive, a breaking up and destroying of the root of corrupt nature, and planting in its stead the seed of a divine nature, to spring, and grow, and bring forth fruit to perfection. In the microcosm of the individual believer, there is the perishing of an old world of sin and death, and the establishment of a new world of righteousness and life everlasting.

Such is the proper idea of Christian baptism, and such would be the practical result were the idea fully realized in the experience of the baptised. But this is so far from being the case, that even the idea is apt to suffer in people's minds from the conscious imperfections of their experience. And it might help to check such a tendency—it might, at least, be of service in enabling them to keep themselves well informed as to what *should* be, if they looked occasionally to what actually was, in the outward pattern of these spiritual things, given in the times of Noah. Are you disinclined, we might say to them, to have the axe so unsparingly applied to the old man of corruption? Think, for your warning, how God spared not the old world, but sent its mass of impurity headlong into the gulph of perdition. Seems it a task too formidable, and likely to prove hopeless in the accomplishment, to maintain your ground against the powers of evil in the world? Think again, for your encouragement, how impotent the giants of wickedness were of old to defeat the counsels of God, or prevail over those who held fast their confidence in his word; with all their numbers and their might, they sunk like lead in the waters, while the little household of faith rode secure in the midst of them. Or, does it appear strange, at times perhaps incredible, to your mind, that *you* should be made the subject of a work which requires for its accomplishment the peculiar perfections of Godhead, while others are left entire strangers to it, and even find the Word of God—the chosen instrument for effecting it—the occasion of wrath and condemnation to their souls? Remember " the few, the eight souls" of Noah's family, alone preserved amid the wreck and desolation of a whole world—preserved, too, by faith in a word of God, which carried in its bosom the doom of myriads of their fellow-creatures, and so, finding that, which was to others a minister of condemnation, a source of peace and safety to them. Rest assured, that as God himself remains the same through all generations, so his work for the good of men is essentially the same also; and it ever must be his design and purpose, that Noah's faith and salvation should be perpetually renewing themselves in the hidden life and experience of those who are preparing for the habitations of glory.

SECTION THIRD.

THE NEW WORLD AND ITS INHERITORS—THE MEN OF FAITH.

In one respect the world seemed to have suffered material loss by the visitation of the deluge. Along with the agents and instruments of evil, there had also been swept away by it the emblems of grace and hope—paradise with its tree of life and its cherubim of glory. We can conceive Noah and his household, when they first left the ark, looking around with melancholy feelings on the position they now occupied, not only as being the sole survivors of a numerous offspring, but also as being themselves bereft of the sacred memorials which bore evidence of a happy past, and exhibited the pledge of a still happier future. An important link of communion with heaven, it might well have seemed, was broken by the change thus brought through the deluge on the world. But the loss was soon fully compensated, and, we may even say, more than compensated, by the advantages conferred on Noah and his seed from the higher relation to which they were now raised, in respect to God and the world. There are three points that here, in particular, call for attention.

1. The first is, the new condition of the earth itself, which immediately appears in the freedom allowed and practised in regard to the external worship of God. This was no longer confined to any single region, as seems to have been the case in the age subsequent to the fall. The cherubim were located in a particular spot, on the east of the garden of Eden; and as the symbols of God's presence were there, it was only natural that the celebration of divine worship should there also have found its common centre. Hence, the two sons of Adam are said to have "*brought* their offerings unto the Lord"—which can scarcely be understood otherwise than as pointing to that particular locality which was hallowed by visible symbols of the Lord's presence, and in the

neighbourhood of which life and blessing still lingered. In like manner, it is said of Cain, after he had assumed the attitude of rebellion, that "he went out from the presence of the Lord," obviously implying that there was a certain region with which the divine presence was considered to be more peculiarly connected, and which can be thought of nowhere else than in that sanctuary on the east of Eden. But with the flood the reason for any such restriction vanished. Noah, therefore, reared his altar, and presented his sacrifice to the Lord where the ark rested. There immediately he got the blessing, and entered into covenant with God—proving that, in a sense, old things had passed away, and all had become new. The earth had risen in the divine reckoning to a higher condition; it had passed through the baptism of water, and was now, in a manner, cleansed from defilement; so that every place had become sacred, and might be regarded as suitable for the most solemn acts of worship.[1]

This more sacred and elevated position of the earth after the deluge appears, farther, in the express repeal of the curse originally laid upon the ground for the sin of Adam: "I will not again curse the ground any more for man's sake" (Gen. viii. 21), was the word of God to Noah, on accepting the first offering presented to him in the purified earth. It is, no doubt, to be understood relatively—not as indicating a *total* repeal of the evil, but only a mitigation of it; yet such a mitigation as would render the earth a much less afflicted and more fertile region than it had been before. But this again indicated that, in the estimation of

[1] If we are right as to the centralization of the primitive worship of mankind (and it seems to be only the natural inference from the notices referred to), then the antediluvian population cannot well be supposed to have been of vast extent, or to have wandered to a very great distance from the original centre. The employment also of a special agency after the flood to disperse the descendants of Noah, and scatter them over the earth, seems to indicate, that an indisposition to go to a distance, a tendency to crowd too much about one locality, was one of the sources of evil in the first stage of the world's history, the recurrence of which well deserved to be prevented, even by miraculous interference; and it is perfectly conceivable, indeed most likely, that the tower of Babel, in connection with which this interference took place, was not intended to be a palladium of idolatry, or a mere freak of ambitious folly, but rather a sort of substitution for the loss of the Edenic symbols, and, as such, a centre of union for the human family. It follows, of course, from the same considerations, that the deluge might not absolutely require, so far as the race of man was concerned, to extend over more than a comparatively limited portion of the earth. But its actual compass is not thereby determined.

Heaven, the earth had now assumed a new position; that by the action of God's judgment upon it, it had become hallowed in his sight, and was in a condition to receive tokens of the divine beneficence, which had formerly been withheld from it.

2. The second point to be noticed here, is the heirship given of this new world to Noah and his seed—given to them expressly as the children of faith.

Adam, at his creation, was constituted the lord of this world, and had kingly power and authority given him to subdue it and rule over it. But, on the occasion of his fall, this grant, though not formally recalled, suffered a capital abridgment; since he was sent forth from Eden as a discrowned monarch, to do the part simply of a labourer on the surface of the earth, and with the discouraging assurance, that it should reluctantly yield to him of its fruitfulness. Nor, when he afterwards so distinctly identified himself with God's promise and purpose of grace, by appearing as the head only of that portion of his seed who had faith in God, did there seem any alleviation of the evil; the curse that rested on the ground rested on it still, even for the seed of blessing (Gen. v. 29), and not they, but the ungodly Cainites, acquired in it the ascendancy of physical force and political dominion.

A change, however, appears in the relative position of things, when the flood had swept with its purifying waters over the earth. Man now rises, in the person of Noah, to a higher place in the world; yet not simply as man, but as a child of God, standing in faith. His faith has saved him, amid the general wreck of the old world, to become in the new a second head of mankind, and an inheritor of earth's domain, as now purged and rescued from the pollution of evil. "He is made heir," as it is written in Hebrews, " of the righteousness which is by faith,"—heir, that is, of all that properly belongs to such righteousness, not merely of the righteousness itself, but also of the world, which in the divine purpose it was destined to possess and occupy. Hence, as if there had been a new creation, and a new head brought in to exercise over it the right of sovereignty, the original blessing and grant to Adam are substantially renewed to Noah and his family: " And God blessed Noah and his sons, and said unto them, Be fruitful and multiply, and replenish the earth. And the fear of you, and the dread of you shall be upon every beast of the earth, and upon every fowl of the air, upon all that moveth upon the earth, and upon all the fishes of the sea; into your hand are they delivered." Here, then, the righteousness of faith received direct from the grace of God the dowry that had been originally bestowed upon the righteousness of nature—not a blessing merely, but a blessing coupled with the heirship and dominion of the world.

There was nothing strange or arbitrary in such a proceeding; it was in perfect accordance with the great principles of the divine administration. Adam was too closely connected with the sin that destroyed the world, to be invested, even when he had become through faith a partaker of grace, with the restored heirship of the world. Nor had the world itself passed through such an ordeal of purification, as to fit it, in the personal lifetime of Adam, or of his more immediate offspring, for being at all represented in the light of an inheritance of blessing. The renewed title to the heirship of its fulness was properly reserved to the time when, by the great act of divine judgment at the deluge, it had passed into a new condition; and when one was found of the woman's seed, who had attained in a peculiar degree to the righteousness of faith, and along with the world had undergone a process of salvation. It was precisely such a person that should have been chosen as the first type of the righteousness of faith, in respect to its world-wide heritage of blessing. And having been raised to this higher position, an additional sacredness was thrown around him and his seed:—the fear of them was to be put into the inferior creatures; their life was to be avenged of every one that should wrongfully take it; even the life-blood of irrational animals was to be held sacred, because of its having something in common with man's, while their flesh was now freely surrendered to their use:—the whole evidently fitted, and, we cannot doubt, also intended to convey the idea, that man had by the special gift of God's grace been again constituted heir and lord of the world, that, in the words of the Psalmist, "the earth had been given to the children of men," and given in a larger and fuller sense than had been done since the period of the fall.[1]

---

[1] It presents no contrariety to this, when rightly considered, that the Lord should also have connected his purpose of preserving the earth in future with the corruption of man: "And the Lord smelled a sweet savour (viz. from Noah's sacrifice), and the Lord said in his heart, I will not again curse the ground any more for man's sake, for the

3. The remaining point to be noticed in respect to this new order of things, is the pledge of continuance, notwithstanding all appearances or threatenings to the contrary, given in the covenant made with Noah, and confirmed by a fixed sign in the heavens. "And God spake unto Noah, and to his sons with him, saying, And I, behold, I establish my covenant with you, and with your seed after you; and with every living creature that is with you, of the fowl, of the cattle, and of every beast of the earth with you; from all that go out of the ark, to every beast of the earth. And I will establish my covenant with you; neither shall all flesh be cut off any more by the waters of a flood; neither shall there any more be a flood to destroy the earth. And God said, This is the token of the covenant which I make between me and you and every living creature that is with you, for perpetual generations: I do set my bow in the cloud, and it shall be for a token of a covenant" (more exactly: my bow I have set in the cloud, and it shall be for a covenant-sign,) "between me and the earth. And it shall come to pass, when I bring a cloud over the earth, that the bow shall be seen in the cloud: and I will remember my covenant, which is between me and you and every living creature of all flesh; and the waters shall no more become a flood to destroy all flesh." (Gen. ix. 8–15.)

There can be no doubt, that the natural impression produced by this passage in respect to the sign of the covenant, is, that it now for the first time appeared in the lower heavens. The Lord might, no doubt, then, or at any future time, have taken an existing phenomenon in nature, and by a special appointment made it the instrument of conveying some new and higher meaning to the subjects of his revelation. But, in a matter like the present, when the specific object contemplated was to allay men's fears of the possible recurrence of the deluge, and give them a kind of visible pledge in nature for the permanence of her existing order

---

imagination of man's heart is evil from his youth" (Gen. viii. 21.) The meaning is, that God delighted so much more in the offerings of righteousness than in the inflictions of judgment, that he would now direct his providence, so as more effectually to secure the former—would not allow the imaginations of man's evil heart to get such scope as they had done before, but perceiving and remembering their native existence in the heart, would bring such remedial influences to work that the extremity of the past should not again return.

and constitution, one cannot perceive how a natural phenomenon, common alike to the antediluvian and the postdiluvian world, could have fitly served the purpose. In that case, so far as the external sign was concerned, matters stood precisely where they were; and it was not properly the sign, but the covenant itself, which formed the guarantee of safety for the future. We incline, therefore, to the opinion that, in the announcement here made, intimation is given of a change in the physical relations or temperature of, at least, that portion of the earth where the original inhabitants had their abode; by reason of which the descent of moisture in showers of rain came to take the place of distillation by dew, or other modes of operation different from the present. The supposition is favoured by the mention only of dew before in connection with the moistening of the ground (Gen. ii. 6); and when rain does come to be mentioned, it is rain in such flowing torrents as seems rather to betoken the outpouring of a continuous stream, than the gentle dropping which we are wont to understand by the term, and to associate with the rainbow.

The fitness of the rainbow in other respects to serve as a sign of the covenant made with Noah, is all that could be desired. There is an exact correspondence between the natural phenomenon it presents, and the moral use to which it is applied. The promise in the covenant was not that there should be no future visitations of judgment upon the earth, but that they should not proceed to the extent of again destroying the world. In the moral, as in the natural sphere, there might still be congregating vapours and descending torrents; indeed, the terms of the covenant imply, that there should be such, and that by means of them God would not fail to testify his displeasure against sin, and keep in awe the workers of iniquity. But there should be no second deluge to diffuse universal ruin; mercy should always so far rejoice against judgment. And so precisely it is in nature with the rainbow, which is formed by the lustre of the sun's rays shining on the dark cloud as it recedes; so that it may fitly be called, in the somewhat poetical language of Lange, " the sun's triumph over the floods; the glitter of his beams imprinted on the rain-cloud as a mark of subjection." How appropriate an emblem of the action of divine grace always returning after wrath! Grace still sparing and preserving even when clouds of judgment have been threatening to desolate and destroy! And as the rainbow throws its radiant arch over the expanse between heaven and earth, and as with a wreath of beauty unites the two together again, after they have been engaged in an elemental war, it strikingly images to the thoughtful eye the essential harmony that is still to subsist between the higher and the lower spheres. Such undoubtedly is its symbolic import, as the sign peculiarly connected with the Noachic covenant; it holds out, by means of its very form and nature, an assurance of God's mercy, as engaged to keep perpetually in check the floods of deserved wrath, and continue to the world the manifestation of his grace and goodness. Such also is the import attached to it, when forming a part of prophetic imagery, in the visions of Ezekiel (ch. i. 28), and of St John (Rev. iv. 3); it is the symbol of grace, as ever ready to return after judgment, and to stay the evil from proceeding so far as to accomplish a complete destruction.

[1] Far too general is the explanation often given of the symbolic import of the rainbow by writers on such topics—as when it is described to be "in general a symbol of God's willingness to receive men into favour again" (Wemyss' Clavis Symbolica), or that "it indicates the faithfulness of the Almighty in fulfilling the promises that he has made to his people" (Mill's Sacred Symbology). Sound Christian feeling, with something of a poetic eye for the imagery of nature, finds its way better to the meaning—as in the following simple lines of John Newton:—

> "When the sun with cheerful beams
>   Smiles upon a low'ring sky,
> Soon its aspect softened seems,
>   And a rainbow meets the eye;
> While the sky remains serene,
> This bright arch is never seen.
>
> Thus the Lord's supporting power
>   Brightest to his saints appears,
> When affliction's threat'ning hour
>   Fills their sky with clouds and fears;
> He can wonders then perform,
> Paint a rainbow on the storm.
>
> Favoured John a rainbow saw
>   Circling round the throne above;
> Hence the saints a pledge may draw
>   Of unchanging covenant-love:
> Clouds awhile may intervene,
> But the bow shall still be seen.

Yet gracious as this covenant with Noah was, and appropriate and beautiful the sign that ratified it, all bore on it still the stamp of imperfection; there was an indication and a prelude of the better things needed to make man truly and permanently blessed, not these things themselves. For, what was this new world, which had its perpetuity secured, and over which Noah was set to reign, as heir of the righteousness that is by faith? To Noah himself, and each one in succession of his seed, it was still a region of corruption and death. It had been sanctified, indeed, by the judgment of God, and as thus sanctified it was not to perish again as it had done before. But this sanctification was only by water—enough to sweep away into the gulf of perdition the mass of impurity that festered on its surface, but not penetrating inwards, to the elements of evil which were bound up with its very framework. Another agency, more thoroughly pervasive in its nature, and in its effects more nobly sublimating, the agency of fire, is required to purge out the dross of its earthliness, and render it a home and an inheritance fit for those who are made like to the Son of God (2 Pet. iii. 7–13). And Noah himself, though acknowledged heir of the righteousness by faith, and receiving on it the seal of heaven, in the salvation granted to him and his household, yet how far from being perfect in that righteousness, or by this salvation placed beyond the reach of evil! How mournfully did he afterwards fall under the power of temptation! and how much of the serpent's seed still lurked in the members of his household! High, therefore, as Noah stood compared with those who had gone before him, he was after all but the representative of an imperfect righteousness, and the heir of a corruptible and transitory inheritance. He was the type, but no more than the type, of Him who was to come—in whom the righteousness of God should be perfected, salvation should rise to its higher sphere, and all, both in the heirs of glory, and the inheritance they are to occupy, should by the baptism of fire be rendered incorruptible and undefiled, and fading not away.

SECTION FOURTH.

THE CHANGE IN THE DIVINE CALL FROM THE GENERAL TO THE PARTICULAR
—SHEM, ABRAHAM.

The obvious imperfections just noticed, both in the righteousness of the new head of the human family, and in the constitution of the world over which he was placed, clearly enough indicated, that the divine plan had only advanced a stage in its progress, but had by no means reached its perfection. As the world, however, in its altered condition, had become *naturally* superior to its former state, so—in necessary and causal connection with this—it was to stand superior to it also in a *spiritual* respect: secured against the return of a general perdition, it was also secured against the return of universal apostacy and corruption. The cause of righteousness was not to be trodden down as it had been before, nay, was to hold on its way and ultimately rise to the ascendant in the affairs of men.

Not only was this pre-supposed in the covenant of perpetuity established for the world, as the internal ground on which it rested, but it was also distinctly announced by the father of the new world, in the prophetic intimation he gave of the future destinies of his children. It was a melancholy occasion which drew this prophecy forth, as it was alike connected with the mournful backsliding of Noah himself, and the wanton indecency of his youngest son. When Noah recovered from his sin, and understood how this son had exposed, while the other two had covered his nakedness, he said, "Cursed is Canaan; a servant of servants (*i. e.* a servant of the lowest grade) shall he be to his brethren. And he said, Blessed is the Lord God of Shem, and Canaan shall be his servant. God shall enlarge Japheth, and he shall dwell in the tents of Shem; and Canaan shall be his servant" (Gen. ix. 25–27).

There are various points of interest connected with this prophecy, and the occurrence that gave rise to it, which it does not fall within our province to notice. But the leading scope of it, as bearing on the prospective destinies of mankind, is manifestly of a hopeful description; and in that respect it differs materially from the first historical incident, that revealed the conflict of nature and grace in the family of Adam. The triumph of Cain over righteous Abel, and his stout-hearted resistance to the voice of God, gave ominous indication of the bad pre-eminence which sin was to acquire, and the fearful results which it was to achieve in the old world. But the milder form of this outbreak of evil in the family of Noah, the immediate discouragement it meets with from the older members of the family, the strong denunciation it draws down from the venerable parent, above all, the clear and emphatic prediction it elicits of the ascendancy of the good over the evil in these seminal divisions of the human family, one and all perfectly accorded with the better state to which the world had now risen; they bespoke the cheering fact, that righteousness should now hold its ground in the world, and that the dominant powers and races should be in league with it, while servility and degradation should rest upon its adversaries.

This, any one may see at a glance, is the general tendency and design of what was uttered on the occasion; but there is a marked peculiarity in the form given to it, such as plainly intimates the commencement of a change in the divine economy. There is a striking particularism in the prophetic announcement. It does not, as previously, give forth broad principles, or foretel merely general results of evil and of good; but it explicitly announces—though still, no doubt, in wide and comprehensive terms—the characteristic outlines of the future state and relative positions of Noah's descendants. Such is the decided tendency here to the particular, that in the dark side of the picture, it is not Ham, the offending son and the general head of the worse portion of the postdiluvian family, who is selected as the special object of vengeance, nor the sons of Ham generally, but specifically Canaan, who, it seems all but certain, was the youngest son (Gen. x. 6). Why this son, rather than the offending father, should have been singled out for denunciation, has been ascribed to various reasons; and resort has not unfrequently been had to conjecture, by supposing that this son may probably have been present with the father, or some way participated with him in the offence. Even, however, if we had been certified of this participation, it could at most have accounted for the introduction of the name of Canaan, but not for that being substituted in the room of the father's. Nor can we allow much more weight to another supposition, that the omission of the name of Ham may have been intended for the very purpose of proving the absence of all vindictive feeling, and shewing that these were the words, not of a justly indignant parent giving vent to the emotions of the passing moment, but of a divinely inspired prophet calmly anticipating the events of a remote futurity. Undoubtedly such is their character; but no extenuating consideration of this kind is needed to prove it, if we only keep in view the judicial nature of this part of the prophecy. The curse pronounced is not an ebullition of wrathful feeling, not a wish for the infliction of evil, but the announcement of a doom, or punishment for a particular offence; and one that was to take, as so often happens in divine chastisements, the specific form of the offence committed. Noah's affliction from the conduct of Ham was in the most peculiar manner to find its parallel in the case of Ham himself: He, the youngest son of Noah,[1] had proved a vexation and disgrace to his father, and in meet retaliation his own youngest son was to have his name in history coupled with the most humiliating and abject degradation.

It was, therefore, in the first instance at least, for the purpose of marking more distinctly the connection between the sin and its punishment, that Canaan only was mentioned in the curse. Viewed as spoken to Ham, the word virtually said, I am pained to the heart on account of you, my youngest son, and you in turn, shall have good cause to be pained on account of your youngest son—your own measure shall be meted back with increase to

---

[1] Gen. ix. 24. The expression in the original is בְּנוֹ הַקָּטָן, and is the same that is applied to David in 1 Sam. xvii. 14. There can, therefore, be no reasonable doubt that it means youngest, and not tender or dear, as some would take it. It is not so expressly said, that Canaan was Ham's youngest son, but the inference that he was such is fair and natural, as he is mentioned last in the genealogy, ch. x. 6, where no sufficient reason can be thought of for deviating from the natural order.

yourself. It may be true—as Hävernick states in his Introduction to the Pentateuch—that the curse, properly belonging to Ham, was to concentrate itself in the line of Canaan; and, beyond doubt, it is more especially in connection with that line that Scripture itself traces the execution of the curse. But these are somewhat remote and incidental considerations; the more natural and direct is the one already given—which Hofmann, we believe, was the first to suggest.[1] And as the word took the precise form it did, for the purpose more particularly of marking the connection between the sin and the punishment, it plainly indicated, that the evil could not be confined to the line of Ham's descendants by Canaan; the same polluted fountain could not fail to send forth its bitter streams also in other directions. The connection is entirely a moral one. Even in the case of Canaan there was no arbitrary and hapless appointment to inevitable degradation and slavery; as is clearly proved by the long forbearance and delay in the execution of the threatened doom, expressly on the ground of the iniquity of the people not having become full, and also from the examples of individual Canaanites, who rose even to distinguished favour and blessing, such as Melchizedec and Rahab in earlier, and the Syrophenician woman in later times. Noah, however, saw with prophetic insight, that in a general point of view the principle should here hold, like father like child; and that the irreverent and wanton spirit, which so strikingly betrayed itself in the conduct of the progenitor, should infallibly give rise to an offspring, whose dissolute and profligate manners would in due time bring upon them a doom of degradation and servitude. Such a posterity, with such a doom, beyond all question were the Canaanites, to whom we may add also the Tyrians and Sidonians, with their descendants the Carthagenians. The connection of sin and punishment might be traced to other sections besides, but it is not necessary that we pursue the subject farther.

Our course of inquiry rather leads us to notice the turn the prophecy takes in regard to the other side of the representation, and to mark the signs it contains of a tendency toward the particular, in connection with the future developement of the scheme

---

[1] Weissagung und Erfüllung, i. p. 89.

of grace. This comes out first and pre-eminently in the case of Shem: "And he said, Blessed is (or be) Jehovah, the God of Shem,"—a blessing not directly upon Shem, but upon Jehovah as his God! Why such a peculiarity as this? No doubt, in the first instance, to make the contrast more palpable between this case and the preceding; the connection with God, which was utterly wanting in the one, presenting itself as everything, in a manner, in the other. Then, it proclaims the identity as to spiritual state between Noah and Shem, and designates this son as in the full sense the heir of blessing: "Blessed be Jehovah, the God of Shem." My God is also the God of my son; I adore him for himself; and now, before I leave the world, declare him to be the covenant God of Shem. Nor of Shem only as an individual, but as the head of a certain portion of the world's inhabitants. It was with this portion that God was to stand in the nearest relation. Here he was to find his peculiar representatives, and his select instruments of working among men—here emphatically were to be the priestly people. A spiritual distinction, therefore—the highest spiritual distinction, a state of blessed nearness to God, and special interest in his fulness—is what is predicated of the line of Shem. And in the same sense, namely, as denoting a fellowship in this *spiritual* distinction, should that part of the prophecy on Japheth also be understood, which points to a connection with Shem: "God shall enlarge Japheth, and he shall dwell in the tents of Shem." It obviously, indeed, designates his stock generally as the most spreading and energetic of the three—pre-eminent, so far as concerns diffusive operations and active labour in occupying the lands and carrying forward the business of the world—and thus naturally tending, as the event has proved, to push their way, even in a civil and territorial respect, into the tents of Shem. This last thought may therefore not unfairly be included in the compass of the prediction, but it can at most be regarded as the subordinate idea. The prospect, as descried from the sacred heights of prophecy, of dwelling in the tents of Shem, must have been eyed, not as an intrusive conquest on the part of Japheth, subjecting Shem in a measure to the degrading lot of Canaan, but rather as a sacred privilege—an admission of this less honoured race under the shelter of the same divine protection, and into the partnership of the same ennobling benefits with himself. In a word, it was through the line of Shem that the gifts of grace and the blessings of salvation were more immediately to flow—the Shemites were to have them at first hand ; but the descendants of Japheth were also to participate largely in the good. And by reason of their more extensive ramifications and more active energies, were to be mainly instrumental in working upon the condition of the world.

It is evident, even from this general intimation of the divine purposes, that the more particular direction which was now to be given to the call of God, was not to be particular in the sense of *exclusive*, but particular only for the sake of a more efficient working and a more expansive result. The exaltation of Shem's progeny into the nearest relationship to God, was not that they might keep the privilege to themselves, but that first getting it, they should admit the sons of Japheth, the inhabitants of the isles, to share with them in the boon, and spread it as wide as their scattered race should extend. The principle announced was *an immediate particularism for the sake of an ultimate universalism.* And this change in the manner of working was not introduced arbitrarily, but in consequence of the proved inadequacy of the other, and, as we may say, more natural course that had hitherto been pursued. Formally considered, the earlier revelations of God made no difference between one person and another, or even between one stem and another. They spoke the same language, and held out the same invitations to all. The weekly call to enter into God's rest—the promise of victory to the woman's seed—the exhibition of grace and hope in the symbols at the east of Eden—the instituted means of access to God in sacrificial worship—even the more specific promises and pledges of the Noachic covenant, were offered and addressed to men without distinction. Practically, however, they narrowed themselves ; and when the effect is looked to, it is found that there was only a portion, an elect seed, that really had faith in the divine testimony, and entered into possession of the offered good. Not only so, but there was a downward tendency in the process. The elect seed did not grow as time advanced, but proportionally decreased ; the cause and party that flourished was the one opposed to God's. And the same result was beginning to take place after the flood, as is evident from what occurred in the family of Noah itself, and from other notices of the early appearance of corruption. The tendency in this direction was too strong to be effectually met by such general revelations and overtures of mercy. The plan was too vague and indeterminate. A more specific line of operations was needed—from the particular to the general; so that a certain amount of good, within a definite range, might in the first instance be secured; and that from this, as a fixed position, other advantages might be gained, and more extensive results achieved.

It is carefully to be noted, then, that a comprehensive object was as much contemplated in this new plan as in the other; it differed only in the mode of reaching the end in view. The earth was to be possessed and peopled by the three sons of Noah; and of the three Shem is the one who was selected as the peculiar channel of divine gifts and communications—but not for his own exclusive benefit; rather to the end that others might share with him in the blessing. The real nature and bearing of the plan, however, became more clearly manifest, when it began to be actually carried into execution. Its proper commencement dates from the call of Abraham, who was of the line of Shem, and in whom, as an individual, the purpose of God began practically to take effect. Why the divine choice should have fixed specially upon him as the first individual link in this grand chain of providences, is not stated; and from the references subsequently made to it, we are plainly instructed to regard it as an example of the absolutely free grace and sovereign election of God (Josh. xxiv. 2; Neh. ix. 7.) That he had nothing whereof to boast in respect to it, we are expressly told; and yet we may not doubt, that in the line of Shem's posterity, to which he belonged, there was more knowledge of God, and less corruption in his worship, than among other branches of the same stem. Hence, perhaps, as being addressed to one, who was perfectly cognizant of what had taken place in the history of his progenitors, the revelation made to him takes a form, which bears evident respect to the blessing pronounced on Shem, and appears only, indeed, as the giving of a more specific direction to Shem's high calling, or chalking out a definite way for its accomplishment. Jehovah was the God of Shem—*that* in the word of Noah was declared to be his peculiar distinction. In like manner Jehovah from the first made himself known to Abraham as his God, nay even took the name of " God of Abraham" as a distinctive epithet, and made the promise, "I will be a God to thee and to thy seed after thee," a leading article in the covenant established with him. And as the peculiar blessing of Shem was to be held with no exclusive design, but that the sons of Japheth far and wide might share in it, so Abraham is called, not only to be himself blessed, but also that he might be a blessing; a blessing to such an extent, that those should be blessed who blessed him, and in him all the families of the earth should be blessed. Yet with this general similarity between the earlier and the later announcement, what a striking advance does the divine plan now make in breadth of meaning and explicitness of purpose? How wonderfully does it combine together the little and the great, the individual and the universal? Its *terminus a quo* the son of a Mesopotamian shepherd; and its *terminus ad quem* the entire brotherhood of humanity, and the round circumference of the globe! What a divine-like grasp and expansiveness! The very projection of such a scheme bespoke the infinite understanding of Godhead; and minds altogether the reverse of narrow and exclusive, minds attempered to noble aims and inspired by generous feeling, alone could carry it into execution.

By this call Abraham was raised to a very singular pre-eminence, and constituted in a manner the root and centre of the world's future history, as concerns the attainment of real blessing. Still, even in that respect not exclusively. The blessing was to come chiefly to Abraham and through him; but, as already indicated also in the prophecy on Shem, others were to stand, though in a subordinate rank, on the same line; since those also were to be blessed who blessed him; that is, who held substantially the same faith, and occupied the same friendly relation to God. The cases of such persons in the patriarch's own day, as his kinsman Lot, who was not formally admitted into Abraham's covenant, and still more of Melchizedec, who was not even of Abraham's line, and yet individually stood in some sense higher than Abraham himself, clearly shewed, and were no doubt partly provided for the express purpose of shewing, that there was nothing arbitrary in Abraham's position, and that the ground he occupied was to a certain extent common to believers generally. The peculiar honour conceded to him was, that the great trunk of blessing was to be of him, while only some isolated twigs or scattered branches were to be found elsewhere; and even these could only be found, by persons coming, in a manner, to make common cause with him. In regard to himself, however, the large dowry of good conveyed to him in the divine promise could manifestly not be realised through himself personally. There could at the most be but a beginning made in his own experience and history; and the widening of the circle of blessing to other kindreds and regions, till it reached the most distant families of the earth, could only be effected by means of those who were to spring from him. Hence, the original word of promise, which was "in thee shall all families of the earth be blessed," was afterwards changed into this, "in thy seed shall all the nations of the earth be blessed" (Gen. xxii. 18.)

Yet the original expression is not without an important meaning, and it takes the two, the earlier as well as the later form, to bring out the full design of God in the calling of Abraham. From the very nature of the case, first, as having respect to so extensive a field to be operated on, and then from the explicit mention of the patriarch's seed in the promise, no doubt whatever could be entertained, that the good in its larger sense was to be wrought out, not by himself individually and directly, but by him in connection with the seed to be given to him. And when the high character, as well as the comprehensive reach of the good was taken into account, it might well have seemed, as if even that seed were somehow going to have qualities associated with it, which he could not perceive in himself—as if another and higher connection with the heavenly and divine should in due time be given to it, than any he was conscious of enjoying in his state of noblest elevation. We, at least, know from the better light we possess, that such actually was the case; that the good promised neither did, nor could have come into realization but by a personal commingling of the divine with the human; and that it has become capable of reaching to the most exalted height, and of diffusing itself through the widest bounds, simply by reason of this union in Christ. He, therefore, is the essential kernel of the promise; and the seed of Abraham, rather than Abraham himself, was to have the honour of blessing all the families of the earth. This, however, by no means makes void the *in thee* of the original promise; for by so expressly connecting the good with Abraham, as well as with his seed, the organic connection was marked between the one and the other, and the things that belonged to him were made known as the beginning of the end. The blessing to be brought to the world through his line had even in his time a present though small realization—precisely as the kingdom of Christ had its commencement in that of David, and the one ultimately merged into the other. And so, in Abraham as the living root of all that was to follow, the whole and every part may be said to take its rise; and not only was Christ after the flesh of the seed of Abraham, but each believer in Christ is a son of Abraham, and the entire company of the redeemed shall have their place and their portion with Abraham in the kingdom of God.

Such being the case with the call of Abraham—in its objects so high, and its results so grand and comprehensive,—it is manifest, that the immediate limitations connected with it, in regard to a fleshly offspring and a worldly inheritance, must only have been intended to serve as temporary expedients and fit stepping-stones for the ulterior purposes in view. And such statements regarding the covenant with Abraham, as that it merely secured to Abraham a posterity, and to that posterity the possession of the land of Canaan for an inheritance, on the condition of their acknowledging Jehovah as their God, is to read the terms of the covenant with a microscope—magnifying the little, and leaving utterly unnoticed the great—in the preliminary means losing sight of the prospective end.[1] Another thing also, and one more closely connected with our present subject, is equally manifest; which is, that since the entire scheme of blessing had its root in Abraham, it must also have had its representation in him—he, in his position and character and fortunes must have been the type of that which was to come. Such uniformly is God's plan, in respect to those whom it constitutes heads of a class, or founders of a particular dispensation. It was so, first of all, with Adam,

---

[1] This is precisely what is done in a late volume, *Israel after the Flesh*, by Mr William H. Johnstone—p. 7, 8. He appears also to slump together the covenant with Abraham and the covenant at Sinai, as if the one were simply a renewal of the other. And this notwithstanding the distinction drawn so pointedly between them in the epistle to the Galatians, and while the author, too, professes to have gone to work with the thorough determination to be guided only by Scripture!

in whom humanity itself was imaged. It was so again in a measure with the three sons of Noah, whose respective states and procedure gave prophetic indication of the more prominent characteristics that should distinguish their offspring. Such, too, at a future period, and much more remarkably, was the case with David, in whom, as the beginning and root of the everlasting kingdom, there was presented the foreshadowing type of all that should essentially belong to the kingdom, when represented by its divine head, and set up in its proper dimensions. Nor could it now be properly otherwise with Abraham. The very terms of the call, which singled him out from the mass of the world, and set him on high, constrain us to regard him as in the strictest sense a representative man—in himself and the things belonging to his immediate heirs, the type at once of the subjective and the objective design of the covenant, or, in other words, of the kind of persons who were to be the subjects and channels of blessing, and of the kind of inheritance with which they were to be blessed. It is for the purpose of exhibiting this clearly and distinctly, and thereby rendering the things written of Abraham and his immediate offspring a revelation, in the strictest sense, of God's mind and will regarding the more distant future, that this portion of patriarchal history was constructed. Abraham himself, in the first instance, was the covenant head and the type of what was to come ; but as the family of the Israelites were to be the collective bearers and representatives of the covenant, so, not Abraham alone, but the whole of their immediate progenitors, who were alike heads of the covenant-people,—besides Abraham, Isaac also, and Jacob, and the twelve patriarchs, possess a typical character. It shall be our object, therefore, in the two remaining sections—which must necessarily be rather long ones—to present the more prominent features of the instruction intended to be conveyed in both of the respects now mentioned—first in regard to the subjects and channels of blessing, and then in regard to the inheritance destined for their possession.

SECTION FIFTH.

THE SUBJECTS AND CHANNELS OF BLESSING—ABRAHAM AND ISAAC, JACOB AND THE TWELVE PATRIARCHS.

WHILE we class the whole of these together, on account of their being alike covenant heads to the children of Israel, who became in due time the covenant-people, we are not to lose sight of the fact, that Abraham was more especially the person in whom the covenant had its original root and representation. It is in his case, accordingly, that we might expect to find, and that we actually have, the most specific and varied information respecting the nature of the covenant, and the manner in which it was to reach its higher ends. We shall therefore look, in the first instance, to what is written of him, coupling Isaac, however, with him; since what is chiefly interesting and important about Isaac concerns him as the seed, for which Abraham was immediately called to look and wait; so that, as to the greater lines of instruction, which are all we can at present notice, the lives of the two are knit inseparably together. And the same is, to a considerable extent, the case also with Jacob and the twelve patriarchs. The whole may be said to be of one piece, viewed as a special instruction for the covenant-people, and through them for the church at large, in respect to her calling and position in the world.

I. Abraham, then, is called to be in a peculiar sense the possessor and dispenser of blessing; to be himself blessed, and through the seed that is to spring from him, to be a blessing to the whole race of mankind. A divine-like calling and destiny! for it is God alone who is properly the source and giver of blessing. Abraham, therefore, by his very appointment, is raised into a supra-natural relationship to God; he is to be in direct communication with heaven, and to receive all from above; God is to work, in a special manner, for him and by him; and the people that are to spring out of him, for a blessing to other peoples, are to arise, not in the ordinary course of nature, but above and beyond it, as the benefits also they should be called to diffuse belong to a higher region than that of nature. As a necessary counterpart to this, as the indispensable condition of its accomplishment, there must be in Abraham a principle of faith, such as might qualify him for transacting with God, in regard to the higher things of the covenant. These were not seen or present, and were also strange, supernatural, to the eye of flesh unlikely or even impossible—yet were not the less to be anticipated as certain on the testimony of God, and looked, waited, or, if need be, also striven and suffered for. This principle of faith must evidently be the fundamental and formative power in Abraham's bosom—the very root of his new being, the life of his life—at once making him properly receptive of the divine goodness, and readily obedient to the divine will—in the one respect giving scope for the display of God's wonders in his behalf, and in the other prompting him to act in accordance with God's righteous ends and purposes. So it actually was. Abraham was pre-eminently a man of faith—so pre-eminently as to gain the title of the Father of the Faithful. And faith in him proved not only a handle to receive, but a hand also to work; and is scarcely less remarkable for what it brought to his experience from the grace and power of God, as for the sustaining, elevating, and sanctifying influence which it shed over his life and conduct. There are particularly three stages, each rising in succession above the other, in which it is important for us to mark this.

1. The first is that of the divine call itself, which came to Abraham while still living among his kindred in the land of Mesopotamia. (Gen. xii. 1–3.) Even in this original form of the divine purpose concerning him, the supernatural element is conspicuous. To say nothing of its more general provisions, that he, a Mesopotamian shepherd, should be made surpassingly great, and should even be a source of blessing to all the families of the earth —to say nothing of these, which might appear incredible only from their indefinite vastness and comprehension, the two specific promises in the call, that a great nation should be made of him, and that another land—presently afterwards determined to be the

land of Canaan—should be given him for an inheritance, both lay beyond the bounds of the natural and the probable. At the time the call was addressed to Abraham, he was already seventy-five years old, and his wife Sarah, being only ten years younger, must have been sixty-five. (Gen. xii. 5, xvii. 17.) For such persons to be constituted parents, and parents of an offspring that should become a great nation, involved at the very outset a natural impossibility, and could only be made good by a supernatural exercise of divine omnipotence—a miracle. Nor was it materially different in regard to the other part of the promise; for it is expressly stated, when the precise land to be given was pointed out to him, that the Canaanite was then in the land. (Gen. xii. 6.) It was even then an inhabited territory, and by no ordinary concurrence of events could be expected to become the heritage of the yet unborn posterity of Abraham. It could only be looked for as the result of God's direct and special interposition in their behalf.

Yet, incredible as the promise seemed in both of its departments, Abraham believed the word spoken to him; he had faith to accredit the divine testimony, and to take the part which it assigned him. Both were required—a receiving of the promise first, and then an acting with a view to it; for, on the ground of such great things being destined for him, he was commanded to leave his natural home and kindred, and go forth under the divine guidance to the new territory to be assigned him. In this command was discovered the inseparable connection between faith and holiness; or between the call of Abraham to receive distinguishing and supernatural blessing, and his call to lead a life of supernatural and distinguishing holiness. He was singled out from the world's inhabitants to begin a new order of things, which were to bear throughout the impress of God's special grace and almighty power; and he must separate himself from the old things of nature, to be in his life the representative of God's holiness, as in his destiny he was to be the monument of God's power and goodness.

It is this exercise of faith in Abraham which is first exhibited in the epistle to the Hebrews, as bespeaking a mighty energy in its working; the more especially as the exchange in the case of

Abraham and his immediate descendants did not prove by any means agreeable to nature. "By faith Abraham, when he was called to go out into a place, which he should after receive for an inheritance, obeyed; and he went out, not knowing whither he went. By faith he sojourned in the land of promise, as in a strange country, dwelling in tabernacles with Isaac and Jacob, the heirs with him of the same promise." It may seem, indeed, at this distance of place and time, as if there were no great difference in the condition of Abraham and his household, in the one place as compared with the other. But it was quite otherwise in reality. They had, first of all, to break asunder the ties of home and kindred, which nature always feels painful, especially in mature age, even though it may have the prospect before it of a comfortable settlement in another region. This sacrifice they had to make in the fullest sense; it was in *their* case a strictly final separation; they were to be absolutely done with the old and its endearments, and to cleave henceforth to the new. Nor only so, but their immediate position in the new was not like that which they had before in the old; settled possessions in the one, but none in the other; in their stead mere lodging-room among strangers, and a life on providence. Nature does not love a change like that, and can only regard it as quitting the certainties of sight for the seeming *un*certainties of faith and hope. These, however, were still but the smaller trials which Abraham's faith had to encounter; for, along with the change in his outward condition, there came responsibilities and duties altogether alien to nature's feelings, and contrary to its spirit. In his old country he followed his own way, and walked after the course of the world, having no special work to do, nor any calling of a more solemn kind to fulfil. But now, by obeying the call of heaven, he was brought into immediate connection with a spiritual and holy God, became charged, in a manner, with his interest in the world, and bound, in the face of surrounding enmity or scorn, faithfully to maintain his cause, and promote the glory of his name. To do this was in truth to renounce nature, and rise superior to it. And it *was* done, let it be remembered, out of regard to prospects which could only be realized, if the power of God should forsake its wonted channels of working, and perform what the carnal mind would have deemed it infatuation to look for. Even in that first stage of the patriarch's course, there was a noble triumph of faith, and the earnest of a life replenished with the fruits of righteousness.

It is true, the promise thus given at the commencement was not uniformly sustained; and Abraham was not long in Canaan till there *seemed* to be a failure on the part of God toward him, and there actually *was* a failure on his part toward God. The occurrence of a famine leads him to take refuge for a time in Egypt, which was even then the granary of that portion of the east, and he is tempted, through fear for his personal safety, to equivocate regarding Sarah, and call her his sister. The equivocation is certainly not to be justified, either on this or on the future occasion on which it was again resorted to; for, though it contained a half truth, this was so employed as to render "the half truth a whole lie." We are rather to refer both circumstances—his repairing to Egypt, and when there betaking to such a worldly expedient for safety—as betraying the imperfection of his faith, which had strength to enable him to enter on his new course of separation from the world and devotedness to God, but still wanted clearness of discernment and implicitness of trust, sufficient to meet the unexpected difficulties that so early presented themselves in the way. Strange indeed had it been otherwise. It was necessary that the faith of Abraham, like that of believers generally, should learn by experience, and even grow by its temporary defeats. The first failure on the present occasion stood in his seeking relief from the emergency that arose by withdrawing, without the divine sanction, to another country than that into which he had been conducted by the special providence of God. Instead of looking up for direction and support, he betook to worldly shifts and expedients, and thus became entangled in difficulties, out of which the immediate interposition of God alone could have rescued him. In this way, however, the result proved beneficial. Abraham was made to feel, in the first instance, that his backsliding had reproved him; and then the merciful interposition of Heaven, rebuking even a king for his sake, taught him the lesson, that with the God of heaven upon his side, he had no need to be afraid for the outward evils that might beset him in his course. He had but to look up in faith, and get the direction or support that he needed,

The conduct of Abraham, immediately after his return to Canaan, gave ample evidence of the general steadfastness and elevated purity of his course. Though travelling about as a stranger in the land, he makes all around him feel, that it is a blessed thing to be connected with him, and that it would be well for them if the land really were in his possession. The quarrel that presently arose between Lot's herdsmen and his own, merely furnished the occasion for his disinterested generosity, in waiving his own rights, and allowing to his kinsman the priority and freedom of choice. And another quarrel of a graver kind, that of the war between the four kings in higher Asia, and of the five small dependent sovereigns in the south of Canaan, drew forth still nobler manifestations of the large and self-sacrificing spirit that filled his bosom. Regarding the unjust capture of Lot as an adequate reason for taking part in the conflict, he went courageously forth with his little band of trained servants, overthrew the conquerors, and recovered all that had been lost. Yet, at the very moment he displayed the victorious energy of his faith, by discomfiting this mighty army, how strikingly did he, at the same time, exhibit its patience in declining to use the advantage he then gained to hasten forward the purposes of God concerning his possession of the land, and its moderation of spirit, its commanding superiority to merely worldly ends and objects, in refusing to take even the smallest portion of the goods of the king of Sodom ! Nay, so far from seeking to exalt self by pressing outward advantages and worldly resources, his spirit of faith, leading him to recognise the hand of God in the success that had been won, causes him to bow down in humility, and do homage to the Most High God in the person of his priest Melchizedec. He gave this Melchizedec tithes of all, and as himself the less, received blessing from Melchizedec as the greater.

Viewed thus merely as a mark of the humble and reverent spirit of Abraham, the offspring of his faith in God, this notice of his relation to Melchizedec is interesting. But other things of a profounder nature were wrapt up in the transaction, which the pen of inspiration did not fail afterwards to notice (Ps. cx. 4 ; Heb. vii.), and which it is proper to glance at before we pass on to another stage of the patriarch's history. The extraordinary circumstance of such a person as a priest of the Most High God, whom even Abraham acknowledged to be such, starting up all at once in the devoted land of Canaan, and vanishing out of sight almost as soon as he appeared, has given rise, from the earliest times, to numberless conjectures. Ham, Shem, Noah, Enoch, an angel, Christ, the Holy Spirit, have each, in the hands of different persons, been identified with this Melchizedec; but the view now almost universally acquiesced in is, that he was simply a Canaanite sovereign, who combined with his royal dignity as king of Salem[1] the office of a true priest of God. No other supposition, indeed, affords a satisfactory explanation of the narrative. The very silence observed regarding his origin, and the manner of his appointment to the priesthood, was intentional, and served to draw more particular attention to the facts of the case, as also to admit of a closer correspondence with the ultimate realities. The more remarkable peculiarity was, that to this person, simply because he was a righteous king and priest of the Most High God, Abraham, the elect of God, the possessor of the promises, paid tithes, and received from him a blessing—and did it, too, at the very time he stood so high in honour, and kept himself so carefully aloof from another king then present—the king of Sodom. He placed himself as conspicuously below the one personage as he raised himself above the other. Why should he have done so? Because Melchizedec already in a measure possessed what Abraham still only hoped for—he reigned where Abraham's seed were destined to reign, and exercised a priesthood which in future generations was to be committed to them. The union of the two in Melchizedec was in itself a great thing —greater than the separate offices of king and priest in the houses respectively of David and Aaron; but it was an expiring

---

[1] No stress is laid on the particular place of which he was king, excepting that in the epistle to the Hebrews, its meaning (Peace) is viewed as emphatic;—only, however, for the purpose of bringing out the idea, that this singular person was really what his name and the name of his place imported. He was in reality a righteous king, and a prince of peace. But there seems good reason to believe the Jewish tradition well-founded, that it is but the abbreviated name of Jerusalem. Hence the name Salem is also applied to it in Ps. lxxvi. 3. And the correctness of the opinion is confirmed by the mention of the king's dale, in Gen. xiv. 17, which from 2 Sam. xviii. 18 can scarcely be supposed to have been far from Jerusalem. The name also of Adonaizedec, synonymous with Melchizedec, as that of the king of Jerusalem in Joshua's time (Jos. x. 3), is a still farther confirmation.

greatness; it was like the last blossom on the old rod of Noah, which thenceforth became as a dry tree. In Abraham, on the other hand, was the germ of a new and higher order of things; the promise, though still only the budding promise, of a better inheritance of blessing; and when the seed should come, in whom the promise was more especially to stand, then the more general and comprehensive aspect of the Melchizedec order was to reappear—and reappear in one who could at once place it on firmer ground, and carry it to unspeakably higher results. Here, then, was a sacred enigma for the heart of faith to ponder, and for the spirit of truth gradually to unfold: Abraham, in one respect, relatively great, and in another relatively little; personally inferior to Melchizedec, and yet the root of a seed that was to do for the world incomparably more than Melchizedec had done; himself the type of a higher than Melchizedec, and yet Melchizedec a more peculiar type than he! It was a mystery that could be disclosed only in partial glimpses beforehand, but which now has become comparatively plain by the person and work of Immanuel. What but the wonder-working finger of God could have so admirably fitted the past to be such a singular image of the future!

There are points connected with this subject that will naturally fall to be noticed at a later period, when we come to treat of the Aaronic priesthood, and other points also, though of a minor kind, belonging to this earlier portion of Abraham's history, which we cannot particularly notice. We proceed to the second stage in the developement of his spiritual life.

2. This consisted in the establishment of the covenant between him and God; which falls, however, into two parts—one earlier in point of time, and in its own nature incomplete; the other, both the later and the more perfect form.

It would seem, as if after the stirring transactions connected with the victory over Chedorlaomer and his associates, and the interview with Melchizedec, the spirit of Abraham had sunk into depression and fear; for the next notice we have respecting him represents God as appearing to him in vision, and bidding him not to be afraid, since God himself was his shield and his exceeding great reward. It is not improbable that some apprehension of a revenge on the part of Chedorlaomer might haunt his bosom, and that he might begin to dread the result of such an unequal contest as he had entered on with the powers of the world. But it is clear also, from the sequel, that another thing preyed upon his spirits, and that he was filled with concern on account of the long delay that was allowed to intervene before the appearance of the promised seed. He still went about childless; and the thought could not but press upon his mind, of what use were other things to him, even of the most honourable kind, if the great thing, on which all his hopes for the future turned, were still withheld? The Lord graciously met this natural misgiving by the assurance, that, not any son by adoption merely, but one from his own loins, should be given him for an heir. And to make the matter more palpable to his mind, and take external nature, as it were, to witness, for the fulfilment of the word, the Lord brought him forth, and, pointing to the stars of heaven, declared to him, "So shall thy seed be." "And he believed in the Lord," it is said, "and he counted it to him for righteousness."

This historical statement regarding Abraham's faith is remarkable, as it is the one so strenuously urged by the apostle Paul in his argument for justification by faith alone in the righteousness of Christ (Rom. iv. 18-22). And the question has been keenly debated, whether it was the faith itself which was in God's account taken for righteousness, or the righteousness of God in Christ, which that faith prospectively laid hold of. Our wisdom here, however, and in all similar cases, is not to press the statements of Old Testament Scripture so as to render them explicit categorical deliverances on Christian doctrine—in which case violence must inevitably be done to them—but rather to catch the general principle embodied in them, and give it a fair application to the more distinct revelations of the Gospel. This is precisely what is done by St Paul. He does not say a word about the specific manifestation of the righteousness of God in Christ, when arguing from the statement respecting the righteousness of faith in Abraham. He lays stress simply upon the natural impossibilities that stood in the way of God's promise of a numerous offspring to Abraham being fulfilled—the comparative deadness both of his own body and of Sarah's—and on the implicit confidence Abraham had, notwithstanding, in the power and faithfulness of

God, that he would perform what he had promised. "Therefore," adds the apostle, "it was imputed to him for righteousness." *Therefore*—namely, because through faith he so completely lost sight of nature and self, and realised with undoubting confidence the sufficiency of the divine arm, and the certainty of its working. His faith was nothing more, nothing else than the renunciation of all virtue and strength in himself, and a hanging in childlike trust upon God for what he was able and willing to do. Not, therefore, a mere substitute for a righteousness that was wanting, an acceptance of something that could be had for something better that failed, but rather the vital principle of a righteousness in God—the beating of a soul in unison with the mind of God, and finding its life, its hope, its all in him. Transfer such a faith to the field of the New Testament—bring it into contact with the manifestation of God in the person and work of Christ for the salvation of the world, and what would or could be its language but that of the apostle, "God forbid that I should glory save in the cross of the Lord Jesus Christ,"—"not my own righteousness, which is of the law, but that which is of God through faith!"

To return to Abraham—when he had attained to such confiding faith in the divine word respecting the promised seed, the Lord gave him an equally distinct assurance respecting the promised land; and in answer to Abraham's question, "Lord God, whereby shall I know that I shall inherit it," the Lord "made a covenant with him" respecting it, by means of a symbolical sacrificial action. It was a covenant by sacrifice; for in the very act of establishing the union, there must be a reference to the guilt of man, and a provision for purging it away. The very materials of the sacrifice have here a specific meaning; the greater sacrifices, those of the heifer, the goat, and the ram, being expressly fixed to be of three years old—pointing to the three generations which Abraham's posterity were to pass in Egypt; and these, together with the turtle-dove and the young pigeon, comprising a full representation of the animals afterwards offered in sacrifice under the law. As the materials, so also the form of the sacrifice was symbolical—the animals being divided asunder, and one piece laid over against another; for the purpose of more distinctly representing the two parties in the transaction—two, and yet one—meeting and acting together in one solemn offering. Recognising

THE SUBJECTS AND CHANNELS OF BLESSING. 317

Jehovah as the chief party in what was taking place, Abraham waits for the divine manifestation, and contents himself with meanwhile driving away the ill-omened birds of prey that flocked around the sacrifice. At last, when the shades of night had fallen, "a smoking furnace and a burning lamp passed between those pieces"—the glory of the Lord himself, as so often afterwards, in a pillar of cloud and fire. Passing under this emblem through the divided sacrifice, he formally accepted it, and struck the covenant with his servant (Jer. xxxiv. 18-19). At the same time also, a profound sleep had fallen upon Abraham, and a horror of great darkness—symbolical of the outward humiliations and sufferings through which the covenant was to reach its accomplishment; and in explanation the announcement was expressly made to him, that his posterity should be in bondage and affliction four hundred years in a foreign land, and should then, in the fourth generation, be brought up to it with great substance.[1] In justification also of the long delay, the specific reason was given, that "the iniquity of the Amorites was not yet full,"—plainly importing, that this part of the divine procedure had a moral aim, and could only be carried into effect in accordance with the great principles of the divine righteousness.

The covenant was thus established in both its branches, yet only in an imperfect manner, if respect were had to the coming future, and even to the full bearing and import of the covenant itself. Abraham had got a present sign of God's formally entering into covenant with him for the possession of the land of Canaan; but it came and went like a troubled vision of the

[1] The notes of time here given for the period of the sojourn in Egypt are somewhat indefinite. The 400 years is plainly mentioned as a round sum; it was afterwards more precisely and historically defined as 430 (Ex. xii. 40-41). From the juxtaposition of the 400 years and the fourth generation in the words to Abraham, the one must be understood as nearly equivalent to the other, and the period must consequently be regarded as that of the actual residence of the children of Israel in Egypt, from the descent of Jacob—not, as many after the Septuagint, from the time of Abraham. For the shortest genealogies exhibit four generations between that period and the exodus. Looking at the genealogical table of Levi (Ex. vi. 16, sq.), 120 years might not unfairly be taken as an average lifetime or generation; so that three of these complete, and a part of a fourth, would easily make 430. In Gal. iii. 17, the law is spoken of as only 430 years after the covenant with Abraham; but the apostle merely refers to the known historical period, and regards the first formation of the covenant with Abraham as all one with its final ratification with Jacob.

night. There was needed something of a more tangible and permanent kind, an abiding, sacramental covenant-signature, which by its formal institution on God's part, and its regular observance on the part of Abraham and his seed, might serve as a mutual sign of covenant-engagements. This was the more necessary, as the next step in Abraham's procedure but too clearly manifested, that he still wanted light regarding the nature of the covenant, and in particular regarding the supernatural, the essentially divine character of its provisions. From the prolonged barrenness of Sarah, and her now advanced age, it began to be imagined, that Sarah possibly might not be included in the promise, the rather so as no express mention had been made of her in the previous intimations of the divine purpose; and so despairing of having herself any share in the fulfilment of the promised word, she suggested, and Abraham fell in with the suggestion, that the fulfilment should be sought by the substitution of her bondmaid Hagar. This was again resorting to an expedient of the flesh to get over a present difficulty, and it was soon followed by its meet retribution in providence—domestic troubles and vexations. The bondmaid had been raised out of her proper place, and began to treat Sarah, the legitimate spouse of Abraham, with contempt. And had she even repressed her improper feelings, and brought forth a child in the midst of domestic peace and harmony, yet a son so born—after the ordinary course of nature, and in compliance with one of her corrupter usages—could not have been allowed to stand as the representative of that seed, through which blessing was to come to the world.

On both accounts, therefore—first, to give more explicit information regarding the son to be born, and then to provide a significant and lasting signature of the covenant, another and more perfect ratification of it took place. The word, which introduced this new scene, expressed the substance and design of the whole transaction: "I am God Almighty, walk before me, and be thou perfect" (Gen. xvii. 1):—On my part there is power amply sufficient to accomplish what I have promised, whatever natural difficulties may stand in the way—the whole shall assuredly be done; only see, that on your part there be a habitual recognition of my presence, and a steadfast adherence to the path of rectitude and purity. What follows is simply a filling up of this general outline—a more particular announcement of what God on his part should do, and then of what Abraham and his posterity were to do on the other. "As for me," (literally, I—*i. e.* on my part,) "behold, my covenant is with thee, and thou shalt be a father of many nations. Neither shall thy name any more be called Abram, but thy name shall be Abraham; for a father of many nations have I made thee. And I will make thee exceeding fruitful, and I will make nations of thee, and kings shall come out of thee. And I will establish my covenant between me and thee, and thy seed after thee, in their generations for an everlasting covenant, to be a God unto thee, and to thy seed after thee. And I will give unto thee, and to thy seed after thee, the land wherein thou art a stranger, all the land of Canaan, for an everlasting possession; and I will be their God." This was God's part in the covenant, to which he immediately subjoined, by way of explanation, that the seed more especially meant in the promise was to be of Sarah, as well as Abraham; that she was to renew her youth, and have a son, and that her name also was to be changed in accordance with her new position. Then follows what was expected and required on the other side: "And God said unto Abraham, And thou," (this now is thy part) "my covenant shalt thou keep, thou and thy seed after thee: Every male among you shall be circumcised; and ye shall circumcise the flesh of your foreskin; and it shall be for a covenant-sign betwixt me and you. And he that is eight days old shall be circumcised to you, every male in your generations; he that is born in the house, or bought with money of any stranger that is not of thy seed. . . . And my covenant shall be in your flesh for an everlasting covenant. And uncircumcision" (*i. e.* pollution, abomination,) "is the male who is not circumcised in the flesh of his foreskin; and cut off is that soul from his people; he has broken my covenant."

There is no need for going into the question, whether this ordinance of circumcision was now for the first time introduced among men; or whether it already existed as a practice to some extent, and was simply adopted by God as a fit and significant token of his covenant. It is comparatively of little moment how such a question may be decided. The same principle *may* have been acted on here, which undoubtedly had a place in the modelling of the Mosaic institutions, and which shall be discussed and vindicated, when we come to consider the influence exercised by the learning of Moses on his subsequent legislation—the principle, namely, of taking from the province of religion generally a symbolical sign or action, that was capable, when associated with the true religion, of fitly expressing its higher truths and principles. The probability is, that this principle was recognised and acted on here. Circumcision has been practised among classes of people and nations, who cannot reasonably be supposed to have derived it from the family of Abraham—among the ancients, for example, by the Egyptian priesthood, and among the moderns by native tribes in America and the islands of the Pacific. Its extensive prevalence and long continuance can only be accounted for on the ground, that it has a foundation in the feelings of the natural conscience, which, like the distinctions into clean and unclean, or the payment of tithes, may have led to its employment before the time of Abraham, and also fitted it afterwards for serving as the peculiar sign of God's covenant with him. At the same time, as it was henceforth intended to be a distinctive badge of covenant-relationship, it could not have been *generally* practised in the region where the chosen family were called to live and act. From the purpose to which it was applied, we may certainly infer, that it formed at once an appropriate and an easily-recognised distinction between the race of Abraham and the families and nations by whom they were more immediately surrounded.

Among the race of Abraham, however, it had the widest application given to it. While God so far identified it with his covenant, as to suspend men's interest in the one upon their observance of the other, it was with his covenant in its wider aspect and bearing—not simply as securing, either an offspring after the flesh, or the inheritance for that offspring of the land of Canaan. It was comparatively but a limited portion of Abraham's actual offspring, who were destined to grow into a separate nation, and occupy as their home the territory of Canaan. At the very outset Ishmael was excluded, though constituted the head of a great nation. And yet not only he, but all the members of Abraham's household, were alike ordered to receive the covenant-signature. Nay, even in later times, when the children of Israel had grown into a distinct people, and everything was placed under the strict administration of law, it was always left open to people of other lands and tribes to enter into the bonds of the covenant through the rite of circumcision. This rite, therefore, must have had a significance for them, as well as for the more favoured seed of Jacob. It spoke also to *their* hearts and consciences, and virtually declared that the covenant, which it symbolized, had nothing in its main design of an exclusive and contracted spirit; that its greater things lay open to all who were willing to seek them in the appointed way; and that if at first there were individual persons, and afterwards a single people, who were more especially identified with the covenant, it was only to mark them out as the chosen representatives of its nature and objects, and to constitute them lights for the instruction and benefit of others. There never was a more evident misreading of the palpable facts of history, than in the disposition so often manifested to limit the rite of circumcision to one line merely of Abraham's posterity, and to regard it as the mere outward badge of an external national distinction.

It is to be held, then, as certain in regard to the sign of the covenant, as in regard to the covenant itself, that its more special and marked connection with individuals was only for the sake of more effectually helping forward its general objects. And not less firmly is it to be held, that the outwardness in the rite was for the sake of the inward and spiritual truths it symbolized. It was appointed as the distinctive badge of the covenant, because it was peculiarly fitted for symbolically expressing the spiritual character and design of the covenant. It marked the condition of every one who received it, as having to do both with higher powers and higher objects than those of corrupt nature, as the condition of one brought into blessed fellowship with God, and therefore called to walk before him and be perfect. There would be no difficulty in perceiving this, nor any material difference of opinion upon the subject, if people would but look beneath the surface, and in the true spirit of the ancient religion, would contemplate the outward as an image of the inward. The general purport of the covenant was, that from Abraham as an individual there was to be generated a seed of blessing, in which all real blessing was to centre, and from which it was to flow to the ends of the earth. There could not, therefore, be a more appropriate sign of the covenant, than such a rite as circumcision—so directly connected with the generation of offspring, and so distinctly marking the necessary purification of nature—the removal of the filth of the flesh—that the offspring might be such as really to constitute a seed of blessing. It is through ordinary generation that the corruption incident on the fall is propagated; and hence, under the law, which contained a regular system of symbolical teaching, there were so many occasions of defilement traced to this source, and so many means of purification appointed for them. Now, therefore, when God was establishing a covenant, the great object of which was, to reverse the propagation of evil, to secure for the world a blessed and a blessed-making seed, he affixed to it this symbolical rite—to shew, that the end was to be reached, not as the result of nature's ordinary productiveness, but of nature purged from its uncleanness—nature raised above itself, in league with the grace of God, and bearing on it the distinctive impress of his character and working. It said to the circumcised man, that he had Jehovah for his bridegroom, to whom he had become espoused, as it were, by blood (Ex. iv. 25), and that he must no longer follow the unregulated will and impulse of nature, but live in accordance with the high relation he occupied, and the sacred calling he had received.[1]

Most truly, therefore, does the apostle say, that Abraham received circumcision, as a seal of the righteousness of the faith which he had (Rom. iv. 11)—a divine token in his own case that he had attained through faith to such fellowship with God, and righteousness in him—and a token for every child that should afterwards receive it, not indeed that he actually possessed the same, but that he was called to possess it, and had a right to the privileges and hopes, which might enable him to attain to the possession. Most truly also does the apostle say in another place (Rom. ii. 28, 29)

---

[1] It may also be noted, that by this quite natural and fundamental view of the ordinance, subordinate peculiarities admit of an easy explanation. For example, the limitation of the sign to males—which in the circumstances could not be otherwise; though the special purifications under the law for women might justly be regarded as providing for them a sort of counterpart. Then, the fixing on the eighth day as the proper one for the rite—that being the first day after the revolution of an entire week of separation from the mother, and when fully withdrawn from connection with the parent's blood, it began to live and breathe in its own impurity.

"He is not a Jew which is one outwardly (*i. e.* not a Jew in the right sense, not such an one as God would recognise and own), neither is that circumcision which is outward in the flesh ; but he is a Jew, which is one inwardly, and circumcision is that of the heart, in the spirit, and not in the letter ; whose praise is not of men, but of God." The very design of the covenant was to secure a seed with these inward and spiritual characteristics, and the sign of the covenant, the outward impression in the flesh, was worthless, a mere external concision—as the apostle calls it, when it came to be alone, Phil. iii. 2—excepting in so far as it was the expression of the corresponding reality. Isaac, the first child of promise, was the fitting type of such a covenant. In the very manner and time of his production he was a sign to all coming ages of what the covenant required and sought ;—not begotten till Abraham himself bore the symbol of nature's purification, nor born till it was evident the powers of nature must have been miraculously vivified for the purpose ; so that in his very being and birth Isaac was emphatically a child of God. But in being so he was the exact type of what the covenant properly aimed at, and what its expressive symbol betokened, viz. a spiritual seed, in which the divine and human, grace and nature, should meet together in producing true subjects and channels of blessing. But its actual representation—the one complete and perfect embodiment of all it symbolized and sought—was the Lord Jesus Christ, in whom the divine and human met from the first, not in co-operative merely, but in organic union, and consequently the result produced was a Being free from all taint of corruption, holy, harmless, undefiled, the express image of the Father, the very righteousness of God. He alone fully realized the conditions of blessing exhibited in the covenant, and was qualified to be in the largest sense the seed-corn of a harvest of blessing for the whole field of humanity.

It is true—and those who take their notions of realities from appearances alone, will doubtless reckon it a sufficient reply to what has been said—that the portion of Abraham's seed, who afterwards became distinctively the covenant people—Israel after the flesh—were by no means such subjects and channels of blessing as we have described, but were to a large extent carnal, having only that circumcision which is outward in the flesh. What then? Had they still a title to be recognised as the children of the covenant, and a right, as such, to the temporal inheritance connected with it? By no means. This were substantially to make void God's ordinance, which could not, any more than his other ordinances, be *merely* outward. It arises from his essential nature, as the spiritual and holy God, that he should ever require from his people what is accordant with his own character, and that when he appoints outward signs and ordinances, it is only with a view to spiritual and moral ends. Where the outward alone exists, he cannot own its validity. Christ certainly did not. For, when arguing with Jews of his own day, he denied on this very ground that their circumcision made them the children of Abraham; they were not of his spirit, and did not perform his works; and so, in Christ's account, their natural connection both with Abraham and with the covenant went for nothing (John viii. 34–44.) Their circumcision was a sign without any signification. And if so, then it must equally have been so in former times. The children of Israel had no right to the benefits of the covenant merely because they had been outwardly circumcised; nor were any promises made to them simply as the natural seed of Abraham. Both elements had to meet in their condition, the natural and the spiritual; the spiritual, however, more especially, and the natural only as connected with the spiritual, and a means for securing it. Hence Moses urged them so earnestly to circumcise their *hearts*, as absolutely necessary to their getting the fulfilment of what was promised (Deut. x. 16); and when the people as a whole had manifestly not done this, circumcision itself, the sign of the covenant, was suspended for a season, and the promises of the covenant were held in abeyance, till they should come to learn aright the real nature of their calling (Josh. v. 3–9.) Throughout, it was the election, within the election, who really had the promises and the covenants; and none but those in whom, through the special working of God's grace, nature was sanctified and raised to another position than itself could ever have attained, were entitled to the blessing. If in the land of Canaan, they existed by sufferance merely, and not by right.

The bearing of all this on the ordinance of Christian baptism cannot be overlooked, but it may still be mistaken. The relation between circumcision and baptism is not properly that of type and antitype; the one is a symbolical ordinance as well as the other, and both alike have an outward form and an inward reality. It is precisely in such ordinances that the Old and the New dispensations approach nearest to each other, and, we might almost say, stand formally upon the same level. The difference does not so much lie in the ordinances themselves, as in the comparative amount of grace and truth respectively exhibited in them—necessarily less in the earlier, and more in the later. The difference in external form was in each case conditioned by the circumstances of the time. In circumcision it bore respect to the propagation of offspring, as it was through the production of a seed of blessing that the covenant, in its preparatory form, was to attain its realisation. But when the seed in that respect had reached its culminating point in Christ, and the objects of the covenant were no longer dependent on natural propagation of seed, but were to be carried forward by spiritual means and influences used in connection with the faith of Christ, the external ordinance was fitly altered, so as to express simply a change of nature and state in the individual that received it. Undoubtedly the New Testament form less distinctly recognises the connection between parent and child—we should rather say, does not of itself recognise that connection at all: so much ought to be frankly conceded to those who disapprove of the practice of infant baptism, and *will* be conceded by all whose object is to ascertain the truth rather than contend for an opinion.

On the other hand, however, if we look, not to the form, but to the substance, which ought here, as in other things, to be chiefly regarded, we perceive an essential agreement—such as is, indeed, marked by the Apostle, when, with reference to the spiritual import of baptism, he calls it "the circumcision of Christ" (Col. ii. 11.) So far from being less indicative of a change of nature in the proper subjects of it, circumcision was even more so; in a more obvious and palpable manner it bespoke the necessity of a deliverance from the native corruption of the soul in those who should become the true possessors of blessing. Hence the Apostle makes use of the earlier rite to explain the symbolical import of the later, and describes the spiritual change indicated and required by it, as "a putting off the body of the sins of the flesh by the circumcision of Christ," and "having the uncircumcision of the flesh quickened together with Christ." It would have been travelling entirely in the wrong direction, to use such language for purposes of explanation in Christian times—if the ordinance of circumcision had not shadowed forth this spiritual quickening and purification even more palpably and impressively than baptism itself—and shadowed it forth, not prospectively merely for future times, but immediately and personally for the members of the old covenant. For, by the terms of the covenant, these were ordained to be, not *types* of blessing only, but also *partakers* of blessing. The good contemplated in the covenant was to have its present commencement in their experience, as well as in the future a deeper foundation and a more enlarged developement. And the outward putting away of the filth of the flesh in circumcision could never have symbolized a corresponding inward purification for the members of the new covenant, if it had not first done this for the members of the old. The shadow must have a substance in the one case as well as in the other.

Such being the case as to the essential agreement between the two ordinances, an important element for deciding in regard to the propriety of infant baptism, may still be derived from the practice established in the rite of circumcision. The grand principle of connecting parent and child together for the attainment of spiritual objects, and marking the connection by an impressive signature, was there most distinctly and broadly sanctioned. And if the parental bond and its attendant obligations be not weakened, but rather elevated and strengthened, by the higher revelations of the Gospel, it would be strange indeed if the liberty, at least the propriety and right, if not the actual obligation, to have their children brought by an initiatory ordinance under the bond of the covenant, did not belong to parents under the Gospel. The one ordinance no more than the other insures the actual transmission of the grace necessary to effect the requisite change; but it exhibits that grace—on the part of God pledges it—and takes the subject of the ordinance bound to use it for the accomplishment of the proper end. Baptism does this now, as circumcision did of old; and if it was done in the one case through the medium of the parent to the child, one does not see why it may not be done now, unless positively prohibited, in the other. But since this is matter of inference ratherthan of positive enactment, those who do not feel warranted to make such an application of the principle of the Old Testament ordinance to the New, should unquestionably be allowed their liberty of thought and action—if only, in the vindication of that liberty, they do not seek to degrade circumcision to a mere outward and political distinction, and thereby break the continuity of the church through successive dispensations.[1]

---

[1] It is not necessary to do more than notice the statements of Coleridge regarding circumcision (Aids to Reflection, I. p. 296), in which, as in some others on purely theological subjects in his writings, one is even more struck with the unaccountable ignoring of fact displayed in the deliverance given, than with the tone of assurance in which it is announced. "Circumcision was no sacrament at all, but the means and mark of national distinction. . . . Nor was it ever pretended that any grace was conferred with it, or that the rite was significant of any inward or spiritual operation." Delitzsch, however, so far coincides with this view, as to deny (Genesis Ausgelegt, p. 281) the sacramental character of circumcision. But he does so on grounds that, in regard to circumcision, will not stand examination; and, in regard to baptism, evidently proceed on the high Lutheran view of the sacraments. He says, that while circumcision had a moral and mystical meaning, and was intended ever to remind the subject of it of his near relation to Jehovah, and his obligation to walk worthy of this, still it was "no vehicle of heavenly grace, of divine sanctifying power," "in itself a mere sign without substance,"—as if it were ever designed to be *by itself!* or, as if baptism with water by itself were anything more than a mere sign! Circumcision being stamped upon Abraham and his seed as the sign of the covenant, and so far identified with the covenant, in the appointment of God, must have been a sign on God's part as well as theirs—it could not otherwise have been the sign of a covenant, or mutual compact; it must, therefore, have borne respect to what God promised to be to his people, not less than what his people were to be to him. This is manifestly what the apostle means, when he calls it a seal which Abraham received—a pledge from God of the ratification of the covenant, and consequently of all the grace that covenant promised. It had otherwise been no privilege to be circumcised; since to be bound to do righteously, without being entitled to look for grace corresponding, is simply to be placed under an intolerable yoke.—We regret to find Mr Litton, in his recent, and, as a whole, admirable work on the Church of Christ, espousing the same view regarding circumcision, and disavowing any proper connection between it and baptism. He thinks "the parallel holds good only in the accidental, and fails in the essential properties of the ordinances. Baptism is a means of grace, circumcision was not; baptism is the rite of admission to the privileges connected with incorporation in Christ, circumcision was not to the Jewish infant an analogous ordinance" (p. 704). He means, that circumcision was not to the Jew, as baptism is to the Christian, a properly initiatory ordinance, and that it was rather for securing his continuance in the possession of the blessings of the covenant, than the rite of admission to them. And distinguishing between the two ordinances in this respect, he says: "Whatever part we assign to the Word in the work of regeneration, no one would maintain that a believer is, by virtue of his faith merely, in Christ" (p. 704). Why, no one has said this more expressly than Mr Litton himself. At p. 226 he says,

3. But we must now hasten to the third stage of Abraham's career, which presents him on a still higher moral elevation than he has yet reached, and view him as connected with the sacrifice of Isaac. Between the establishment of the covenant by the rite of circumcision, and this last stage of developement, there were not wanting occasions fitted to bring out the pre-eminently holy character of his calling, and the dependence on his maintaining this toward God of what God should be and do toward him. This appears in the order he received from God to cast Ishmael out of his house, when the envious, mocking spirit of the youth too clearly shewed, that he had not the heart of a true child of the covenant, and would not submit aright to the arrangements of God concerning it. It appears also, in the free and familiar fellowship to which Abraham was admitted with the three heavenly visitants, whom he entertained in his tent on the plains of Mamre, and the disclosure that was made to him of the divine counsel respecting Sodom and Gomorrah, expressly on the ground that the Lord " knew he would command his children and his household after him to keep the way of the Lord, to do justice and judgment." And most of all it appears in the pleading of Abraham for the preservation of the cities of the plain—a pleading based upon the principles of righteousness, that the Judge of all the earth would do right, and would not destroy the righteous with

---

" If the recorded cases of Scripture are to decide the point, the first occasion of spiritual life to the soul does not come from visible union with the church. The church cannot, in the first instance, introduce him to Christ, who has already come to Christ; for he that believes upon Christ, has come to Christ." It might, therefore, on Mr Litton's own views, be affirmed as well regarding baptism, as regarding circumcision, that it is for confirmation, rather than for initiation, in the gifts and privileges of grace. In truth, it is not in respect to the soul's inward and personal state, that either ordinance can properly be called initiatory (for in that respect blessing might be had initially without the one as well as the other), but in respect to the person's recognised connection with the corporate society of those who are subjects of blessing. This begins now with baptism, and it began of old with circumcision; till the individual was circumcised he was not reckoned as belonging to that society, and if passing the proper time for the ordinance without it, he was to be held as *ipso facto* cut off. Under both covenants there is an inward and an outward bond of connection with the peculiar blessing—the inward, faith in God's word of promise (of old, faith in God, now more specifically, faith in Christ); the outward, circumcision formerly, now baptism. Yet the two in neither case should be viewed as altogether apart, but the one should rather be held as the formal expression and seal of the other.

the wicked—and a pleading that proved in vain only from there not being found the ten righteous persons in the place mentioned in the patriarch's last supposition. So that the awful scene of desolation which the region of those cities afterwards presented on the very borders of the land of Canaan, stood perpetually before the Jewish people, not only as a monument of the divine indignation against sin, but also as a witness that the father of their nation would have sought their preservation from a like judgment only on the principles of righteousness, and would have even ceased to plead in their behalf, if righteousness should sink as low among them as he ultimately supposed it might have come in Sodom.

But the topstone of Abraham's history as the spiritual head of a seed of blessing, is only reached in the divine command to offer up Isaac, and the obedience which the patriarch rendered to it. "Take now thy son, thine only son Isaac, whom thou lovest, and get thee into the land of Moriah; and offer him there for a burnt-offering upon one of the mountains, which I will tell thee of." That Abraham understood this command rightly, when he supposed it to mean a literal offering of his son upon the altar, and not as Hengstenberg and Langé have contended, a simple dedication to a religious life, needs no particular proof. Had anything but a literal surrender been meant, the mention of a burnt-offering as the character in which Isaac was to be offered to God, and of a mountain in Moriah as the particular spot where the offering was to be presented, would have been entirely out of place. But why should such a demand have been made of Abraham? And what precisely were the lessons it was intended to convey to his posterity, or its typical bearing on future times?

In the form given to the required act, special emphasis is laid on the endeared nature of the object demanded: thine *only* son, and the son whom thou *lovest*. It was, therefore, a trial in the strongest sense, a trial of Abraham's faith, whether it was capable of such implicit confidence in God—such profound regard to his will, and such self-denial in his service, as at the divine bidding to give up the best and dearest—what in the circumstances must even have been dearer to him than his own life. Not that God really intended the surrender of Isaac to death, but only the proof of such a surrender in the heart of his servant; and such a proof could only have been found in an unconditional command to sacrifice, and an unresisting compliance with the command up to the final step in the process. This, however, was not all. In the command to perform such a sacrifice, there was a *tempting* as well as a *trying* of Abraham; since the thing required at his hands seemed to be an enacting of the most revolting rite of heathenism; and, at the same time, to war with the oracle already given concerning Isaac, "In Isaac shall thy seed be called." According to this word, God's purpose to bless was destined to have its accomplishment especially and peculiarly through Isaac; so that to slay such a son appeared like slaying the very word of God, and extinguishing the hope of the world. And yet, in heart and purpose at least, it must be done. It was no freak of arbitrary power to command the sacrifice, nor for the purpose merely of raising the patriarch to a kind of romantic moral elevation. It was for the purpose of exhibiting outwardly and palpably the great truth, that God's method of working in the covenant of grace must have its counterpart in man's. The one must be the reflex of the other. God in blessing Abraham triumphs over nature, and Abraham triumphs after the same manner in proportion as he is blessed. He receives a special gift from the grace of God, and he freely surrenders it again to Him who gave it. He is pre-eminently honoured by God's word of promise, and he is ready in turn to hazard all for its honour. And Isaac, the child of promise—the type in his outward history of all who should be proper subjects or channels of blessing—he also must concur in the act—on the altar must sanctify himself to God—as a sign to all who would possess the higher life in God, that it implies and carries along with it a devout surrender of the natural life to the service and glory of God.

We have no account of the workings of Abraham's mind, when going forth to the performance of this extraordinary act of devotedness to God; and the record of the transaction is, from the very simplicity with which it narrates the facts of the case, the most touching and impressive in Old Testament history. But we are informed on inspired authority, that the principle on which he acted, and which enabled him—as indeed it alone could enable him—to fulfil such a service, was faith: "By faith Abraham, when he was tried, offered up Isaac, and he that received the promises offered up his only begotten son; of whom it was said, That in Isaac shall thy seed be called; accounting that God was able to raise him up, even from the dead—from whence also he received him in a figure" (Heb. xi. 17-19). His noblest act of obedience was nothing more than the highest exercise and triumph of his faith. It was this which removed the mountains that stood before him, and hewed out a path for him to walk in. Grasping with firm hand that word of promise which assured him of a numerous seed by the line of Isaac, and taught by past experience to trust its faithfulness even in the face of natural impossibilities, his faith enabled him to see light, where all had otherwise been darkness, to hope while in the very act of destroying the great object of his hope. I know—so he must have argued with himself—that the word of God, which commands this sacrifice, is faithfulness and truth; and though to stretch forth my hand against this child of promise is apparently destructive to my hopes, yet I may safely risk it, since He commands it who gave the promise. It is as easy for the Almighty arm to give me back my son from the domain of death, as it was at first to bring him forth out of the dead womb of Sarah; and what He *can* do, His declared purpose makes me sure that he *will* and *must* do. Thus nature, even in its best and strongest feelings, was overcome, and the sublimest heights of holiness were reached, simply because faith had struck its roots so deeply within, and had so closely united the soul of the patriarch to the mind and perfections of Jehovah.

This high surrender of the human to the divine, and holy self-consecration to the will and service of God, was beyond all doubt, like the other things recorded in Abraham's life, of the nature of a revelation. It was not intended to terminate in the patriarch and his son, but in them as the sacred roots of the covenant-people, to shew in outward and corporeal representation, what in spirit ought to be perpetually repeating itself in their individual and collective history. It proclaimed to them through all their generations, that the covenant required of its members lives of unshrinking and devoted application to the service of God—yielding to no weak misgivings or corrupt solicitations of the flesh—staggering at no difficulties presented by the world; and also that it rendered such a course possible by the ground and scope it afforded for the exercise of faith in the sustaining grace and might of God. And undoubtedly, as the human here was the reflex of the divine, whence it drew its source and reason, so inversely, and as regards the ulterior objects of the covenant, the divine might justly be regarded as imaged in the human. An organic union between the two was indispensable to the effectual accomplishment of the promised good; and the seed, in which the blessing of Heaven was to concentrate, and from which it was to flow throughout the families of the earth, must on the one side be as really the Son of God, as on the other he was to be the offspring of Abraham. Since, therefore, the two lines were ultimately to meet in one, and that one, by the joint operation of the divine and human, was once for all to make good the provision of blessing promised in the covenant, it was meet, and it may reasonably be supposed, was one end of the transaction, that they should be seen from the first to coalesce in principle; that the surrender Abraham made of *his* son, for the world's good, in the line after the flesh, and the consecration willingly made by the son of himself on the altar of God, was designed to foreshadow in the other and higher line the wonderful gift of God in yielding up *his* Son, and the free-will offering and consecration of the Son himself to bring in eternal life for the lost. Here, too, as the things done were in their nature unspeakably higher than in the other, so were they thoroughly and intensely real in their character. The representative in the Old becomes the actual in the New; and the sacrifice performed there merely in the spirit, passes here into that one full and complete atonement, which for ever perfects them that are sanctified.[1]

---

[1] In my former edition I missed the typical connection between the Old and the New here exhibited; missed it, from looking too exclusively, on the one hand, to the merely formal resemblances usually pressed by typological writers, and on the other, to the ostensible differences. Presented as it is above, the typical relationship is both quite natural, and easy of apprehension, if only one keeps distinctly in view the necessary connection between the divine and the human for accomplishing the ends of the covenant—a connection influential and co-operative as regards the immediate ends—organic and personal, as regards the ultimate. That the action was, as Warburton represents, a scenical representation of the death and resurrection of Christ, appointed expressly to satisfy the mind of Abraham, who longed to see Christ's day, is to present it in a fanciful and arbitrary light; and what is actually recorded requires to be supplemented by much that is not. Nor do we need to lay any stress on the precise locality where the offering was appointed to be made. It must always remain somewhat doubtful whether the "land of Moriah"

In the preparatory and typical line, however, Abraham's conduct on this occasion was the perfect exemplar of what should follow; he stood now on the highest elevation of the righteousness of faith; and to shew the weight God attached to that righteousness, and how inseparably it was to be bound up with the provisions of the covenant, the Lord consummated the transaction by a new ratification of the covenant. After the angel of Jehovah had staid the hand of Abraham from slaying Isaac, and provided the ram for a burnt-offering, he again appeared and spake to Abraham, " By myself have I sworn, saith the Lord; for because thou hast done this thing, and hast not withheld thy son, thine only son, that in blessing I will bliss thee, and in multiplying I will multiply thy seed, as the stars of heaven, and as the sand which is upon the sea-shore; and thy seed shall possess the gate of thine enemies; and in thy seed shall the nations of the earth be blessed; because thou hast obeyed my voice." The things promised, it will be observed, are precisely the things which God had already of his own goodness engaged in covenant to bestow upon Abraham: these, indeed, to their largest extent, but still no more, no other than these—a seed numerous as the sand upon the sea-shore, or the stars of heaven, shielded from the malice of enemies, itself blessed, and destined to be the channel of blessing to all nations. But it is also to be observed, that while the same promises of good are renewed, they are now connected with Abraham's surrender to the will of God, and are given as the reward of his obedience. To render this more clear and express, it is announced both at the beginning and the end of the address: " Because thou hast done this...because thou hast obeyed my voice." And even afterwards, when the covenant was established with Isaac, an explicit reference is made to the same thing. The Lord said, he would perform the oath he had sworn to Abraham, " because he obeyed my voice, and kept my charge, my commandments, my statutes, and my laws" (Gen. xxvi. 5). What could have more impressively exhi-

was the same with "Mount Moriah," on which the temple was afterwards built, as the one, indeed, is evidently a more general designation than the other. And the minor circumstances, excepting in so far as they indicate the implicit obedience of the father, and the filial submission and devotedness of the son, should be considered as of no moment.

bited the truth, that though the covenant, with all its blessings, was of grace, on the part of God, and to be appropriated by faith on the part of men, yet the good promised should not be actually conferred by Him, unless there appeared in them the righteousness of faith! Their faith would otherwise be accounted dead, the mere semblance of what it should be. And as if to bind the two more solemnly and conspicuously together, the Lord takes this occasion to superadd his oath to the covenant—not to render the word of promise more sure in itself, but more palpably sure to the heirs of promise—and to imprint it upon their hearts, that nothing should fail of all that had been spoken, if only the future faith and obedience should accord with the present!

II. We must leave to the reflection of our readers the application of this to Christian times and relations, which is indeed so obvious as to need no particular explanation; and we proceed to take a rapid glance at the leading features of the other branch of the subject—that which concerns Jacob and the twelve patriarchs. This forms the continuation of what took place in the lives of Abraham and Isaac, and a continuation, not only embodying the same great principles, but also carrying them forward with more special adaptation to the prospective condition of the Israelites as a people. Towards the close of the patriarchal period, the covenant, even in its more specific line of operations, began to widen and expand, to rise more from the particular to the general, to embrace a family circle, and that circle the commencement of a future nation. And the dealings of God were all directed to the one great end of shewing, that while this people should stand alike outwardly related to the covenant, yet their real connection with its promises, and their actual possession of its blessings, should infallibly turn upon their being followers in faith and holiness of the first fathers of their race.

Unfortunately, the later part of Isaac's life did not altogether fulfil the promise of the earlier. Knowing little of the trials of faith, he did not reach high in its attainments. And in the more advanced stage of his history he fell into a state of general feebleness and decay, in which the moral but too closely corresponded with the bodily decline. Notwithstanding the very singular and marked exemplification that had been given in his own case of the pre-eminent respect had in the covenant to something higher than nature, he failed so much in discernment, that he was disposed only to make account of the natural element in judging of the respective states and fortunes of his sons. To the neglect of a divine oracle going before, and the neglect also of the plainest indications afforded by the subsequent behaviour of the sons themselves, he resolved to give the more distinctive blessing of the covenant to Esau, in preference to Jacob, and so to make him the more peculiar type and representative of the covenant. In this, however, he was thwarted by the overruling providence of God—not, indeed, without sin on the part of those who were the immediate agents in accomplishing it—but yet, so as to bring out more clearly and impressively the fact, that mere natural descent and priority of birth was not here the principal, but only the secondary thing, and that higher and more important than any natural advantage was the grace of God manifesting itself in the faith and holiness of men. Jacob, therefore, though the younges by birth—yet from the first the child of faith, of spiritual desire, of heart-felt longings after the things of God, ultimately the man of deep discernment, ripened experience, prophetic insight, wrestling and victorious energy in the divine life—*he* must stand first in the purpose of Heaven, and exhibit in his personal career a living representation of the covenant, as to what it properly is, and really requires. Nay, opportunity was taken from his case, as the immediate founder of the Israelitish nation, to begin the covenant history anew; and starting, as it were, from nothing in his natural position and circumstances, it was shewn how God, by his supernatural grace and sufficiency, could vanquish the difficulties in the way, and more than compensate for the loss of nature's advantages. In reference partly to this instructive portion of Jacob's history, and to deepen upon their minds the lesson it was designed to teach, the children of Israel were appointed to go to the priest in after times with their basket of first-fruits in their hand, and the confession in their mouth, A Syrian ready to perish was my father (Deut. xxvi. 5). It was clear, clear as noon-day, that all Jacob had to distinguish him outwardly from others, the sole foundation and spring of his greatness, was the promise of God in the covenant, received by him in humble faith, and taken as the ground of prayerful and holy striving. As the head of the covenant-people, he was not less really, though by a different mode of operation, the child of divine grace and power, than his father Isaac. And as his whole life, in its better aspects, was a lesson to his posterity respecting the superiority of the spiritual to the merely natural element in things pertaining to the covenant of God, so when his history drew toward its close, there were lessons of a more special kind, and in the same direction, pressed with singular force and emphasis upon his family.

It was a time when such were peculiarly needed. The covenant was now to assume more of a communal aspect. It was to have a national membership and representation, as the more immediate designs, which God sought to accomplish by means of it, could not be otherwise effected. Jacob was the last separate impersonation of its spirit and character. His family in their collective capacity were henceforth to take this position. But they had first to learn, that they could take it, only if their *natural* relation to the covenant was made the means of forming them to its *spiritual* characteristics, and fitting them for the fulfilment of its righteous ends. They must even learn, that their individual relation to the covenant in these respects, should determine their relative place in the administration of its affairs and interests. And for this end Reuben the first-born, is made to lose his natural pre-eminence, because, like Esau, he *presumed* upon his natural position, and in the lawless impetuosity of nature broke through the restraints of filial piety. Judah, on the other hand, obtains one of the prerogatives Reuben had lost—Judah who became so distinguished for that filial piety as to hazard his own life for the sake of his father. Simeon and Levi, in like manner, are all but excluded from the blessings of the covenant on account of their unrighteous and cruel behaviour:—a curse is solemnly pronounced upon their sin, and a mark of inferiority stamped upon their condition—while, again, at a later period, and for the purpose still of shewing how the spiritual was to rule the natural, rather than the natural the spiritual, the curse in the case of Levi was turned into a blessing. The tribe was, indeed, according to the word of Jacob, scattered in Israel, and was thereby rendered politically weak; but the more immediate reason of the scattering was the zeal and devotedness which the members of that tribe had exhibited in the wilderness, on account of which they were dispersed as lights among Israel, bearing on them the more peculiar and sacred distinctions of the covenant—and thus became morally strong. Most strikingly, however, does the truth break forth in connection with Joseph, who in the earlier history of the family was the *only* proper representative of the covenant. He was the one child of God in the family, though, with a single exception, the least and youngest of its members. God, therefore, after allowing the contrast between him and the rest to be sharply exhibited, ordered his providence so as to make him pre-eminently the son of blessing. The faith and piety of the youth draw around him the protection and loving-kindness of heaven wherever he goes, and throw a charm around everything he does. At length he rises to the highest position of honour and influence—blessed most remarkably himself, and on the largest scale made a blessing to others—the noblest and most conspicuous personal embodiment of the nature of the covenant, as first rooting itself in the principles of a spiritual life, and then diffusing itself in healthful and blessed energy on all around. At the same time, and as a foil to set off more brightly the better side of the truth represented in him, while he was thus seen riding upon the high places of the earth, his unsanctified brethren were famishing for want; the promised blessing of the covenant has almost dried up in their experience, because they possessed so little of the true character of children of the covenant. And when the needful relief comes, they have to be indebted for it to the hand of him in whom that character is most luminously displayed. Nay, in the very mode of getting it, they are conducted through a train of humiliating and soul-stirring providences, tending to force on them the conviction that they were in the hands of an angry God, and to bring them to repentance of sin and amendment of life. So that, by the time they are raised to a position of honour and comfort, and settled as covenant-patriarchs in Egypt, they present the appearance of men chastened, subdued, brought to the knowledge of God, fitted each to take his place as a head of the future covenant-people, while the double portion, which Reuben lost by his iniquity, descends on him, who was, under God, the instrument of accomplishing so much good for them and for others.

And here, again, we cannot but notice, that when the chosen

family were in the process of assuming the rudimentary form of that people, through whom salvation and blessing were to come to other peoples of the earth, the beginning was rendered prophetic of the end; the operations both of the evil and the good in the infancy of the nation, were made to image the prospective manifestation that was to be given of them when the things of the divine kingdom should rise to their destined maturity. Especially in the history of Joseph, the representative of the covenant in its earlier stage, was there given a wonderful similitude of him in whom its powers and blessings were to be concentrated in their entire fulness, and who was therefore in all things to obtain the pre-eminence among his brethren. Like Joseph, the Son of Mary, though born among brethren after the flesh, was treated as an alien; envied and persecuted even from his infancy, and obliged to find a temporary refuge in the very land that shielded Joseph from the fury of his kindred. His supernatural and unblemished righteousness continually provoked the malice of the world, and, at the same time, received the most unequivocal tokens of the divine favour and blessing. That very righteousness, exhibited amid the greatest trials and indignities, in the deepest debasement, and in worse than prison-house affliction, procured his elevation to the right hand of power and glory, from which he was thenceforth to dispense the means of salvation to the world. In the dispensation, too, of these blessings, it was the hardened and cruel enmity of his immediate kindred which opened the door of grace and blessing to the heathen; and the sold, hated, and crucified One becomes a Prince and Saviour to the nations of the earth, while his famishing brethren reap in bitterness of soul the fruit of their injurious treatment toward him. Nor is there a door of escape to be found for them until they come to acknowledge, in contrition of heart, that they are verily guilty concerning their brother; but then, looking unto him whom they have pierced, and owning him as by God's appointment the one channel of life and blessing, they shall be repaid with love for hatred, and shall be admitted to share in the inexhaustible fulness that belongs to him.

What a succession, then, of lessons for the children of the covenant in regard to what constituted their greatest danger—lessons stretching through four generations—ever varying in their precise form, yet always bearing most directly and impressively upon the same point—writing out on the very foundations of their history, and emblazoning on the banner of their covenant the important truth, that the spiritual element was ever to be held the thing of first and most essential moment, and that the natural was only to be regarded as the channel through which the other was chiefly to come, and the safeguard by which it was to be fenced and kept! From the first the call of God made itself known as no merely outward distinction; and the covenant that grew out of it, instead of being but a formal bond of interconnection between its members and God, was framed especially to meet the spiritual evil in the world, and required as an indispensable condition, a sanctified heart, in all who were to experience its blessings and to work out its beneficent results. How, indeed, could it be otherwise? How could the spiritual Jehovah, who has, from the first creation of man upon the earth, been ever manifesting himself as the Holy One, and directing his administration so as to promote the ends of righteousness, enter into a covenant of life and blessing on any other principle? It is impossible—as impossible as it is for the unchangeable God to act contrary to his nature, that the covenant of Abraham, Isaac, and Jacob—the covenant of grace and blessing, which embraces in its bosom Christ himself, and the benefits of his eternal redemption—could ever have contemplated as its real members any but spiritual and righteous persons. And the whole tenor and current of the divine dealings in establishing the covenant seem to have been alike designed and calculated to shut up every thoughtful mind to the conclusion, that none but such could either fulfil its higher purposes, or have an interest in its more essential provisions.

What thus appears to be taught in the historical revelations of God connected with the establishment of the covenant, is also perpetually re-echoed in the later communications of the prophets. Their great aim, in the monitory part of their writings, is to bring home to men's minds the conviction, that the covenant had pre-eminently in view moral ends, and that in so far as the people degenerated from these, they failed in respect to the main design of their calling. Let us point, in proof of this, merely to the last of the prophets, that we may see how the closing witness of the Old Covenant coincides with the testimony delivered at the beginning. In the second chapter of his writings, the prophet Malachi, addressing himself to the corruptions of the time, as appearing first in the priesthood, and then among the people generally, charges both parties expressly with a breach of covenant, and a subversion of the ends for which it was established. In regard to the priests, he points to their ancestral holiness in the personified tribe of Levi, and says, " My covenant was with him of life and peace; and I gave them to him for the fear wherewith he feared me, and was afraid before my name. The law of truth was in his mouth, and iniquity was not found in his lips: he walked with me in peace and equity, and did turn many away from iniquity.... But ye are departed out of the way; ye have caused many to stumble at the law; ye have corrupted the covenant of Levi, saith the Lord of Hosts. Therefore have I also made you contemptible and base before all the people, according as ye have not kept my ways, but have been partial in the law." In a word, the covenant in this particular branch of it, had been made expressly on moral grounds and for moral ends, and in practically losing sight of these, the priests of that time had made void the covenant, even though externally complying with its appointments, and were consequently visited with chastisement instead of blessing. Then, in regard to the people, a reproof is first of all administered on account of the unfaithfulness, which had become comparatively common, in putting away their Israelitish wives, and taking outlandish women in their stead, " the daughters of a strange God." This the prophet calls " profaning the covenant of their fathers." And then pointing in this case, as in the former, to the original design and purport of their covenant-calling, he asks, in a question which has been entirely misunderstood, from not being viewed in relation to the precise object of the prophet, " And did not He make one? Yet had he the residue of the Spirit. And wherefore one? That he might seek a godly seed. Therefore take heed to your spirit, and let none deal treacherously against the wife of his youth." The *one*, which God made, is not Adam, nor Abraham, to either of whom the commentators refer it, though the case of neither of them properly suits the point more immediately in question. The oneness referred to is that distinctive species of it, on which the whole section proceeds as its basis—Israel's oneness as a family. God had chosen them—them alone of all the nations of the earth—to be his peculiar treasure. If he had pleased, he might have chosen more; the residue of the Spirit was, with him, by no means exhausted by that single effort. He could have either left them like others, or chosen others besides them. But he did not; he made one—one alone, to be peculiarly his own, setting it apart from the rest; and wherefore that one? Simply that he might have a godly seed; that they might be an holy people, and transmit the true fear of God from generation to generation. How base, then, how utterly subversive of God's purposes concerning them, to act as if no such separation had taken place? to put away their proper wives, and by heathenish alliances bring into the bosom of their families the very defilement and corruption, against which God had especially called them to contend? Such was this prophet's understanding of the covenant made with the fathers of the Israelitish people; and no other view of it, we venture to say, would ever have prevailed, if its nature had been sought primarily in those fundamental records, which describe the procedure of God in bringing it originally into existence.

SECTION SIXTH.

THE INHERITANCE DESTINED FOR THE HEIRS OF BLESSING.

The covenant made with Abraham, Isaac, and Jacob, was connected not only with a seed of blessing, but also with an inheritance of blessing destined for their possession. And in order to get a correct view both of the immediate and of the ultimate bearing of this part of the covenant-promise, it is not less necessary than in the other case, to consider the specific object proposed in its relation to the entire scheme of God, and especially to bear in mind, that it forms part of a series of arrangements, in which the particular or the individual was selected with a view to the general, the universal. In respect to the good to be inherited, as well as in respect to the persons who might be called to inherit it, the end proposed on the part of God was from the first of the most comprehensive nature; and if for a time there was an immediate narrowing of the field of promise, it could only be for the sake of an ultimate expansion. To see more distinctly the truth of this, it may be proper to take a brief retrospect of the past.

From the outset, the earth, in its entire extent and compass, was given for the domain and the heritage of man. He was placed in paradise as his proper home. There he had the throne of his kingdom, but not that he might be pent up within that narrow region; rather that he might from that, as the seat of his empire, and the centre of his operations, go forth upon the world around, and bring it under his sway. His calling was to multiply and replenish the earth, and subdue it; so that it might become to its utmost bounds an extended and peopled paradise. But when the fall entered, though the calling was not withdrawn, nor the possession finally lost, yet man's relative position was changed. He had now, not to work from paradise as a rightful king and lord, but from the blighted outfield of nature's barrenness to work as a servant, in the hope of ultimately reaching a new and better paradise than he had lost. The first promise of grace, and the original symbols of worship, viewed in connection with the facts of history, out of which they grew, presented him with the prospect of an ultimate recovery from the evils of sin and death, and put him in the position of an expectant through faith in God, and toil and suffering in the flesh, of good things yet to come. The precise hope he cherished respecting these good things, or the inheritance he actually looked for, would at first naturally take shape in his imagination from what he had lost. He would fancy, that though he must bear the deserved doom for his transgression, and return again to dust, yet the time would come, when, according to the revealed mercy and loving-kindness of God, the triumph of the adversary would be reversed, the dust of death would be again quickened into life, and the paradise of delight be re-occupied anew, with better hopes of continuance, and with enlarged dimensions suited to its destined possessors. He could scarcely have expected more with the scanty materials which faith and hope yet had to build upon; and with the grace revealed to him, he could scarcely, if really standing in faith and hope, have expected less.

We deem it incredible, that with the grant of the earth so distinctly made to man for his possession, and death so expressly appointed as the penalty of his yielding to the tempter, he should, as a subject of restoring grace, have looked for any other domain as the result of the divine work in his behalf, than the earth itself, or for any other mode of entering on the recovered possession of it, than through a resurrection from the dead. For, how should he have dreamt of a victory over evil in any other region than that where the evil had prevailed? Or, how could the hope of restitution have formed itself in his bosom, excepting as a prospective re-instatement in the benefits he had forfeited? A paradise such as he had originally occupied—but prepared now for the occupation of redeemed multitudes—made to embrace, it may be, the entire territory of the globe—wrested for ever from the serpent's brood, and rendered through all its borders beautiful and good—that, and nothing else, we conceive, must have been what the first race of patriarchal believers hoped and waited for, as the objective portion of good reserved for them.

But in process of time the deluge came, changing to a considerable extent the outward appearance of the earth, and in certain respects also the government under which it was placed, and so preparing the way for a corresponding change in the hopes that were to be cherished of a coming inheritance. The old world then perished, leaving no remnant of its original paradise, any more than of the giant enormities which had caused it to groan, as in pain, to be delivered. But the new world, cleansed and purified by the judgment of God, was now, without limit or restriction, given to Noah, as the saved head of mankind, that he might keep it for God, replenish and subdue it,—might work it, if such a thing were possible, into the condition of a second paradise. It soon became too manifest, however, that this was not possible; and that the righteousness of faith, of which Noah was heir, was still not that which could prevail to banish sin and death, corruption and misery, from the world. Another and better foundation yet remained to be laid for such a blessed prospect to be realized. But the promise of this very earth was nevertheless given for man's inheritance, and with a promise securing it against any fresh destruction. The needed righteousness was somehow to be wrought upon it, and the region itself reclaimed so as to become a habitation of blessing. This was now the heritage of good set before mankind; to have this realized was the object which they were called of God to hope and strive for. And it was with this object before them, an object, however, to which the events immediately subsequent to the deluge did not seem to be bringing them nearer, but rather to be carrying them more remote, that the call to Abraham entered. This call, as we have already seen, was of the largest and most comprehensive nature as to the personal and subjective good it contemplated. It aimed at the bestowal of blessing—blessing, of course, in the divine sense, including the fullest triumph over sin and death, (for where these are, there can be but the beginnings or smaller drops of blessing;) and the bestowal of them on Abraham and his lineal offspring, first and most copiously, but only as the more effectual way of extending them to all the families of mankind. The grand object of the covenant made with him was to render the world truly blessed in its inhabitants, himself forming the immediate starting-point of the design, which was thereafter to grow and germinate, till the whole circle of humanity were embraced in its beneficent provisions. But in connection with this higher and grander object, there was singled out a portion of the earth for the occupation of his immediate descendants in a particular line—the more special line of blessing; and the conclusion is obvious, even before we go into an examination of particulars, that unless this select portion of the world were placed in utter disagreement with the higher ends of the covenant, it must have been but a stepping-stone to their accomplishment—a kind of first-fruits of the proper good—the occupation of a *part* of the promised inheritance by a *portion* of the heirs of blessing to image and prepare for the inheritance of the whole by the entire company of the blessed. The particular must here also have been for the sake of the general, the universal, the ultimate.

Proceeding, however, to a closer view of the subject, we notice, first, the region actually selected for a possession of an inheritance to the covenant-people. The land of Canaan occupied a place in the ancient world that entirely corresponded with the calling of such a people. It was of all lands the best adapted for a people who were at once to dwell in comparative isolation, and yet were to be in a position for acting with effect upon the other nations of the world. Hence it was said by Ezekiel, ch. v. 5, to have been "set in the midst of the countries and the nations"— the *umbilicus terrarum*. In its immediate vicinity lay both the most densely-peopled countries, and the greater and more influential states of antiquity—on the south, Egypt, and on the north and east, Assyria and Babylon, the Medes and the Persians. Still closer were the maritime states of Tyre and Sidon, whose vessels frequented every harbour then known to navigation, and whose colonies were planted in each of the three continents of the old world. And the great routes of inland commerce between the civilized nations of Asia and Africa, lay either through a portion of the territory itself, or within a short distance of its borders. Yet bounded as it was on the west by the Mediterranean, on the south by the desert, on the east by the valley of the Jordan, with its two seas of Tiberias and Sodom, and on the north by the towering heights of Lebanon, the people who inhabited it might justly be said to dwell alone, while they had on every side points of contact with the most influential and distant nations. Then, the land itself, in its rich soil and plentiful resources, its varieties of hill and dale, of river and mountain, its connection with the sea on one side, and with the desert on another, rendered it a kind of epitome of the natural world, and fitted it peculiarly for being the home of those who were to be a pattern-people to the nations of the earth. Altogether, it were impossible to conceive a region more wisely selected, and in itself more thoroughly adapted, for the purposes on account of which the family of Abraham were to be set apart. If they were faithful to their covenant engagements, they might there have exhibited, as on an elevated platform before the world, the bright exemplar of a people possessing the characteristics, and enjoying the advantages of a seed of blessing. And the finest opportunities were, at the same time, placed within their reach of proving in the highest sense benefactors to mankind, and extending far and wide the interests of truth and righteousness. Possessing the elements of the world's blessing, they were placed where these elements might tell most readily and powerfully on the world's inhabitants; and the present possession of such a region was at once an earnest of the whole inheritance, and, as the world then stood, an effectual step toward its realization. Abraham, as the heir of Canaan, was thus also "the heir of the world" as a heritage of blessing. (Rom. iv. 13.)[1]

But, next, let us mark the precise words of the promise to Abraham concerning this inheritance. As it first occurs, it runs, "Get thee out of thy country, and from thy kindred, and from

---

[1] We assume, that the land promised in the covenant to Abraham, and afterwards occupied by his posterity in the line of Isaac and Jacob, was simply what is known as the land of Canaan, lying between the Jordan and the Mediterranean sea, and between Lebanon and the wilderness below Kadesh. This is so clearly and definitely marked out in a multitude of historical passages, and the inhabitants of that precise region are so often named as those whom Israel dispossessed, that any considerations which would assign other limits, cannot possibly be well grounded. There are two or three prophetical passages which mention the Nile and the Euphrates as the two extremities of Israel's possession (Gen. xv. 18; xxiii. 31; Deut. i. 7). But, as in later prophecy, these rivers are merely used as representatives of the countries of Egypt and Assyria, and the meaning is, that in the region lying between, Israel alone should have the dominion—though still the portion to be actually possessed by them was of much narrower dimensions.

thy father's house, unto a land that I will shew thee, and I will make of thee a great nation," &c. Gen. xii. 1. Then, when he reached Canaan, the promise was renewed to him in these terms: "Unto thy seed will I give this land," v. 7. More fully and definitely, after Lot separated from Abraham, was it again given: "Lift up now thine eyes, and look from the place where thou art northward, and southward, and eastward, and westward: for all the land which thou seest, to thee will I give it, and to thy seed for ever," xiii. 14, 15. Again, in chap. xv. 7, "I am the Lord that brought thee out of Ur of the Chaldees, to give thee this land to inherit it ;" and toward the close of the same chapter, it is said, "In the same day the Lord made a covenant with Abram, saying, Unto thy seed have I given this land, from the river of Egypt unto the great river." In chap. 17th, the promise was formally ratified as a covenant, and sealed by the ordinance of circumcision; and there the words used respecting the inheritance are, "I will give unto thee, and to thy seed after thee, the land wherein thou art a stranger, all the land of Canaan for an everlasting possession, and I will be their God." We read only of one occasion in the life of Isaac, when he received the promise of the inheritance, and the words then used were, "Unto thee, and unto thy seed, will I give all these countries, and I will perform the oath which I sware unto Abraham thy father," chap. xxvi. 3. Such also were the words addressed to Jacob at Bethel, "I am the Lord God of Abraham thy father, and the God of Isaac, the land whereon thou liest, to thee will I give it, and to thy seed ;" and in precisely the same terms was the promise again made to Jacob many years afterwards, as recorded in chap. xxxv. 12.

It cannot but appear striking, that to each one of these patriarchs successively, the promise of the land of Canaan should have been given, first to themselves, and then to their posterity; while, during their own lifetimes, they never were permitted to get beyond the condition of strangers and pilgrims, having no right to any possession within its borders, and obliged to purchase, at the marketable value, a small field for a burying-ground. How shall we account for the promise, then, so uniformly running, "to thee," and to "thy seed?" Some, as Ainsworth and Bush, tell us that *and* here is the same as *even*, to thee, even to thy seed; as if a man were all one with his offspring, or the name of the latter were but another name for himself! Gill gives a somewhat more plausible turn to it, thus: "God gave Abram the title to it now, and to them the possession of it for future times; gave him it to sojourn in now where he pleased, and for his posterity to dwell in hereafter." But the gift was the land for an inheritance, not for a place of sojourn; and a title, which left him personally without a foot's-breadth of possession, could not be regarded in that light as any real boon to him. Warburton, as usual, confronts the difficulty more boldly: "In the literal sense, it is a promise of the land of Canaan to Abraham and to his posterity; and in this sense it was literally fulfilled, though Abraham was never personally in possession of it; since Abraham and his posterity, put collectively, signify the RACE OF ABRAHAM; and that race possessed the land of Canaan. And surely God may be allowed to explain his own promise: now, though he tells Abraham, he would give *him* the land, yet, at the same time, he assures him, that it would be many hundred years before his *posterity* should be put in possession of it, Gen. xv. 13, &c. And as concerning himself, that he should go to his fathers in peace, and be buried in a good old age. Thus we see, that both what God explained to be his meaning, and what Abraham understood him to mean, was, that his posterity, after a certain time, should be led into possession of the land."[1]

But if this were really the whole meaning, the thought naturally occurs, it is strange so plain a meaning should have been so ambiguously expressed. Why not simply say, " thy posterity," if posterity alone were intended, and so render unnecessary the somewhat awkward expedient of sinking the patriarch's individuality in the history of his race? Why, also, should the promise have been renewed at a later period, with a pointed distinction between Abraham and his posterity, yet with an assurance that the promise was to him as well as to them: "And I will give unto thee, and to thy seed after thee, the land wherein thou art a stranger?" And why should Stephen have made such special reference to the apparent incongruity between the personal condition of Abraham and the promise given to him, as if there were some further meaning in what was said than lay on the sur-

---

[1] Legation of Moses, B. VI. sec. 3.

face—" He gave him none inheritance in it, no not so much as to set his foot on, yet he promised to give it to him for a possession, and to his seed after him ?" Acts vii. 5.

We do not see how these questions can receive any satisfactory explanation, so long as no account is made of the personal standing of the patriarchs in regard to the promise. And there are others equally left without explanation. For no sufficient reason can be assigned on that hypothesis, for the extreme anxiety of Jacob and Joseph to have their bones carried to the sepulchre of their fathers, in the land of Canaan—betokening, as it evidently seemed to do, a conviction, that to them also belonged a personal interest in the land. Neither does it appear how the fact of Abraham and his immediate offspring, " confessing that they were strangers and pilgrims on the earth," which they did no otherwise, that we are aware of, than by living as strangers and pilgrims in Canaan, should have proved that they were looking for and desiring a better country, that is, an heavenly one. And then, strange to think, if nothing more were meant by the promise than the view now under consideration would imply, when the posterity who were to occupy the land *did* obtain possession of it, we find the men of faith taking up precisely the same confession as to their being strangers and pilgrims in it, which was witnessed by their forefathers, who never had it in possession. Even after they became possessors, it seems, they were still like their wandering ancestors, expectants and heirs of something better, and faith had to be exercised, lest they should lose the proper fulfilment of the promise, (Ps. xxxix. 12, xcv., cxix. 19 ; 1 Chron xxix. 15.) Surely if the earthly Canaan had been the whole inheritance they were warranted to look for, after they were settled in it, the condition of pilgrims and strangers no longer was theirs—they had reached their proper destiny—they were dwelling in their appointed home—the promise had received its due fulfilment.

These manifold difficulties and apparent inconsistencies will vanish—(and we see no other way in which they can be satisfactorily removed)—by supposing, what is certainly in accordance with the tenor of revelation, that the promise of Canaan as an inheritance to the people of God was part of a connected and growing scheme of preparatory arrangements, which were to have their proper outgoing and final termination in the establishment of Christ's everlasting kingdom. Viewed thus, the grant of Canaan must be regarded as a kind of second Eden, a sacred region once more possessed in this fallen world—God's own land—out of which life and blessing were to come for all lands—the present type of a world restored and blessed. And if so, then we may naturally expect the following consequences to have arisen:—First, that whatever transactions may have taken place concerning the actual Canaan, these would be all ordered so as to subserve the higher design, in connection with which the appointment was made; and second, that as a sort of vail must have been allowed meanwhile to hang over this ultimate design, (for the issue of redemption could not be made fully manifest till the redemption itself was brought in), a certain degree of dubiety would attach to some of the things spoken regarding it—these would appear strange, or impossible, if viewed only in reference to the temporary inheritance—and would have the effect, with men of faith, as no doubt they were intended, to compel the mind to break through the outward shell of the promise, and contemplate the rich kernel enclosed within. Thus the promise being made so distinctly and repeatedly to Abraham, Isaac, and Jacob, while personally they were allowed no settled footing in the inheritance bestowed, could scarcely fail to impress them, and their more pious descendants, with the conviction, that higher and more important relations were included under those in which they stood to the land of Canaan during their earthly sojourn, and such as required another order of things to fulfil them. They must have been convinced, that for some great and substantial reason, not by a mere fiction of the imagination, they had been identified by God with their posterity as to their interest in the promised inheritance. And so, they must have felt shut up to the belief, that when God's purposes were completely fulfilled, his word of promise would be literally verified, and that their respective deaths should ultimately be found to raise no effectual barrier in the way of their actual share in the inheritance; as the same God who would have raised Isaac from the dead, had he been put to death, to maintain the integrity of his word, was equally able, on the same account, to raise them up.

Certainly the exact and perfect manner in which the other line of promise, that which respected a seed to Abraham, was fulfilled, gave reason to expect a fulfilment in regard to this also, in the most proper and complete sense. Abraham did not at first understand how closely God's words were to be interpreted; and after waiting in vain for some years for the promised seed by Sarah, he began to think, that God must have meant an offspring that should be his only by adoption, and seems to have thought of constituting the son of his steward his heir. Then, when admonished of his error in entertaining such a thought, and informed, that the seed was to spring from his own loins, he acceded, after another long period of fruitless waiting, to the proposal of Sarah regarding Hagar, under the impression, that though *he* was to be the father of the seed, yet it should not be by his proper wife; the expected good was to be obtained by a worldly expedient, and to be his only in a kind of secondary sense. Here again, however, he was admonished of error, commanded to cease from such unworthy devices, and walk in uprightness before God; reminded that He, who made the promise, was the Almighty God, to whom, therefore, no impossibility connected with the age of Sarah could be of any moment, and assured that the long promised child was to be the son of him and his lawful spouse.[1] And when Abraham was thus taught to interpret one part of the promise in the most exact and literal sense, how natural was it to infer, that he must do the same also with the other part? If when God said, "Thou shalt be the father of a seed," it became clear that the word could receive nothing short of the strictest fulfilment; what else, what less could be expected, when God said, "Thou shalt inherit this land," than that the fulfilment was to be equally proper and complete? The providence of God, which furnished such an interpretation in the one case, could not but beget the conviction, that a similar principle of interpretation was to be applied to the other, and that as the promise of the inheritance was given to Abraham, Isaac, and Jacob, as well as to their seed, so it should be made good in their experience, not less than in that of their posterity.

No doubt, such a belief implied, that there must be a resurrection from the dead before the promise could be realized; and to those, who conceive that immortality was altogether a blank page

[1] Gen. xvii. 1—17.

to the eye of an ancient Israelite, the idea may seem to carry its own refutation along with it. The Rabbis, however, with all their blindness, seemed to have had juster, because more scriptural, notions of the truth and purposes of God, in this respect. For, on Ex. vi. 4, the Talmud in Gemara, in reply to the question, "Where does the law teach the resurrection of the dead?" thus distinctly answers, "In that place where it is said, I have established my covenant with thee, to give thee the land of Canaan. For it is not said, with *you*, but with *thee*, (lit. yourselves.)"[1] The same answer substantially, we are told, was returned by Rabbi Gamaliel, when the Sadducees pressed him with a similar question. And in a passage quoted by Warburton (B. vi. sec. 3,) from Manasseh Ben-Israel, we find the argument still more fully stated: "God said to Abraham, I will give to thee, and to thy seed after thee, the land wherein thou art a stranger. But it appears, that Abraham and the other patriarchs did not possess that land; therefore it is of necessity that they should be raised up to enjoy the good promises,—else the promises of God should be vain and false. So that we have here a proof, not only of the immortality of the soul, but also of the essential foundation of the law, namely, the resurrection of the dead." It is surely not too much to suppose, that what Jewish Rabbis could so certainly draw from the word of God, may have been perceived by wise and holy patriarchs. And the fact, of which an inspired writer assures us, that Abraham so readily believed in the possible resurrection of Isaac to a present life, is itself conclusive proof, that he would not be slow to believe in his own resurrection to a future life, when the word of promise seemed no otherwise capable of receiving its proper fulfilment. Indeed, the doctrine of a resurrection from the dead—not that of the immortality of the soul—is the form which the prospect of an after-state of being must have chiefly assumed in the minds of the earlier believers, because that which most obviously and naturally grew out of the promises made to them, as well as most accordant with their native cast of thought. And nothing but the undue influence of

---

[1] Sic habetur traditio Rab. Simai; quo loco astruit Lex resurrectionem mortuorum? Nempe ubi dicitur, "Aque etiam constabilivi foedus meum cum ipsis, ut dem ipsis terram Canaan." Non enim dicitur *vobis* sed *ipsis*.

the Gentile philosophy on men's minds could have led them to imagine, as they generally have done, the reverse to have been the case.

In the writings of the Greeks and Romans, especially those of the former, we find the distinction constantly drawn between matter and spirit, body and soul,—and the one generally represented as having only elements of evil inhering in it, and the other elements of good. So far from looking for the resurrection of the body, as necessary to the final well-being of men, full and complete happiness was held to be impossible so long as the soul was united to the body. Death was so far considered by them a boon, that it emancipated the ethereal principle from its prison-house; and their visions of future bliss, when such visions were entertained, presented to the eye of hope, scenes of delight, in which the disembodied spirit alone was to find its satisfaction and repose. Hence it is quite natural to hear the better part of them speaking with contempt of all that concerned the body, looking upon death as a final, as well as a happy, release from its vile affections, and promising themselves a perennial enjoyment in the world of spirits. "In what way shall we bury you?" said Crito to Socrates, immediately before his death. "As you please," was the reply. "I cannot, my friends, persuade Crito, that I am the Socrates that is now conversing, and ordering every thing that has been said; but he thinks I am that man, whom he will shortly see a corpse, and asks how you should bury me. But what I have all along been talking so much about,—that when I shall have drunk the poison, I shall no longer stay with you, but shall, forsooth, go away to certain felicities of the blest,—this I seem to myself to have been saying in vain, whilst comforting at the same time you and myself." And in another part of the same dialogue (Phædo), after speaking of the impossibility of attaining to the true knowledge and discernment of things, so long as the soul is kept in the lumpish and impure body, he is represented as congratulating himself on the prospect now immediately before him: "If these things are true, there is much reason to hope, that he who has reached my present position, shall there soon abundantly obtain that, for the sake of which I have laboured so hard during this life; so that I encounter with a lively hope my appointed removal." No doubt such representations give a highly coloured and far too favourable view of the expectations which the more speculative part of the heathen world cherished of a future state of being,—for to most of them the whole was overshadowed with doubt and uncertainty, too often, indeed, the subject of absolute unbelief. But in this respect the idea it presents is perfectly correct, that so far as hope *was* exercised toward the future, it connected itself altogether with the condition and destiny of the soul; and so abhorrent was the thought of a resurrection of the body to their notions of future good, that Tertullian did not hesitate to affirm the heresy, which denied that Christian doctrine to be the common result of the whole Gentile philosophy.[1]

It was precisely the reverse with believers in ancient and primitive times. *Their* prospects of a blessed immortality were mainly associated with the resurrection of the body; and the dark period to them was the intermediate state between death and the resurrection, which even at a comparatively late stage in their history, presented itself to their view as a state of gloom, silence, and forgetfulness. They contemplated man, not in the light in which an airy, speculative philosophy might regard him, but in the more natural and proper one of a compound being, to which matter as essentially belongs as spirit, and in the wellbeing of which there must unite the happy condition both of soul and body. Nay, the materials from which they had to form their views and prospects of a future state of being, pointed most directly to the resurrection, and passed over in silence the period intervening between that and death. Thus, the primeval promise, that the seed of the woman should bruise the head of the serpent, taught them to live in expectation of a time when death should be swallowed up in victory; for death being the fruit of the serpent's triumph, what else could his complete overthrow be than the reversal of death—the resurrection from the dead? So also the prophecy embodied in the emblems of the tree of life, still standing in the midst of the garden of Eden, with its way of approach meanwhile guarded by the flaming sword, and possessed by the cherubim of glory—implying, that when the spoiler should be himself spoiled, and the way of life should again be laid open for the children of promise, they should have access to the food of

[1] Ut carnis restitutio negetur, de una omnium philosophorum schola sumitur, De Praesc. adv. Haeret. § 7.

immortality, which they could only do by rising out of death and entering on the resurrection-state. The same conclusion grew, as we have just seen, most naturally, and we may say inevitably, out of that portion of the promises made to the fathers of the Jewish race, which assured them of a *personal* inheritance in the land of Canaan; for dying, as they did, without having obtained any inheritance in it, how could the word of promise be verified to them, but by their being raised from the dead to receive what it warranted them to expect? In perfect accordance with these earlier intimations, or ground-promises, as they may be called, we find, as we descend the stream of time, and listen to the more express utterances of prophecy regarding the hopes of the church, that the grand point on which they are all made to centre, is the resurrection from the dead; and it is so, no doubt, for the reason, that as death is from the first represented as the wages of sin, the evil pre-eminently under which humanity groans, so the abolition of death by mortality being swallowed up of life, is understood to carry in its train the restitution of all things.

The Psalms, which are so full of the experiences and hopes of David, and other holy men of old, while they express only fear and discomfort in regard to the state after death, not unfrequently point to the resurrection from the dead as the great consummation of desire and expectation: " My flesh also shall rest in hope, for thou wilt not leave my soul in hell, neither wilt thou suffer thine holy one to see corruption," Ps. xvi. 9, 10. " Like sheep they are laid in the grave; death shall feed on them; and the upright shall have dominion over them in the morning; and their beauty shall consume in the grave from their dwelling; but God will redeem my soul from the power of the grave, for he shall receive me," xlix. 14, 15. The prophets, who are utterly silent regarding the state of the disembodied soul, speak still more explicitly of a resurrection from the dead, and evidently connect with it the brightest hopes of the church. Thus Isaiah, " He will swallow up death in victory," xxv. 8; and again, " Thy dead men shall live, together with my dead body shall they arise; awake and sing, ye that dwell in the dust," xxvi. 19. To the like effect, Hosea xiii. 14, " I will ransom them from the power of the grave, I will redeem them from death; O death, I will be thy plagues; O grave, I will be thy destruction." The vision of the dry bones, in the thirty-seventh chapter of Ezekiel, whether understood of a literal resurrection from the state of the dead, or of a figurative resurrection, a political resuscitation from a downcast and degraded condition, strongly indicates, in either case, the characteristic nature of their future prospects. Then, finally, in Daniel, we read, ch. xii., not only that he was himself, after resting for a season among the dead, " to stand in his lot at the end of the days," but also that at the great crisis of the church's history, when they should be for ever rescued from the power of the enemy, " many of them that sleep in the dust of the earth should awake, some to everlasting life, and some to shame and everlasting contempt."

Besides these direct and palpable proofs of a resurrection in the Jewish scriptures, and of the peculiar place it holds there, the Rabbinical and modern Jews, it is well known, refer to many others as inferentially teaching the same doctrine. That the earlier Jews were not behind them, either in the importance they attached to the doctrine, or in their persuasion of its frequent recurrence in the Old Testament scriptures, we may assuredly gather from the tenacity with which all but the Sadducees evidently held it in our Lord's time, and the ready approval which he met with when inferring it from the declaration made to Moses, " I am the God of Abraham, of Isaac, and of Jacob." It is nothing to the purpose, therefore, to allege, as has often been done, against any clear or well-grounded belief, on the part of the ancient Jews, regarding a future and immortal state of being, such passages as speak of the darkness, silence, and nothingness of the condition immediately subsequent to death, and during the sojourn of the body in the tomb. For that precisely was the period in respect to which their light failed them. Of a heathenish immortality, which ascribed to the soul a perpetual existence separate from the body, and considered its happiness, when thus separate, as the ultimate good of man, they certainly knew and believed nothing. But we are persuaded, no tenet was more firmly and sacredly held among them from the earliest periods of their history, than that of the resurrection from the dead, as the commencement of a final and everlasting portion of good to the people of God. And when the Jewish doctors gave to the resurrection of the dead a place among the thirteen fundamental articles of their faith, and cut off from all inheritance in a future state of felicity, those who deny it, we have no reason to regard the doctrine as attaining to a higher place in their hands, than it did with their fathers before the Christian era.[1]

There was something more, however, in the Jewish faith concerning the resurrection, than its being simply held as an article in their creed, and held to be a fact that should one day be realized in the history of the church. It stood in the closest connection with the promise made to the fathers, as some of the foregoing testimonies shew, and especially with the work and advent of Messiah. They not only believed that there would be a resurrection of the dead, to a greater or less extent, when Messiah came (see Lightfoot, Hor. Heb. John i. 21, v. 25), but that his work, especially as regards the promised inheritance, could only be carried into effect through the resurrection. Levi[2] holds it as a settled point, that "the resurrection of the dead will be very near the time of the redemption," meaning by the redemption the full and final enjoyment of all blessing in the land of promise, and that such is the united sense of all the prophets who have spoken of the times of Messiah. In this, indeed, he only expresses the opinion commonly entertained by Jewish writers, who constantly assert that there will be a resurrection of the whole Jewish race, to meet and rejoice with Christ, when he comes to Jerusalem, and who often thrust forward their views regarding it, when there is no proper occasion to do so. Thus, in Sohar, Genes. fol. 77, as quoted by Schoettgen, II. p. 367, R. Nehorai is reported to have said, on Abraham's speaking to his servant, Gen. xxiv. 2, "We are to understand the servant of God, his senior domus. And who is he? Metatron (Messiah), who, as we have said, will bring forth the souls from their sepulchres." But a higher authority still may be appealed to. For the apostle to the Gentiles thus expresses—and with evident approval as to the general principle—the mind of his countrymen in regard to the Messiah and the resurrection: "I now stand and am judged for the hope of the promise made of God unto our fathers; unto which promise our twelve tribes, instantly serving God day and

---

[1] See Appendix C.
[2] Dissertations on the Prophecies of Old Test., vol. i. p. 56.

night, hope to come—for which hope's sake, king Agrippa, I am accused of the Jews. Why should it be thought a thing incredible with you, that God should raise the dead?"[1] The connection, in which the resurrection of the dead is here placed with the great promise of a Messiah, for which the Jews are represented as so eagerly and intently looking, evidently implies, that the two were usually coupled together in the Jewish faith, nay that the one could reach its proper fulfilment only through the performance of the other, and that in believing on a Messiah risen from the dead, the apostle was acting in perfect accordance with the hopes of his nation.

But now, to apply all this to the subject under consideration, the promised inheritance,—if that inheritance was promised in a way, which from the very first implied a resurrection from the dead, before it could be rightly enjoyed,—and if all along, even when Canaan was possessed by the seed of Abraham, the men of faith still looked forward to another inheritance, when the curse should be utterly abolished, the blessing fully received, and death finally swallowed up in victory—then, a twofold boon must have been conveyed to Abraham and his seed, under the promise of the land of Canaan; one to be realized in the natural, and the other in the resurrection state,—a mingled and temporary good before, and a complete and permanent one after, the restitution of all things by the Messiah. So that, in regard to the ultimate designs of God, the land of Canaan would serve much the same purpose as the garden of Eden, with its tree of life and cherubim of glory—the same, and yet more,—for it not only presented to the eye of faith a type, but also gave in its possession an earnest of the inheritance of a paradisiacal world. The difference, however, is not essential, and only indicates an advance in God's revelations and purposes of grace, making what was ultimately designed for the faithful more sure to them by an instalment, through a singular train of providential arrangements, in a present inheritance of good. They thus enjoyed a real and substantial pledge of the better things to come, which were to be fulfilled in the kingdom of God.

But what were these better things themselves? What was

[1] Acts xxvi. 6-8.

thus indicated to Abraham and his believing posterity, as their coming inheritance of good? If it was clear that they must have attained to the resurrection from the dead, before they could properly enjoy the possession, it could not be Canaan in its natural state, as a region of the present earth, that was to be inherited. For that considered as the abode of Abraham and all his elect posterity, when raised from the tomb and collected into an innumerable multitude, must have appeared of far too limited dimensions, as well as of unsuitable character. Though it might well seem a vast inheritance for any living generation that should spring from the loins of Abraham, yet it was palpably inadequate for the possession of his collected seed, when it should have become like the stars of heaven for multitude. And not only so, but as the risen body is to be, not a natural, but a glorified one, the inheritance it is to occupy must be a glorified one too. The fairest portions of the earth, in its present fallen and corruptible state, could be a fit possession for men only so long as in their persons they are themselves fallen and corruptible. When redeemed from the power of the grave, and entered on the glories of the new creation, the natural Canaan will be as unfit to be their proper home and possession, as the original Eden would have been with its tree of life. Much more so, indeed—for the earth in its present state is adapted to the support and enjoyment of man, as constituted, not only after the earthly Adam, but after him as underlying the pernicious effects of the curse. And the ultimate inheritance destined for Abraham and the heirs of promise, which was to become theirs after the resurrection from the dead, must be as much higher and better than any thing which the earth, in its present state, can furnish, as man's nature, when glorified, shall be higher and better than it is while in bondage to sin and death.

Nothing less than this certainly is taught in what is said of the inheritance, as expected by the patriarchs, in the Epistle to the Hebrews: "These all died in faith, not having received the promises, but having seen them afar off, and were persuaded of them, and embraced them, and confessed that they were strangers and pilgrims on the earth. For they that say such things, declare plainly, that they seek a country. And truly, if they had been mindful of that country from whence they came out, they might have had opportunity to have returned. But now they desire a better country, that is, an heavenly; wherefore God is not ashamed to be called their God, for he hath prepared for them a city." Without entering into any minute commentary on this passage, it cannot but be regarded as perfectly conclusive of two points: First, that Abraham, and the heirs with him of the same promise, did understand and believe, that the inheritance secured to them under the promise of Canaan (for that was the only word spoken to them of an inheritance), was one in which they had a personal interest. And then, secondly, that the inheritance as it was to be occupied and enjoyed by them, was to be not a temporary, but a final one,—one that might fitly be designated a "heavenly country," a city built by divine hands, and based on immoveable foundations,—in short, the ultimate and proper resting-place of redeemed and risen natures. This was what these holy patriarchs expected and desired,—what they were *warranted* to expect and desire;—for their conduct in this respect is the subject of commendation, and is justified on the special ground, that otherwise God must have been ashamed to be called their God. And, finally, it was what they found contained in the promise to them, of an inheritance in the land, in which they were pilgrims and strangers; for to that promise alone could they look for the special ground of the hopes they cherished of a sure and final possession.

But the question again returns, what is that possession itself really to be? That it cannot be the country itself of Palestine, either in its present condition, or as it might become under any system of culture of which nature is capable, is too obvious to require any lengthened proof. The twofold fact, that the possession was to be man's ultimate, heavenly inheritance, and that it could be attained only after the resurrection from the dead, clearly forbids the supposition of its being the literal land of Canaan, under any conceivable form of renovated fruitfulness and beauty. This is also evident from the nature of the promise, that formed the ground of Abraham's hope,—which made mention only of the land of Canaan,—and which, as pointing to an ulterior inheritance, must have belonged to that combination of

[1] Heb. xi. 13-16.

type with prophecy, which we placed first, viz. having the promise, or prediction, not in the language employed, but in the typical character of the object which that language described. The promise made to Abraham was simple enough in itself. It gave assurance of a land distinctly marked off by certain geographical boundaries. It was not properly in the words of that promise that he could read his destiny to any future and ultimate inheritance; but putting together the two things, that the promised good could only be realized fully in an after-state of being, and that all the relations of the church then were preparative and temporary representations of better things to come, he might then perceive, that the earthly Canaan was a type of what was finally to be enjoyed. Thus the establishment of his offspring there would be regarded as a prophecy, *in fact*, of the exaltation of the whole of an elect seed to their destined state of blessing and glory. But such being the case,—the prediction standing altogether in the type,—the thing predicted and promised must in conformity with all typical relations, have been another and far higher thing than that which served to predict and promise it, —Canaan could not be the type of itself,—it could only represent, on the lower platform of nature, what was hereafter to be developed on the loftier arena of God's everlasting kingdom,—and as far as the things of fallen and corrupt nature differ from, and are inferior to, those of redemption, so far must the rest of Canaan have differed from, and been inferior to, " that rest which remaineth for the people of God."

What that final rest or inheritance, which forms the antitype to Canaan, really is, we may gather from the words of the apostle concerning it in Eph. i. 14, where he calls the Spirit " the earnest of our inheritance, until the redemption of the purchased possession."[1] It is plain, that the subject here discoursed of, is not our

---

[1] That the received translation gives here the sense of the original with substantial correctness, I am fully satisfied. The latter part of it, εἰς ἀπολύτρωσιν τῆς περιποιήσεως, has been variously understood, and its natural import too commonly overlooked. Robinson in his Lexicon makes it, ἀπολύτρωσιν τὴν περιποιηθεῖσαν, the redemption acquired for us,—a violent change, which could only be justified if absolutely necessary. The only two senses, in which the word occurs in the New Testament, are, 1. *Acquiring, acquisition, obtaining*, 1 Thess. v. 9 ; 2 Thess. ii. 14 ; Heb. x. 39 ; 2. *The thing obtained or acquired, possession*, in which sense, unquestionably, it is used in Mal. iii. 17, and in

persons, but our goods; not what believers in their souls and bodies are to be hereafter, but what is prepared for their enjoyment. For the inheritance which belongs to a person, must always be separate from the person himself. And as that which is called an inheritance in the one clause, is undoubtedly the same with that which in the other is named a possession, purchased or acquired, but not yet redeemed, the redemption of the possession must be a work to be accomplished *for* us, and not to be wrought *in* us. It must be a change to the better, effected not upon our persons, but upon the outward provision secured for their ulterior happiness and well-being.

It is true, that the church of God, the company of sound and genuine believers, is sometimes called the inheritance or purchased possession of God. In Old Testament Scripture his people are styled his " heritage," " his treasure;" and in New Testament Scripture we find St Peter addressing them as " a peculiar people,"

---

1 Pet. ii. 9. In both of these places it is applied to the church, as God's acquired, purchased possession, and is equal to his peculium, or property in the stricter sense, his select treasure, which is related to him as nothing else is, which he has acquired or purchased, περιποιήσατο, by his own blood, Acts xx. 28, comp. also Ex. xix. 6; Deut. vii. 6; Tit. ii. 14. The great majority of interpreters, from Calvin to Harless, are of opinion, that because in these passages περιποίησις is used as a designation of the church, considered as God's peculiar property, it has the same meaning here, " unto, or until the redemption of his purchased people," as Boothroyd expressly renders. But this view is liable to three objections. 1. The word περιποίησις, is nowhere absolutely and by itself put for " purchased people," or " church;" when so used, it has the addition of λαός. 2. The redemption of the church would then be regarded as future, whereas it is always represented as past. We read of the redemption of the *bodies* of believers as yet to take place, but never of the redemption of the *church;* that is uniformly spoken of as having been effected by the death of Christ. 3. It does not suit the connection; for the apostle is speaking of the in-dwelling of the spirit as the earnest of the inheritance, to which believers are destined, and as an earnest is given as a temporary substitute for the inheritance or possession, the term to which, or the end in respect to which it is given, must be, not some other event of a collateral nature, but the coming or receiving of the possession itself. Then, while these objections apply to the common view, there is no need for resorting to it; while it does violence to the word, it only obscures the sense. Εις περιποίησιν both Œcumenius and Theophylact on 1 Pet. ii. 9, hold to be εἰς κτῆσιν, εἰς κληρονομίαν, for a possession, for an inheritance. And Didymus on the same place, as quoted by Steiger, says, " that is περιποίησις, which, by way of distinction, is reckoned among our substance and possessions." Therefore, the correct meaning here is that given by Calov: " Περιποίησις, the abstract being placed for the concrete, is to be understood of the acquired inheritance, for the Holy Spirit is the pledge and earnest until the full redemption of the acquired inheritance."

or literally, a people for a possession—namely, a possession of God, acquired or purchased by the precious blood of his dear Son. The question here, however, is not of what may be called God's inheritance, but of ours; not of our redemption from the bondage of evil as a possession of God, which he seeks to enjoy free from all evil, but of that which we are ourselves to possess and occupy as our final portion. And as we could with no propriety be called our own inheritance, or our own possession, it must be something apart from, and out of ourselves, which is here to be understood, —not a state of being to be held, but a portion of blessing and glory to be enjoyed.

Now, whatever the inheritance or possession may be in itself, and whatever the region where it is to be enjoyed, when it is spoken of as needing to be redeemed, we are evidently taught to regard it, as something that has been alienated from us, but is again to be made ours; not a possession altogether new, but an old possession, lost, and again to be reclaimed from the powers of evil, which now overmaster and destroy it. So was it certainly with our persons. They were sold under sin. With our loss of righteousness before God, we lost, at the same time, our spiritual freedom, and all that essentially belonged to the pure and blessed life, in the possession of which we were created. Instead of this we became subject to the tyrannous dominion of the prince of darkness, holding us captive in our souls to the foul and wretched bondage of sin, and in our bodies to the mortality and corruption of death. The redemption of our persons is just their recovery from this lost and ruinous state, to the freedom of God's children, and the blessedness of immortal life in his presence and glory. It proceeds at every step by acts of judgment upon the great adversary and oppressor, who took advantage of the evil, and ever seeks to drive it to the uttermost. And when the work shall be completed by the redemption of the body from the power of the grave, there shall then be the breaking up of the last bond of oppression that lay upon our natures,—the putting down of the last enemy, that the son of wickedness may no longer vex or injure us.

In this redemption-process, which is already begun upon the people of God, and shall be consummated in the glories of the resurrection, it is the same persons, the same soul and body, which have experience both of the evil and of the good. Though the change is so great and wonderful, that it is sometimes called a new creation, it is not in the sense of any thing being brought into existence, which previously had no being. Such language is simply used on account of the happy and glorious transformation, that is made to pass upon the natures which already exist, but exist only in a state of misery and oppression. And when the same language is applied to the inheritance, which is used of the persons of those who are to enjoy it, what can this indicate, but that the same things are true concerning it? The bringing in of that inheritance, in its finished state of fulness and glory, is in like manner called "the making of all things new;" but it is so called only in respect to the wonderful transformation which is to be wrought upon the old things, which are thereby to receive another constitution, and present another aspect, than they were wont to do before. For that the possession is to be *redeemed*, bespeaks it as a thing to be recovered, not to be made,—a thing already in being, though so changed from its original destination, so marred and spoiled, overlaid with so many forms of evil, and so far from serving the ends for which it is required, that it may be said to be alienated from us, in the hands of the enemy, for the prosecution of his purposes of evil.

Now, what is it, of which this can be affirmed? If it is said heaven, and by that is meant what is commonly understood, some region far removed from this lower world, in the sightless realms of ether, then, we ask, was heaven in that sense ever man's? Has it become obnoxious to any evils, from which it must be delivered? or has it fallen into the hands of an enemy and an oppressor, from whose evil sway it must again be redeemed? None of these things surely can be said of *such* a heaven. It would be an altogether new inheritance, a possession never held, consequently never lost, and incapable of being redeemed. And there is nothing that answers such a description, or can possibly realize the conditions of such an inheritance, but what lies within the bounds and compass of this earth itself, with which the history of man has hitherto been connected both in good and evil, and where all the possession is, that he can properly be said either to have held or to have lost.

Let us again recur to the past. Man's original inheritance was a lordship or dominion, stretching over the whole earth, but extending no farther. It entitled him to the ministry of all creatures within its borders, and the enjoyment of all fruits and productions upon its surface—one only excepted, for the trial of his obedience (Gen. i. 28–31; Ps. viii.) When he fell, he fell from his dominion, as well as from his purity; the inheritance departed from him; he was driven from paradise, the throne and palace of his kingdom; labour, servitude, and suffering, became his portion in the world; he was doomed to be a bondsman, a hewer of wood and drawer of water, on what was formed to be his inheritance, and all that he has since been able, by hard toil and industry, to acquire, is but a partial and temporary command over some fragments of what was at first all his own. Nor is that the whole. For with man's loss of the inheritance, Satan was permitted to enter, and extend his usurped sway over the domain, from which man has been expelled as its proper lord. And this he does by filling the world with agencies and works of evil,—spreading disorder through the elements of nature, and disaffection among the several orders of being,—above all, corrupting the minds of men, so as to lead them to cast off the authority of God, and to use the things he confers on them for their own selfish ends and purposes, for the injury and oppression of their fellow-men, for the encouragement of sin and suppression of the truth of God, for rendering the world, in short, as far as possible, a region of darkness and not of light, a kingdom of Satan and not of God, a theatre of malice, corruption, and disorder, not of love, harmony, and blessedness.

Now, as the redemption of man's *person* consists in his being rescued from the dominion of Satan, from the power of sin in his soul, and from the reign of death in his body, which are the two forms of Satan's dominion over man's nature; what can the redemption of the *inheritance* be, but the rescuing of this earth from the manifold ills, which through the instrumentality of Satan have come to lodge in its bosom,—purging its elements of all mischief and disorder,—changing it from being the vale of tears and the charnel-house of death, into a paradise of life and blessing,—restoring to man, himself then redeemed, and fitted for the honour, the sceptre of a real dominion over all its fulness,—in a word, rendering it in character and design what it was on creation's morn, when the sons of God shouted for joy, and God himself looked with satisfaction on the goodness and order and beauty, which pervaded this portion of his universe? To do such a work as this upon the earth, would manifestly be to redeem the possession, which man by disobedience forfeited and lost, and a new title to which has been purchased by Christ for all his spiritual seed; for were that done, the enemy would be completely foiled and cast out, and man's proper inheritance restored.

But some are perhaps ready to ask, is that, then, *all* the inheritance that the redeemed have to look for? Is their abode still to be upon earth, and their portion of good to be confined to what may be derived from its material joys and occupations? Is paradise restored, to be simply the re-establishment and enlargement of paradise lost? We might reply to such questions by putting similar ones regarding the persons of the redeemed. Are these still, after all, to be the same persons they were during the days of their sojourn on earth? Is the soul, when expatiating amid the glorious scenes of eternity, to live in the exercise of the same powers and faculties, which it employed on the things of time? And is the outward frame, in which it is to lodge and act and enjoy itself, to be that very tabernacle, which it bore here in weakness, and which it left behind to rot and perish in the tomb? Would any one feel at a moment's loss to answer such questions in the affirmative? Does it in any respect shock our feelings, or lower the expectations we feel warranted to cherish concerning our future state, when we think, that the very soul and body, which together constitute and make up the being we now are, shall also constitute and make up the being we are to be hereafter? Assuredly not; for however little we know what we are to be hereafter, we are not left in ignorance, that both soul and body shall be freed from all evil; and not only so, but in the process shall be unspeakably refined and elevated. We know it is the purpose of God to magnify in us the riches of his grace by raising our natures higher than the fall has brought them low—to glorify, while he redeems them, and so to render them capable of spheres of action and enjoyment beyond, not only what eye has seen or ear has heard, but even what has entered into the mind of man to conceive.

And why may we not think and reason thus also, concerning

the inheritance which these redeemed natures are to occupy? Why may not God do a like work of purification and refinement on this solid earth, so as to transform and adapt it into a fit residence for man in glory? Why may not, why *should* not that, which has become for man as fallen, the house of bondage, and the field of ruin, become also for man redeemed the habitation of peace, and the region of pre-eminent delight? Surely He, who from the very stones can raise up children unto Abraham, and who *will* bring forth from the noisome corruption of the tomb, forms clothed with honour and majesty, can equally change the vile and disordered condition of the world, as it now is, and make it fit to be " the house of the glory of his kingdom,"—a world, where the eye of redeemed manhood shall be regaled with sights of surpassing loveliness, and his ear ravished with sounds of sweetest melody, and his desires satisfied with purest delight,— aye, a world, it may be, which, as it alone of all creation's orbs has been honoured to bear the footsteps of an incarnate God, and witness the performance of his noblest work, so shall it be chosen as the region, around which he will pour the richest manifestations of his glorious presence, and possibly send from it, by the ministry of his redeemed, communications of love and kindness, to the farthest bounds of his habitable universe!

No; when rightly considered, it is not a low and degrading view of the inheritance, which is reserved for the heirs of salvation, to place it in the possession of this very earth, which we now inhabit, after it shall have been redeemed and glorified. I feel it for myself to be rather an ennobling and comforting thought; and were I left to choose, out of all creation's bounds, the place where my redeemed nature is to find its local habitation, enjoy its redeemer's presence, and reap the fruits of his costly purchase, I would prefer none to this. For if destined to so high a purpose, I know it will be made in all respects what it should be,— the paradise of delight, the very heaven of glory and blessing, which I desire and need. And, then, the connection between what it now is, and what it shall have become, must impart to it an interest, which can belong to no other region in the universe. If any thing could enhance our exaltation to the lordship of a glorious and blessed inheritance, it would surely be the feeling of possessing it in the very place, where we were once miserable bondsmen of sin and corruption. And if any thing should dispose us to bear meekly our present heritage of evil, to quicken our aspirations after the period of deliverance, and to raise our affections above the vain and perishable things around us, it should be the thought, that all we can now either have or experience from the world is part of a possession forfeited and accursed, but that it only waits for the transforming power of God to be changed into the inheritance of the saints in light, when heaven and earth shall be mingled into one.

But if this renovated earth is to be itself the inheritance of the redeemed,—if it, in the first instance at least, is to be the heaven where they are to reap life everlasting, how, it may be asked, can heaven be spoken of as above us, and represented as the higher region of God's presence? Such language is never, that we are aware of, used in Scripture to denote the final dwelling-place of God's people; and if it were used there, as it often is in popular discourse, it would need, of course, to be understood with that limitation, which requires to be put upon all our more definite descriptions of a future world. To regard expressions of the kind referred to, as determining our final abode to be over our heads, were to betray a childish ignorance of the fact, that what is such by day, is the reverse of what is so by night. Such language properly denotes the superior nature of the heavenly inheritance, and not its relative position. God can make any region of his universe a heaven, since heaven is there, where he manifests his presence and glory; and why might he not do so here, as well as in any other part of creation?—But is it not said, that the kingdom, in which the redeemed are to live and reign for ever, was prepared for them before the foundation of the world; and how, then, can the scene of it be placed on this earth, still waiting to be redeemed for the purpose? The preparation there meant, however, cannot possibly be an actual fitting up of the place which believers are to occupy with their Lord; for wherever it is, the apostle tells us, it still needs to be redeemed; in that sense it is not yet ready; and Christ himself said, in reference to his leaving the world, that he was going to prepare it, which he does by directing, on his throne of glory, the events which are to issue in its full establishment. Still, from the first it might be said to be prepared, because destined for Christ and his elect people in the mind of God, even as they were all chosen in him before the foundation of the world; and every successive act in the history of the mediatorial kingdom is another step toward the accomplishment of the purpose.—Are we not again told, however, that the earth is to be destroyed, its elements made to melt with fervent heat, and all its works consumed? Unquestionably this *is* said—though not by any means necessarily implying, that the earth is really to be annihilated. We know, that God is perpetually causing changes to pass over the works of his hands, but that he actually annihilates any, we have no ground, either in nature or in Scripture, to suppose. If in the latter we are told of man's body, that it perishes, and is consumed by the moth, yet of what are we more distinctly assured, than that it is not doomed to absolute destruction, but shall live again? When we read of the old world being destroyed by the flood, we know that the material fabric of the earth continued as before. Indeed, much the same language that is applied to the earth in this respect, is also extended to the heavens themselves; for they too are represented as ready to pass away, and to be changed as a vesture, and the promise speaks of new heavens as well as a new earth. And in regard to this earth in particular, there is nothing in the language used concerning it to prevent us from believing, that the fire which, in the day of God's judgment, is to burst forth with consuming violence, may, like the waters of the deluge, and in a far higher respect than they, act as an element of purification—dissolving, indeed, the present constitution of things, and leaving not a wreck behind of all we now see and handle, but at the same time rectifying and improving the powers of nature, refining and elevating the whole framework of the earth, and impressing on all that belongs to it a transcendent, imperishable glory—so that in condition and appearance it shall be substantially a new world, and one as far above what it now is, as heaven is above the earth.

There is nothing, then, in the other representations of Scripture, which appears, when fairly considered, to raise any valid objection against the renovated earth being the ultimate inheritance of the heirs of promise. And there is much to shut us up to the conclusion that it is so. We have enlarged on one testimony of inspiration, not because it is the only, or the chief one on the subject, but because it is so explicit, that it seems decisive of the question. For, an inheritance, which has been already acquired or purchased, but which must be redeemed before it can really be our possession, can be understood of nothing but that original domain, which with man himself sin brought into the bondage of evil at the fall. And of what else can we understand the representation in the 8th Psalm, as interpreted by the pen of inspiration itself, in the Epistle to the Hebrews, chap. ii. 5–9, and in 1 Cor. xv. 27, 28 ? These passages in the New Testament put it beyond a doubt, that the idea of perfect and universal dominion, delineated in the Psalm, is to be realized in the world to come, over which Christ, as the head of redeemed humanity, is to rule, in company with his redeemed people. The representation itself in the Psalm, is evidently borrowed from the first chapter of Genesis, and considered as a prophecy of good things to come, or a prediction of the dignity and honour already obtained for man in Christ, and hereafter to be revealed, it may be regarded as simply presenting to our view the picture of a restored and renovated creation. " It is just that passage in Genesis, which describes the original condition of the earth," to use the words of Hengstenberg, " turned into a prayer for us," and we may add, into an object of hope and expectation. When that prayer is fulfilled—in other words, when the natural and moral evils entailed by the fall have been abolished, and the earth shall stand to man, when redeemed and glorified, in a similar relation to what it did at the birth of creation, then shall the hope we now possess of an inheritance of glory be turned into enjoyment. In Isa. xi. 6–9, the final results of Messiah's reign are in like manner delineated under the aspect of a world, which has obtained riddance of all the disorders introduced by sin, and is restored to the blessed harmony and peace which characterized it, when God pronounced it very good. And still more definitely, though with reference to the same aspect of things, the apostle Peter (Acts iii. 21), represents the time of Christ's second coming as " the time of the restitution of all things," that is, when every thing should be restored to its pristine condition,—the same condition in kind, all pure and good, glorious and blessed, but higher in degree, as it is the design and tendency of redemption to ennoble whatsoever it touches.

¹· That this is simply the force of the original here, it may be enough to give the mean-

It is precisely on the same object, a redeemed and glorified earth, that the apostle Paul, in the 8th chap. of the Romans, fixes the mind of believers as the terminating point of their hopes of glory. An incomparable glory is to be revealed in them, and in connection with that "the deliverance of a suffering creation from the bondage of corruption, into the glorious liberty of the sons of God." What can this deliverance be, but what is marked in the Epistle to the Ephesians, as "the redemption of the purchased possession?" Nor is it possible to connect with any thing else the words of Peter in his second Epistle, where, after speaking of the dreadful conflagration which is to consume all that belongs to the earth in its present form, he adds,—as if expressly to guard against supposing, that he meant the actual and entire destruction of this world as the abode of man,—"Nevertheless we, according to his promise, look for new heavens, and a new earth, wherein dwelleth righteousness."

It is only by understanding the words of Christ himself, "the meek shall inherit the earth," of the earth in that new condition, its state of blessedness and glory, that any full or adequate sense can be attached to them. He could not surely mean the earth as it then was, or as it is to be during any period of its existence, while sin and death reign in it. So long as it is in that condition, not only will the saints of God have many things to suffer in it, as our Lord immediately foretold, when he spake of the persecutions for righteousness' sake, which his people should have to endure, and on account of which he bade them look for their "reward in heaven;" but all the treasure it contains must be of the moth-eaten, perishable kind, which they are expressly forbidden to covet, and the earth itself must be that city without continuance, in contrast to which they are called to seek one to come. To speak, therefore, as many commentators do, of the tendency of piety in general, and of a mild and gracious disposition in particular, to secure for men a prosperous and happy life on earth, is to say comparatively little as regards the fulfilment of the promise, that they shall "inherit the earth." If it could even command for them the whole that earth now can give, would Christ

ing of the main word from the lexicographer Hesychius: ἀποκατάστασις, "is the restoration of a thing to its former state, or to a better; restitution, consummation, a revolution of the grander kind, from which a new order of things arises, rest after turmoil."

on that account have called them *blessed?* Would he not rather have warned them to beware of the deceitfulness of riches, and the abundance of honours thus likely to flow into their bosom? To be blessed in the earth as an inheritance, must import, that the earth has become to them a real and proper good, such as it shall be, when it has been transformed into a fit abode for redeemed natures. This view is also confirmed, and apparently rendered as clear and certain as language can make it, by the representations constantly made by Christ and the inspired writers, of his return to the earth and manifestation on it in glory, as connected with the last scenes and final issues of his kingdom. When he left the world, it was as a man going into a far country, from which he was to come again;[1] the heaven received him at his resurrection, but only until the times of the restitution of all things;[2] the period of his residence within the veil, is coincident with that during which his people have to maintain a hidden life, and is to be followed by another, in which they and he together are to be manifested in glory.[3] And in the book of Revelation, while unquestionably the scenes are described in typical language, yet when exact localities are mentioned as the places where the scenes are to be realized, and that in connection with a plain description of the condition of those who are to have part in them, we are compelled by all the ordinary rules of composition, to regard such localities as real and proper habitations. What, then, can we make of the ascription of praise from the elders, representatives of a redeemed church, when they give glory to the Messiah, as "having made them kings and priests unto God, and they shall reign with him upon the earth?" Or, what of the closing scenes, where the Evangelist sees a new heaven and a new earth, in the room of those which had passed away, and the new Jerusalem coming down out of heaven to settle on the renovated earth, and the tabernacle of God fixed amongst men?[4] Granting that the delineations of the book are a succession of pictures, drawn from the relations of things in

---

[1] Math. xxv. 14; Luke xix. 12; John xiv. 3.
[2] Acts iii. 21.
[3] Col. iii. 4; Heb. ix. 28; 1 John iii. 2; Rev. i. 7.
[4] Rev. v. 9, 10, xxi. 1—5.

the former ages of the world, and especially under the Old Testament economy, and that the fulfilment to be looked for is not as of a literal description, but as of a symbolical representation, yet there must be certain fixed landmarks as to time and place, persons and objects, which, in their natures or their names, are so clearly defined, that by them the relation of one part to another, must be arranged and interpreted. For example, in the above quotations, we cannot doubt who are kings and priests, or with whom they are to reign; and it were surely strange, if there could be any doubt of the theatre of their dominion, when it is so expressly denominated *the earth*. And still more strange if, when heaven and earth are mentioned relatively to each other, and the scene of the church's future glory fixed upon the latter as contradistinguished from the former, still earth should stand for heaven, and not for itself. Indeed the most striking feature in the representations of the Apocalypse, is the uniformity with which they connect the higher grade of blessing with earth, and the lower with the world of spirits. As Hengstenberg has justly remarked on ch. xx. 4, 5, it invariably points to a double stage of blessedness, the one awaiting believers immediately after their departure out of this life, the other what they are to receive when they enter the New Jerusalem, and reign with Christ in glory. But we find the same in our Lord's teaching, as when he said to the thief on the cross, " To-day shalt thou be with me in Paradise," and yet pointed his disciples to the state of things on earth after the resurrection for their highest reward (Matth. xix. 28). And, on the whole, we are forced to conclude with Usteri, that " the conception of a transference of the perfected kingdom of God into the heavens, is properly speaking modern, seeing that according to Paul, and the Apocalypse, (and, he might also have added, Peter and Christ himself,) the seat of the kingdom of God is the earth, inasmuch as that likewise partakes in the general renovation."[1]

---

[1] The above passage is quoted by Tholuck, on Rom. viii. 19, who himself there, and on Heb. ii., concurs in the same view. He also states, what cannot be denied, that it is the view, which has been adopted by the greatest number, and the most ancient of the expositors, amongst whom he mentions, though he does not cite, Chrysostom, Theodoret, Jerome, Augustine, Ambrose, Luther, &c. And Rivet, on Gen. viii. 22, states, that the opinion, which maintains only a change, and not an utter destruction of the

Having now closed our investigation, we draw the following conclusions from it.

1. The earthly Canaan was neither designed by God, nor from the first was it understood by his people, to be the ultimate and proper inheritance, which they were to occupy; things having

world, has most supporters, both among the older and the more recent writers, so that it may be called, says he, " the common one, and be said to prevail by the number of its adherents." In the present day, the opposite opinion would probably be entitled to be regarded as by much the most common; and the view here set forth, will perhaps by some be eyed with jealousy, if not condemned as novel. It may be proper, therefore, to give a few quotations from the more eminent commentators. Jerome, on Isa. lxv. 17, quotes Ps. cii. 26 and 27, which he thinks " clearly demonstrates, that the perdition spoken of, is not a reducing to nothing, but a change to the better;" and having referred to what Peter says of the new heavens, and the new earth, he remarks, that the Apostle " does not say, we look for other heavens and another earth, but for the old and original ones transformed into a better state." Of the fathers generally, as of Justin Martyr in particular, Semish states, that they regarded the future destruction of the world by fire, " far more frequently, as a transformation, than as an annihilation." (Life and Times of Justin, Bib. Cab. Vol. XLII. p. 366.) Calvin, while he discourages minute inquiries and vain speculations regarding the future state, expresses himself with confidence, on Rom. viii. 21, as to this world being the destined theatre of glory, and considers it as a proof of the incomparable glory to which the sons of God are to be raised, that the lower creation is to be renewed for the purpose of manifesting and ennobling it, just as the disorders and troubles of creation have testified to the appalling evil of our sin. So also Haldane, a man of peculiarly sober judgment, on the same passage, after quoting from 2 Pet. and Rev. continues : " The destruction of the substance of things differs from a change in their qualities. When metal of a certain shape is subjected to fire, it is destroyed as to its figure, but not as to its substance. Thus the heavens and the earth will pass through the fire, but only that they may be purified and come forth anew, more excellent than before. This hope—the hope of deliverance—was held out in the sentence pronounced on man, for in the doom of our first parents the divine purpose of providing a deliverer was revealed. We know not the circumstances of this change, how it will be effected, or in what form the creation—those new heavens and that new earth, wherein dwelleth righteousness, suited for the abode of the sons of God—shall then exist; but we are sure it shall be worthy of the divine wisdom, although at present beyond our comprehension." To the same effect Fuller, in his Gospel its own Witness, ch. v. Thiersch says of the promise to Abraham, " Undoubtedly it pointed to a kingdom of God upon earth, not in an invisible world of spirits. Paradise itself had been upon earth, much more should the earth be the centre of the world to come." (History, I. p. 20). See Olshausen also on Matth. viii. Mr Stuart, in his work on Romans, expresses his strong dissent from such views, on the ground of their being opposed to the declarations of Christ, and requiring such a literal interpretation of prophecy, as would lead to absurd and ridiculous expectations in regard to other predictions. We can perceive no contrariety in our opinion to any declaration of Christ or his apostles, and the other predictions he refers to belong to quite another class, and do not require, or even admit, as might quite easily be shewn, of a strictly literal fulfilment.

been spoken and hoped for concerning it, which plainly could not be realized within the bounds of Canaan.

2. The inheritance was one which could be enjoyed only by those who had become the children of the resurrection, themselves fully redeemed in soul and body from all the effects and consequences of sin, made more glorious and blessed, indeed, than if they had never sinned, because constituted after the image of the heavenly Adam. And as the inheritance must correspond with the inheritor, it can only be man's original possession restored,—the earth redeemed from the curse which sin brought on it, and, like man himself, rendered exceedingly more beautiful and glorious, than in its primeval state,—the fit abode of a church, made like, in all its members, to the Son of God.

3. The occupation of the earthly Canaan by the natural seed of Abraham, was a type, and no more than a type, of this occupation by a redeemed church, of her destined inheritance of glory; and consequently every thing concerning the entrance of the former on their temporary possession, was ordered so as to represent and foreshadow the things which belong to the church's establishment in her permanent possession. Hence, between the giving of the promise, which though it did not terminate in the land of Canaan, yet included that, and through it prospectively exhibited the better inheritance, a series of important events intervened, which are capable of being fully and properly explained in no other way, than by means of their typical bearing on the things hereafter to be disclosed respecting that better inheritance. If we ask, why did the heirs of promise wander about so long as pilgrims, and withdraw to a foreign region, before they were allowed to possess the land, and not rather, like a modern colony, quietly spread, without strife or bloodshed, over its surface, till the whole was possessed? Or, why were they suffered to fall under the dominion of a foreign power, from whose cruel oppression they needed to be redeemed, with terrible executions of judgment on the oppressor, before the possession could become theirs? Or why, before that event also should they have been put under the discipline of law, having the covenant of Sinai, with its strict requirements and manifold obligations of service, superadded to the covenant of grace and promise? Or, why again should their right to the inheritance itself, have to be vindicated from a race of occupants, who

had been allowed for a time to keep possession of it, and whose multiplied abominations had so polluted it, that nothing short of their extermination could render it a fitting abode for the heirs of promise? The full and satisfactory answer to all such questions, can only be given, by viewing the whole in connection with the better things of a higher dispensation,—as the first part of a plan, which was to have its counterpart and issue in the glories of a redeemed creation, and for the final results of which the church needed to be prepared by standing in similar relations, and passing through like experiences, in regard to an earthly inheritance. No doubt, with one and all of these, there were connected reasons and results for the time then present, amply sufficient to justify every step in the process, when considered simply by itself. But it is only when we take the whole as a glass, in which to see mirrored the far greater things, which from the first were in prospect, that we can get a comprehensive view of the mind of God in appointing them, and know the purposes which he chiefly contemplated.

For example, the fact of Abraham and his immediate descendants, being appointed to wander as pilgrims through the land of Canaan, without being allowed to occupy any part of it as their own possession, may be partly explained, though in that view it must appear somewhat capricious, by its being considered as a trial to their own faith, and an act of forbearance and mercy toward the original possessors, whose iniquities were not yet full. But if we thus find grounds of reason to explain, why it *may* have been so ordered, when we come to look upon the things which happened to them, as designed to image other things, which were afterwards to belong to the relation of God's people to a higher and better inheritance, we see it was even *necessary* that those transactions should have been so ordered, and that it would have been unsuitable for the heirs of promise, either entering at once on the possession, or living as pilgrims and expectants, any where but within its borders. For thus alone could their experience fitly represent the case of God's people in gospel times, who have not only to wait long for the redemption of the purchased possession, but while they wait, must walk up and down as pilgrims in the very region, which they are hereafter to use as their own, when it shall have been delivered from the powers of evil who now hold it in bondage, and purged from their abominations. Hence, if they know aright their relation to the world as it now is, and their calling as the heirs of promise, they must sit loose to the things of earth, even as the patriarchs did to the land of their sojourn,—must feel, that it cannot be the place of their rest, so long as it is polluted, and that they must steadfastly look for the world to come as their proper home and possession. And thus also the whole series of transactions, which took place between the confirmation of the covenant of promise with Jacob, and the actual possession of the land promised, and more especially the things which concerned that greatest of all the transactions, the revelation of the law from Sinai, is to be regarded as a delineation in the type, of the way and manner in which the heirs of God are to obtain the inheritance of the purchased possession. Meanwhile, apart from these later transactions, there are two important lessons, which the church may clearly gather from what appears in the first heirs of promise, and which she ought never to lose sight of:—First, that the inheritance, come when and how it may, is the free gift of God, bestowed by him, as sovereign lord and proprietor, on those whom he calls to the fellowship of his grace: And, second, that the hope of the inheritance must exist as an animating principle in their hearts, influencing all their procedure. Their spirit and character must be such as become those who are the expectants, as well as heirs, of that better country, which is an heavenly. And Christ is never truly formed in the heart, until he be formed as "the hope of glory."

APPENDIX A.

TYPICAL FORMS IN NATURE.—P. 94.

It is scarcely possible, within the compass of a few pages, to exhibit the prevalence of Typical Forms in Nature, so as to make it tell in the manner it is capable of doing on our general argument. For as it rests upon a multiplicity of facts, bearing a certain relation to each other, and these facts such as have been but recently, and some of them as yet only partially ascertained—the subject must inevitably suffer, when presented in a great measure apart from these, in a brief and imperfect outline. But such an outline is all that can be given here. Those who desire to enter more fully into the investigation may have recourse to the works of Professor Owen, especially to his Treatises on *Limbs*, and on the *Archetype and Homologies of the Vertebrate Skeleton*; to Mr Hugh Miller's *Footprints of the Creator*; and the ingenious and interesting article on *Typical Forms* in the 30th Number of the North British Review, understood to be the production of the author of the *Method of the Divine Government*. The writer of this article pursues the subject even into the vegetable field of nature, and endeavours to shew that in plants which have leaves that strike the eye, the leaf and plant are typically analogous: the leaf is a typical plant or branch, and the tree or branch a typical leaf. In this field, however, the facts are neither so fully established, nor do they appear so perfectly uniform, as in the higher region of animal forms, or comparative anatomy. Here it is found, by a wide and satisfactory induction, that the human is what may be called the *pattern* form of animal existences—the archetype of the vertebrate division of animated nature. In the structure of all other animal forms there are observable striking resemblances to that of man, and resemblances of a kind that seem plainly designed to assimilate the lower, as near as circumstances would admit, to the higher. It is found, that in all vertebrate animals, from fishes to man, the vertebrate skeleton is composed of a series of parts of essentially the same order, though modified in a great variety of ways to suit the particular functions which each organ has to perform in the different animals respectively. Thus, to give only a single instance, every segment, and almost every bone present in the human hand and arm, exist also in the fin of the whale, though they do not seem required for the support and movement of that undivided and inflexible paddle; and one can think of no specific reason for such a peculiarity of structure, excepting the intention of having it brought into the nearest possible conformity to the archetype. Most strikingly does the similarity to the human type, coupled with its relative superiority to the others, appear in regard to the brain, which is the most peculiar and distinguishing part of the animal frame. "Nature," says Mr Miller, "in constructing this curious organ in man, first lays down a grooved cord, as the carpenter lays down the keel of his vessel; and on this narrow base the perfect brain, as month after month passes by, is gradually built up, like the vessel from the keel. First it grows up into a brain closely resembling that of a fish; a few additions more convert it into a brain undistinguishable from that of a reptile; a few additions more impart to it the perfect appearance of the brain of a bird; it then developes into a brain exceedingly like that of a mammiferous quadruped; and finally, expanding atop, and spreading out its deeply corrugated lobes, till they project widely over the base, it assumes its unique character as a human brain. Radically such at the first, it passes through all the inferior forms, from that of the fish upwards, as if each man were in himself, not the microcosm of the old fanciful philosopher, but something greatly more wonderful—a compendium of all animated nature, and of kin to every creature that lives. Hence the remark, that man is the sum total of all animals—'the animal equivalent,' says Oken, 'to the whole animal kingdom.' "—(*Footprints*, p. 291.)

This, however, is not the whole. For, as geology has now learned to read with sufficient accuracy the stony records of the past to be able to tell of successive creations of vertebrate animals, from fish, the first and lowest, up to man, the last and highest; so here also we have a kind of typical history—the animal productions of nature during those earlier geological periods bore, as the imperfect, a prospective reference to man, as the complete and ultimate form of animal existence. They were the types, and he is the antitype in the mundane system. In the words of Professor Owen, " all the parts and organs of man had been sketched out in anticipation, so to speak, in the inferior animals; and the recognition of an ideal exemplar in the vertebrated animals proves, that the knowledge of such a being as man must have existed before man appeared. For the divine mind, which planned the archetype, also foreknew all its modifications. The archetypal idea was manifested in the flesh long prior to the existence of those animal species that actually exemplify it. To what natural laws or secondary causes the orderly succession and progression of such organic phenomena may have been committed, we are as yet ignorant. But if, without derogation of the divine power we may conceive the existence of such ministers, and personify them by the term NATURE, we learn from the past history of our globe that she has advanced with slow and stately steps, guided by the archetypal light amidst the wreck of worlds, from the first embodiment of the vertebrate idea under its old ichthyic vestment, until it became arrayed in the glorious garb of the human form."

In this view of the matter, what a striking analogy does the history of God's operations in nature furnish to his plan in providence, as brought out in the history of redemption! Here, in like manner, there is a grand archetypal idea in the person and kingdom of Christ, towards which for ages the divine plan was continually working. Partial exhibitions of it appear from time to time in certain personages, events, and institutions that rise prominently into view as the course of providence proceeds, but all marred with obvious faults and imperfections in respect to the great object contemplated; until, at length, the idea in its entire length and breadth is seen embodied in Him to whom all the prophets gave witness—*the God-man foreordained before the foundation of the world.* " The Creator "—to adopt again the language of Mr Miller, who, in an article in the *Witness* newspaper of 2d August 1851, has very felicitously described the analogy in this respect between the natural and the moral departments of God's plan—" The Creator, in the first ages of his workings, appears to have been associated with what he wrought simply as the producer or author of all things. But even in those ages, as scene after scene, and one dynasty of the inferior animals succeeded another, there were strange typical indications which pre-Adamite students of prophecy among the spiritual existences of the universe might possibly have aspired to read—symbolical indications to the effect that the Creator was in the future to be more intimately connected with his material works than in the past, through a glorious creature made in his own image and likeness. And to this semblance and portraiture of the Deity—the first Adam—all the merely natural symbols seem to refer. But in the eternal decrees it had been for ever determined that the union of the Creator with creation was not to be a mere union by proxy or semblance. And no sooner had the first Adam appeared and fallen, than a new school of prophecy began, in which type and symbol were mingled with what had now its first existence on earth—verbal enunciations; and all pointed to the second Adam, 'the Lord from heaven.' In him creation and the Creator meet in reality and not in semblance. On the very apex of the finished pyramid of being sits the adorable Monarch of all:—as the Son of Mary—of David—of the first Adam, the created of God; as God and the Son of God, the eternal Creator of the universe. And these—the two Adams—form the main theme of all prophecy, natural and revealed. And that type and symbol should have been employed with reference not only to the second, but—as held by men like Agassiz and Owen—to the first Adam also, exemplifies, we are disposed to think, the unity of the style of Deity, and serves to shew that it was He who created the worlds that dictated the Scriptures."

The subject might even be prosecuted farther still, for it is as well fitted to stimulate the aspirations of hope toward the future, as to strengthen the foundations of faith in the past. If the archetypal idea in animated nature has been wrought at, through long periods and successive stages of being, till it found its proper realization in man; now that the nature of man is linked in personal union with the Godhead, for the purpose of repairing what is evil, and raising manhood to a higher than its original condition, who can conceive to what peerless glory and perfection it may yet attain? The divine power is no longer to be displayed in creating what is new, but in a work of " regeneration " upon the old, to the intent that the earthly and human in us may be brought to the nearest possible conformity to the spiritual and divine in Christ. The frame and condition of redeemed men, therefore, though relatively perfect as compared with the past, is yet but in embryo when viewed with respect to the more elevated future. All has still to assume the form and impress of a more glorious type, which eye hath not seen nor ear heard; of which the whole we can now say is—" We know not what we shall be, but we know that when he appears we shall be like him, for we shall see him as he is."

APPENDIX B.

THE OLD TESTAMENT IN THE NEW.—P. 102.

I.—THE HISTORICAL AND DIDACTIC PORTIONS.

BESIDES numberless allusions of various kinds in the New Testament to the Old, there are somewhat more than two hundred and fifty express citations in the writings of the one from those of the other. These citations are of unequal length; they consist often of a single clause, but sometimes also extend to several verses. They are taken indiscriminately from the different parts of Old Testament Scripture; though, with very few exceptions, they belong to the five books of Moses, the Psalms, and the writings of the prophets.

Not a few of these citations from the Old Testament are citations of the simplest kind; they appear merely as passages quoted in their plain sense from the previously existing canon of Scripture. Such, for example, are the passages out of the books of Moses, with which our Lord, after the simple notification, "It is written," thrice met the assaults of the tempter in the wilderness; and such also are those with which Stephen, in his historical speech before the Jewish council, sought, through appropriate references to the past, to enlighten the minds and alarm the consciences of his judges. In examples of this description, there is nothing that can be said to wear even the semblance of a difficulty, unless it may be regarded as such, that occasionally a slight difference appears in the passages as quoted, from what they are as they stand in the original Scripture. But the difference is never more than a verbal one; the sense of the original is always given with substantial correctness by the inspired writers in the New Testament; and so far as the great principles of interpretation are concerned, there is no need for lingering about the discussion of a matter so comparatively minute.

But there still remains a considerable variety of Old Testament passages, so cited in the New, as plainly to involve certain principles of interpretation; because they are cited as grounds of inference for some authoritative conclusion, or as proofs of doctrine respecting something connected with the person, the work, or the kingdom of Christ. And on the supposition of the authors of the New Testament being inspired teachers, the character of these citations is of the gravest importance—first, as providing in the hermeneutical principles they involve, a test to some extent of the inspiration of the writers; and then as furnishing in those principles, an infallible direction for the general interpretation of ancient Scripture. For, there can be no doubt that the manner in which our Lord and his apostles understood and applied the Scriptures of the Old Testament, was as much intended to throw light generally on the principles of interpretation, as to administer instruction on the specific points, for the sake of which they were more immediately appealed to. What, then, is the kind of use made of the passages in question, and the spirit in which they are explained? Is it natural and proper? Is there nothing strained, nothing paradoxical, nothing arbitrary and capricious in the matter? Does it altogether commend itself to our understandings and consciences? Undoubtedly it does so in the great majority of cases. And yet it is not to be denied that there are certain peculiarities connected with the treatment of the Old Testament in the New, which are very apt to stagger inquirers in their first attention to the subject. Nay, there are real difficulties attaching to some parts of it, which have long exercised the ingenuity of the ablest interpreters, and of which no satisfactory solution can be given, without a clear and comprehensive insight being first obtained into the connection subsisting between the preparatory and the ultimate things in God's kingdom.

In a small publication, which materially contributed to the solution of some of these difficulties, issued so far back as 1824, Olshausen remarks concerning the use made of the Old Testament in the New:—

"This has been for all more recent expositors a stone of stumbling, over which not a few of them have actually fallen. It has appeared to them difficult and even impossible to discover a proper unity and connection in the constructions put upon the passages by the New Testament writers, or to refer them to rules and principles. Without being able to refer them to these, they could not properly justify and approve of them; neither could they, on the other hand, altogether disapprove and reject them, without abandoning every thing. So that in explaining the passages of the Old Testament which pointed to the New, and again explaining the passages of the New Testament which expressly referred to and applied the Old, expositors for the most part found themselves involved in the greatest difficulties, and, on the one side or the other, resorted to the most violent expedients. But the explanation of the Old Testament in the New is the very point from which alone all exposition that listens to the voice of divine wisdom must set out. For we have here presented to us the sense of Holy Scripture as understood by inspired men themselves, and are furnished with the true key of knowledge." [1]

It is more especially, however, in the application made by New Testament writers of the *prophecies* of the Old Testament that the difficulties in question present themselves. Nor are they by any means of one kind; they are marked by a considerable diversity, and the passages will require to be taken in due order and connection, if we are to arrive at a well-grounded and

---

[1] Ein Wort über tiefern Schriftsinn, pp. 7, 8.

satisfactory view of the subject. This is what we mean to do. But, as there are other portions of Old Testament Scripture, besides the prophecies, referred to and quoted in the New—as much use also is made there of the historical and didactic portions—it is important, in the first instance, to notice that this use, with only one or two apparent, and no real exceptions, is always of a quite natural and unsophisticated character; free from any ridiculous or extravagant conceits, and entirely approving itself to the judgments of profound and thoughtful readers. Such readers, indeed, so naturally expect it to be so, that they scarcely take cognisance of the fact, or ever think of the possibility of its having been otherwise. But it is the rather to be noted, as, at the period the New Testament was written, there was, both in the age generally, and in the Jewish section of it in particular, a strong tendency to the allegorical in interpretation—to the strained, the fanciful, the puerile. The records of gospel history contain many plain indications of this. Our Lord even charged the Jewish scholars and interpreters of his day with rendering of no effect the law of God by their traditions (Mark vii. 11, 12); and evidently had it as his chief aim, in a considerable part of his public teaching, to vindicate the real sense of ancient Scripture from their false glosses and sophistical perversions. The oldest Rabbinical writings extant, which profess to deliver the traditional interpretations of the leading doctors of the synagogue, sufficiently evince what need there was for our Lord adopting such a course. Such as know these only from the quotations adduced by Ainsworth, Lightfoot, and similar writers, see them only in what is at once by far their best side, and their smallest proportions. For, to a large extent, they consist of absurd, incredible, and impure stories; abound with the most arbitrary and ridiculous conceits; and, as a whole, tend much more to obscure and perplex the meaning of Old Testament Scripture, than explain it. It was even regarded as a piece of laudable ingenuity to multiply as much as possible the meanings of every clause and text; for, as Jeremiah had compared the Word of God to a hammer that breaks the rock in pieces, so, it was thought, the Word must admit of as many senses as the rock smitten with the hammer might produce splinters. Some Rabbinical authorities, therefore, contend for forty-nine, and others for as many as seventy meanings to each verse.[1]

---

[1] Eisenmenger Entwectes Judenthum, vol. i. ch. 9. This laborious investigator of Jewish writings justly calls their expositions "foolish and perverted," and supports the assertion with ample proof. Thus—to refer only to one or two—on the passage which narrates the meeting of Esau and Jacob, it is gathered in the Bereschith Rabba, from a small peculiarity in one of the words, that Esau did not come to kiss, but to bite, and that "our father Jacob's neck was changed into marble, so that the teeth of the ungodly man were broken." The passage in Ps. xcii. 10—"My horn shalt thou exalt like the horn of an unicorn. I shall be anointed with fresh oil," is explained in the Jalkut Chudash by the statement, that while in "anointing the other sons of Jesse, the oil was poured out, when David's turn came, the oil of itself flowed and ran upon his head." These, indeed, are among the simpler specimens; for, by giving a numerical value to the letters, the most extravagant and senseless opinions were thus obtained. The fact, however, is of importance, as it provides a sufficient answer to the mode of interpretation adopted by many modern expositors, who think it enough to justify the evangelists in putting what they regard as a false meaning upon words of prophecy, to say, that the Jewish writers were in the habit of applying Scripture in the same way—applying it in a sense different from its original import. It is forgotten in this case that the Jewish writers actually believed Scripture to have many senses, and that when they speak of its being fulfilled, they meant that the words really had the sense they ascribe to them.

When we pass out of the strictly Jewish territory to the other theological writings of the first ages, we are seldom allowed to travel far without stumbling on something of the same description. To say nothing of the writings of Philo, which are replete with fanciful allegorical meanings, but which could have little if any influence in Judea, in the epistle of Barnabas (ascribed to the pen of that Barnabas who was the companion of St Paul, and an acknowledged production of the first age), we find among other frivolous things, the circumcision of 318 persons in Abraham's house interpreted as indicating that the patriarch had received the mystery of three letters. For, the numerical value of the two leading letters that stand for the name of Jesus is 18, and the letter T, the figure of the cross, is 300; "wherefore by two letters he signified Jesus, and by the third his cross. He who has put the engrafted gift of his doctrine within us, knows that I never taught to any one a more certain truth." In the epistle of Clement, another production of the apostolical age, the scarlet thread which Rahab suspended from her window, is made to signify that there should be redemption through the blood of Jesus to all that believe and hope in him; and the fable of the Phœnix, dying after five hundred years, and giving birth, when dead, to another destined to live for the same period, is gravely treated as a fact in natural science, and held up as a proof of the resurrection. Some things of a similar nature are also to be met with in Irenæus, and many in the writings of Justin Martyr. Let the following suffice for a specimen:—

"When the people fought with Amalek, and the son of Nun, called Jesus, led on the battle, Moses was praying to God, having his arms extended in the form of a cross; as long as he remained in that posture, Amalek was beaten; but if he ceased in any degree to preserve it, the people were worsted,—all owing to the power of the cross; for the people did not conquer because Moses prayed, but because the name of Jesus was at the head of the battle, and Moses himself made the figure of the cross."
—(*Dial. Tryph.* p. 248, *Ed. Sylburg*).

Now, it is surely no small proof of the divine character of the New Testament writings, that they stand entirely clear from such strained and puerile interpretations, notwithstanding that they were the production of the very age and people peculiarly addicted to such things. Though Jesus of Nazareth, from the circumstances of his early life, could not have enjoyed more than the commonest advantages, he yet came forth as a public teacher nobly superior to the false spirit of the times; never seeking for the frivolous or the fanciful, but penetrating with the profoundest discernment into the real import of the divine testimony. And even the apostle Paul, though brought up at the feet of Gamaliel, whose name is still held in veneration in the schools of Rabbinical learning, betrays nothing of the sinister bias in this respect, which his early training must have tended to impart; he writes as one well skilled, indeed, to reason and dispute, but still always as one thoroughly versant in the real meaning of Scripture, and incapable of stooping to any thing trifling and fantastical. And that there should thus have been, in persons so circumstanced, along with a frequent handling of Old Testament Scripture, a perfectly sober and intelligent use of it—a spirit of interpretation pervading and directing that use, which can stand even the searching investigations of the nineteenth century, cannot fail to raise the question in candid and thoughtful minds, "Whence had these men this wisdom?" It is alone fitted to impress us with the conviction, that they were men specially taught by God, and that the inspiration of the Almighty gave them understanding.

We have stated, however, that though there are no real departures in the writings of the New Testament from a sound and judicious explanation of the historical and didactic parts of the Old, there are a few apparent ones —a few that may seem to be such on a superficial consideration. One passage, and only one, in our Lord's history, belongs to this class. It is his scriptural proof of the resurrection, in reply to the shallow objection of the Sadducees, which he drew from the declaration of God to Moses at the bush, "I am the God of Abraham, the God of Isaac, and the God of Jacob." It is clear from this alone, our Lord argued, that the dead are raised; "for God is not the God of the dead but of the living; for all live unto him"—(Matt. xxii. 32 ; Luke xx. 38). The argument was plainly stigmatised by the notorious Wolfenbuttle-fragmentist of the last century, as of the Rabbinical hair-splitting kind; and more recently Strauss, with some others of a kindred spirit in Germany, have both regarded it as a "cabalistical exposition," and urged as an additional reason for so regarding it, that the doctrine of a future state was derived by the Jews from other nations, and cannot be proved from the writings of the Old Testament. Most worthy successors truly to those Sadducean objectors whom our Lord sought to confute—equally shallow in their notions of God, and equally at fault in their reading of his written word! So far from deriving the notion of a future state, in the particular aspect of it now under consideration—a resurrection from the dead—from the heathen nations around them, the Jews were the only people in antiquity who held it; the Gentile philosophy in all its branches rejected it as incredible. And the construction put by our Lord on the words spoken to Moses, so far from being cabalistical or hair-splitting, simply penetrates to the fundamental principles involved in the relation they indicate between God and his servants. "The God of Abraham, of Isaac, and of Jacob"—*theirs* in the full and proper sense, to be to them, and to do for them, whatever such a Being, standing in such a relation, could be and do; therefore, most assuredly, to raise them from the dead, since, if one part of their natures were to be left there the prey of corruption, he might justly be ashamed to be called their God—(Heb. xi. 16). "How could God," Neander properly asks, "place himself in so near a relation to individual men, and ascribe to them so high a dignity, if they were mere perishable appearances, if they had not an essence akin to his own, and destined for immortality? The living God can only be conceived of as the God of the living."[1] Yes, the whole law, in a sense, bore witness to that; for there death constantly appears as the embodiment of foulness and corruption, with which the pure and holy One cannot dwell in union. So that for those who are really his, he must manifest himself as the conqueror of death; their relation to him, as his peculiar people, is a nonentity, if it

---

[1] Life of Jesus, § 248.

does not carry this in its train. How profound, then, yet how simple and how true, is the insight which our Lord here discovers into the realities of things, compared either with his ancient adversaries or his modern assailants! And how little does his argument need such diluted explanations to recommend it as those of Kuinoel,—" God is called the God of any one, in so far as he endows them with benefits; but he cannot bestow benefits upon the dead, therefore they live!" Nay, that is but a part; be not afraid to go a little deeper. There is more water in the well than is fetched up by such a bucket. It is clear still at a lower depth.

A passage that has much more commonly been regarded by commentators as breathing the dialectics of the Jewish schools, is Gal. iv. 21–31, where the apostle, in arguing against the legal and fleshly tendencies of the Galatians, summons them to " hear the law." And then he calls to their remembrance the circumstances recorded of the two wives of Abraham and their offspring; the one Sarah, the free-woman, the mother of the children of promise, or the spiritual seed, corresponding to the heavenly Jerusalem and its true worshippers; the other, Hagar, the bond-woman, the mother of a seed born after the flesh, carnal and ungodly in spirit, and so corresponding to the earthly Jerusalem, or Sinai, with its covenant of law, and its slavish carnal worshippers. And the apostle declares it as certain, that worshippers of this class must all be cast out from any inheritance in the kingdom of God, even as Hagar and her fleshly son were, by divine command, driven out of Abraham's house, that the true child of promise might dwell in peace, and inherit the blessing. It is true, the apostle himself calls this an allegorizing of the history, which is quite enough with some to stamp it as fanciful and weak. And there are others, looking merely to the superficial appearances, who allege that the exposition fails, since the child of Hagar had nothing to do with the law, while it was precisely the posterity of Sarah, by the line of Isaac, who stood bound by its requirements. This is an objection that could be urged only by those who did not perceive the real drift of the apostle's statement. We shall have occasion to unfold this in a subsequent part of our inquiry, when we come to speak of what the law could not do. Meanwhile, we affirm that the apostle's comment proceeds on the sound principle, that the things which took place in Abraham's house in regard to a seed of promise and blessing, were all ordered specially and peculiarly to exhibit at the very outset the truth, that such a seed must be begotten from above, and that all not thus begotten, though encompassed, it might be, with the solemnities and privileges of the covenant, were born after the flesh—Ishmaelites in spirit, and strangers to the promise. The apostle merely reads out the spiritual lessons that lay infolded in the history of Abraham's family as significant of things to come; and, to say that the similitude fails, because the law was given to the posterity of Sarah and not of Hagar, betrays a lamentable ignorance of what the real design of the law was, and what should have been expected from it. The interpretation of the apostle alone brings out the fundamental principles involved in the transactions, and it does no more.

Those who would fasten on the apostle the charge of resorting to Rabbinical arbitrariness and conceit, point with considerable confidence to a passage in the first epistle to the Corinthians. The passage is 1 Cor. x. 1–4, where the apostle reminds the Corinthians how their fathers had been under the cloud, and had passed through the sea; and had been baptised into Moses in the cloud and in the sea; and had all eaten the same spiritual food, and all drunk of the same spiritual drink; for they drank of that spiritual Rock which followed them, and that Rock was Christ. In this latter part of the description, it has been alleged (and is still by De Wette, Rückert, Meyer), that the apostle adopts the Jewish legends respecting the rock at Horeb having actually followed the Israelites in their wanderings, and puts a feigned allegorical construction on the other parts to suit his purpose. The passage will naturally present itself for explanation when we come to the period in Israel's history to which it refers.[1] At present we merely say, that it only requires us to take the apostle's statements in their proper connection, and make due allowance for the figurative use of language. He is representing the position of the Israelites in the desert as substantially one with that of the Corinthians. And, to make it more manifest, he even applies the terms fitted to express the condition of the Corinthians to the case of the Israelites:—These, says he, were baptized like you, had Christ among them like you, and like you were privileged to eat and drink as guests in the Lord's house. Of course, language transferred thus from one part of God's dispensations to another, could never be meant to be taken very strictly—no more could it be so, when the *new* things of the Christian dispensation were applied to the Israelites, than when the *old* things of the Jewish are applied to the members of the Christian Church. In this latter mode of application, the Christian Church is spoken of as having a temple as Israel had, an altar, a passover-lamb and feast, a sprinkling with blood, a circumcision. Yet every one knows that what is meant by such language is, not that the very things themselves, the things in their outward form and appearance, but that the inward realities signified by them, belong to the Church of Christ. The old name is retained, though actually denoting something higher and better. And we must interpret in the same way, when the transference is made in the reverse order—when the new things of the Christian Church are ascribed to the ancient Israelites. By the cloud passing over and resting between them and the Egyptians, and afterwards by their passing under its protection through the Red sea in safety, they were baptised into Moses— for thus the line of demarcation was drawn between their old vassalage and the new state and prospects on which, under Moses, they had entered; and Christ himself, whose servant Moses was, was present with them, feeding them as from his own hand with direct supplies of meat and drink, till they reached the promised inheritance. In short, these were to them relatively what Christian baptism and the Lord's supper are to believers now. But not in themselves formally the same. Christ was there only in a mystery; Gospel ordinances were possessed only under the shadow of means and provisions, adapted immediately to their bodily wants and temporal condition. Yet still Christ and the Gospel were there; for all that was then given and done linked itself by a spiritual bond with the better things to come, and as

---

[1] See Book III., § 4.

in a glass darkly reflected the benefits of redemption. So that, as the Israelites in the desert stood relatively in the same position with the professing Church under the Gospel, the language here used by the apostle merely shews how clearly he perceived the points of resemblance, and how profoundly he looked into the connection between them.

II.—PROPHECIES REFERRED TO BY CHRIST.

We no sooner open the evangelical narratives of New Testament Scripture than we meet with references and appeals to the *prophecies* of the Old. The leading personages and transactions of gospel times are constantly presented to our view as those that had been foreseen and described by ancient seers; and at every important turn in the evolution of affairs, we find particular passages of prophecy quoted as receiving their fulfilment in what was taking place. But we soon perceive, that the connection between the predictions referred to and their alleged fulfilment, is by no means always of the same kind. It appears sometimes as more natural and obvious in its nature, and sometimes as more mystical and recondite. The latter, of course, in an inquiry like the present, are such as more especially call for consideration and remark; but the others are not on that account to be passed over in silence. For they are so far at least of importance, that they shew what class of predictions, in the estimation of our Lord and his apostles, most obviously point to the affairs of the Messiah's kingdom, and afford also an opportunity of marking how the transition began to be made to a further and freer application of Old Testament prophecy.

In this line of inquiry, however, it will not do to take up the references to the prophets precisely as they occur in the gospels; for the evangelists did not write their narratives of our Lord's personal history till a considerable time after the events that compose it had taken place—not till the deeper, as well as the more obvious things connected with it had become known to them; and not a few of the prophetical references found in their narratives were only understood by themselves at a period much later than that at which the events occurred. It is in Christ's own teaching, communicated as the events were actually in progress, that we may expect to find the most simple and direct applications of prophecy, and the key to the entire use of it subsequently made by his apostles. For the present, therefore, we shall throw ourselves back upon the transactions of the gospel age, and with our eye upon him who was at once the centre and the prime agent of the whole, we shall note the manner in which he reads to those around him the prophecies that bore on himself and his times. We shall take them, not in the historical order they occupy in the narratives of the evangelists, but in the antecedent order which belonged to them, as quoted in the public ministry of Christ. We shall thus see how he led those around him, step by step, to a right understanding of the prophecies in their evangelical import.

At the very commencement of our Lord's public ministry, and on the occasion, as it would seem, of his first public appearance in the synagogue of Nazareth, he opened the book of the prophet Isaiah that had been put into his hands, and read from chap. lxi. the following words: "The Spirit of the Lord is upon me, because he hath anointed me to preach the Gospel to the poor: he hath sent me to heal the broken-hearted, to preach deliverance to the captives, and recovering of sight to the blind, to set at liberty them that are bruised; to preach the acceptable year of the Lord. And he closed the book," it is added by the evangelist, "and began to say unto them, This day is this Scripture fulfilled in your ears." The passage thus quoted, and so emphatically applied by Jesus to himself, is one of those in the latter portion of Isaiah's writings (comprehending also chap. xlii., xlix., liii.), which evidently treat of one grand theme,—"the Lord's servant," his "elect" one, him "in whom his soul delighted;" unfolding what this wonderful and mysterious personage was to be, to do, and to suffer for the redemption of the Lord's people, and the vindication of his cause in the earth. It is matter of certainty that, in the judgment of the ancient Jewish church, the person spoken of in all these passages was the Messiah;[1] so that in applying to himself that particular passage in Isaiah, Jesus not only advanced the claim, but he must have been perfectly understood by those present to advance the claim, to be the Messiah of the Jewish prophets. The modern Jews, and a considerable number also of Christian expositors (chiefly on the continent), have endeavoured to prove that the immediate and proper reference in this, and the other passages in Isaiah connected with it, is to the Jewish nation as a whole, or to the prophetical part of it in particular. But these attempts have signally failed. It stands fast, as the result of the most careful and searching criticism, that the words of the prophet can only be understood of a single individual, in whom far higher than human powers were to develope themselves, and who was to do, as well for Israel as for the world at large, what Israel had been found utterly incompetent, even in the lighter departments of the work, to accomplish. In a word, they can be understood only of the promised Messiah. And of all that had been spoken concerning him by the prophet Isaiah, there is not a passage to be found that could more fitly have been appropriated by Jesus than the one he read at that opening stage of his career; as it describes him in respect to the whole reach and compass of his divine commission, with all its restorative energies and beneficent results. We see as well the wisdom of the selection as the justness of the application. It is also to be noted, that the appropriation by our Lord of the passage in this sixty-first chapter of Isaiah, gives the virtual sanction of his authority to the applications elsewhere made of other passages in the same prophetical discourse to gospel-times—such as Matt. xii. 18-21; Acts viii. 32-35; xiii. 47; Rom. x. 21; 1 Peter ii. 23-25, where portions of Isa. xlii., xlix., liii. are so applied.

The next *open and public* appeal made by our Lord to an ancient prophecy, was made with immediate respect to John the Baptist. It was probably about the middle of Christ's ministry, and shortly before the death of John. Taking occasion from John's message to speak of the distinguished place he held among God's servants, the Lord said: "This is he, of whom

---

[1] See Lightfoot, Hor. Heb. on Matt. xii. 20, and John v. 19; Schöttgen de Messia, pp. 113, 192; Hengstenberg's Christology on Isa. xlii. 1-9, xlix., liii. 2. Also Alexander on the same passages, and lxi.

it is written, Behold, I send my messenger before thy face, and he shall prepare thy way before thee." The words are taken from the beginning of the third chapter of Malachi—with no other difference than that he who there sends is also the one before whom the way was to be prepared: "He shall prepare the way before *me*." The reason of this variation will be noticed presently. But, in regard to John, that he was the person specially intended by the prophet as the herald-messenger of the Lord, can admit of no doubt on the part of any one who sincerely believes that Jesus was God manifest in the flesh, and personally tabernacling among men. John himself does not appear to have formally appropriated this passage in Malachi. But he virtually did so when he described himself in the words of a passage in Isaiah, "I am the voice of one crying in the wilderness, Prepare ye the way of the Lord;" for the passage in Malachi is merely a resumption, with a few additional characteristics, of that more ancient one in Isaiah. And on this account they are both thrown together at the commencement of St Mark's Gospel, as if they formed indeed but one prediction: "As it is written in the prophets (many copies even read 'by Isaiah the prophet'), Behold, I send my messenger before thy face, which shall prepare thy way before thee. The voice of one crying in the wilderness, Prepare ye the way of the Lord, make his paths straight." And there is still another prediction—one at the very close of Malachi—which is but a new, and, in some respects, more specific announcement of what was already uttered in these earlier prophecies. In this last prediction, the preparatory messenger is expressly called by the name of Elias the prophet, and the work he had to do "before the coming of the Lord," is described as that of turning "the heart of the fathers (or making it return) to the children, and the heart of the children to their fathers." As this was the last word of the Old Testament, so it is in a manner the first word of the New; for the prophecy was taken up by the angel, who announced to Zacharias the birth of John, and at once applied and explained it in connection with the mission of John. "Many of the children of Israel," said the angel, "shall he turn to the Lord their God; and he shall go before him in the spirit and power of Elias, to turn the hearts of the fathers to the children, and the disobedient to the wisdom of the just; to make ready a people prepared for the Lord" (Luke i. 16, 17). Here the coming of the Lord, as in all the passages under consideration, was the grand terminating point of the prophecy, and, as preparatory to this, the making ready of a people for it. This making ready of the people, or turning them back again (with reference to the words of Elijah in 1 Kings xviii. 37) to the Lord their God, is twice mentioned by the angel as the object of John's mission. And, between the two, there is given what is properly but another view of the same thing, only with express reference to the Elijah-like character of the work: John was to go before the Lord as a new Elias, in the spirit and power of that great prophet, and for the purpose of effecting a reconciliation between the degenerate seed of Israel and their pious forefathers—making them again of one heart and soul, so that the fathers might not be ashamed of their children, nor the children of their fathers; in a word, that he might effect a real reformation, by turning "the disobedient (offspring) to the wisdom of the just (ancestors)." Thus in all these passages—to which we may also add the private testimony of our Lord to the disciples as to Elias having indeed come (Mark ix. 13)—there is a direct application of the Old Testament prophecy, in a series of closely-related predictions, to the person and mission of John the Baptist. And, so far from any violence or constraint appearing in this application, the predictions are all taken in their most natural and obvious meaning. For that the literal Elias was no more to be expected from the last of these predictions, than the literal David from Ezek. xxxiv. 23, seems plain enough; the person meant could only be one coming in the spirit of Elias, and commissioned to do substantially his work. So also, Jezebel and Balaam are spoken of as reviving in the teachers of false doctrine and the patrons of corruption, who appeared in some of the churches of Asia (Rev. ii. 14, 20).

But we must pass on to another instance of fulfilled prophecy. It will be observed, that in all those passages out of Isaiah and Malachi applied to John the Baptist, there was involved an application also to Christ himself, as being the person whose way John was sent to prepare. The assertion, that John was the herald-messenger foretold in them, clearly implied, that Jesus of Nazareth was the Lord who was to come to his people, or "the Angel of the Covenant that was to come suddenly to *his* temple." He, therefore, was the Lord of the temple, or the divine head and proprietor of the covenant people whom that temple symbolized, and in the midst of whom he appeared as God manifest in the flesh. But this the Lord merely left to be inferred from what he said of John; he even seems to have purposely drawn a sort of veil over it, by the slight change he introduced into the words of Malachi, saying, Not "before *me*," but "before *thy face*." For he well knew, that those to whom he spake could not bear in this respect the plain announcement of the truth, indeed, least of all here; they could not even bear to hear Jesus call himself by the milder epithet of the Son of God. Sometime, however, if not at present, the Lord must give them to know, that in this rooted antipathy to the essentially divine character of Messiah, they had their own Scriptures against them. And so, in the next public appeal he made to the prophetical Scriptures, he selected this point in particular for proof. But that the appeal might come with more power to their consciences, he threw it into the form, not of an assertion, but of an interrogation; he put it to themselves: "What think ye of Christ? whose son is he? They say unto him, The son of David. He saith unto them, How then doth David in spirit call him Lord, saying, The Lord said unto my Lord, Sit thou on my right hand, till I make thine enemies thy footstool. If David then call him Lord, how is he his son?" (Matt. xxii. 42-45). The familiar allusion here, and in other passages of the New Testament, to this psalm as descriptive of the Messiah, clearly evinces what was the view taken of it by the ancient Jewish church; such an argumentative use of it could only have been made on the ground that it was held by general consent to be a prophecy of Christ. Efforts have again and again been made in modern times to controvert this view, but without any measure of success. And, indeed, apart altogether from the explicit testimony of our Lord and his apostles, looking merely to what is said of the hero of this psalm—that he stood to David himself in the relation of Lord; that he was to sit on Jehovah's right hand, that is, should be invested with the power and sovereignty of God; that he should, like Melchizedec, be a priest on the throne, and that for ever—it is impossible to take these parts of the description in their natural meaning, and understand them of any one but the Messiah—a Messiah, too, combining in his mysterious person properties at once human and divine. The silence of our Lord's adversaries then, and the fruitless labours of his detractors since, are confirmatory testimonies to the soundness of this application of the psalm, as the only tenable one.

Another purpose—one immediately connected with his humiliation—led our Lord, very shortly after the occasion last referred to, to point to another prophecy as presently going to meet with its fulfilment. It was when fresh from the celebration of the paschal feast and his own supper, he had retired with his disciples, under the shade of night, to the Mount of Olives: " Then said Jesus unto them, All ye shall be offended because of me this night; for it is written, I will smite the shepherd, and the sheep of the flock shall be scattered abroad" (Matt. xxvi. 31). So it had been written in Zachariah, xiii. 7, respecting that peculiar shepherd and his flock, who was to be Jehovah's fellow, or rather his near relation—for so the word in the original imports; and hence, when spoken of any one's relation to God, it cannot possibly denote a mere man, but can only be understood of one who, by virtue of his divine nature, stands on a footing of essential nearness and equality toward God. All other interpretations, whether by Jews or Christians, can only be regarded as shifts, devised to explain away or get rid of the plain meaning of the prophecy. And it was here more especially chosen by our Lord, as, more distinctly and emphatically perhaps than any other prediction in Old Testament Scripture, it combined with the peerless dignity of Christ's nature the fearful depth of his humiliation and suffering; and so was at once fitted to instruct and comfort the disciples in respect to the season of tribulation that was before them. It told them, indeed, that the suffering was inevitable; but at the same time imparted the consolation, that so exalted a sufferer could only suffer for a time. But though this was the only prophetical passage particularly noticed, as having been explained by Christ with reference to his sufferings, we are expressly informed that, after his resurrection at least, he made a similar application of many others. He reproved the two disciples on their way to Emmaus, for their dulness and incredulity, because they had not learned from the prophets how Christ must suffer before entering into his glory: "And beginning at Moses and all the prophets, he expounded unto them in all the Scriptures the things concerning himself." Indeed, it would appear that, even before his death, he had referred to various Scriptures bearing on this point; for, at Luke xxiv. 44, we find him saying to the disciples as a body: " These are the words which I spake unto you, while I was yet with you, that all things must be fulfilled which were written in the law of Moses, and in the prophets, and in the psalms, concerning me." But as what had been spoken previously had been spoken to little purpose, he then " opened their understandings, that they might understand the Scriptures;" and said unto them, " Thus it is written, and thus it behoved Christ to suffer, and to rise from the dead on the third day," &c.

Nor are we left altogether without the means of knowing what portions of Old Testament Scripture our Lord thus applied to himself. The apostles undoubtedly proceeded to act upon the instruction they had received, and to make use of the light that had been imparted to them. And when, on opening the Acts of the Apostles, we find Peter, in chap. i., applying without hesitation or reserve what is written in Ps. cix., of the persecutions of Jesus and the apostacy of Judas: again, in chap. ii., applying in like manner, what is written in Ps. xvi. to Christ's speedy resurrection; Ps. cx., to his exaltation to power and glory; and Joel ii. 28-32, to the gift of the Spirit; in chap. iii., affirming Jesus to be the prophet that Moses had foretold should be raised up like to himself; in chap. iv., speaking of Jesus as the stone rejected by the builders, but raised by God to the head of the corner, as written in Ps. cxviii. (an application that had already been indicated, at least, by Christ in a public discourse with the Jews, Matt. xxi. 42), and, along with the other apostles, describing Christ as the anointed king in Ps. ii., against whom the heathen raged, and the people imagined vain things;—when we read these things, it would be folly to doubt that we have in them the fruit of that more special instruction which our Lord gave to his disciples, when he opened their understanding that they might understand the Scriptures. It is Christ's own teaching made known to us through the report of those who had received it from his lips. And any interpretation of those passages of Old Testament Scripture, which would deny their fair and legitimate application to Christ and the things of his kingdom, must be regarded as a virtual reflection on the wisdom and authority of Christ himself.

But it does not follow from this, that Christ and Gospel events must in all of them have been *exclusively* intended: it may be enough if in some they were more peculiarly included. More could scarcely be meant, especially in respect to Ps. cix. and cxviii., in both of which the language is such as to comprehend classes of persons, and whole series of events. That the proper culmination of what is written should be found in Christ and his Gospel dispensation, is all that could justly be expected. But of this it will be necessary to speak more fully, as it touches on a more profound and hidden application of Old Testament things to those of the New. There were other parts also of our Lord's personal teaching which still more strikingly bore on such an application, but which, from their enigmatical character, we have purposely omitted referring to in this section. Meanwhile, in those more obvious and direct references which have chiefly passed under our review, what a body of well-selected proof has our Lord given from the prophecies of the Old Testament, to the truth of his own Messiahship! And how clear and penetrating an insight did he exhibit into the meaning of those prophecies, compared with what then prevailed among his countrymen!

III.—THE DEEPER PRINCIPLES INVOLVED IN CHRIST'S USE OF THE OLD TESTAMENT.

We have seen that nearly all the prophecies of Old Testament Scripture, which our Lord applied to himself and the affairs of his kingdom, during the period of his earthly ministry, were such as admitted of being so applied in their most direct and obvious sense. In nothing else could they have found a proper and adequate fulfilment. This can scarcely, however, be said of the whole of them. When his ministry was drawing to a close, he on one occasion publicly, and on several occasions with the disciples privately, made application to himself and the things of his kingdom, of prophecies which could not be said to bear immediate and exclusive respect to New Testament times. And we have now to examine these later and more peculiar applications of prophetical Scripture, in order to perceive the deeper principles of connection between the Old and the New, involved in our Lord's occasional use of the word of prophecy.

The *public* occasion we have referred to was when, a few days before his death, Christ solemnly pointed the attention of the Jews to a passage in Ps. cxviii. "Did ye never read," he asked (Matt. xxi. 42), "in the Scriptures, The stone which the builders rejected, the same is become the head of the corner: this is the Lord's doing, and it is marvellous in our eyes?" Though Jesus did not say in respect to this psalm, as he said shortly after in respect to the 110th, that in inditing it the Psalmist spake through the Spirit of Christ; yet both the question itself he put regarding the passage, and the personal application he presently afterwards made of it, clearly implied, that he considered himself and the Jewish authorities of his time, to be distinctly embraced in the Psalmist's announcement. And the same opinion was still more explicitly avowed by the Apostle Peter, after he had been instructed more fully by Christ respecting the Old Testament Scriptures, when, standing before the Jewish council, he exclaimed, "This is the stone which was set at nought by you builders, which is become the head of the corner."— (Acts iv. 11.)

Yet, when we turn to the psalm itself, the passage thus quoted and applied to Christ, in his relation to the Jewish rulers, has the appearance rather of a statement then actually verified in the history and experience of the covenant-people, than of a prediction still waiting to be fulfilled. The psalm throughout has the appearance of a national song, in which priests and people joined together to celebrate the praise of God, on some memorable occasion when they saw enlargement and prosperity return after a period of depression and contempt. It was peculiarly an occasion of this kind, when the little remnant that escaped from Babylon, amid singular tokens of divine favour, found themselves in a condition to set about the restoration of God's house and kingdom in Jerusalem. Indeed, Ezra iii. 11 leaves very little room to doubt, that the psalm owes its origin to that happy occasion, as we are there told, that when they met to lay anew the foundation of the temple, the assembled multitude began to praise the Lord in the very words which form the commencement of this psalm. There could not be a more seasonable moment for the joyous burst of thanksgiving, which the people seem in the psalm, as with one heart and soul, to pour forth to God, on account of his distinguishing goodness in having rescued them from the deadly grasp of their heathen adversaries, and for the elevating and assured hope they express of the final and complete ascendency of his kingdom. Of this, the eye of faith was presented with an encouraging pledge in current events. By a remarkable turn in God's providence, the apparently dead had become alive again; the stone rejected by the mighty builders of this world, as worthless and contemptible, was marvellously raised to the head of the corner; and, in connection with it, a commencement was made, however feebly, toward the universal triumph of the truth of God over the corruption and idolatry of the world. But such being the natural and direct purport of the psalm, how could the sentiment uttered in it concerning the stone be so unconditionally applied to Christ? The right answer to this question presupposes the existence of a peculiarly close relation between the commonwealth of Israel and Christ; and such a relation as can only be understood aright, when we have first correctly apprehended the real calling and destiny of Israel.

Now, this was declared at the outset by anticipation to Abraham, when the Lord said concerning his seed, that it should be blessed and made a blessing—made so peculiarly the channel of blessing, that in it *all* the families of the earth were to be blessed. To fulfil this high destination, was the calling of Israel as an elect people. Viewed, therefore, according to their calling, they were the children of God, Jehovah's first-born (Deut. xiv. 1; Exod. iv. 22); Jehovah was the father that begot them—that is, raised them into the condition of a people, possessing a kind of filial relationship to himself (Deut. xxxii. 6, 18; Jer. xxxi. 9); but possessing it only in so far as they were a spiritual and holy people, abiding near to God, and fitted for executing his righteous purposes—for so far only did their actual state correspond with their destination.—(Exod. xix. 5, 6; Deut. xiv. 2; Ps. lxxiii. 15.) For the most part, this correspondence palpably failed. God was true to *his* engagements, but not Israel to *theirs*. He gave freely to them of his goodness; gave often when he might have withheld; but *their* history is replete with backslidings and apostasies, shame and reproach. Even within the limits of Canaan, the real children of God—the seed of blessing—were usually in a grievous minority; they were, for the most part, the comparatively poor, the afflicted, the needy, amid multitudes of an opposite spirit—the internal heathen, who differed only in name and outward position from the heathen abroad. But this very imperfection in the reality, as compared with the idea, was here, as in other things, made to contribute toward the great end in contemplation. For it was this especially that shewed the necessity of something higher and better to accomplish what was in prospect. So long as God stood related to them, merely as he did, or had done to their fathers, believers in Israel felt that they had to wage an unequal conflict, in which fearful odds were generally against them, even on Israelitish ground. And how could they expect to attain to a righteousness, and acquire a position, that should enable them to bless the whole world? For this, manifestly, there was needed another and still closer union than yet existed between Israel and God—a union that should somehow impenetrate their condition with the very power and sufficiency of Godhead. Only if the relation between earth and heaven could be made to assume a more vital and organic form—only if the divine and human, the angel of the covenant and the seed of Abraham, Jehovah and Israel, could become truly and personally one—then only could it seem possible to raise the interest of righteousness in Israel to such an elevation as should bring the lofty destination of Abraham's seed to bless the world within the bounds of probability. It was one leading object of prophecy to give to such thoughts and anticipations a definite shape, and convert what might otherwise have been but the vague surmises, or uncertain conjectures of nature, into a distinct article of faith. Especially does this object come prominently out in the latter portion of Isaiah's writings, where, in a lengthened and varied discourse concerning the calling and destiny of Israel, we find the Lord perpetually turning from Israel in one sense, to Israel in another; from an Israel full of imperfection, false, backsliding, feeble, and perverse, (for example, in chap. xlii. 19; xliii. 22; xlviii. 4; lviii.; lix.), to an Israel full of excellence and might, the beloved of Jehovah, the very impersonation of divine life and goodness, in whom all righteousness should be fulfilled, and salvation for ever made sure to a numerous and blessed offspring.—(Chap. xlii. 1–7; xlix.; lii. 13–15, liii.; lv.; lxi. 1–3.) So that what Israel, as a whole, had completely failed to realize—what, even in the *spiritual* portion of Israel, had been realized in a very partial and inadequate manner, *that*, the prophet gave it to be understood, was one day to be accomplished without either failure or imperfection. But let it be marked well how it was to be accomplished;—simply by there being raised up in Israel One who should link together in his mysterious person the properties of the seed of Abraham and the perfections of Jehovah; in whom, by the singular providence of God, should meet on the one side all that distinctively belonged to Israel of calling and privilege, and all, on the other, that was needed of divine power and sufficiency to make good the determinate counsel of Heaven to bless all the families of the earth.

But this is still only one, and what may be called the more general, aspect of the matter. Within the circle of the chosen seed, a special arrangement was, from the first, contemplated (Gen. xlix. 8–10), and came at last to be actually made, which was rendered yet more remarkably subservient to the design of at once nourishing the expectation of a Messiah, and exhibiting the difference, the antagonism even, that should exist between him and the fleshly Israel. We refer to the appointment of a royal house, in which Israel's peculiar calling to bless the world was to rise to its highest sphere, and by which it was more especially to reach its fulfilment. To render more clearly manifest God's real purpose in this respect, he allowed a false movement to be made, in the first instance, concerning it. The choice was virtually given to the people, who sought merely to have a king and kingdom like the nations around them (1 Sam. viii. 5; ix. 20; xii. 13); and so the king they got, being carnal, like themselves, soon proved incapable, notwithstanding the peculiar means that were employed to elevate his spiritual condition, of reigning as God's vicegerent, and his kingdom equally incapable of establishing righteousness within, or resisting assaults from without. It was but a human institution, and fell alike unblessed and unblessing. Therefore, the Lord stepped in to exercise *his* choice in the matter, and found David, who, by special training and gifts, was prepared to wield the kingdom for the Lord. So thoroughly did he enter into the Lord's mind in the matter, and act as the Lord's servant, that the kingdom was made to stand in him as its living root, and the right to administer a kingdom of blessing in the earth was connected in perpetuity with his line.—(2 Sam. vii.) But here, again, the same kind of results presently began to discover themselves, as in the former case. It was with the utmost difficulty at first, and never more than in the most imperfect manner, that David himself, or any of his successors, could succeed in establishing righteousness and dispensing blessing even among the families of Israel. The kingdom, too, with all its imperfections, lasted but for a brief period, and then fell into hopeless confusion. So that if the divine purpose in this matter was really to stand; if there was to be a kingdom of truly divine character, administered by the house of David, and encompassing the whole earth with its verdant and fruitful boughs (Ezek. xvii. 22-24; Dan. vii. 13, 14), it was manifest that some other link of connection must be formed than any that still existed, between the divine source and the earthly possessor of the sovereignty—a connection not merely of delegated authority, but of personal contact and efficient working; on the one side humanizing the Deity, and on the other deifying humanity. For no otherwise than through such intermingling of the divine and human could the necessary power be constituted for establishing and directing such a kingdom throughout the nations of the earth.

Now, this destined rise in the kingdom founded in David, and its culmination in a divine-human Head, is also the theme of many prophecies. David himself took the lead in announcing it; for he already foresaw, through the Spirit, what, in this respect, would be required to verify the wonderful promise made to him.—(2 Sam. vii.; Ps. ii., xlv., lxxii., cx.; also Isa. vii. 14; ix. 6, &c.) But as David was himself the root of this new order of things, and the whole was to take the form of a verification of the word spoken to him, or of the perfectionment of the germ that was planted in him, so in his personal history there was given a compendious representation of the nature and prospects of the kingdom. In the first brief stage was exhibited the embryo of what it should ultimately become. Thus, the absoluteness of the divine choice in appointing the king—his *seeming* want, but *real* possession of the qualities required for administering the affairs of the kingdom—the growth from small, because necessarily *spiritual*, beginnings of the interests belonging to it—still growing, however, in the face of an inveterate and ungodly opposition, until judgment was brought forth unto victory,—these leading elements in the history of the first possessor of the kingdom must appear again—they must have their counterpart in Him, on whom the prerogatives and blessings of the kingdom were finally to settle. There was a real necessity in the case, such as always exists where the end is but the developement and perfection of the beginning; and we may not hesitate to say, that if they had failed in Christ, he could not have been the anointed king of David's line, in whom the purpose of God to govern and bless the world in righteousness, was destined to stand. Here, again, we have another and lengthened series of predictions, connecting, in this respect, the past with the future, the beginning with the ending (for example, Ps. xvi., xxii., xl., lxix., cix.; Isa. liii.; Zech. ix. 9; xii. 10; xiii. 1-7.)

Such, then, is the close and organic connection, in two important respects, between God's purpose concerning Israel, and his purpose in Christ. And if we only keep this distinctly in view, we shall have no difficulty in perceiving that a valid and satisfactory ground existed for the application of Ps. cxviii. 22 to Christ, and many applications of a similar kind made both by him and by the apostles. In the psalm now mentioned, the calling and destination of Israel to be blessed, and to bless mankind, notwithstanding that they were in themselves so small in number, and had to carry it against all the might and power of the world—this is the theme which is chiefly unfolded there, and it is unfolded in connection with the singular manifestation of divine power and goodness, which had even then given such a striking token of the full accomplishment of the design. But this accomplishment, as we have seen, could only be found in Christ, in whom was to meet what distinctively belonged to Israel, on the one side, and, on the other, what exclusively belongs to God. In him, therefore, the grand theme of the psalm must embody itself, and through him reach its complete realization. He pre-eminently and peculiarly is the stone, rejected in the first instance by the carnalism of the world, as represented in the Jewish rulers, but at length raised by God, on account of its spiritual and divine qualities, to be the head of the corner. And all that formerly occurred of a like nature in the history of Israel, was but the germ of what must again, and in a far higher manner, be developed in the work and kingdom of the Lord Jesus Christ.

The same thing, with no material difference, holds of an entire class of passages in the Psalms, only, in most of them, respect is chiefly had to the covenant made with the house of David, rather than to the more general calling and destination of Israel. Such, for example, are the two closely-related Psalms lxix. and cix., parts of which were first privately applied by Christ, and afterwards more publicly by Peter, to the case of Judas (John xv. 25; Acts i. 20, comp. with Ps. lxix. 4, 25; cix. 3, 8); but to him only as the worst embodiment and most palpable representative of the malice and opposition of which the Messiah was the object: for such Judas was in reality, and such also is the kind of enmity described in the Psalms—an enmity that had many abettors, though concentrating itself in one or more individuals. Hence St Paul applies the description to the Jews generally.—(Rom. xi. 9, 10.) Other passages in the same two psalms are applied by the evangelists and apostles to Christ—Matt. xxvii. 34, 48; John ii. 17; Rom. xv. 3.) And to these psalms we may add, as belonging to the same class, Ps. xli., a verse of which, " He that did eat of my bread, lifted up his heel against me," is pointed to by our Lord as finding its fulfilment in the treachery of Judas (John xiii. 18); Ps. xxii., of which several similar appropriations are made concerning Christ (Matt. xxvii. 46; John xix. 24, &c.); and Ps. xl., which contains the passage regarding the insufficiency of animal sacrifices, and the necessity of a sublime act of self-devotion, quite unconditionally applied to Christ in Heb. x. 4-10. The references to these psalms, it will be observed, were made either by Christ, near the close of his ministry, when seeking to give the disciples a deeper insight into the bearing of Old Testament Scripture on gospel-times, or by the evangelists and apostles after his work on earth was finished, and all had become plain to them. The Psalms themselves are so far alike, that they are all the productions of David, and productions in which he, as the founder and root of the kingdom, endeavoured, through the Spirit, out of the lines of his own eventful history, to set forth the light it furnished respecting the more important and momentous future. That his eye was chiefly upon this future is evident, as well from the extremity of the sufferings described, which greatly exceeded what David personally underwent (Ps. xxii. 8, 14-18 ; lxix. 8, 21 ; cix. 24, 25), as from the world-wide results, the everlasting and universal benefits that are spoken of as flowing from the salvation wrought, far beyond any thing that David could have contemplated respecting himself.—(Ps. xxii. 27 ; xl. 5, 10, 16 ; xli. 12 ; lxix. 35.) But still, while the future is mainly regarded, it is seen by the Psalmist under the form and lineaments of the past ;—his own sufferings and deliverances were like the book from which he read forth the similar, but greater things to come. And why should not David, who so clearly foresaw the brighter, have foreseen also the darker and more troubled aspect of the future ? If it was given him through the Spirit to descry, as the proper heir and possessor of the kingdom, One, so much higher in nature and dignity than himself, that he felt it right to call him Lord and God (Ps. xlv., cx.), why should it not also have been given him to see that this glorious personage, *as his son*, should bear his father's image alike in the more afflicting and troubled, and in the better and more glorious part of his career ? This is simply what David did see, and what he expressed, with great fulness and variety, in the portion of his writings now under consideration. And hence their peculiar form and structure, as partaking so much of the personal. When unfolding the more *divine* aspect and relations of the kingdom, the Psalmist speaks of the possessor of it as of another than himself, nearly related to him, but still different, higher and greater—(Ps. ii., xlv., lxxii., cx.) But when he discourses, in the psalms above referred to, concerning its more *human* aspect and relations, he speaks as of himself ; the sufferings to be borne and overcome seemed like a prolongation, or rather like a renewal in an intenser form, of his own ; the father, in a manner, identifies himself with the son, as the son again, in alluding to what was written, identifies himself with the father ; for so it behoved to be—the past *must* here foreshadow the future, and the future take its shape from the past.

The view now given of this series of psalms, it will be observed, differs materially, not only from that which regards them as properly applicable only to David, and merely accommodated to Christ and gospel things, but also from that of Hengstenberg and others, according to which the psalms in question describe the suffering righteous person in general, and apply to Christ only in so far as he was pre-eminently a righteous sufferer. We hold them to be, in a much closer sense, prophecies of Christ, and regard them as delineations of what, in its full sense, could only be expected to take place in him who was to fulfil the calling and destination, of which the mere foreshadow and announcement was to be seen in David. And this connection between David and Christ, on which the delineation proceeds, seems to us satisfactorily to account for two peculiarities in the structure of these psalms, which have always been the occasion of embarrassment. The first is the one already noticed—their being written as in the person of the

Psalmist. This arose from his being led by the Spirit to contemplate the coming future as the continuation and only adequate completion of what pertained to himself—to descry the Messiah as the second and higher David. The other peculiarity is the mention that is made in some of these psalms of sin as belonging to the person who speaks in them; as in Ps. xl., for example, where he confesses his sins to be more in number than the hairs of his head—and that, too, presently after he had declared it to be his purpose and delight to do the will of God in a way more acceptable than all sacrifice. This has been deemed inexplicable, on the supposition of Christ being the speaker. And if Christ alone, directly and exclusively, had been contemplated, we think it *would* have been inexplicable. His connection with sin would not have been represented exactly in that form. But let the ground of the representation be what we have described; let it be understood that David wrote of the Messiah as the Son, who, however higher and greater than himself, was still to be a kind of second self, then the description *must* have taken its form from the history and position of David, and should be read as from that point of view. If it is true in some respects that "things take the signature of thought" (*Coleridge*), here the reverse necessarily happened —the thought, imaging to itself the future as the reflection and final developement of the past, naturally took the signature of *things;* and sin, with which the second as well as the first David had much to do in establishing the kingdom, must be confessed as from the bosom of the royal Psalmist. It is merely a part of the relatively imperfect nature of all the representations of Christ's work and kingdom, which were unfolded under the image and shadow of past and inferior, but closely related circumstances. And this imperfection in the form was the more necessary in psalms, since, being destined for public use in the worship of God, they could only express such views and feelings as the congregation might be expected to sympathise with, and should, even when carrying forward the desires and expectations of the soul to better things to come, still touch a chord in every believer's bosom.

There is, however, another and more peculiar, indeed the *most* peculiar, application made by our Lord of the Old Testament Scriptures;—but an application proceeding on a quite similar, though more specific, connection between the past and the future in God's kingdom. We refer to what our Lord said after the transfiguration respecting John the Baptist. Before this, he had even publicly asserted John to be the Elias predicted by Malachi: "And if ye will receive it, this is Elias which was for to come: He that hath ears to hear, let him hear."—(Matt. xi. 14, 15.) It was a profound truth, our Lord would have them to know, which he was now delivering— one that did not lie upon the surface, and could only be received by spiritual and divinely-enlightened souls. This much is implied in the words, "If ye will receive it,"—if ye have spiritual discernment so far as to know the mind of God; and still more by the call that follows, "He that hath ears to hear, let him hear;" a call which is never uttered but when something enigmatical, or difficult to the natural mind, requires to be understood. The disciples themselves, however, still wanted the capacity for understanding what was said, as they betrayed, when putting the question to Christ after the transfiguration, "Why, then, do the scribes say, that Elias must first come?" This led our Lord again to assert what he had done before, and also to give some explanation of the matter: "And he answered and said unto them, Elias verily cometh first and restoreth all things. . . . But I say unto you, that Elias has indeed come, and they have done to him whatsoever they listed; as it is written of him." (Mark ix. 12, 13.) Here he so nearly identifies John with Elias, that what had been recorded of the one he holds to have been written of the other; for certainly the things that had happened to this second Elias, were no otherwise written of him, than as things of a similar kind were recorded in the life of the first. The essential connection between the two characters, rendered the history of the one, in its main elements, a prophecy of the other. If John had to do the work of Elias, he must also enter into the experience of Elias; coming as emphatically the preacher of repentance, he must have trial of hatred and persecution from the ungodly; and the greater he was than Elias in the one respect, it might be expected he should also be the greater in the other. It must, therefore, have been merely in regard to his commission from above, that he was said to "come and restore all things;" for here again, as of old, the sins of the people—headed at last by a new Ahab and Jezebel, in Herod and Herodias—cut short the process; "they rejected the counsel of God against themselves," and only in a very limited degree experienced the benefit, which the mission of John was in itself designed and fitted to impart. Nor *could* John have been the new Elias, unless, amid all outward differences, there had been such essential agreements as these between his case and that of his great predecessor.

We have now adverted to all the applications of Old Testament prophecy which are expressly mentioned by the evangelists to have been made by our Lord to himself and gospel-times, with the exception of a mere reference in Matt. xxiv. 15 to Daniel's "abomination of desolation," and the use made of Isa. vi. 9, 10, as describing the blind and hardened state of the men of his own generation, not less than of those of Isaiah's. Besides those passages, however, expressly quoted and applied by our Lord, it is right to notice, as preparatory to the consideration of what was done in this respect by evangelists and apostles, that he not unfrequently appropriated to himself, as peculiarly true of him, the language and ideas of the Old Testament. As when he takes the words descriptive of Jacob's vision, and says to Nathanael, "Verily, verily, I say unto you, hereafter ye shall see heaven open, and the angels of God ascending and descending on the Son of Man;" or when he said to the Jews of his own body, "Destroy this temple, and in three days I will raise it up;" or when he speaks of himself as going to be lifted up for the salvation of men, as the serpent was lifted up in the wilderness, and of the sign of the prophet Jonas going to appear again in him. Such appropriations of Old Testament language and ideas evidently proceeded on the ground of that close connection between the Old and the New, which we have endeavoured to unfold, as one that admitted of being carried out to many particulars. If, therefore, we shall find the evangelists and apostles so carrying it out, they have the full sanction of Christ's authority as to the *principle* of their interpretation. And on the ground even of Christ's own expositions, we may surely see how necessary it is in explaining Scripture to keep in view the pre-eminent place which Christ from the first was destined to hold in the divine plan, and how every thing in the earlier arrangements of God tended to him as the grand centre of the whole. Let us indeed beware of wresting any passages of the Old Testament for the purpose of finding Christ where he is not to be found; but let us also beware of adopting such imperfect views as would prevent us from finding him where he really is. And especially let it never be forgotten, that the union of the divine and the human in Christ, while in itself the great mystery of godliness, is, at the same time, the grand key to the interpretation of what else is mysterious in the divine dispensations; and that in this stands the common basis of what ancient seers were taught to anticipate, and what the church now is in the course of realizing.

IV.—THE APPLICATIONS MADE BY THE EVANGELISTS OF OLD TESTAMENT PROPHECIES.

It is to be borne carefully in mind, then, that the stream of Old Testament prophecy respecting the Messiah, in its two great branches—the one originating in the calling and destination of Israel, the other in the purpose to set up a kingdom of righteousness and blessing for the world in the house of David—flowed in the same direction, and pointed to the same great event. The announcements in both lines plainly contemplated and required an organic or personal connection between the divine and human natures as the necessary condition of their fulfilment; so that if there was any truth in the pretensions of Jesus of Nazareth—if he was indeed that concentrated Israel, and that peerless son of David, in whom the two lines of prophecy were to meet and be carried out to their destined completion, the indwelling of the divine in his human nature must have existed as the one foundation of the whole building. That very truth which the Jews of our Lord's time could not bear even to be mentioned in their presence—the truth of his proper deity—was the indispensable preliminary to the realization of all that was predicted. Hence it is that the four evangelists, each in his own peculiar way, but with a common insight into the import of Old Testament prophecy, and the real necessities of the case, all begin with laying this foundation. St John opens his narrative with a formal and lengthened statement of Christ's relation to the Godhead, and broadly asserts that in him the divine Word was made flesh. St Luke also relates at length the circumstances of the miraculous conception, and with the view evidently of conveying the impression, that this mode of being born into the world stood in essential connection with Christ's being, in the strictest sense, "the son of the Highest." Even Mark, while observing the greatest possible brevity, does not omit the essential point, and begins his narrative with the most startling announcement that ever headed an historical composition:—" The beginning of the gospel of Jesus Christ *the Son of God.*" And the first evangelist, who wrote more immediately for his Jewish brethren, and continually selects the points that were best fitted to exhibit Jesus as the Messiah of the Jewish Scriptures, characteristically enters on *his* narrative by describing the circumstances of Christ's miraculous birth as the necessary fulfilment of one of the most marvellous prophecies of the incarnation :—" Now all this was done that it might be fulfilled which was spoken of the Lord by the prophet, saying, Behold a virgin shall conceive and shall bring forth a son, and they shall call his name Immanuel, which, being interpreted, is God with us."

Commentators, it is well known, are not agreed as to the precise manner in which this prediction should be applied to Christ; and not a few hold that it is to be understood, in the first instance, of an ordinary child born after the usual manner in the prophet's own time, and only in a secondary, though higher and more complete sense, applicable to the Messiah. Their chief reason for this is, that they see no other way of understanding how the facts announced in the prophecy could properly have been a sign to Ahaz and his people, as they were expressly called by the prophet. Without entering into the discussion of this point, we simply state it as our conviction, that the difficulty felt arises mainly from a wrong view of what is there meant by a *sign*—as if the prophet intended by it something which would be a ground of comfort to the wicked king and kingdom of Judah. On the contrary, the prediction manifestly bears the character of a threatening to these, though with a rich and precious promise inclosed for a future generation. Between the promise of the child and its fulfilment, there was to be a period of sweeping desolation—for the child was to be born in a land distinguished for " butter and honey," the spontaneous products of a desolated region, as opposed to one well-peopled and cultivated (comp. Isa. vii. 15 with v. 22), and was to be fed of these. This state of desolation the prophet describes to the end of the chapter as ready to fall on the kingdom of Judah, and inevitably certain, notwithstanding that a present temporary deliverance was to be granted to it; so that, from the connection in which the promise of the child stands, coupled with the loftiness of the terms in which it is expressed, there appears no adequate occasion for it till the impending calamities were overpast, and the real Immanuel should come. Indeed, as Dr Alexander justly states (on Isa. vii. 14), " There is no ground, grammatical, historical, or logical, for doubt as to the main point, that the church, in all ages, has been right in regarding the passage as a signal and explicit prediction of the miraculous conception and nativity of Jesus Christ." Even Ewald, whose views are certainly low enough as to his mode of explaining the prediction, yet does not scruple to say, that " every interpretation is false which does not admit that the prophet speaks of the coming Messias."

We have no hesitation, therefore, in regarding the application of this prophecy of Isaiah to Christ as an application of the more direct and obvious kind. And such also is the next prophecy referred to by St Matthew, the prophecy of Micah regarding Bethlehem as the Messiah's birth-place. The evangelist does not formally quote this prophecy as from himself, but gives it from the mouth of the chief priests and scribes, of whom Herod demanded where Christ should be born. The prediction is so plain, that there was no room for diversity of opinion about it. And as both the prediction itself, and its connection with Isa. vii. 14, have already been commented on in the body of the work (p. 134), there is no need that we should further refer to it here.

Presently, however, we come in the second chapter of St Matthew to another and different application of a prophecy. For, when relating the providential circumstances connected with Christ's temporary removal to Egypt, and his abode there till the death of Herod, he says it took place, " that it might be fulfilled which was spoken of the Lord by the prophet, saying, Out of Egypt have I called my Son."—(Chap. ii. 15.) It admits of no doubt, that this word of the prophet Hosea was uttered by him rather as an historical record of the past, than as a prophetical announcement of the future. It pointed to God's faithfulness and love in delivering Israel from his place of temporary sojourn,—" When Israel was a child, then I loved him, and called my Son out of Egypt." When regarded by the evangelist, therefore, as a word needing to have its accomplishment in Christ, it manifestly could not be because the word itself was prophetical, but only because the event it recorded was typical. Describing a prophetical circumstance or event, it is hence, by a very common figure of speech, itself called a prophecy; since what it records to have been done in the type, must again be done in the antitype. And the only point of moment respecting it is, how could the calling of Israel out of Egypt be regarded as a prophetical action in such a sense, that it must be repeated in the personal history of Jesus?

This question has already been answered by anticipation, as to its more important part, in the last section, where the relation was pointed out between Christ and Israel. This relation was such that the high calling and destination of Israel to be not only blessed, but also the channel of blessing to the world, necessarily stood over for its proper accomplishment till He should come, who was to combine with the distinctive characteristics of a child of Abraham, the essential properties of the Godhead. All that could be done before this, was no more than the first feeble sproutings of the tree, as compared with the gigantic stature and expansion of its full growth. So that, viewed in respect to the purpose and appointment of God, Israel, in so far as they were the people of God, possessed the beginnings of what was in its completeness to be developed in Jesus; they, God's Son in the feebleness and imperfection of infancy, he the Israel of God in realized and concentrated fulness of blessing. And hence to make manifest this connection between the old and the new, between Israel in the lower and Israel in the higher sense, it was necessary, not only that there should belong to Christ, in its highest perfection, all that was required to fulfil the calling and destination of Israel, as described in prophetic Scripture, but that there should also be such palpable and designed correspondences between his history and that of ancient Israel, as would be like the signature of heaven to his pretensions, and the matter-of-fact testimony to his true Israelite destiny. Such a correspondence was found especially in the temporary sojourn in Egypt, and subsequent recal from it to the proper field of covenant-life and blessing. If, as our Lord himself testified, even the things that befel the Elias of the Old Testament, were a prophecy in action of the similar things that were to befal the still greater Elias of the New, how much more might Israel's former experience in this respect be taken for a prophecy of what was substantially to recur in the so closely related history of Jesus! That the old things were thus so palpably returning again, was God's sign in providence to a slumbering church, that the great end of the old was at length passing into fulfilment. It proclaimed—and as matters stood there was a moral necessity that it should proclaim—that He, who of old loved Israel, so as to preserve him for a time in Egypt, and then called him out for the *lower* service he had to render, was now going to revive his work, and carry it forward to its destined completion by that Child of Hope, to whom all the history and promises of Israel pointed as their common centre.

In such a case, of course, when both the prophecy and the fulfilment are deeds, and deeds connected, the one with a lower, the other with a higher sphere of service, there could only be a general, not a complete and detailed agreement. There must be many differences as well as coincidences. It was so in the case of John the Baptist as compared with his prototype Elias. It was so, too, with our Lord, in his temporary connection with Egypt, as compared with that of ancient Israel. Amid essential agreements there are obvious circumstantial differences—but these such only as the altered circumstances of the case naturally, and, indeed, necessarily gave rise to. Enough, if there were such palpable correspondences as clearly bespoke the same overruling hand in Providence, working toward the accomplishment of the same great end. These limitations hold also, and, indeed, with still greater force, in respect to the next application made by St Matthew, when he says of the slaughter by Herod of the infants at Bethlehem, "Then was fulfilled that which was spoken by Jeremy the prophet, saying, In Rama was there a voice heard, lamentation, and weeping, and great mourning; Rachel weeping for her children, and would not be comforted, because they are not." Here the relation is not so close between the Old and the New as in the former case; and the words of the evangelist imply as much, when he puts it merely, "Then was fulfilled," not as before, "That it might be fulfilled." It is manifest, indeed, that, when a word originally spoken respecting an event at Rama (a place some miles north of Jerusalem) is applied to another event, which took place ages afterwards at Bethlehem (another place lying to the south of it), the fulfilment meant in the latter case must have been of an inferior and secondary kind. Yet there must also have been some such relation between the two events, as rendered the one substantially a repetition of the other; and something, too, in the whole circumstances, to make it of importance that the connection between them should be marked by their being ranged under one and the same prophetical testimony.

Now, the matter may be briefly stated thus: It was at Rama, as we learn incidentally from Jer. xl. 1, that the Chaldean conqueror of old assembled the last band of Israelitish captives before sending them into exile. And being a place within the territory of Benjamin, the ancestral mother of the tribe, Rachel, is poetically represented by the prophet as raising a loud cry of distress, and giving way to a disconsolate grief, because getting there, as she thought, the last look of her hapless children, seeing them ruthlessly torn from her grasp, and doomed to an apparently hopeless exile. The wail was that of a fond mother, whose family prospects seemed now to be entirely blasted. And, amid all the outward diversities that existed, the evangelist descried substantially the same ground for such a disconsolate grief in the event at Bethlehem. For here, again, there was another, though more disguised enemy, of the real hope of Israel, who struck with relentless severity, and struck what was certainly meant to be an equally fatal blow. Though it was but a handful of children that actually perished, yet, as among these the Child of Promise was supposed to be included, it might well seem as if all were lost; Rachel's offspring, as the heritage of God, had ceased to exist; and the new covenant, with all its promises of grace and glory, was for ever buried in the grave of that Son of the virgin—if so be that he *had* fallen a victim to the ruthless jealousy of the tyrant. So that, viewed in regard to the main thing, the Chaldean conqueror had again revived in the cruel Edomite, who then held the government of Judea, and the slaughter at Bethlehem was, in spirit and design, as fatal a catastrophe as the sweeping away of the last remnant of Jews into the devouring gulph of Babylon. As vain, therefore, for the church of the New Testament to look for a friend in Herod, in respect to the needed redemption, as for the church of old to have looked for such in Nebuchadnezzar. Such is the instruction briefly contained in the evangelist's application of the prophecy of Jeremiah; an instruction much needed then, when so many were disposed to look for great things from the Herods, instead of regarding them as the deadliest enemies of the truth, and the manifest rods of God's displeasure. The lesson, indeed, was needed for all times, that the church might be warned not to expect prosperity and triumph to the cause of Christ from the succour of ungodly rulers of this world, but from God, who alone could defend her from their ceaseless machinations and violence.

In this last application of a prophetic word by St Matthew to the events of the gospel, there is a remarkable disregard of external and superficial differences, for the sake of the more inward and vital marks of agreement. It is somewhat singular, that, in his next application, the reverse seems rather to be the case—a deep spiritual characteristic of Messiah is connected with the mere name of a city. The settling of Joseph and Mary at Nazareth, it is said, at the close of chap. ii., took place "that it might be fulfilled, which was spoken by the prophets, He shall be called a Nazarene." There is here a preliminary difficulty in regard to the thing said to have been spoken by the prophets, which is not in so many words to be found in any prophetical book of the Old Testament; and, indeed, from its being said to have been spoken by the prophets generally, we are led to suppose, that the evangelist does not mean to give us the precise statement of any single prophet, but rather the collected sense of several. He seems chiefly to refer to those passages in Isaiah and Zechariah, where the Messiah was announced as the *Nezer* or sprouting branch of the house of David, pointing to the unpretending lowliness of his appearance and his kingdom. It is understood that the town Nazareth had its name from the same root, and on account of its poor and despised condition. That it was generally regarded with feelings of contempt even in Galilee, appears from the question of Nathanael, "Can any good thing come out of Nazareth?"— (John i. 46.) And it is quite natural to suppose, that this may have been expressed in its very name. So that the meaning of the evangelist here comes to be, that the providence of God directed Joseph to Nazareth, as a place in name, as well as general repute, peculiarly low and despised, that the prophecies respecting Jesus as the tender shoot of David's stem might be fulfilled. The meaning, indeed, thus becomes plain enough; but it seems strange that so outward and comparatively unimportant a circumstance should be pointed to as a fulfilment of prophecy. In this, however, we are apt to judge too much from the present advanced position of Christ's cause and kingdom; and also from the greatly altered tone of thinking in respect to the significance of names. The Jews were accustomed to mark every thing by an appropriate name; with them the appellations of men, towns, and localities every where uttered a sentiment or told a history. A respect to this prevalent tone of thinking pervades the whole gospel narrative, and appears especially in the names given to the place of Christ's birth (Bethlehem, house of bread), to the Baptist (John, the Lord's favour), and Jesus, (Saviour); in the surnames applied by Christ to Simon, (Cephas), to James and John (Boanerges); in the fact of the traitor, who among the disciples represented the cupidity, and blindness, and treachery of the Jewish people, also bearing the name of Judas (the Jew.) So natural was this mode of viewing things to the disciples, that the evangelist John even finds a significance in the name of Siloam as connected with one of the miracles of Jesus. (Chap. ix. 7.) It was fitly called Siloam, *sent*, since one was now sent to it for such a miracle of mercy; its name would henceforth acquire a new significancy. It might, therefore, be perfectly natural for those who lived in our Lord's time, to attach considerable importance to the name of the town where he was brought up, and whence he was to manifest himself to Israel. And in that state of comparative infancy, when a feeble faith and a low spiritual sense required even outward marks, like finger-posts, to guide them into the right direction, it was no small token of the overruling providence of God, that he made the very name of Christ's residence point so distinctly to the lowly condition in which ancient prophets had foretold he should appear. By no profound sagacity, or deep spiritual insight, but even as with their bodily eyesight they might behold the truth, that Jesus was the predicted *Nezer*, or tender shoot of David. Thus the word of the prophets was fulfilled in a way peculiarly adapted to the times.

The same kind of outwardness and apparent superficiality, but coupled with the same tender consideration and spiritual discernment, discovers itself in some of the other applications made by the evangelists of ancient prophecy. Thus in Matt. viii. 17, Christ is said to have wrought his miraculous cures on the diseases of men, "that it might be fulfilled, which was spoken by Esaias the prophet, saying, Himself took our infirmities and bare our sicknesses." Was this the whole that the prophet meant? Was it even the main thing? The evangelist does not, in fact, say that it was; he merely says, that Christ was now engaged in the work, of which the prophet spake in these words; and so, indeed, he was. Christ was sent into the world to remove by his mediatorial agency the evil that sin had brought into the world. He began this work when he cured bodily diseases, as these were the fruits of sin; and the removal of them was intended to serve as a kind of ladder to guide men to the higher and more spiritual part that still remained to be done. It was this very connection which our Lord himself marked, when he said alternately to the sick man of the palsy, "Thy sins be forgiven thee," and, "Arise, take up thy bed and walk;" it was as much as to say, the doing of the one goes hand in hand with the other; they are but different parts of the same process. That Matthew knew well enough which was the greater and more important part of the process, is evident from the explanation he records of the name of Jesus (chap. i. 21, "He shall save his people from their sins"); and his reporting such a declaration of Christ as this, "The Son of Man came to give his life a ransom for many." (Chap. xx. 28.) We have similar examples in John xix. 36, where the preservation of our Lord's limbs from violence is regarded as a fulfilment of the prophecy in type—"A bone of him (the Paschal Lamb) shall not be broken;" and in ver. 37, where the piercing of Christ's side is connected with the prediction in Zechariah—"They shall look on Him whom they pierced." It is evident that in both cases alike the original word looked farther than the mere outward circumstances here noticed, and had respect mainly to spiritual characteristics. But this evangelist, who had a quick eye to the discerning of the spiritual in the external, who could even see in the slight elevation of the cross something that pointed, as it were, to heaven (chap. xii. 33), saw also the hand of God in those apparently accidental and superficial distinctions in Christ's crucified body—the finger-mark of heaven, giving visible form and expression to the great truths they embodied, that they might be the more readily apprehended. It was not as if these outward things were the whole in his view, but that they were the heaven-appointed signs and indications of the whole; seeing these, he, in the simplicity of faith, saw all—in the unbroken leg the all-perfect Victim; in the pierced side the unutterable agony and distress of the bleeding heart of Jesus.

We need do little more than refer to the other applications made of Old Testament prophecy to Jesus by the evangelists. They are either applications in the most direct and obvious sense of predictions, that can be understood of no other circumstances and events than those they are applied to, or applications of some of the psalms and other prophecies, which had already been employed in part by Christ himself. Thus, Matt. iv. 15, 16, which regards the light diffused by the preaching of Jesus in the land of Naphtali and Zebulun, as a fulfilment of the prophecy in Isa. ix. 1, 2; Matt. xxi. 4, John xii. 15, which connect Christ's riding into Jerusalem on an ass with the prophecy in Zech. ix. 9; Matt. xxvii. 9, which, in like manner, connects the transactions about the thirty pieces of money given to Judas with the prophecy in Zech. xi. 13—these are admitted by all the more learned and judicious interpreters of the present day to be applications of prophecy of the most direct and simple kind. Portions of Ps. xxii. and of Isa. xlii. 1–4; liii. 1, 12, of which we have already had occasion to speak, in connection with our Lord's own use of ancient Scripture, are referred to, as finding their fulfilment in Christ, in Matt. xxvii. 35; John xii. 38, 40; xix. 24; Mark xv. 28. The only remaining passage in the Gospels, in which there is anything like a peculiar application of Old Testament Scripture, is Matt. xiii. 34, 35, where the evangelist represents our Lord's resorting to the parabolical method of instruction as a fulfilment of what is written in Ps. lxxviii. 2, and which has been explained in the chapter to which this Appendix refers. See p. 103.

Thus we see, that no arbitrary or unregulated use is made by the evangelists of ancient prophecy in regard to the events of gospel history, but such only as evinced a profound and comprehensive view of the connection between the Old and the New in God's dispensations. They had Christ's own authority for all they did—either as to the principle on which their applications were made, or the precise portions of Scripture applied by them. And nothing more is needed to ensure for them our entire sympathy and concurrence, than first, that we clearly apprehend the relation of Christ, as the God-man, to the whole scheme and purposes of God, and then that we realize the peculiar circumstances of the church, at the time when the higher and more spiritual things of the Gospel began to take the place of those that were more outward and preparatory. The want of these has been the chief source of the embarrassment that has been experienced on the subject.

V.—APPLICATIONS IN THE WRITINGS OF THE APOSTLE PAUL.

No one can fail to perceive that very frequent use is made of Old Testament Scripture in the writings of the Apostle Paul. Sometimes the use he makes of it is quite similar to that made by the Apostle Peter in his epistles— one, namely, of simple reference or appropriation. He adopts the language of Old Testament Scripture as his own, as finding in that the most suitable expression of the thoughts he wished to convey (Rom. ii. 24, x. 18, xii. 19, 20; Eph. iv. 26, v. 14, &c.); or he refers to the utterances it contained of God's mind and will, as having new and higher exemplifications given to them under the Gospel (Rom. i. 17; 1 Cor. i. 19, 31; 2 Cor. vi. 16, 17, viii. 15, ix. 9, &c). Of this latter sort also, substantially, is the application he makes to Christ in Eph. iv. 8 of a passage in Ps. lxviii. ("He ascended up on high, he led captivity captive," &c.)—a psalm which is nowhere else in New Testament Scripture applied to Christ, nor is it one of those which, from their clear and pointed reference to the things of Christ's kingdom, are usually distinguished as Messianic psalms. In applying the words of the psalm to the ascension of Christ, and his subsequent bestowal of divine gifts, the Apostle can hardly be understood to mean more than that what was done figuratively and in an inferior sense in the times of David by God, was now most really and gloriously done in Christ.

And there is also another application of an Old Testament Scripture by the Apostle Paul, which might, perhaps, without violence be understood, and by some evangelical interpreters is understood, in a similar manner, not as a direct prophecy, uttered in respect to Christian times, but as the announcement of a principle in God's dealing with his ancient people, which came again to be most strikingly exemplified under the Gospel. We allude to the passage in Isa. xxviii. 16 (combined with ch. viii. 14, 15), which is adduced by Paul in Rom. ix. 33 (as it is also, and still more emphatically by Peter in his first epistle, ch. ii. 7, 8) as bearing upon Christ, and the twofold effect of his manifestation upon the souls of men, "Behold, I lay in Zion a stone," &c. We regard it, however, as by much the most natural method, to take the word of the prophet there as a direct prediction of gospel-times. The difficulty in finding a specific object of reference otherwise, is itself no small proof of the correctness of this view—some understanding it of the temple, some of the law, others of Zion, and others still again, of Hezekiah. The prophet, we are persuaded, is looking above and beyond all these. Contemplating the people in their guilt and waywardness as engaged in contriving, by counsels and projects of their own, to secure the perpetuity of their covenant blessings, he introduces the Lord as declaring that there *was* to be a secure and abiding perpetuity—but not by such vain and lying devices as theirs, nor for the men who followed such corrupt courses as they were doing —but God himself would lay the sure and immoveable foundation in Zion, by means of which every humble believer would find ample confidence and safety; while to the perverse and unbelieving this also should become but a new occasion of stumbling and perdition. It can be understood of nothing properly but Christ. And we therefore have no hesitation in considering the word as a direct prediction of gospel-times, of which the only proper fulfilment was to be found in the events of Christ's history.

It is not so much, however, by way of simple reference or application, that Paul makes either his most frequent or his most peculiar application of Old Testament Scripture; he is more remarkable for the argumentative use he makes of it. He often introduces it in express and formal citations to establish his doctrinal positions, or to shew the entire conformity of the views he unfolded of divine truth with those which had been propounded by the servants of God in former times. It is in connection with this use of ancient Scripture by Paul, that the only difficulties of any moment in his application of it are to be found. And as we have already referred (in the first section) to his use, in this respect, of the historical and didactic portions, we have at present only to do with his employment of the prophecies. In respect to these also, the subject, in so far as it calls for consideration here, narrows itself to a comparatively limited field; for it is only in the application made of a few prophecies, and these bearing on the questions agitated in the apostle's day between Jew and Gentile, that any marked peculiarity strikes us. In saying this, however, we must be understood as leaving out of view the Epistle to the Hebrews, in which such a distinctive use of Old Testament Scripture is made as will require a separate consideration.

Now, the chief peculiarity is this, that while the Apostle, in the portions of his writings referred to, wrote argumentatively, and consequently behoved to employ his weapons in the most unequivocal and uniform manner, he seems to vary considerably in his manner of handling the prophecies; he even seems to use a strange freedom with the literal and spiritual mode of interpretation; now, apparently, taking them in the one, and now, again, in the other sense, as suited his convenience. So, at least, the depreciators of the Apostle's influence have not unfrequently alleged it to be. But is it so in reality? The matter certainly demands a close and attentive consideration.

I. The passage that naturally comes first in order is that in Rom. iv. 11–16, where the Apostle refers to the promises of blessing made to Abraham, and in particular to the two declarations, that he should be a father of many nations, and should have a seed of blessing—or rather, should be the head of *the* seed of blessing throughout all the families of the earth. In reasoning upon these promises, the object of the Apostle is plainly to shew, that as they were made to Abraham before he received circumcision, that is, while he was still, as to any legal ground of distinction, in a heathen state, so they bore respect to a posterity as well without as within the bounds of lineal descent and legal prescription; to those, indeed, within, but even there only to those who believed as he did, and attained to the righteousness of faith; and besides these, to all who should tread "in the steps of that faith of our father Abraham, which he had when still uncircumcised." According, therefore, to the Apostle's interpretation, the seed promised to Abraham in the original prophecy was essentially of a spiritual kind; it comprehended all the children of faith, wherever they might be found,—as well the children of faith apart from the law, as the children of faith under the law. The justness of this wide and profoundly spiritual interpretation, the Apostle specially bases, as we have said, on the time when circumcision—the sign and seal of the covenant—began to be administered; not before, but after the promises were given. And he might also have added, as a collateral argument, the persons to whom it was administered—not to that portion only of Abraham's lineal descendants, of whom the Jews sprung, nor even to his lineal descendants alone as a body; but to all collectively, who belonged to him at the first as a household, and all afterwards who should enter into the faith of the covenant, and should seek to belong to him (Ex. xii. 48, &c.) What could more evidently shew that Abraham's seed, viewed in the light contemplated in the promise as a seed of blessing, was to be pre-eminently of a spiritual nature? a seed, that was only in part to be found among the corporeal offspring of the patriarch; but, wherever found, was to have for its essential and most distinctive characteristic his faith and righteousness?

It is the *positive* side of the matter, that the Apostle seeks to bring out at this stage of his argument: his object is to manifest *how far* the spiritual element in the promise reaches. But at another stage, in chap. ix. 6–13, he exhibits with equal distinctness the *negative* side; he shews how the same spiritual element excludes from the promised seed all, even within the corporeal descent and the outward legal boundary, who at any period did not possess the faith and righteousness of Abraham. All along the blessing was to descend through grace by faith; and such as might be destitute of these were not, in the sense of the original prophecy, the children of Abraham; they were rather, as our Lord expressly called the Jews of his day, the children of the devil, John viii. 44,—a declaration that rests on the same fundamental view of the promise as that unfolded in the argument of the Apostle.

II. But now, if we turn to another portion of the Apostle's writings—to the Epistle to the Galatians—where he is substantially handling the same argument as to the alone sufficiency of faith in the matter of justification, we find what, at first sight, appears to be in one respect a quite opposite principle of interpretation; we find the mere letter of the promise so much insisted on, that even the word *seed*, being in the singular, is regarded as limiting it to an individual. In chap. iii. 6-18 of this epistle, the argument of the Apostle is of the following nature:—Abraham himself attained to blessing simply through faith; and when he was told that even all nations should come to partake in his blessing, it was implied that they also should attain to it through the same faith that dwelt in him. The law entered long after this promise of blessing had been given; and if the blessing were now made to depend upon the fulfilment of the law, then the promise would be virtually disannulled. Not only so, but the promise was expressly made to Abraham's seed, as of one, not as of many—" to thy seed," which, says the Apostle " is Christ ;" thus, apparently, making the promise point exclusively to the Messiah, and in order to this, forcing on the collective noun *seed*, a properly singular meaning.

Yet, on the other hand, it would be very strange if the Apostle had actually done so. For every one knows, who is in the least degree acquainted with the language of the Old Testament, that *seed*, when used of a person's offspring, is always taken collectively; it never denotes a single individual, unless that individual were the whole of the offspring. Educated as Paul was, it was impossible he could be ignorant of this; nay, in this very chapter, he shews himself to be perfectly cognizant of the comprehensive meaning of the word *seed*; and the drift of his whole argument is to prove that *every child of faith* is a component part of the seed promised to Abraham—that " they which be of faith, are blessed with faithful Abraham ;" or, as he again puts it at the close, " if ye be Christ's, then are ye Abraham's seed, and heirs according to the promise."

It is thus clear as day, that the Apostle here took the same comprehensive view of the promise to Abraham that he did in the fourth chapter of Romans; so that the distinction between *seed* and *seeds*, when properly understood, can only be meant to draw the line of demarcation between one class of Abraham's family and another—between posterity and posterity. For, though it would be quite against the ordinary usage to speak of *individuals in the same line* as so many seeds, it would by no means be so to speak thus of so many *distinct lines of offspring;* these might fitly enough be regarded as so many seeds or posterities. Such, precisely, is the meaning of the Apostle here. In his view Abraham's seed of blessing in the promise are his believing posterity—these alone, and not the descendants of Abraham in every sense. " Had this latter been expressed in the words," as Tholuck justly remarks, " seeds would require to have been used; as then only could it have been inferred that all the posterity of Abraham, including those by natural descent, were embraced. But since the singular is used, this shews that the prophecy had a *definite* posterity in view, namely, a *believing* posterity. The Jew must have been the more disposed to admit this, as for him also it would have proved too much, if the prophecy had been made to embrace absolutely the whole of Abraham's offspring. He, too, would have wished the lines by Ishmael and Esau excluded." So that, viewed in respect to the promised inheritance of blessing, those, on the one hand, who were merely born after the flesh, in the common course of nature, were not reckoned of the seed—they were still, in a sense, unborn, because they wanted the indispensable spiritual element; while, on the other hand, those are reckoned, who, though they want the natural descent, have come to possess the more important spiritual affinity—they have been born from above, and have their standing and inheritance among the children.

But if such be the import of the Apostle's statement, why, then, it may be asked, does he in v. 16, so expressly limit the seed of blessing to Christ? He does it, we reply, in the very same sense in which at v. 8 he limited the blessing to Abraham—in the one case he identifies Abraham with all the posterity of blessing, and in the other Christ; in both cases alike the two heads comprehend all who are bound up with them in the same bundle of life. "The Scripture foreseeing," he says at v. 8, "that God would justify the heathen through faith, preached before the gospel unto Abraham, saying, 'In thee shall all nations be blessed.'" *In thee*, combining the blessing of Abraham and all his spiritual progeny of believers into compact unity; he, the head, and those who spiritually make one person with him, being viewed together, and blessed in the same act of God. In like manner, when at v. 16, the Apostle passes from the parent to the seed, and regards the seed as existing simply in Christ, it is because he views Christ as forming one body with his people; in him alone the blessing stands as to its ground and merit, and in him, therefore, the whole seed of blessing have their life and being. So that the term *seed* is still used collectively by the Apostle; it is applied to Christ, not as an individual, but to Christ, as comprehending in himself all who form with him a great spiritual unity—those who in this same chapter of the Galatians are said to have " put on Christ," and to have become "all one in him" (a personal, mystical unity, v. 27, 28). We find precisely the same identification of Christ and his people, when the Apostle elsewhere says of the church, that it is " his body, the fulness of Him that filleth all in all" (Eph. i. 23); and yet again, when he says in 1 Cor. xii. 12, "As the body is one, and hath many members, and all the members of that one body being many, are one body, so also is Christ"— that is, Christ taken in connection with his church; he and they together.

III. Reverting again to the Epistle to the Romans, to that part of it in which the Apostle discusses the subject of the present unbelief and rejection, together with the future conversion of the Jews, chap. ix. x. xi., we find an apparent want of uniformity somewhat more difficult to explain. If we look at one part, there is the greatest freeness, but if at another, there seems the greatest strictness and literality in the manner he handles and applies the words of prophecy. In chap. ix. 25, 26, he introduces from Hosea what was unquestionably spoken in immediate reference to ancient Israel, and gives it a quite general application. Speaking of Israel as now apostate and rejected, but afterwards to be converted, the prophet had said that those who had been treated without mercy should yet obtain mercy, and those who had been called, " Not my people," should yet be called, " The children of the living God" (chap. i. 10; ii. 23). This the Apostle adduces in proof of the statement, that God was now calling to the blessings of salvation vessels of mercy, " not of the Jews only, but also of the Gentiles." It is certainly possible, that in applying the words thus, the Apostle did not mean to press them as in the strict sense a prophecy of the calling and conversion of the Gentiles. He may have referred to them simply as exhibiting a display of divine mercy, precisely similar in kind to what was now exemplified in the salvation of the Gentiles; that is, mercy exercised on persons who previously were cut off from any interest in its provisions, and in themselves had lost all claims to its enjoyment. That was to be done, according to the prophet, in the case of many in Israel; and if it was now also done in the case of a people called alike from among Jews and Gentiles, it was no new thing; it was but the old principle of the prophecy finding a new exemplification. Such, perhaps, is all the Apostle means by this application of prophecy to gospel-times.

But we cannot so explain another application made in the next chapter of the epistle. There, in proof of the declaration that " there is no difference between the Jew and the Greek, the same Lord over all being rich unto all that call upon him," he quotes what is said in Joel ii. 32, " For whosoever shall call upon the name of the Lord shall be saved." As found in Joel, the prediction has throughout an Israelitish aspect. It is " in Mount Zion and in Jerusalem," that the deliverance or salvation is said to be provided; and while the Spirit is spoken of as going to be poured out on " all flesh," still it seems to be flesh only as belonging to the Israelitish territory; for in describing the effect of the outpouring, the prophet says, " *Your* sons and *your* daughters shall prophecy; *your* old men," &c. Referring to it, therefore, as the Apostle does, for a formal proof of the position, that there is no difference between the Jew and the Greek in the matter of salvation, he must have considered the prophet as simply addressing the church of God, without respect to the Jewish element, which at that time so largely entered into its composition. He must have understood the prophecy as uttered respecting the visible church of God—no matter of what element composed, or how constituted—otherwise there would have been room for plying him with the objection, that by the connection the " all flesh," and the " every one that calleth," should be understood of such only among the circumcised Jews, not of those who belonged to the uncircumcised Gentiles. In this more restricted sense, St Peter plainly applied the words of the prediction on the day of Pentecost, for not till some years afterwards did he entertain any thought of comprehending in its provisions the Gentiles as such. Paul's application of it, therefore, is much freer than Peter's, and proceeds on the ground of converted Gentiles, not less than believing Jews, being interested in the promises of salvation addressed to the Israelitish church.

We find precisely the same broad principle in the fourth chapter of Galatians, where, in regard to the church of the New Testament, the Apostle quotes Isa. liv. 1, " Sing, O barren, thou that didst not bear; break forth into singing and cry aloud, thou that didst not travail with child; for more are the children of the desolate, than the children of the married wife, saith the Lord." It is distinctly as a proof text, that the Apostle introduces this verse of Isaiah, prefacing it with the words, " For it is written," a proof that the " Jerusalem that is above," in other words, the real church, is " the mother of us all" who are Christians, and as such is " free," the real and proper spouse of the Lord. Yet there can be no doubt, that in uttering the word the prophet addressed more immediately the Jewish Church; of that no one who reads the prophecy in its original connection, can entertain the slightest doubt. Hence, according to the interpretation of St Paul, it is not the Jewish element at that time existing in the church, which is now to be respected; it is simply the element of her being the spouse of God (" For thy maker is thine husband"), which consequently gives to the church of the New Testament, though formed mainly of believers from among the Gentiles, an equal interest in the grace promised in that prophetic word, with the church as it was, when composed almost exclusively of the descendants of Jacob.

But then the Apostle seems suddenly to abandon this broad principle of prophetical application, when in Rom. xi. 26, he comes to speak of the future conversion of the natural Israel,—" And so (that is, after the fulness of the Gentiles has come in, till which blindness in part has happened to Israel) all Israel shall be saved: as it is written, There shall come out of Zion the deliverer, and shall turn away ungodliness from Jacob; for this is my covenant unto them, when I shall take away their sins." Appealed to as in itself a sufficient proof that the natural seed of Israel, as a whole, shall be saved, is not this prophecy from Isa. lix. 20, 21, here understood as spoken to the Jewish people not as a church, but merely as a race? Are not those "in Jacob" the fleshly descendants merely of the patriarch, with the literal Zion as the centre of their commonwealth? And if so here, why not elsewhere? Why not also in the prophecies already referred to? And how, then, should the Apostle in them have made account only of the *spiritual* element in Israel as the church of God, and regarded the *natural* (as expressed in the words, Jacob, Zion, Jerusalem) as but incidental and temporary?

Such questions not unnaturally arise here; and the rather so, as the Apostle has materially altered the words of the prophecy, apparently as if to make them suit better the immediate object to which he applied it. In the prophet it is *to* Zion, not out of it, that the Redeemer was to come; and he was to come, not to turn away ungodliness from Jacob, but " to those that turn from transgression in Jacob." Such deviations from the scope and purport of the original have appeared to some so material, that they have come to regard the Apostle here, not so properly interpreting an old prediction, as uttering a prediction of his own, clothed as nearly as possible in the familiar language of an ancient prophecy. An untenable view, however, this; for how, then, can we vindicate the apostle from the want of godly simplicity, using, as he must then have done, his accustomed formula for prophetical quotations (" As it is written,") only to disguise and recommend an announcement properly his own?

We repudiate any such solution of the difficulty, which would represent the Apostle as sailing under false colours. Nor can we regard the alterations as the result of accident or forgetfulness. They have manifestly sprung from design. The correct view both of the use made of the prediction, and of the line of thought connected with it, we take to be this:—The Apostle gives the substantial import of the prophecy in Isaiah, but in accordance with his design gives it also a more special direction, and one that pointed to the kind of fulfilment it must now be expected in that direction to receive. According to the prophet, the Redeemer was to come, literally *for* Zion— somehow in its behalf; and in the behalf also of penitent souls in it—those turning from transgression. So, indeed, he had come already, in the most literal and exact manner, and the small remnant who turned from transgression recognised him and hailed his coming. But the Apostle is here looking beyond these; he is looking to the posterity of Jacob generally, for whom, in this and other similar predictions, he descries a purpose of mercy still in reserve. For, while he strenuously contends that the promise of a seed of blessing to Abraham, through the line of Jacob, was not confined to the natural offspring, he explicitly declares this to have been always included—not the whole, indeed, yet an elect portion out of it. At that very time, when so many were rejected, he tells us there was such an elect portion; and there must still continue to be so, " for the gifts and calling of God are without repentance;" that is, God having connected a blessing with Abraham and his seed in perpetuity, he could never recal it again; there should never cease to be *some* in whom that blessing was realised. But besides, here also there must be a fulness: the first fruits of blessing give promise of a coming harvest; and the fulness of the Gentiles itself is a pledge of it; for if there was to be a fulness of these coming in to inherit the blessing, because of the purpose of God to bless the families of the earth in Abraham and his seed, how much more must there be such a fulness in the seed itself? *The overflowings of the stream could not possibly reach farther than the direct channel.* But then this fulness, in the case of the natural Israel, was not to be (as they themselves imagined, and as many along with them still imagine) separate and apart; as if by providing some channel, or appointing for them some place of their own. Of this the Apostle gives no intimation whatever. Nay, on purpose, we believe, to exclude that very idea, he gives a more special turn to the prophecy so as to make it *out of* Zion that the Redeemer was to come, and to turn away ungodliness *from* those in Jacob. For the old literal Zion, in the Apostle's view, was now gone; its external framework was presently to be laid in ruins, and the only Zion, in connection with which the Redeemer could henceforth come, was that Zion in which he now dwells, which is the same with the heavenly Jerusalem, the church of the New Testament. He must come *out of* it, at the same time that he comes *for* it, in behalf of the natural seed of Jacob; and this is all one with saying, that these could only now attain to blessing in connection with the Christian church; or, as the Apostle himself puts it, could only obtain mercy through *their* mercy—namely, by the reflux of that mercy which has been bearing in the fulness of believing Gentiles. Thus alone, now, could the prophecy reach its fulfilment in the case of the natural Israel generally, as the result of a Saviour's gracious presence coming forth from his dwelling-place in Zion, and acting through the instrumentality of a Christian church.

So explained, this part of the Apostle's argument is in perfect accordance with his principles of interpretation and reasoning elsewhere. And it holds out the amplest encouragement in respect to the good yet in store for the natural Israel. It holds out none, indeed, in respect to the cherished hope of a literal re-establishment of their ancient polity. It rather tends to discourage any such expectations; for the Zion, in connection with which it tells us the Messiah is to come, is the one in which he at present dwells—the Zion of the New Testament church; *to* which he can no longer come, except at the same time by coming *out of* it. Let the church, therefore, that already dwells with him in this Zion (Heb. xii. 22), go forth in his name, and deal in faith and love with these descendants of the natural Israel. Let her feel that the presence and the blessing of the Lord are with her, that she may bring his word to bear with living power on the outcasts of Jacob, as well as on those ready to perish among the heathen. Let her do it *now*, not waiting for things that, if they shall ever happen, lie beyond the limits alike of her responsibility and her control; and remembering, that for any thing we can tell, the fulness of converted Israel may come in as gradually as the fulness of converted Gentiles. This also was spoken of as one great event by our Lord, when he warned the Jews that the Gospel would be taken from them, and given to a nation bringing forth the fruits thereof (Matt. xxi. 43.) Yet how slow and progressive the accomplishment! Converted Jews gradually diffused the leaven of the kingdom among the Gentiles, and converted Gentiles may have to do the part of as gradually diffusing it among the Jews that still remain in unbelief. And so " the life from the dead," which the conversion of Israel is to bring to the Christian church, may be no single revival done at a stroke, but a succession of reviving and refreshing influences coming in with every new blessing vouchsafed to the means used for turning away ungodliness from Jacob.

VI.—THE APPLICATIONS MADE IN THE EPISTLE TO THE HEBREWS—CONCLUSION.

The Epistle to the Hebrews has, in this country, been usually regarded as an inspired production of the Apostle Paul. This opinion, however, has never been universally acquiesced in. The early church itself appears to have been divided on the subject,—the Greek or Eastern church generally ascribing it to St Paul, and the Western regarding it as the production of some other person. From the middle of the fourth or the beginning of the fifth century, the opinion became almost universal, that it had proceeded from the pen of the Apostle to the Gentiles. But in more modern times, very great diversity of opinion has again prevailed; and on the continent, the preponderance among the more learned commentators has rather been in favour of some other person than Paul—probably Luke, Timothy, Apollos, or Clement. The chief source of this disposition to find another author than Paul, arises from the marked difference in the style of this epistle, as compared with the acknowledged writings of the Apostle—a difference so marked, that it is impossible for any one acquainted with the original not to be struck with it, and the more noticeable as the much purer Greek idiom that distinguishes this epistle, is found where we should least have expected it—in a writing addressed, not to Greek readers, as the greater part of

Paul's epistles were, but to those whose native language was Syriac. This circumstance is so very singular in itself, and so unlike the course that is usually adopted in such cases, that if the epistle did proceed from the Apostle, he must have on purpose departed considerably from his usual style, and possibly allowed this to be chiefly modelled by some Grecian coadjutor, and none more likely than Luke, who went with Paul to Rome. And we think a sufficient reason may be discovered for such a procedure, in the jealousy that was entertained towards Paul personally among the Jewish churches. If the epistle had either borne his name expressly on its front, or had been marked by his well-known characteristics of style, the parties to whom it was addressed might have been disposed to cast it aside at once, or would have listened with prejudiced feelings to the line of argument, by which it sought to win them from their dangerous attachment to the decayed formalities of Judaism. Certainly, the argument itself, no one might have been expected so readily to handle as the Apostle Paul, as no one could be supposed more deeply alive to the importance of the object it aimed at. And his very eagerness to attain this object might quite naturally have led him to court the kind of disguise, which appears in the withholding of his name, and the adoption of another style than what was properly his own.

The epistle abounds with references to Old Testament Scripture, and with direct quotations from it; as was, indeed, unavoidable from the nature of the subject it discusses. It is in its main theme a reasoning from the Old to the New; not, however, for the purpose of proving that Jesus was the Christ promised to the fathers, but rather, taking for granted this as a point mutually held, and shewing from the dignity of Christ's person, and the perfection of his work, as indicated even in Old Testament Scripture, the completeness of his dispensation in itself, and the mingled folly and danger of keeping up the shadowy services of Judaism, which had lost all their importance when their design was accomplished in Christ. To continue still to adhere to them, of necessity betokened at the very outset defective views of the superlative glory of Christ, and a tendency to look to those merely temporary representations of it for more than they were ever intended to impart; and the probability was, that, if persevered in, the carnal element would carry it entirely over the spiritual, and complete shipwreck of the faith would be made amid the dead observances of an obsolete and now annulled Judaism. Such briefly is the aim and drift of this epistle; and it very naturally leads us to expect that the author, in treating the subject, would make considerable use of passages in Old Testament Scripture bearing on gospel-times; that he would lay especial emphasis on those passages which either substantially implied or expressly announced the pre-eminent greatness of Christ's person, and work, and kingdom; and that he would also draw largely upon the accredited memorials of the past for warnings and expostulations against the danger of backsliding and apostacy, and for incentives to progress in the higher degrees of knowledge and virtue. All this we might have expected, and all this we find, in an epistle full of doctrinal expositions, happily combined with the earnest enforcement of practical duty. But there are some peculiarities in the application of Old Testament passages that appear in the course of the argument, which are not to be met with, at least to the same extent, in any other portions of the New Testament, and which call for some explanation.

1. First of all, there is a peculiarity in the mode of selection. Out of thirty-two or three passages in all that are quoted from the Scriptures, no fewer than sixteen, or one-half, are taken from the book of Psalms; and these, with only one or two exceptions in the two first chapters, comprise all that are referred to as bearing immediately on the person or work of Christ. There is something very singular in this, and something, we are disposed to think, which should have a degree of importance attached to it in connection with the author's manner of dealing with Scripture. For some reason or another he felt himself, if not absolutely shut up, yet practically influenced to confine almost entirely his proof passages respecting Christ as the head of the new dispensation, to such as might be found in the book of Psalms. What that reason might be we can only conjecture, or probably conclude from the nature and object of the epistle. Possibly it arose from the constant use made of the psalter in the Jewish worship, whereby it was not only rendered more familiar to the minds of the Judaizing Christians than any other portion of ancient Scripture, but was also most naturally regarded as of special authority in matters connected with the devotional service of God. So that arguments drawn from this source in behalf of a more spiritual worship, and for the disuse of those fleshly services with which it had been wont to be associated, could scarcely fail to tell with peculiar force on the subject of controversy—might even seem to come like a voice from the temple itself in testimony against its antiquated usages. At all events, the fact of the Apostle's quotations on this point being derived almost wholly from the Psalms, may justly be regarded as resting on some important consideration which it was necessary to keep in view. And this being the case, we should not so much wonder at testimonies respecting Christ being taken from passages there where he is not so plainly exhibited, while no reference is made to others in the prophetical books of Scripture more direct and explicit. The author deemed it right to draw his materials from a limited field, and he naturally pressed these as far as he properly could.

2. But does he not press them too far? Does he not really seek for materials in proof of Christ's personal or mediatorial greatness where they are not to be found? So it has been supposed; and it is not to be denied that another peculiarity meets us here, in the extent to which the book of Psalms is used in this epistle for testimonies respecting Christ. Particular psalms are employed in the discussion which are nowhere else in the New Testament applied to Christ. Not, however, it should be observed, to the neglect of those which *are* elsewhere applied to him; not as if the author were hunting for *concealed* treasures, and making light of such as lay *open* to his view. The more remarkable Messianic psalms, the 2d, the 22d, the 40th, the 45th, the 110th, are all referred to at different places as testifying of the things belonging to the Messiah. But besides these (to which we do not need now to refer more particularly), we find in the first chapter alone two other psalms, the 97th and the 102d, quoted without a note of explanation as portions bearing respect to Christ. Thus, at ver. 6, it is said, "When he

bringeth in the first begotten into the world, he saith, And let all the angels of God worship him," quoting the latter clause of Ps. xcvii. 7. And the concluding part of Ps. cii. is brought forward as spoken directly to the Son, "To the Son he saith, Thou, Lord, in the beginning hast laid the foundation of the earth, and the heavens are the works of thy hands," &c.

It should be carefully remembered, however, in respect to the use made of such passages, that the Apostle is not appealing to them for the purpose of proving that Jesus was the Messiah, or that he who became the Messiah in the fulness of time originally brought the universe into being. The Apostle is writing to persons who understood and believed these points—believed both that Jesus was the Christ, and that by him, as God's Word and Son, the worlds had been at first made, as well as redemption now accomplished for a believing people. The question was, what honour and respect might be due to him as such? and whether there was not a glory in him that overshadowed, and, in a manner, extinguished the glory of all preceding revelations? Now, for this purpose the passages referred to were perfectly in point, and contained a testimony which must have been quite valid with believing Hebrews. According to *their* belief also (in fact they could not have been in any proper sense Christians without having first come to the belief that), the Messiah was, as to his divine nature, the Son of God, and the immediate agent of Godhead in the creation of the world. Hence, as a matter of course, the word, in the concluding portion of the 102d Psalm, addressed to God as the Creator, must have been held as immediately applicable to the Son; it is of necessity *his* creative energy, and uncreated, unchangeable existence that is there more directly celebrated. No one can doubt this who knows the relation of the Son to the Father as the revealer of Godhead in the works of creation and of providence. And in like manner the 97th Psalm, which points to the manifestation of God's power and glory in the world, as going to bring discomfiture on all the worshippers of idols, and joy to the Church. What believer can really doubt that this was mainly to be accomplished in the person and the work of Christ? Even Rabbinical writers have understood it of Messiah. There is no other manifestation of God, either past or to come, fitted to produce such results but the personal manifestation given in Christ; and the call to worship God, written in the psalm, was most properly connected with the incarnation of the Divine Word. When by that event the First-begotten was literally brought into the world, there was the loudest matter-of-fact proclamation, calling upon all to worship him. It was only then, indeed, that the peculiar displays of divine power and glory began to be put forth, which the psalm announces; and the spiritual results it speaks of always appear according as Christ comes to be known and honoured as the manifested God.

But the use made in the second chapter of the eighth Psalm is thought by some still more peculiar and difficult of explanation. For in that psalm the glory of God is celebrated in the most general way, as connected with the place and dignity of man upon the earth; and how can it be produced as a testimony for Christ? But is it so produced? As far as we can see, the Apostle does not understand what is written in that psalm as pointing at all, directly or exclusively, to Christ. He is answering an objection, which, though not formally proposed, yet was plainly anticipated as ready to start up in the minds of his readers, to what he had advanced concerning the divine honour and glory due to Christ, as the Eternal Son of God. However he may be so when viewed simply in respect to his divine nature, yet as known to us, he was a man like ourselves; yea, a man compassed about with infirmity, and subject to suffering above the common lot of humanity; and might not the consideration of this detract somewhat from his dignity? Might it not even be justly regarded as placing him below the angels? By no means, says the Apostle, there is a glory of God connected also with man's estate; the Psalmist was filled with wonder and admiration at the imperfect indications he beheld of it in his day, regarding these as pledges of the more complete realisations of it yet to come; and it must be realised and perfected, not in connection with the nature of angels, but in connection with the nature of man. In allying himself with man, the Son of God, indeed, stooped for a time below the dignity of angels, but it was only that he might raise manhood to a higher position even than theirs; he humanized the Godhead, that he might, in a manner, deify humanity, that is, raise it to a participation in his own peerless majesty and fulness of blessing. In a word, the lordship of this world, which from the first was destined for man, and the thought of which filled the Psalmist with rapture and astonishment—this, in all its perfection and completeness, is still to be the inheritance of redeemed man, because the Eternal Son, as Redeemer, has, by becoming man, secured the title to it for himself and as many as are joined to him by a living faith. So that Christ has lost nothing of his proper glory by assuming the nature of man, but has simply made provision for a redeemed people sharing with him in it.

It is in connection with this branch of the argument also that the Apostle refers to a passage in Isaiah, which has been thought not strictly applicable to Christ. It is Isa viii. 17, 18, where the prophet, in his own name or another, says, "I will wait (or trust) upon the Lord; behold, I and the children which the Lord hath given me are for signs and wonders," &c. The prophet, it has been thought, speaks there of himself, and of his own proper children, as specially raised up by the Lord, to encourage the people to trust in the divine power and faithfulness for deliverance. That, however, is by no means so clear as some would have it. It is fully as probable, and the opinion is certainly growing among commentators, that the prophet rather rises here above himself and his children to those whom they represented, to the Angel of the Covenant, and his spiritual seed. For he says immediately before, "Bind up the testimony, seal the law among my disciples, and I will wait," &c. Who could speak thus of *his* disciples, and command the testimony to be bound up? Surely a higher than Isaiah is there. But even supposing that the prophet spoke of himself, supposing that in what follows, at least in the words quoted here, he does speak of himself and his own children; yet, as these must unquestionably have been viewed as personating the Immanuel and his spiritual offspring, the passage, even in that view of it, was a perfectly valid proof of the point for which it is quoted. It plainly indicates a oneness of nature in the Head and the members of the Lord's covenant people, and a common exposure to the ills of humanity.

3. A third peculiarity, and one that has been thought still more characteristic of the Old Testament quotations in this epistle from those elsewhere made in the New Testament, is, that they are uniformly taken from the Septuagint (*i. e.* the old Greek translation of the Old Testament), even where that differs materially from the original Hebrew. The New Testament writers generally, and the Apostle Paul in particular, very frequently quoted from that version, because it was in common use in the synagogues, and had acquired a kind of standard value. But they also, in many cases, departed from it, when it did not give at least the general sense of the original. This, however, is never done in the Epistle to the Hebrews; the Septuagint version is almost uniformly quoted from, whether it comes near or not to the exact meaning. Thus the words of the ninety-seventh Psalm, rendered in chap. i. 6, "Let all the angels of God worship him," are literally "Worship him all ye gods." So again in the quotation from the eighth Psalm in the second chapter, what is literally "Thou hast made him want a little of God," is given from the Septuagint, "Thou hast made him a little lower than the angels." A still greater deviation occurs in chap. x. 5, where the words from Psalm xl., which are in the original, "Mine ears hast thou bored," or opened, stand thus, "A body hast thou prepared me." And once more, a passage taken from Habakkuk, in chap. x. 38, which, accordding to the Hebrew, is, "Behold, his soul is lifted up, it is not upright in him," appears in the much altered form of the Greek version, "If any man draw back, my soul shall have no pleasure in him."

We omit other and less important variations. Those we have adduced undoubtedly shew a close adherence to the Greek version, even where it is not strictly correct. At the same time, it is to be observed, that nothing in the way of argument is built upon the differences between that version and the original, and the sentiment it expresses, so far as used by the Apostle, would not have been materially affected by a more literal translation. Indeed, in the last instance referred to, the passage from the prophet Habakkuk is not formally given as a citation at all; and as the order of the clauses also stands differently in the epistle from what it does in the Septuagint, so as to suit more exactly the object of the writer, we may rather regard him as adopting for his own what was found in the Septuagint, and giving it the sanction of his authority, than intending to convey the precise sense of the ancient prophet. And, after all, it is only a differently expressed, not by any means a discordant, sense with that of the prophet. The swollen, puffed-up soul is not upright, or does not maintain the even course of integrity. When the prophet says this, he only expresses more generally what is more fully and specifically intimated by the Apostle, when he speaks of such as draw back in times of trial, and incur thereby the displeasure of God. The passage taken from the fortieth Psalm admits of a similar explanation. The Apostle lays no stress upon the words, "A body hast thou prepared me;" he lays stress only on the declared readiness of the speaker in the psalm to do the will of God, by a personal surrender to its requirements; and as to say, "Mine ears hast thou opened," means, Thou hast made me ready to listen to all the demands of thy service; so to say, "A body hast thou prepared me," is but to turn it from a part of the body to the whole, and to intimate that his body itself was provided for the purpose of yielding the obedience required. The difference is quite a superficial one as regards the vein of thought running through the passage. And such also is the case with the other quotations, in which the angels are substituted for God or gods. It is plain that, in such expressions as "Worship him ye gods," and, "Thou hast made him to want but a little of God," something else than the supreme Jehovah is meant by the *Elohim* of the original—it must denote more generally something divine, or divine-like in condition and dignity, whether esteemed such on earth, or actually such in heavenly places. And the angels being the creatures nearest to God that we are acquainted with, they were not unnaturally regarded as substantially answering to the idea indicated in the expression. Many, even of the most learned interpreters, still think, that it is best to abide by the word *angels* in the passages referred to.

4. In conclusion, we shall make only two remarks—the one more immediately applicable to the peculiarity just noticed in this epistle, and the other common to it with the New Testament generally, in respect to the use of the Old Testament Scriptures.

The first is, that it perfectly consists with a profound regard to Scripture as given by inspiration of God, to employ a measure of freedom in quoting it, if no violence is done to its general import. There are cases in which much hangs on a particular expression; and in these cases the utmost exactness is necessary. In this very epistle a striking example is furnished of the pregnancy of single words, in the comment made upon those of the 110th Psalm, "The Lord hath sworn and will not repent, Thou art a priest for ever after the order of Melchizedec," where every expression is shewn to be important. And it is not too much to affirm, from such specimens of inspired interpretation, that the very words of Scripture are to be held as bearing on them the stamp of the Spirit's diction. On the other hand, the free renderings adopted in other places, where it was enough to obtain the general import, teach us to avoid the errors of superstitious Jews and learned pedants, and to be more anxious to imbibe the spirit of Scripture, than to canonize its mere words and letters. We must contend for every jot and tittle of the word, when the adversary seeks, by encroaching on these, to impair or corrupt the truth of God. But we are not absolutely bound up to that; we may freely use even a general or incomplete representation of its meaning, if by so doing we are more likely to get a favourable hearing for the important truths it unfolds. Correctness without scrupulosity should be the rule here, as in the Christian life generally.

Our second remark is, that the chief thing necessary for enabling us to go heartily along with the applications made both here and elsewhere of the Old Testament in the New, is a correct apprehension of the relation between the Jewish and the Christian dispensations. It is because the inspired writers went so much farther in this respect, than many of their readers and commentators are disposed to do now, that the great difficulty is experienced in sympathizing with this part of their writings. They saw every thing in the Old pointing and tending towards the manifestation of God in Christ, so that not only a few leading prophecies and more prominent institutions, but even subordinate arrangements and apparently incidental notices in matters connected with the ancient economy, were regarded as having a significance in respect to Christ and the Gospel. No one can see eye to eye with them in this, if he has been wont practically to divorce Christ from the Old Testament. And in proportion as an intelligent discernment of the connection between the two economies is acquired, the course actually adopted by the New Testament writers will appear the more natural and justifiable. Let there only be a just appreciation of the things written and done in former times, as preparatory to the better things to come in Christ, and there will be found nothing to offend even the science and the taste of the nineteenth century in the principles of interpretation sanctioned in the writings of the New Testament.

APPENDIX C.

THE DOCTRINE OF A FUTURE STATE.—P. 176.

In the text we have merely vindicated the Old Testament Scriptures from any charge of inconsistence in the reserve these maintained regarding the doctrine of a future state. It is desirable, however, to present the subject in a fuller light, and to consider both the state of opinion that prevailed respecting it in heathen antiquity, and the relation in which the Old and the New Testament Scriptures alike stand to it. We shall thus have an opportunity of pointing out several erroneous views, as we conceive, that are still of frequent occurrence in discussions upon the subject.

1. First of all, we look to the general fact—that somehow, and in some form or another, a belief in the doctrine of the soul's immortality has prevailed in nations, which had only natural resources to guide them in their religious views and tenets. We are not aware of any considerable people, either in ancient or in modern times, of whom this might not be affirmed; and among all nations that have reached any degree of intelligence and civilization, it is notorious, that the doctrine has always held a recognised and prominent place in the articles of popular belief. In no age or country has a public religion existed, which did not associate with it the prospect of a future state of happiness or misery as one of its leading elements and most influential considerations. So much is this the case, that the fear of the gods in heathen states was very commonly looked upon as identified with the expectation of good and evil in a life after the present; and the ancient legislators, who established, and the sages who vindicated the importance of religion, with one consent agree in deriving its main virtue from the salutary hopes and terrors it inspired respecting the life to come.[1] We are perfectly

[1] See Warburton's Div. Leg., B. III. s. 1, for the proof of this; and Russell's Connexion, vol. i. p. 308, seq.

entitled, therefore, from the existence and prevalence of religion among men, to infer, in a corresponding degree, the existence and prevalence of a belief in the immortality of the soul, or its destination in some form hereafter to a better or a worse state than belongs to it here. And as nothing ever attains to the rank of a universal belief, or general characteristic of mankind, which is not rooted in some common instinct of man's nature, we may further assert it as an undoubted fact, that this idea of a future state is one that springs from the spiritual instincts which belong to man as man; or, in the expressive language of Coleridge, that " its fibres are to be traced to the tap-root of humanity."

Exceptions, no doubt, are to be found to it, even among those who externally joined in the popular religion of their country—but only in the case of persons, or parties, who were unfavourably situated for the developement of their spiritual instincts, and who have seldom, in any age or country, formed more than a small minority of their generation. Such an exception, for example, appeared in the case of the Sadducees in the latter days of the Hebrew commonwealth—a sect small in point of numbers, and one that sprung up, partly as a reaction from the superstitions and frivolities of Pharisaism, and partly from the spread of Grecian culture among the richer and more ambitious classes in Judea. It was essentially a sect of philosophy, and had drunk too deeply of the sceptical influences of heathenism to be much impressed with *any* religious beliefs; though its repulsion to Pharisaism probably led it to take up more of an extreme position in respect to them, than it might otherwise have done. But it is impossible for any one to read the occasional notices given of the sect in Josephus, without perceiving that, as a party, they habitually did violence to the moral, as well as the spiritual instincts of their nature; that they exhibited the usual characteristics of the infidel spirit, and would very soon have ceased even from the profession of religion, if they had not been surrounded by a religious atmosphere. So that they can scarcely be regarded as exceptions to the natural union of the religious sentiment with the prospect of an hereafter; for the religious sentiment had no proper place in their bosom.

Substantially the same explanation is to be given of the views entertained by individual writers, and by some whole sects of heathen philosophers. Their intellectual culture unfitted them for sympathizing with the popular forms, into which either the worship of the gods, or the belief of a future state of existence had thrown itself. They saw the grossness and manifold absurdity of what had obtained the general assent, without having anything of their own clearly defined and thoroughly ascertained to put in its place; and the inevitable result was, that many of them became sceptical on the whole subject of religion, and others wavered from side to side in a kind of half-belief—sometimes giving utterance to the hopes and fears that naturally sprung from the conviction of a Supreme Governor, and again expressing themselves as if all heaven were a fable, and all futurity a blank. It was not that nature in them wanted the spiritual instincts it seems to possess in other men, or that these instincts failed to link themselves with the prospect of a future existence; but that, situated as they were, the instincts wanted appropriate forms, in which to clothe their feelings and expectations, and thus had either to hew out a channel of their own for faith and hope to flow in (which they were often too weak to do), or collapsed into a state of painful uncertainty or sceptical disbelief.

We take this to be both a fairer and a more rational account of the state of opinion prevalent among the more thoughtful and speculative part of ancient heathens, than that given by Bishop Warburton, and re-echoed in our own times by Archbishop Whately. Warburton has laboured with a great profusion of learning to shew, that all the ancient philosophers, with the exception of Socrates, were in their real sentiments disbelievers in a future state of reward and punishment, and only taught it in their exoteric writings as a doctrine profitable to the vulgar. We think it is impossible to make out this by any fair interpretation of the better writings of heathen antiquity; and, without giving far too much weight to the explanations and statements of the later Sophists and Neo-Platonists, who are no proper authorities on such questions. The doctrine of the soul's immortality, and of its destination to a future state of reward or punishment, comes out too frequently in the higher and even more philosophical productions of the ancients, to admit of being explained on the ground of a mere paltering to vulgar superstition and prejudice. And both the frequency of its recurrence, and the variety of forms in which the belief is uttered, force on us the conviction that the writers, in uttering it, often expressed the native sentiments of their hearts. But then the crude representations and incredible absurdities with which the doctrine was mixed up in the only authoritative form known to them, as often again drove them back from the ground they were inclined to occupy, and set speculation, with her daughters, doubt and uncertainty, wholly adrift. They could not fall in, heart and soul, with what had been embodied in the religion of their country, and had established itself in the popular belief; and it was, therefore, perfectly natural, that many inconsistences on the subject should appear in their writings; that they should be found retracting at one time what they seemed to have conceded at another; and that in their recoil of feeling from the palpably erroneous on one side, they should often have lost themselves in thick darkness on the other.

All this, however, is to be understood only of the more learned and speculative portion of heathen antiquity; of those, who either formally attached themselves to some sect of philosophy, or were, to a certain extent, imbued with the spirit of philosophy. Such persons were manifestly in the most unfavourable position for the free developement of their spiritual instincts. Policy alone, or a sense of public duty, led them to take any part in defending the existence, or in observing the rites of the prevailing religion; so that they were continually doing the part of dissemblers and hypocrites. But undoubtedly they would not have done in this respect what they did, or avowed so often their belief in a moral government above, and a state of recompense before them, unless these ideas had been interwoven with the established religion, and had come, through it, to pervade the minds of their countrymen. Warburton's declarations to this effect may be regarded as substantially correct, when he lays down the position, that a future state of rewards and punishments was not only taught and propagated by lawgivers, priests, and philosophers, but was also universally received by the people throughout the whole earth.[1]

Dr Whately, however, who, in his Essay on the Revelation of a Future State, generally re-echoes, as before stated, the sentiments of Warburton, expresses discordant views on this part of the subject. He seems to think that the people generally had as little belief in the existence of a future state of reward and punishment as the philosophers. From an expression in Plato, that " men in general were highly incredulous as to the soul's future existence," he concludes it to have been "notoriously the state of popular opinion," at the time, that " the accounts of Elysium and Tartarus were regarded as mere poetical fables, calculated to amuse the imagination, but unworthy of serious belief." Let us test this conclusion by a parallel declaration from a Platonic English philosopher—Lord Shaftesbury. This nobleman, ridiculing the fear of future punishment as fit at best only for the vulgar, adds regarding others, " Such is the nature of the liberal, polished, and refined part of mankind; so far are they from the mere simplicity of babes and sucklings, that, instead of applying the notion of a future reward or punishment to their immediate behaviour in society, they are apt much rather, through the whole course of their lives, to shew evidently that they look on the pious narrations to be indeed no better than children's tales, and the amusement of the mere vulgar."[2] This is, in fact, a far stronger and more sweeping assertion of a general disbelief among the learned now regarding the expectation of a future state, than that made by Plato of the generality of men in ancient times; but who would think of founding on such a statement, though uttered with the greatest assurance, as if no one could doubt what was said, a conclusion as to the all but universal rejection by educated men in modern times of the Scripture representations of the future world? Who does not know, that the conclusion would be notoriously false? But the inference drawn from the remark of Plato rests on a still looser foundation. And, indeed, if the matter had been as Dr Whately represents it, even in Plato's time, where should have been the temptation to the philosophers who lived then and afterwards, for so often speaking and writing differently, as is alleged, from what they really thought, respecting the world to come? They did so, we are told, in accommodation to the popular belief—that is (if this representation were correct), in accommodation to a belief which was known to have had no actual existence.

Dr Whately lays special stress in this part of his essay on the account given by Thucydides, of the effects produced among the Athenians by the memorable plague, which ravaged the city and neighbourhood. Many at first, the historian tells us, " had recourse to the offices of their religion, with a view to appease the gods; but when they found their sacrifices and ceremonies availed nothing against the disease, and that the pious and impious alike fell victims to it, they at once concluded, that piety and impiety were altogether indifferent, and cast off all religious and moral obligations." " Is it not evident from this," the archbishop asks, " that those who did rever-

[1] Div. Leg. B. III. sec. 2.   [2] Characteristics, vol. iii. p. 177.

ence the gods had been accustomed to look for none but *temporal* rewards and punishments from them ? Can we conceive that men who expected that virtue should be rewarded, and vice punished, in the other world, would, just at their entrance into that world, *begin* to regard virtue and vice as indifferent?" We hold this to be an entire misapplication of the historian's facts; and a misapplication that has arisen from an error very prevalent among English theologians, and shared in by Archbishop Whately, in the mode of contemplating the doctrine of a future recompense—as if the expectation of a *future* were somehow incompatible with the experience of a *present* recompense. We shall have occasion to expose this error by and by. But, meanwhile, we assert, that such a dissolution of manners and general lawlessness as took place at Athens under the awful visitation of the plague, and as always to some extent attends similar calamities, is rather a proof of men's expecting a future state of reward and punishment than the reverse—that is, of their doing so in their regular and ordinary state of mind, when they appear to pay some regard to virtue, and to wait on the offices of religion. The recklessness of what may be called their abnormal condition, bespeaks how much their normal one was under the restraining and regulating influences of fear and hope.

We hold it, then, as an established fact, that the expectation of a future state of reward and punishment, has been the general characteristic of men in every age—wherever they have been so situated as to find free scope to the spiritual instincts of their nature. The general prevalence alone of religious worship is a proof of it—for religion, whether in the nation or the individual, has never long flourished—it soon languishes and expires when divorced from the belief of a coming state of happiness or misery. The expectation, no doubt, of such a state, in all heathen forms of belief, has never failed to connect itself with many grievous errors—especially as to the mode of existence in the future world, and the kinds of reward and punishment that have been anticipated. *There* human reason and conjecture have always proved miserable guides; and the doctrines of the metempsychosis, from one fleshly form to another, the higher doctrine of the absorption into the divine unity, and the fables of Tartarus and Elysium, were but so many efforts on the part of the human mind to give distinct shape and form to its expectations of the future. These efforts were necessarily abortive. And the facts of the case will bear us no farther in the right direction, than in enabling us to assert the prevalence of a wide-spread, well-nigh universal, belief of a future existence, mainly depending for the good or evil to be experienced in it, on the conduct maintained during the present life. But *so far*, we are thoroughly satisfied, they do bear us.

Before leaving this point, we must be allowed to say, that there is a manifest unfairness in the way in which the sentiments of heathen antiquity, especially of its more profound thinkers, are very commonly represented by Warburton and his followers. This is particularly apparent in the use that is made of the alleged secret doctrine amongst them. It cannot be denied, that their writings contain strong statements in favour of a future state; but then, it is affirmed, these were only the writings that contained their exoteric doctrines—their real, or more strictly philosophical and esoteric doctrines, must be sought elsewhere. In this way the whole argumentation in Plato's Phædo goes for nothing; because that, it is alleged, belonged to the exoteric class, or his writings for the vulgar. A strange sort of vulgar it must have been, that could be supposed to enter with relish into the line of argumentation pursued in that discourse! We should like also, on that supposition, to see the line described that separates, as to form and style, between the philosophical and the popular, the esoteric and the exoteric in ancient writings. But the ground for such a distinction at all has been enormously exaggerated, and was very much the invention of the later Platonists. And so we find Professor Brandis, in the article on Plato in Smith's Dictionary, treating " the assumption of a secret doctrine as groundless, and destitute of support even from the passages brought forward out of the insitious Platonic letters." We cannot but reckon it unfair, also, in regard to Cicero, the next great writer of antiquity, who has treated at large of the question of the soul's immortality, to set against his deliberate and formal statements on the subject a few occasional sentences culled from his private letters, and but too commonly written when the calamities of life had enveloped him in gloom and despondency. In the first book of the Tusculan Disputations, c. 15, he enunciates both his own and the general belief, as one growing out of the rational instincts of humanity; and we have no reason to question the sincerity of the statement: *Nescio quomodo, inhæret in mentibus quasi seculorum quoddam augurium futurorum; idque in maximis ingeniis, altissimisque animis, et existit maxime, et apparet facillime.* He ridicules, indeed, the popular belief about Hades, as contrary to reason, and says enough to indicate how much of darkness and uncertainty mingled with his anticipations of the future; but the belief itself of a state of being after the present, is never disparaged or denied, but rather clung to throughout. It admits, however, of no doubt, that in the age of Cicero, the general tone of society at Rome among the more refined and influential classes, was deeply tinctured with infidelity. The sceptical spirit of the later philosophy of Greece, which regarded nothing as true, except that everything was involved in uncertainty, had become extensively prevalent among the rulers of the world. And such public disclaimers respecting the future punishments of Hades as are to be found in Cæsar's speech against Catiline, ascribed to him by Sallust, or in Cicero's oration for Cluentius, and the *nox est perpetua, una dormienda*, of the loose epicurean and debauchee Catullus (on which Dr Whately lays stress), are no more to be regarded as fair indications o the general belief of heathendom, than the infidel utterances of the French philosophers of last century are to be taken as just representations of the general belief of Christendom.

2. Let us proceed, however, in the next place, to look at the natural grounds for this belief.

And here, at the outset, we are to bear in mind a truth which is often verified in respect to men's convictions and judgments, as well in secular matters as in those of a moral and spiritual kind, viz. that a belief may be correctly formed, or a fact may be truly stated, and yet the reasons assigned for it in individual cases may be, if not absolutely wrong, at least very inadequate and inconclusive. It was the advice of a learned judge to a man of much natural shrewdness and sagacity, when appointed to a judicial function in the colonies, to give his decisions with firmness, but to withhold the reasons on which they were grounded; for in all probability the decisions would be right, while the reasons would be incapable of standing a close examination. We need not wonder, therefore, if in the higher field of religious thought and inquiry—if, especially in respect to those anticipations which men are prompted to form respecting a future existence—anticipations originating in the instincts of their rational nature, and nourished by a great variety of thoughts and considerations insensibly working upon their minds, both from within and from without—here especially we need not wonder if, when men began to reason out the matter in their own minds, they should often have rested their views on partial or erroneous grounds. This is what has actually happened, both in ancient and in modern times.

If we look, for example, into the most systematic and far-famed treatise, which has come down to us from heathen antiquity on this subject—the Phædo of Plato—we can scarcely help feeling some surprise at the manifest fancifulness of some of the reasons advanced for a future state of existence, and their utter inconclusiveness as a whole. It is the greatest of Grecian sages who is represented as unfolding them—Socrates;—Socrates, too, when on the very eve of his martyrdom; and his thoughts have the advantage of being developed by one of the greatest masters of reasoning, and the very greatest master of dialectical skill, of whom antiquity could boast. But what are the arguments adduced? There are altogether five. The first is, the soul's capacity and desire for knowledge, beyond what it can ever attain to in the present life: for, at present, it is encumbered on every side by the body, and obliged to spend a large portion of its time and resources in providing for bodily wants; so that it can never penetrate, as it desires, into the real nature and essence of things, and can even get very imperfectly acquainted with their phenomenal appearances. Hence, the soul being made for the acquisition of knowledge, and having capacities for making indefinite progress in it, there must be a future state of being, where, in happier circumstances, the end of its being in this respect shall be realized. The second argument is from the law of contraries—according to which things in nature are ever producing their opposites—rest issuing in labour, and labour again in rest—heat terminating in cold, and cold returning to heat—unity resolving itself into plurality, and plurality into unity;—and so, since life terminates in death, death must in turn come back to life; not, however, through the body which perishes, but in the soul itself that survives it. Then, thirdly, there are the soul's reminiscences of a previous life—by which are meant the ideas which it possesses, other than those it has derived from the five senses—such as of matter and space, cause and effect, truth and duty—ideas which, it is supposed, must have been brought by the soul from a previous state of existence; and if it has already passed out of one state of existence in coming into this world, the natural supposition is, that in leaving it, the soul shall again pass into another. The simple and indivisible nature of the soul is advanced as a fourth argument for immortality;—the soul in its essence is not, like bodily substances, compounded, divisible, and hence corruptible, but is itself, like the ideas it apprehends, immaterial, spirit-nal, incapable of change or dissolution into other elements. Then, lastly, there is the consideration of the soul's essential vitality—being the principle of life that animates and supports the body—and which, like the element of heat in material substances, may leave its former habitation, but must still retain its own inherent properties—must be vital still, though the body it has left necessarily falls into inertness, corruption, and death.

Such are the arguments advanced in this celebrated discourse for the soul's immortality—every one of them, it will be observed, except the first, of a metaphysical nature; though toward the close a kind of moral application is made of them, by urging the cultivation of mental, as opposed to sensual, desires and properties. "On account of these things," Socrates is made to say, "a man ought to be confident about his soul, who during this life has disregarded all the pleasures and ornaments of the body as foreign from his nature, and who, having thought they do more harm than good, has zealously applied himself to the acquirement of knowledge, and who, having adorned his soul, not with a foreign, but with its own proper ornament, temperance, justice, fortitude, freedom, and truth, thus waits for his passage to Hades, as one who is ready to depart whenever destiny shall summon him." The meaning is—not that the enjoyment of immortality depends upon the cultivation of such tendencies and virtues—for the reasons are all derived from the soul's inherent nature; and if good for any thing are good for every one who possesses a soul—but that, by being so exercised here, the soul becomes ready for at once entering on its better destiny; while, in the case of others, a sort of purgatory has first to be gone through—processes of shame and humiliation to detach it from the grosser elements that have gained the ascendancy over it. But in regard to the arguments themselves, who would *now* be convinced by them? There is manifestly nothing in that derived from the law of contraries—for in how many things does it not hold? how many evils in nature appear to issue in no countervailing good? Neither is there any thing in that derived from the supposed reminiscences of a former life—there being in reality no such reminiscences. And the reason found in the soul's essential vitality, is a simple begging of the question; for, apart from what has appeared of this in its connection with the body, what is known of it? What proof otherwise exists of the soul's vitality?

Of the two remaining arguments, the one placed in the soul's simple and indivisible nature, has often been revived. Not only does it recur in Cicero, among the ancients, and in such modern metaphysical productions as those of Clarke and Cudworth; but the sagacious Bishop Butler also makes use of it in his Analogy. We have it also presented to us in the glowing lines of Tupper:—

> "And corruption, closely noted, is but a dissolving of the parts,
> The parts remain, and nothing lost, to build a better whole;
> Moreover, mind is unity, however versatile and rapid;
> Thou can'st not entertain two coincident ideas, although they quickly follow;
> And unity hath no parts, so that there is nothing to dissolve;
> The element is still unchanged in every searching solvent."

And Dr Thomas Brown even lays the chief stress on it: "The mind," he contends, "is a substance, distinct from the bodily organ, simple, and incapable of addition or subtraction:" that is his first proposition; and his next is, "Nothing which we are capable of observing in the universe has ceased to exist since the world began." The two together, he conceives, establish the conclusion, so far as analogy can have influence, that "the mind does not perish in the dissolution of the body." And he adds, "in judging according to the mere light of nature, it is on the immaterialism of the thinking principle, that I consider the belief of its immortality to be most reasonably founded; since the distinct existence of a spiritual substance, if that be admitted, renders it incumbent on the assertor of the soul's mortality to assign some reason which may have led the only Being, who has the power of annihilation, to exert his power in annihilating the mind, which he is said, in that case, to have created only for a few years of life." As if there were here no alternative between the annihilation of the *substance* of mind, and the destruction of its *existence* and *identity* as a living agent! The matter of the body, it is true, is not annihilated at death; the particles of which it is composed still continue to exist; but not surely as the component elements of an organized structure. In that respect the body is destroyed —as far as our present observation goes, annihilated. And why may it not be so in respect to the mind? Allow that this is an immaterial substance, and as such, essentially different from the body, yet, for aught we can tell, it might be capable of being resolved into some condition as far from a continuation of its present state, as that of the dead body is in respect to its living state. The phenomena of swoons and sleep clearly shew that immateriality is no security against the *suspension* of thought and consciousness: —And who shall be able to assure us, on merely natural considerations, that death is not a *destruction* of them?

In truth, no sure footing can be obtained here on metaphysical grounds. It was the error and misfortune of the ancient philosophers—so far we certainly agree with Bishop Warburton[1]—that they suffered themselves to be determined by metaphysical, rather than by moral arguments on the subject; for this naturally took off their minds from the considerations that have real weight, and involved them in many absurd and subtle speculations, which could not stand with the soul's personal existence hereafter. When he excepts Socrates from the number, and accounts for his firm belief in a future state, on the ground of his avoiding metaphysical, and adhering only to moral, studies, he certainly gives us a very different view of the reasonings of Socrates on the subject from that presented in Plato. And we are persuaded, that neither was Socrates so singular in his belief, nor the others so universal in their disbelief of a future state, as Warburton would have us to believe. But, undoubtedly, there would have been far more of belief among them, if their reasonings had taken less of a metaphysical direction, and they had looked more to those moral considerations, connected with man's nature and God's government, on which the stay of the argument should alone be placed.

Let us now endeavour to indicate briefly the different steps of the ratiocination, which it is possible for unassisted nature, when rightly directed, to take in the way of establishing the belief of the soul's existence after death in a state of reward or punishment.

[1] Div. Leg. B. iii. § 4.

(1.) First of all, there is an argument furnished by the analogies of nature —an argument partly, indeed, of a merely negative character, and amounting to nothing more than that, notwithstanding the visible phenomena of death, the soul may survive and pass into another state of painful or blessed consciousness. For, however nearly connected the soul is with the body, it still is capable of many things that argue the possibility of its maintaining a separate and independent existence. Bodily organs may be lost—even great part of the body be reduced to an inactive lump by paralysis, while the mind exists in full vigour. In dreaming, and the exercise of abstract thought, there is sometimes found the most lively exercise of mind, when its connection with the body is the slightest, and, as far as *we* can discern, mind alone is at work. Why may it not, then, live and act when it is altogether released from the body—especially when we see the period of its release is often the moment of its highest perfection and most active energy? Those preceding analogies render it not unreasonable to imagine, that such at least *may* be the case.

Besides, life here is seen to move in cycles. It proceeds from one stage to another—each end proving only the starting-point of a new beginning. Man himself exists in two entirely different conditions—before and after birth:— And throughout his whole course of life on earth, he is perpetually undergoing change. Other creatures have still more marked changes and progressions in their career. Thus in many insects there is first the egg, then the worm, then the chrysalis, then the fully developed insect. And there are cases (of Aphides) in which as many as six or eight generations of successive change and developement pass away, before a return is made to the original type. Such things appearing in the present operations of nature, afford, indeed, no positive proof that life in man is destined to survive the body and enter on a sphere entirely different from the present; but they are well fitted to suggest the thought—and they meet the objection, which might not unnaturally arise, when the thought *was* suggested, from the great diversity necessarily existing between the present and that supposed future life. For they shew that it is part of the divine plan to continue life through very different circumstances and conditions.

It is manifest, however, that such analogies in nature cannot be pressed farther than this—they simply render possible or conceivable the soul's destination to another life, and answer objections apt to arise against it—but they contain no positive proof of the fact. Indeed, proceeding as they do upon the constitution of man's physical nature, and what is common to him with the inferior creation, they start the objection on the other side—that if on such grounds immortality might be predicated of man, it might also be predicated of all animals alike. But there is another class of analogies, to which this objection does not apply, which bring out the essential difference between man and the inferior animals—and are not simply negative in their character, but contain something of presumptive evidence in favour of a future state, closely connected with the present. We refer to the analogies presented by the adaptations so largely pervading the divine administration on earth, by means of which every being and part of being is wisely fitted to its place and condition. We see this adaptation in the construction of the organs of the human body—the eye, the ear, the taste, the limbs—all so nicely adjusted to the positions they occupy, both in respect to the human frame itself, and to the purposes they have to serve in connection with the material objects around them. We see it in the masticating and digestive apparatus, with which the various kinds of animals are furnished—one after one fashion, another after another—but each most appropriately suited to the nature and habits of the specific animal, and the kind of aliment required for its support. We see it even in the general condition of the inferior creation, which is so ordered in the great majority of instances, that each living creature gets the measure of good, of which it is capable, and with which it is satisfied. And then there are prospective contrivances in connection with all animal natures—contrivances formed at one stage of their existence, and preparing them for entering upon and enjoying another still before them—such as the eyes that are already fashioned in the fœtus, and the second row of teeth that lie for a time buried in the mouth of the child, and spring up only when they are required.

Now, when we turn to man with his large capacities and lofty aspirations—growing and rising as he proceeds through life—but still capable of indefinite expansion, and conscious of desires that can find no satisfaction here—does it not impress itself on our minds, that there would be something anomalous—at variance with the analogies everywhere appearing around us—if man, so formed and constituted, should terminate his existence on earth? He would, in that case, be the only creature that might seem out of place in the world, and that always the more, the higher he rose in the scale of intelligence and purity: in him alone there would be powers implanted, which seemed to fail of their proper end and object. "A brute arrives at a point of perfection that he can never pass: in a few years he has all the endowments he is capable of; and were he to live ten thousand more, would be the same thing he is at present. Were a human soul thus at a stand in her accomplishments, were her faculties to be full blown, and incapable of further enlargements, I could imagine it might fall away insensibly, and drop at once into a state of annihilation. But can we believe a thinking being, that is in a perpetual progress of improvements, and travelling on from perfection to perfection, after having just looked abroad into the works of its Creator, and made a few discoveries of his infinite goodness, wisdom, and power, must perish at her first setting out, and in the very beginning of her inquiries? Would an infinitely wise Being make such glorious creatures for so mean a purpose? Can he delight in such abortive intelligences, such short-lived reasonable beings? How can we find that wisdom, which shines through all his works in the formation of man, without looking on this world as only a nursery for the next, and believing, that the several generations of rational creatures, which rise up and disappear in such quick successions, are only to receive the rudiments of their existence here, and afterwards to be transplanted into a more friendly climate, where they may flourish to all eternity?"[1]

[1] Addison, in Spectator, Brit. Essayists, vi. No. 111. The essay is a fine specimen of that delicate sensibility and admirably-balanced judgment, which enabled Addison often to seize on thoughts that had escaped profounder thinkers. He introduces the argument merely as

This argument might be presented as one merely arising out of the general law of adaptation, and is so presented by Dr Chalmers in his Institutes. But it is the analogies connected with that law, which give it all its power to awaken any presumption in favour of a future state of being for man, as separate and distinct from the inferior creation; for the presumption arises on the contemplation of the apparent discrepancy between man's present condition and his present capacities, viewed in the light of analogous arrangements in providence. It properly belongs, therefore, to the argument from analogy, and shews how that argument is capable also of assuming a positive form. It bears, too, quite appositely on the real state of the question—which is not, as Bishop Butler and most others in his day seemed to think, whether the soul is naturally and essentially immortal—but whether we are warranted to conclude it to be the will and design of God, as indicated in our own natures and his government of the world, that it should have a prolonged existence in a future state, different from, yet closely connected with the present.

(2.) A second, and still stronger ground for the general belief in such a state is furnished by the actings of conscience. For it belongs to this faculty to pronounce authoritatively on what men should, and should not do, and to record in the secret chambers of the breast sentences of approval or condemnation, according as the things done are perceived to have been right or wrong. But there is always a felt incompleteness about these judgments of the moral faculty—viewed simply by themselves; and they rather indicate, that the things so judged are fit subjects of reward and punishment, than that they have thereby received what is properly due. In short, the authority of conscience, by its very nature, stands related to a higher authority, whose will it recognises, whose verdict it anticipates. And, as Bishop Butler justly remarks concerning it in his sermons, " if not forcibly stopt, it naturally and always of course goes on to anticipate a higher and more effectual sentence which shall hereafter second and affirm its own."

It is from the powerful sway that conscience has in awakening such anticipations, and its tendency to connect its own awards with those of a righteous lawgiver, that we are to account for the predominantly fearful and gloomy character of men's *native* thoughts respecting a future state. There is much in their natural condition to dispose them, when looking forward to another region of existence, to clothe the prospect in the most agreeable and fascinating colours, that they might find in it an effectual counterbalance to the manifold troubles of life, and a support amid the approaching agonies of death. But the reverse is so much the case, that it is the *apprehension*, rather than the *expectation* of a future state, which the belief of immortality most commonly awakens. And the vividness with which the mind of heathen antiquity pictured to itself the punishments of Tartarus—appear strangely contrasted with the dim and ghost-like pleasures of Elysium. A ready explanation of this peculiarity presents itself in the common operations of conscience, in

---

a " hint that he had not seen opened and improved by others, who had written on the subject," and as a kind of subsidiary to the reasons derived from the essence and immateriality of the soul, which were then chiefly pressed. Bishop Butler contents himself with those current reasons, and has in consequence left his chapter on a future life the most imperfect and unsatisfactory of his whole Book.

which the notes of condemnation, if not more frequent, are at least greatly more distinct and impressive than those of satisfaction; and hence, as in glancing upwards, its sense of guilt naturally awoke the idea of an offended deity, requiring to be appeased by the blood of sacrifice, so in pointing forward, its sentences of reproof not less naturally cast ominous shadows before them, and threw a sombre and forbidding aspect over the coming eternity.

The convictions thus produced in men's minds respecting a future world by the natural workings of conscience, it is plain, involve the recognition of a moral government of the world, and one that is accompanied with sanctions which are destined to take effect in a state of being after the present. It is, if we may so speak, on the background of such a government with such sanctions, that conscience raises in the bosom its forebodings of a judgment to come.—Nor, indeed, on any other ground could it beget either fear or hope for the future.

(3.) But closely connected with this, and strongly corroborative of the argument, it affords for a coming existence after the present, is the evidence that appears of a moral government in the actual course of things—a government accompanied by present sanctions. And this we announce as a third, and, upon the whole, the most tangible and convincing reason for the anticipation of a future state of retribution. But here it will be necessary to go into some detail, as it is in connection with this part of the argument that divines in this country have most commonly erred, and, by a strange inversion, have sought for proof of a future state of retribution rather in the *inequalities* of the divine government, or its apparent want of moral rectitude and present sanctions, than its possession of these. Thus, it is mentioned by Jeremy Taylor, in his sermon on the death of Sir George Dalston, as one of the things " which God has competently taught to all mankind, that the soul of man does not die; that though things may be ill here, yet to the good, who usually feel most of the evils of this life, they should end in honour and advantages. When virtue," he adds, " made man poor, and free speaking of brave truths made the wise to lose their liberty: when an excellent life hastened an opprobrious death, and the obeying reason and our conscience lost us our lives, or at least all the means and conditions of enjoying them, it was but time to look about for another state of things, where justice should rule, and virtue find her own portion." The want of justice here, and virtue's bereavement of her proper reward, is thus represented as the main reason and impelling motive for anticipating a better state of things hereafter. And a long array of similar representations might be produced from the works of English moralists and theologians.

But we would rather point to the manifestation of this error—the error of overlooking the connection between a present and a future recompense—as exhibited in a more doctrinal form, and with a more direct injustice to the character of Scripture, by those who have treated of the religious tenets and prospects of the Jews. Not unfrequently do we find the one presented as the antithesis of the other—as if the expectation of a future recompense could only begin to take effect when the other began to give way. This is done in the coarsest manner by Spencer in his work, De Leg. Hebræorum (L. I. c. vi.), where, it is alleged the ancient Israelites were so gross and sensual, so addicted to the flesh and the world, as to be incapable of being moved by anything but present rewards and punishments; and—which is but another modification of the same view—since idol-worship owed its influence chiefly to the expectations of present good or ill, which its imaginary deities were supposed to have at their command, so the tendency to idolatry among the Israelites required to be met by temporal threatenings and promises. As if God were willing by any sort of means to attach men to his service, and were content to fight idolatry with its own weapons, provided only he could induce his people to render him a formal and mercenary homage! The view of Warburton, as usual, differs only in a slight degree from Spencer's. It proceeds on the idea, that down to the later periods of the Jewish commonwealth, everything was administered by what he calls an extraordinary providence of present rewards and punishments, which supplied the place of the yet undiscovered and altogether unknown future world; and that in proportion as the extraordinary providence broke down, the belief of a future state of reward and punishment rose in its stead. Dean Graves, in his work on the Pentateuch, follows much in the same track, although he would not so absolutely exclude the belief of a future world from the remoter generations of God's people. Among the secondary reasons which he assigns for the employment of merely temporal sanctions to the law, he mentions " the intellectual and moral character of the Jewish nation, which was totally incapable of that pure and rational faith in the sanctions of a future state, without which these sanctions cannot effectually promote the interests of piety and virtue. Their desires and ideas being confined to the enjoyments of a present world, they would pay little attention to the promises of a future retribution, which they could never be sure of being fulfilled" (Works, II. p. 222). No doubt, *if* their desires and ideas were, and must have been, confined to a present world;—but why such a necessity? Would it not have been the most likely way to give their desires and ideas a loftier direction, to lay open to their view something of the good and evil to be inherited in the world to come? And if it had consisted with the divine plan to impart this, is it to be imagined, that the Israelites, who were so immeasurably superior to all the nations of antiquity in the knowledge of divine truth, should on this point alone have been incapable of entertaining ideas, which the very rudest of these were found in some measure to possess?

But not to spend farther time in the disproof of a notion so manifestly incredible and absurd, we must refer more particularly to what Dean Graves, in common with many British divines, regards as the great reason for the silence observed by Moses in respect to a future state. " I contend," he says (Works, II. p. 208), " that the reality of an extraordinary providence (*i. e.* an administration of present rewards and punishments) being established by unquestioned authority, and by the general nature of the Mosaic code, we can thence satisfactorily account for the omission of a future sanction, and that this is the *only way* in which it can be accounted for." The present administration of rewards and punishments the only way of accounting for the omission of future rewards and punishments! This might have been said with some degree of truth, if it had been meant, that through the present the future might be descried; but not in the sense understood by Dr Graves, as if the one had been to some extent incompatible with the other. The truth and reality of the temporal sanction should rather have been viewed as the necessary foundation and undoubted evidence of a future retribution. On this point Hengstenberg forcibly remarks, "Where this foundation—that, namely, of a moral government on earth, a temporal recompense—is not laid, there the building of a faith in immortality is raised on sand, and must fall before the first blast. He who does not recognise the temporal recompense must necessarily find in his heart a response to the scoff of Vanini at the revelation, ' which indeed, promises retributions for good and bad actions, but only in the life to come, lest the fraud should be discovered.' There is to be found in Barth on Claudian, p. 1078 sq., a rich collection from heathen authors, in which despair as to a future recompense is raised on the ground of unbelief as to a present one. And does not the history of our own age render it clear and palpable, how closely the two must hang together? The doubt was first directed against the temporal recompense; and it seemed, as if the belief of immortality was going to rise, in consequence of this very misapprehension, to a higher significance and greater stability. Supranaturalistic theologians themselves, such as Knapp and Steudel, derived one of their leading proofs of a future retribution from deficiences of the present one. But the *real* consequence was not long in discovering itself. The doctrine of reward, driven from the lower region, could not long maintain its ground in the higher. It became manifest that the hope of immortality had fed itself with its own heart's blood. ' If ye enjoy not such a recompense on earth,' says Richter justly, according to the conceptions of the age, ' God is by no means truly righteous, and you find yourselves in opposition to your own doctrine.' Where the sentiment, that the world's history is a world's judgment, is first of all heartily received in the true, the scriptural sense, there the advance becomes certain and inevitable to faith in *the* (final) judgment of the world." (Pent. II. p. 573.)

Earlier and more appalling illustrations than those referred to in this extract, might have been produced of the certainty with which disbelief in a present, tends to beget disbelief also in a future recompense. In those great and sweeping calamities, in which all distinctions seem to be lost between the good and the bad, all alike standing in jeopardy of life, or ruthlessly mowed down by the destroyer, it is seldom long till a general relaxation of principle, and even total regardlessness of future consequences, comes to prevail. It seems at such times as if the very foundations of religion and virtue were destroyed, and nothing remained but a selfish and convulsive struggle for the interests of the moment: "Let us eat and drink, for to-morrow we die." This is the right reading of the account given by Thucydides of the plague at Athens, formerly adverted to, in which the historian tells us, " men were restrained neither by fear of the gods, nor by human law; deeming it all one whether they paid religious worship or not, since they saw that all perished alike, and not expecting they should live till judgment should be passed on their offences here." Similar visitations in later times have always been observed to produce similar effects, excepting where religious principle has been so deeply rooted and so generally diffused, as to triumph over present appearances. During the plague of Milan in 1630, deeds of savage cruelty and wholesale plunder were committed that would never have been thought of in ordinary times. Even in London during the great plague in 1665, while there were not wanting proofs of sincere devotion and living principle, there was also a terrific display of the worst passions of human nature—a general dissolution of principle and rioting of iniquity, that struck the more thoughtful with dismay, and added immensely to the horrors of the time. The lurid light reflected from such apparent temporary suspensions of God's moral government, abundantly shews what results might be anticipated, if its ordinary sanctions did not exist, and the present recompenses of good and evil were withdrawn. It would no longer be the utterance merely of the fool, but the general sentiment of mankind, that there is no God—none judging in the earth now, and therefore none to judge in eternity hereafter. For, as Hengstenberg remarks again, "what God does not do here, neither will he do hereafter. If he is indeed the living and the righteous God, he cannot merely send forth letters of credit for blessing, nor terrify with simple threatenings of future evil."[1]

The ground, on which we here rest the natural expectation of a future state of reward and punishment, is precisely that which has been so solidly laid by Bishop Butler in the second and third chapters of his Analogy; and it may well excite our wonder, that English divines especially, who must be well acquainted with the train of thought there pursued, should suppose an extraordinary providence, or an exact distribution of reward and punishment on earth, to militate against either the revelation, or the belief of a future state. It is simply the want, the apparent or real want, of exactness in these temporal distributions in the usual course of Providence, which mars the completeness of Butler's argument. Yet as things actually stand, he does not hesitate to draw from the present aspect and constitution of Providence the following conclusions:—*First*, That the Author of nature is not indifferent to virtue and vice; *secondly*, that if God should reward virtue and punish vice, as such, so that every one may upon the whole have his deserts, this distributive justice would not be a thing different in *kind*, but only in *degree*, from what we experience in his present government. It would be that in *effect*, toward which we now see a *tendency*. It would be no more than the *completion* of that moral government, the *principles* and *beginning* of which have been shewn, beyond all dispute, discernible in the present constitution and course of nature. And from hence it follows, *thirdly*, that as under the *natural* government of God, our experience of those kinds and degrees of happiness and misery, which we do experience at present,

---

[1] How strongly the more thinking portion of heathen antiquity clung to the doctrine of a retributive providence as the abiding ground of hope amid appearances fitted to shake it, may be seen alone from the train of argument pursued by Juvenal in his xiiith book, where, treating of the prosperities of bad men, he finds consolation in the thought, that they suffer from the inflictions of an evil conscience, itself the heaviest of punishments; that hence, things naturally pleasant and agreeable, such as delicious food and wines, fail to give them satisfaction; that their sleep is disturbed; that they are frightened with thunder and disease, seeing in such things the signs of an offended deity; and that they go on to worse stages of iniquity, till they are overwhelmed with punishment; and concludes, that if these things are considered,

```
         ——— Poena gaudebis amara
Numinis invisi tandemque fatebere laetus,
Nec surdum, nec Tiresiam quemquam esse Deorum.
```

gives just ground to hope for and to fear higher degrees and other kinds of both in a future state, supposing a future state admitted ; so, under his *moral* government, our experience that virtue and vice are actually rewarded and punished at present, in a certain degree, gives just ground to hope and to fear, that they may be rewarded and punished in a higher degree hereafter. And there is ground to think that they actually *will* be so, from the good and bad tendencies of virtue and vice, which are essential, and founded in the nature of things ; whereas the hindrances to their becoming effect are, in numberless cases, not necessary, but artificial only. And it is much more likely that these tendencies, as well as the actual rewards and punishments of virtue and vice, which arise directly out of the nature of things, will remain hereafter, than that the accidental hindrances of them will.

The solid foundation which these considerations lay for the expectation of a future state of reward and punishment, and which, growing out of the observation of what is constantly taking place here, must be felt in thousands of bosoms that never thought of turning it into the form of an argument, is entirely overlooked by Archbishop Whately in the essay formerly referred to. He does not, indeed, like Warburton and Graves, place the temporal rewards and punishments in direct antagonism to the disclosure of a future state ; but neither does he make any account of the one as constituting a proper ground for the expectation of the other, and forming a kind of natural stepping-stone to it. His line of argument rather implies that it would have the reverse tendency, and that the Jews were only prepared to receive the doctrine of immortality when their present temporal blessings ceased. (§ 10.) He deems it absolutely incredible that the Israelites, as a people, should have looked for an after state of being, seeing that their attention was so very rarely, if at all, directed to such a state, and seeing also that they so seldom believed what was of much easier credence, the temporal promises and threatenings held out to them. The presumption against it he thinks greatly strengthened by the difficulty still experienced in getting people to realise the prospect of a future world, notwithstanding the comparative clearness and frequency with which it is pressed on their notice in the Gospel. In this, however, two things are evidently confounded together—the speculative knowledge or notional belief, and the practical faith of a future state of happiness and misery. For, on the same ground that Dr Whately denies the hope of immortality to those who lived under the Jewish dispensation, he might hold it to be very doubtfully or darkly propounded to believers now. Besides, he is obliged after all to admit, that somehow the doctrine and belief of a future state *did* become prevalent among the Jews long before the revelations of the Gospel—an admission which is totally subversive of his main positions ; for, beyond all dispute, this prevalent belief arose without the doctrine being frequently and directly inculcated in any book of authoritative Scripture. It is fatal, also, to the argument from 2 Tim. i. 10, " Jesus Christ, who hath abolished death, and brought life and immortality to light through the Gospel." For, if the knowledge of a future state existed at all before Christ, this could not have been brought to light by him, as a thing till then wrapt in utter darkness and obscurity. Nor does the statement of the Apostle imply that. It merely declares, that by means of Christ's Gospel a clear light has been shed on the concerns of a future life; they have been brought distinctly into view, and set in the foreground of his spiritual kingdom. And we have no more reason to maintain, from such a declaration, that all was absolute darkness before, than to argue from Christ being called "the true light, which lighteth every man that cometh into the world" (John ii. 9), that a total ignorance reigned before his coming in regard to the things of God's kingdom.

In truth, it is no more the specific object of the Christian, than it was of the earlier dispensations, to disclose and formally establish the doctrine of a future state. They both alike take it for granted, and have it for their grand business to prepare men for entering on its realities. Only, in the dispensation of the Gospel, as there the ultimate provision for eternity is made, and the way laid open into its abiding mansions, a light shines upon its momentous interests, which, from the nature of things, could not be imparted previously, without confounding shadow and substance together, and merging the preparatory in the final. But still the existence of a future state of reward and punishment was implied from the very first in the history of the divine dispensations, and is not doubtfully indicated in many of the earlier notices of Scripture as among the settled beliefs of God's people. It was implied even in the first institution of a religion of mercy and hope for fallen man; since, connecting with God's worship the prospect of a recovery from the ruin of sin, it would have only mocked the worshippers with false expectations, unless an immortal state of blessedness had been the issue it contemplated for such as faithfully complied with the appointed services. It was implied in the special dealings of God with his more honoured servants—such as Abel and Enoch before the flood, and after it Abraham and the patriarchs—whose history, in many of its bearings, is an inexplicable riddle, if viewed apart from the hope of better things to come in their future destiny. It is implied again as an object of well-grounded faith and expectation, to such persons and their spiritual seed, in the relation which God acknowledged himself to hold towards them, as their God and their Father—titles that manifestly bespoke for them an abiding interest in his eternal power and Godhead (Gen. vi. 2; Ex. iii. 6; iv. 22; Matt. xxii. 32; Heb. xi. 16). Could such special dealings and revelations have been made to the ancestors of the Jewish race without awakening a response in the bosoms of those that received them? Could they have failed to stimulate and call forth that instinctive belief in a future state, which even common providences were sufficient to evoke in all other nations of the earth? The idea is utterly incredible; and scanty as the notices are, which are given us of their feelings and prospects (for a supernatural restraint was laid upon the sacred penmen in this respect), they yet tell us of a hope in death, which was enjoyed by the good—a hope, which it was the highest wish of Balaam in his better moods to possess as his own last heritage—the hope of being gathered, in the first instance, to their fathers in the peaceful chambers of Sheol, and of ultimately attaining to a better resurrection (Gen. xxv. 8; xlix. 33; Numb. xxiii. 10; Heb. xi. 13, 35).

These views respecting the earlier dispensations, as connected with the doctrine and belief of a future state, are strongly confirmed by the argument maintained in the epistle to the Romans, and that to the Hebrews. The professed object of these epistles is to prove the necessity of the Christian religion, and its superiority over even the true, though imperfect, forms of religion that existed before it. And if there had been such an utter lack of any just ground for the expectation of a future state in the Old Testament dispensations, as is supposed by those we are now contending against, the chief stress would naturally have been laid upon the great omission in this respect which had been supplied by the Gospel. But is it so in reality? So far from it, that the reverse is frequently stated, and uniformly assumed. Ancient as well as present believers looked and hoped for a better existence after this. The main discussion in both epistles turns on man's relation to the law of God, and (to use the words of Coleridge, "Aids to Reflection," vol. i. p. 293,) "to the point, of which this law, in its own name, offered no solution—the mystery which it left behind the veil, or in the cloudy tabernacle of types and figurative sacrifices. It was not whether there was a judgment to come, and souls to suffer the dread sentence; but rather, what are the means of escape? where may grace be found and redemption? Not, therefore, that there is a life to come, and a future state; but what each individual soul may hope for itself therein; and on what grounds: and that this state has been rendered an object of aspiration and fervent desire, and a source of thanksgiving and exceeding great joy; and by whom, and through whom, and for whom, and by what means, and under what conditions—these are the peculiar and distinguishing fundamentals of the Christian faith. These are the revealed lights and obtained privileges of the Christian dispensation. Not alone the knowledge of the boon, but the precious inestimable boon itself, is the *grace and truth* that came by Jesus Christ."

To return, however, to our main theme—we hold it to be a great and unhappy oversight that has been committed by many, who, in overlooking the connection between a present and a future recompense, have thereby left out of view the very strongest of nature's grounds for anticipating an hereafter of weal or woe. But it is quite possible to err on the one side as well as on the other. "There is no error so crooked as not to have in it some lines of truth." And it seems to us, that Hengstenberg, in the treatise already quoted from, has to some extent overlooked the lines of truth which are in the error he controverts. It is quite true, as he has correctly and vigorously stated, that the temporal is the necessary basis of the future recompense; and that it is from what God does here, men are to argue, and in fact do argue and infer, regarding what he will do hereafter. It is also true, as farther stated by him, that a clear knowledge of the breadth and purity of God's law, and of the various spiritual ends God aims at in his dealings with men on earth, are sufficient to explain many seeming irregularities in his outward providence; as it discovers enough of imperfection in the righteousness of the good to account for their liability to sufferings, and enough of evil in the prosperity of the bad to render their condition destitute of real blessing. All this is admitted, and yet one cannot but feel that there is something which is left unexplained by it, or not thoroughly met. The assertion of a perfect administration of right holds in the full sense, only when eternity is added to time; that is, when the point now under consideration is virtually taken for granted. Looking simply to a present world, it is impossible to maintain that the administration *is* perfect; the more impossible, the clearer and more spiritual our views are of the law of righteousness. For, how then could the doers of righteousness be found to suffer, as is sometimes the case, for their good deeds? or, how could prosperity of any kind be accorded to the enemies of righteousness? True, their prosperity may prove in the long run their punishment; but only in respect to its bearing on the issues of a coming eternity; and even then only as abused on their part, not as given on the part of God. In themselves his gifts are all good; and the commonest bounties of providence, if conferred on the unworthy, mark a relative imperfection, at least, in the administration of justice on earth. Without some measure, even of real imperfection, where would there be room for the cry of an oppressed church, "Lord, how long?" Or, where again the necessity for the righteous looking so much away from the present world, and fixing their expectations on what is to come? In truth, a certain degree of imperfection here is as much to be expected, and, in a sense also, as necessary as in all the preparatory dispensations of God. For it is the feeling of imperfection within definite limits, which more especially prompts the soul to look and long for a more perfect future.

To bring the discussion to a close—it is indispensably necessary, in order to ground the conviction and belief of a future state of reward and punishment, that there should be in the present course of the divine administration palpable and undoubted evidences of a moral government of the world. And in furnishing these in such manifold variety, and with such singular clearness, consisted the peculiar service rendered by the Mosaic dispensation to the doctrine of a future state. But enough being seen in the providence of God to establish this doctrine in the convictions of men, the appearance, along with that, of anomalies and imperfections, must naturally tend to confirm its hold on serious minds, and foster the expectation of its future realities; as they cannot but feel convinced, that a righteousness, which gives such indubitable marks of its stringent operation, shall sometime remove every defect and perfect its work. They deem it certain, that under the government of a God, to whom such righteousness belongs, the apparent must at length be adjusted to the real state of things, and that all instances of prosperous villany and injured worth must be brought to an end. "There is much, therefore," to use the words of Dr Chalmers, "in the state of our present world, when its phenomena are fully read and rightly interpreted, to warrant the expectation, that a time for the final separation of all those grievous unfitnesses and irregularities is yet coming—when the good and the evil shall be separated into two distinct societies, and the same God, who, in virtue of his justice, shall appear to the one in the character of an avenger, shall, in virtue of his love, stand forth to the other as the kind and munificent Father of a duteous offspring, shielded by his paternal care from all that can offend or annoy in mansions of unspotted holiness."[1] Were it not, he justly adds, for the element of justice visible in God's administration, we

---

[1] Institutes, vol. i. p. 131.

should have no stepping-stone to arrive at this conclusion. And yet the partial defects and imperfections apparent in its present exercise have their share in contributing to the result; as they materially tend, when once the conclusion itself is established in the mind, to nourish the expectation of another and more perfect state to come.

APPENDIX D.

ON SACRIFICIAL WORSHIP.—P. 261.

The great, and we may say, fundamental mistake in the sounder portion of English theologians, who have written upon primitive sacrifice, has been their holding the necessity of a divine command to prove the existence of a divine origin. They have conceived, that the absence of such a command would inevitably imply the want of such an origin. And hence the whole strength of the argument, as it has been usually conducted, is directed to shew, that though no command is actually recorded, yet the facts of the case prove it to have been issued. As a specimen of this style of reasoning, we take the following from Delany:—"Nothing but God's command could create a right to take away the lives of his creatures. And it is certain, that the destruction of an innocent creature is not in itself an action acceptable to God; and therefore nothing but duty could make it acceptable, and nothing but the command of God could make it dutiful" (Revelation examined with Candour, vol. i. p. 136). And so generally. Uncommanded sacrifice, it has been presumed, would necessarily have been unwarranted and unacceptable; and therefore the right to kill animals for clothing, but still more the duty of sacrificing their lives in worship, has appeared conclusively to argue the prior existence of a divine command to use them in acts of worship.

The opponents of this view, on the other hand, have maintained, and, we think, have maintained successfully, that if such a command, expressly and positively enjoining the sacrifice of animal life in worship, had actually been given, it is unaccountable that it should not have been recorded—since, to drop it from the record, if so certainly given, and so essentially necessary, as is alleged on the other side, was like leaving out the foundation of the whole edifice of primitive worship. The only warrantable conclusion we can be entitled to draw from the silence of Scripture in such a case, is, that no command of the kind was really given. So with some reason it is alleged; but when the persons, who argue and conclude thus, proceed, as they invariably do, to the farther conclusion, that, since there was no command, there was nothing properly divine in the offerings of sacrificial worship, they unduly contract the boundaries of the divine in human things, and betray, besides, an entire misapprehension of the nature of the first dispensation of God toward fallen man. This, as we have said, is distinguished by the absence of command in every thing; throughout, it exhibits nothing of law in the strict and proper sense; and yet it would surely be a piece of extravagance to maintain that there were not, in the procedure of God, and in the relation man was appointed to hold toward him, the essential grounds and materials of divine obligation. How readily these were discovered in the divine operations, where still there was no divine command, may be inferred from what is written of the formation of Eve, "And Adam said, 'This is now bone of my bones, and flesh of my flesh: she shall be called woman (Isha), because she was taken out of man (Ish).'" He had come to know the manner of her formation; the divine act had been disclosed to him, as it had, doubtless, been in all others in which he was personally interested, because in the act there was contained a revelation of God, involving responsibilities and duties for his creatures. "Therefore," it is added, by way of inference from the act of God, and an inference, if not drawn on the spot by Adam, yet undoubtedly expressing the mind of God, as to what might even then have been drawn, and what actually was drawn, by the better portion of his immediate descendants, "Therefore shall a man leave his father and his mother, and shall cleave unto his wife: and they shall be one flesh." The act of God alone, without any accompanying command, laid the foundation for all coming time of the conjugal relation, and not only entitled, but bound men to hold, as of divine appointment, its virtual incorporation of persons, and corresponding obligations of mutual love and fidelity.

The principle that *ought* to be laid as the foundation of all just reasoning on such subjects, is, that whatever man can plainly learn from the revelations God gives of himself, to be in accordance with the divine mind and will, *that* is of God, and it is man's duty to believe and act accordingly. But the issuing of authoritative commands is not the *only* way God has of revealing his mind and will; nor, to creatures made after his own image, and as such, capable of understanding and imitating his procedure, is it even the first and most natural way of doing so. It is rather the manifestations which God gives of himself in his works and ways, in which they might be expected to find the primary grounds of their faith and practice; and only, when such had proved to be inadequate, might they require to be supplemented by explicit commands and stringent enactments. Holding, therefore, as we do, that the command to sacrifice was not necessary to establish the divine authority of the rite of sacrifice—holding, moreover, that in the divine act of covering man's person by the skins of slain beasts, as the symbol of his guilt being covered before God, there was an actual revelation of the mind of God in regard to his purposes of mercy and forgiveness to the sinful, precisely such as was afterwards embodied in animal sacrifice—we can satisfactorily account for the absence of the command, and, at the same time, maintain the essentially divine origin of the rite. And the reasoning of Davison and others, on the principle of no command, therefore no divine authority, falls to the ground of itself as a false deduction.

Of course the soundness of our own view, respecting the essentially divine origin of sacrifice and its properly expiatory character, depends upon the correctness of the interpretation we have put upon the divine act referred to. Davison, in common with British divines generally, regards it in a merely natural light. He sees in it simply "an instance of the divine wisdom and philanthropy; interposing, by the dictation and provision of a more durable clothing, to veil the nakedness, and cherish the modesty of our fallen nature, by sin made sensible to shame," (p. 24.) This he deems an object worthy of a special intervention of God, worthy also of a sacrifice of animal life to secure its accomplishment; and being so secured, he thinks it quite natural that the first pair might afterwards have felt themselves perfectly at liberty to use, for the sacred purposes of worship, what they had been taught to consider at their service for the lower purposes of corporeal clothing. This inference might certainly have been legitimate, if the premises on which it is founded had been accurately stated. But there we object. If corporeal clothing alone had been the intention of the act, it would have been the fruit of a needless interposition—the more so, as our first parents were themselves powerfully prompted to seek for clothing, and had already found a temporary relief. When the instincts and feelings of nature were manifestly so alive to the object, is it to be conceived that the ingenuity and skill which proved sufficient to accomplish so many other operations for their natural support and comfort, should have been incompetent here? It is altogether incredible. On simply natural grounds, the action admits of no adequate explanation, and must ever appear above the occasion, consequently unworthy of God. Besides, how anomalous, especially in a historical revelation, which ever gives the foremost place to the *moral* element in God's character and ways, if he should have appeared thus solicitous about the decent and comfortable clothing of men's bodies, and yet have left them wholly in the dark as to the way of getting peace and quietness to their consciences? Such must have been the case with our first parents, if they were thrown entirely upon their own resources in the presentation of sacrificial offerings. And so Davison, himself, substantially admits. For, while he endeavours to account naturally, and by means of the ordinary principles and feelings of piety, for the offering of animal life in sacrifice to God, considered simply as an expression of penitence in the offerer, or of his sense of deserved punishment for sin, he denies it could properly be regarded as an expiation or atonement of guilt; and hence postpones this higher aspect of sacrifice altogether, till the law of Moses, when he conceives it was for the first time introduced. Up till that period, therefore, sacrificial worship was but a species of natural religion; and man had no proper ground from God to expect, in answer to his offerings, the assurance of divine pardon and acceptance. But this, we contend, had it been real, would have been anomalous. It would have been to represent God as caring originally more for the bodies than for the souls of his people; and as utterly ignoring at one period of his dealings, what at another he not only respects, but exalts to the highest place of importance. How could we vindicate the pre-eminently moral character of God's principles of dealing, and the unchangeable nature of his administration, if he actually had been at first so indifferent in regard to the removal of guilt from the conscience, and afterwards so concerned about it, as to make all religion hinge on its accomplishment? Any satisfactory vindication, in such a case, must necessarily be hopeless. But we are convinced, it is not needed. The moral element *is* pre-eminent in God's dealings toward men. It was this which gave its significance and worth to his act of clothing our first parents, as painfully conscious of guilt, with the skins of living creatures, whose covering of innocence was in a manner put on them. And on the ground alone of what was moral in the transaction, symbolically disclosing itself (as usual in ancient times) through the natural and corporeal, can we account for the sacrifice of slain victims becoming so soon, and continuing so long, the grand medium of acceptable communion with God? If, in so clothing man, God did mean to give indication respecting the covering of man's guilt, and men of faith understood him to do so, all becomes intelligible, consistent, and even comparatively plain. But if otherwise, all appears strange, irregular, and mysterious.[1]

We are not disposed, in a matter of this kind, to lay much stress upon philological considerations. Yet it is not unimportant to notice, that the technical and constantly recurring expression under the law, for the design of expiatory offerings (לְכַפֵּר עָלָיו), seems to have its most natural explanation by reference to that fundamental act of God, considered in respect to its moral import. *To cover upon him*, as the words really mean, is so singular an expression for making an atonement for guilt, that it could scarcely have arisen without some significant fact in history naturally suggesting it. We certainly have such a fact in the circumstance of God's covering upon our first parents with the skins of animals, slain for them, if that was intended to denote the covering of their guilt and shame, as pardoned and put away by God. The first great act of forgiveness in connection with the sacrifice of life, would thus not unfitly have supplied a sacrificial language, as well as formed the basis of a sacrificial worship.

But if some collateral support may be derived from this quarter to the view we have advanced, we certainly must disclaim being indebted to another philological consideration, more commonly urged by the advocates of the divine origin of sacrifice. We refer to the argument so much pressed by Lightfoot, Magee, and others still in the present day, and based on what is regarded as a more exact rendering of Gen. iv. 7, as if it should be, " If thou doest well, shalt thou not be accepted? and if thou doest not well, *a sin-offering lieth at the door.*" Magee calls this " the plain, natural, and significant interpretation" of the words, and vindicates it at great length—more especially on three grounds, 1. That the word translated sin (חטאה) is very frequently used in the sense of sin-offering; 2. That when so used, it is usually coupled (though a feminine noun) with a verb in the masculine; and, 3. That the verb connected with it here, properly has respect to an animal (רבץ), and literally denotes, *couching* or *lying down*—quite appropriately said of a beast, but not so of sin. A single fact is perfectly suffi-

---

[1] Davison's *internal* reason, as he calls it (p. 84), against the atoning character of the ante-legal oblations—that such oblations, even under the law, atoned only for ceremonial offences, which of necessity had no existence in earlier times, scarcely deserves any notice in the present day. It proceeds on a complete misconception of the law of Moses, which was fundamentally and pervasively moral in its character; so that there was never simply a ceremonial, but always along with that a moral element in the duties it required, and the sins it condemned. If its oblations did not atone for guilt of a moral kind, they atoned for nothing. But on this we refer to what is said of the law in our second volume.

cient to put the whole to flight; the fact, namely, that the Hebrew term for sin never bears the import of sin-offering till the period of the law, and could not indeed do so, as till then what were distinctively called *sin-offerings* were unknown. To give the passage this turn, therefore, is to put an arbitrary and unwarranted sense upon the principal word, as there used, and nothing but the high authority of such men as Lightfoot and Magee could have given it the currency which it has so long obtained in this country. The real explanation of the feminine noun being coupled with a masculine verb, is to be found in the personification of sin as a wild beast, or cunning tempter to evil. And the whole passage, indeed, bears respect to the circumstances of the first temptation, and can only be correctly understood, when these are kept in view: " And Jehovah said unto Cain, why art thou wroth? and why is thy countenance fallen? Shall there not, if thou doest good, (viz. in regard to the sacrifice), be acceptance (or, lifting up)? and if thou doest not good, sin coucheth at the door—and unto thee shall be its desire, and thou shalt rule over it." The last words are simply a transference to sin, in its relation to Cain, of what was originally said of Eve, in her relation to Adam (Gen. iii. 16); and many Jewish (see, for example, the exposition of Sola, Lindenthall, and Raphall) as well as Christian interpreters, have discerned the allusion, and had respect to it in their exposition. Our translators, however, have unhappily understood the parties spoken of to be Cain and Abel, instead of Cain and sin, and thereby greatly obscured the meaning. The object of the divine expostulation with Cain is evidently to shew him, in the first instance, that the evil he frowned at really lay with himself, in his refusing to acknowledge and serve God, as his brother did. If he would still take this course, the ground of complaint should be removed; he would find acceptance, as well as his brother. But if he refused, then there was but one alternative—he could not get rid of sin—like an evil genius, it lay couching at the door, ready to prevail over him; but it was for him to do the manly part, and assert his superiority over it. In short, he is reminded by a silent reference to the sad circumstances of the fall, that giving way to sin, as he was doing, was allowing the weaker principle of his nature (represented by the woman in that memorable transaction), to gain the ascendant, while it became him, by cleaving to the right, to keep it in subjection; and it was implied, that if he failed in this, a second fall should inevitably follow—instead of rising, he must sink.

While, however, we reject the argument commonly derived from this passage in behalf of the divine origin of sacrifice, we derive an argument from it of another kind—viz. from the explicit manner in which it connects doing good with the acceptable presentation of sacrifice, and its representing sin as unforgiven, unsubdued, reigning in the heart and conduct, if sacrifice was not so performed. Had sacrifice not been essentially of God; had it not required the humble and childlike heart of faith to present it aright; had it not carried along with it, when so presented, the blessing of forgiveness and grace from Heaven, we cannot understand how such singular importance should have been attached to it. Like the sacrifice of Christ now, it has all the appearance of having then been the great touchstone of an accepted and blessed, or a sinful and condemned condition; not one of many, like a work of man, but standing comparatively alone as an all-important ordinance of God.

APPENDIX E.

DOES THE ORIGINAL RELATION OF THE SEED OF ABRAHAM TO THE LAND OF CANAAN AFFORD ANY GROUND FOR EXPECTING THEIR FINAL RETURN TO IT?—P. 357.

This question very naturally suggests itself in connection with the subject discussed in the text, although, from its involving matter of controversy, we deemed it better not to enter upon it there. The view presented, however, of the relations of the covenant-people, as connected with the occupation of Canaan, leads naturally to the conclusion, that their peculiar connection with that territory has ceased with the other temporary expedients and shadows to which it belonged. The people had certain ends of an immediate kind to fulfil, by means of their residence in the land—being placed there as representatives and bearers of the covenant, more fully to exhibit its character and tendencies, and to operate with more effect upon the nations around. But while intended to serve this present purpose, their possession of the land was also designed to be to the eye of faith an earnest and a pledge of the final occupation of a redeemed and glorified earth by Christ, and his elect seed of blessing. This is the proper antitype to the possession of the inheritance by the natural seed, in so far as that could justly be accounted typical.

One can easily perceive, therefore, that the representation entirely fails in its foundation, which is often made by recent writers on unfulfilled prophecy, viz. that the original possession of the land of Canaan by the seed of Jacob, was " only a token and earnest of a more glorious occupation of the land hereafter to be enjoyed by them." It is contrary to the nature of prophecies of this sort, as determined by the history of previous fulfilments, to make an event foreshadow itself—to make one occupation of the land of Canaan the type of another and future occupation of it. As well might it be alleged, that the natural Israel having eaten manna in the desert, was a type of their having to eat it again, or that their former killing of the passover-lamb foreshadowed their doing so hereafter in some new style, as that their ancient occupation of the land of Canaan typified a future and better possession of it.

It is possible enough, however, that what we have put here in the form of extravagant suppositions, will be readily embraced by many, who believe in the future restoration of Israel to Canaan. An entire re-production of the old is now contended for, as necessary to establish the literal truthfulness of

Scripture. And among other things to be expected, we are told, in connection with the return of Israel to Canaan, is the building anew, and on a style of higher magnificence, of the material temple, the resuscitation of the Levitical priesthood, and the re-institution of the fleshly sacrifices and pompous ceremonial of the ancient worship. To hold this, indeed, is only to follow to its legitimate results the idea, that the former possession of Canaan was typical of another; since, if that earlier possession gave promise of a later one, the establishment of the religious economy connected with it must have foreshadowed its future restoration. But the notion, in this form of it, stands in direct antithesis to the whole genius of the New Testament dispensation, and to some of the most explicit statements also of New Testament Scripture. If any thing be plain in the Gospel of Jesus Christ, it is, that every thing there assumes a spiritual character and a universal aspect, as contradistinguished from the local and fleshly. Foreseeing this, the prophet Malachi had said, that in the coming age, " incense and a pure offering should in *every* place be offered to the Lord ;" and our Lord himself announced to the woman of Samaria the approaching abolition of all local distinctions. " The hour cometh, when neither in this mountain, nor yet in Jerusalem, shall men worship the Father ;" that is, shall not regard worship rendered in these places as more sacred or more acceptable than worship paid elsewhere. The law with all its limitations of time and place, its bodily lustrations and prescribed services, was for the nonage of the church, and in form falls away, remains only in spirit, when the church reaches her maturity. Such, unquestionably, is the argument of the Apostle in his epistle to the Galatians; and it would surely be to run counter to all sense and reason, if, when the furthest extreme from the nonage condition is attained, the nonage food and discipline should return. As well might one expect to hear of angels being put into leading-strings ! Nay, it is expressly declared, that the abolition of the outward forms and services of Judaism was on account of its "weakness and unprofitableness" (Heb. vii. 18); and that the law, which ordained such things, was *of necessity* changed or disannulled with the introduction of a new priesthood made after the order of Melchizedec (Heb. vii. 12). And hence those who, in the apostolic age insisted on the continued observance of the now antiquated rites of Judaism, were expostulated with by the Apostle as virtually making void the work of Christ, and acting as if the church stood at where it was before he came into the world (Gal. v. 2-4; Col. ii. 14-23).

Where such scriptural testimonies, so plain in their terms, and so conclusive in their import, have failed to produce conviction, it would be vain to expect any thing from further argumentation. It may be proper, however, to present briefly, and more formally than has yet been done, what we deem the proper view of Israel's typical relations, with respect more immediately to the subject now under consideration. The natural Israel, then, as God's chosen people from among the peoples of the earth, were types of the elect seed, the spiritual and royal priesthood, whom Christ was to choose out of the world, and redeem for his everlasting kingdom. When this latter purpose began to be carried into effect, the former, as a matter of course, began to give way—precisely as the shedding of Christ's blood upon the cross antiquated the whole sacrificial system of Moses. Hence, to indicate that the type in this respect has passed into the antitype, believers in Christ, of Gentile as well as of Jewish origin, are called Abraham's seed (Gal. iii. 29); Israelites (ch. vi. 16; Eph. ii. 12, 19); comers unto mount Zion (Heb. xii. 22); citizens of the free or heavenly Jerusalem (Ib. Gal. iv. 26); the circumcision (Phil. iii. 3; Col. ii. 11); and in the Apocalypse, which is written throughout in the language of symbol and type, they are even called Jews (ch. ii. 9); while the sealed company, in ch. vii., who undoubtedly represent the whole multitude of the redeemed, are identified with the sealed of the twelve tribes of Israel. Further, this spiritual Israel of the New Testament are expressly declared to be " heirs according to the promise" (Gal. iii. 29)—the promise, namely, given to Abraham; for it is as Abraham's seed that they are designated heirs; and, of course, the possession of which they are heirs can be no other than that given by promise to Abraham. But then, as the antitypical things have now entered, not the old narrow and transitory inheritance is to be thought of, but that which it typically represented—" the inheritance incorruptible, undefiled, and that fadeth not away," which now takes its place as an object of hope. Accordingly, when the higher things of the Gospel are fairly introduced, it is to this nobler inheritance, as alone remaining, that the desires and expectations of the heirs of salvation are pointed. The apostles never allude to any other, when handling the case either of believing Jews or converted Gentiles; and when that inheritance of endless blessing and glory, the inheritance, as we believe it to be, of this earth itself in a state of heavenly perfection, when this shall become the possession of a redeemed and glorified church, then shall the promise contained in the Old Testament type be fully realised.

But may not something specially belonging to Israel be included in the antitype?—something to distinguish the natural line of believers from those who belong to the seed only by spiritual ties? So, sometimes, it is argued, as in *Israel Restored*, p. 193:—" Do they tell us the literal Israel was a a type of the spiritual? We instantly grant it. Do they tell us again, that therefore there is a spiritual fulfilment of the covenant to believers? We grant it also. But all this, we say, is nothing to the point. You must go farther. What you need to prove is, that Israel of old, whose descendants still exist, was *so* a type of the spiritual Israel, that they were finally to merge, and be lost in them whom they typified." There is no need for any such proof; the point in question is implied in the very fact of their being types; for, *as such*, they of necessity merged and became lost in the antitype. Was not the paschal lamb merged and lost in Christ? And the vail of the temple in Christ's body? And David in the Son of Mary? Every type must, as a matter of necessity, share the same fate; and if any thing peculiar is reserved for the land or people, who served a typical purpose, it must be on some other account than this that it shall belong to them.

More commonly, however, the stress of the argument, as connected with the original position of the Israelites, is laid upon the terms of the covenant with Abraham, in which Canaan is spoken of as their sure and abiding possession. So, among many others, Kurtz (*Geschichte des Alten Bundes*, p. 128), who says — " In the renewed promise (Gen. xvii. 8), the possession

Scripture. And among other things to be expected, we are told, in connection with the return of Israel to Canaan, is the building anew, and on a style of higher magnificence, of the material temple, the resuscitation of the Levitical priesthood, and the re-institution of the fleshly sacrifices and pompous ceremonial of the ancient worship. To hold this, indeed, is only to follow to its legitimate results the idea, that the former possession of Canaan was typical of another; since, if that earlier possession gave promise of a later one, the establishment of the religious economy connected with it must have foreshadowed its future restoration. But the notion, in this form of it, stands in direct antithesis to the whole genius of the New Testament dispensation, and to some of the most explicit statements also of New Testament Scripture. If any thing be plain in the Gospel of Jesus Christ, it is, that every thing there assumes a spiritual character and a universal aspect, as contradistinguished from the local and fleshly. Foreseeing this, the prophet Malachi had said, that in the coming age, " incense and a pure offering should in *every* place be offered to the Lord;" and our Lord himself announced to the woman of Samaria the approaching abolition of all local distinctions. " The hour cometh, when neither in this mountain, nor yet in Jerusalem, shall men worship the Father;" that is, shall not regard worship rendered in these places as more sacred or more acceptable than worship paid elsewhere. The law with all its limitations of time and place, its bodily lustrations and prescribed services, was for the nonage of the church, and in form falls away, remains only in spirit, when the church reaches her maturity. Such, unquestionably, is the argument of the Apostle in his epistle to the Galatians; and it would surely be to run counter to all sense and reason, if, when the furthest extreme from the nonage condition is attained, the nonage food and discipline should return. As well might one expect to hear of angels being put into leading-strings! Nay, it is expressly declared, that the abolition of the outward forms and services of Judaism was on account of its " weakness and unprofitableness" (Heb. vii. 18); and that the law, which ordained such things, was *of necessity* changed or disannulled with the introduction of a new priesthood made after the order of Melchizedec (Heb. vii. 12). And hence those who, in the apostolic age insisted on the continued observance of the now antiquated rites of Judaism, were expostulated with by the Apostle as virtually making void the work of Christ, and acting as if the church stood at where it was before he came into the world (Gal. v. 2-4; Col. ii. 14-23).

Where such scriptural testimonies, so plain in their terms, and so conclusive in their import, have failed to produce conviction, it would be vain to expect any thing from further argumentation. It may be proper, however, to present briefly, and more formally than has yet been done, what we deem the proper view of Israel's typical relations, with respect more immediately to the subject now under consideration. The natural Israel, then, as God's chosen people from among the peoples of the earth, were types of the elect seed, the spiritual and royal priesthood, whom Christ was to choose out of the world, and redeem for his everlasting kingdom. When this latter purpose began to be carried into effect, the former, as a matter of course, began to give way—precisely as the shedding of Christ's blood upon the cross antiquated the whole sacrificial system of Moses. Hence, to indicate that the type in this respect has passed into the antitype, believers in Christ, of Gentile as well as of Jewish origin, are called Abraham's seed (Gal. iii. 29); Israelites (ch. vi. 16; Eph. ii. 12, 19); comers unto mount Zion (Heb. xii. 22); citizens of the free or heavenly Jerusalem (Ib. Gal. iv. 26); the circumcision (Phil. iii. 3; Col. ii. 11); and in the Apocalypse, which is written throughout in the language of symbol and type, they are even called Jews (ch. ii. 9); while the sealed company, in ch. vii., who undoubtedly represent the whole multitude of the redeemed, are identified with the sealed of the twelve tribes of Israel. Further, this spiritual Israel of the New Testament are expressly declared to be "heirs according to the promise" (Gal. iii. 29)—the promise, namely, given to Abraham; for it is as Abraham's seed that they are designated heirs; and, of course, the possession of which they are heirs can be no other than that given by promise to Abraham. But then, as the antitypical things have now entered, not the old narrow and transitory inheritance is to be thought of, but that which it typically represented—"the inheritance incorruptible, undefiled, and that fadeth not away," which now takes its place as an object of hope. Accordingly, when the higher things of the Gospel are fairly introduced, it is to this nobler inheritance, as alone remaining, that the desires and expectations of the heirs of salvation are pointed. The apostles never allude to any other, when handling the case either of believing Jews or converted Gentiles; and when that inheritance of endless blessing and glory, the inheritance, as we believe it to be, of this earth itself in a state of heavenly perfection, when this shall become the possession of a redeemed and glorified church, then shall the promise contained in the Old Testament type be fully realised.

But may not something specially belonging to Israel be included in the antitype?—something to distinguish the natural line of believers from those who belong to the seed only by spiritual ties? So, sometimes, it is argued, as in *Israel Restored*, p. 193 :—" Do they tell us the literal Israel was a a type of the spiritual? We instantly grant it. Do they tell us again, that therefore there is a spiritual fulfilment of the covenant to believers? We grant it also. But all this, we say, is nothing to the point. You must go farther. What you need to prove is, that Israel of old, whose descendants still exist, was *so* a type of the spiritual Israel, that they were finally to merge, and be lost in them whom they typified." There is no need for any such proof; the point in question is implied in the very fact of their being types; for, *as such*, they of necessity merged and became lost in the antitype. Was not the paschal lamb merged and lost in Christ? And the vail of the temple in Christ's body? And David in the Son of Mary? Every type must, as a matter of necessity, share the same fate; and if any thing peculiar is reserved for the land or people, who served a typical purpose, it must be on some other account than this that it shall belong to them.

More commonly, however, the stress of the argument, as connected with the original position of the Israelites, is laid upon the terms of the covenant with Abraham, in which Canaan is spoken of as their sure and abiding possession. So, among many others, Kurtz (*Geschichte des Alten Bundes*, p. 128), who says — " In the renewed promise (Gen. xvii. 8), the possession of the land is called an everlasting possession, as the covenant also is called an everlasting covenant (v. 7, 13). That the covenant should be called an everlasting one, cannot appear strange, as it is a covenant that must reach its end. If the fruit of the covenant is of a permanent kind, such also must be the covenant itself, of which it is the fulfilment. The promise of an everlasting possession of the land had respect primarily to the pilgrim-condition of Abraham, which was such as not to admit of his possessing a single foot-breadth in it as his own. But the land of promise is the inheritance and possession of his seed, and remains so for ever, though Israel may have been exiled from the land, and whether the exile may have lasted seventy or two thousand years." True, no doubt, if the relative position of things continues substantially the same during the longer, as during the shorter period of exile; but not, surely, if they have undergone an essential change. The seed of Abraham has become unspeakably ennobled in Christ, and it is but natural to infer, that the inheritance also should be correspondingly ennobled. The peculiar distinction of Canaan, and that which most of all rendered it an inheritance of blessing, was its being God's land. And if in Christ the whole earth becomes in the same sense the Lord's, that Canaan was of old claimed to be his, then the promise will embrace the earth; nor will it be, in such a case, as if Canaan were lost to any portion of the seed, but rather as if Canaan were indefinitely widened and enlarged to receive them. In like manner, believers have the promise, that they shall worship God in his heavenly temple; and yet, when the heavenly appears to John in its glory, he sees no temple in it. Does the promise therefore fail? On the contrary, it is in the highest sense fulfilled. The no-temple simply means, that all has become temple, alike sacred and glorious; just as we may say, the no-Canaan in Christ has become all-Canaan. The inheritance is not lost; it has only ceased to become a part, and extends as far and wide as Christ's peculiar possession reaches (Ps. ii.) Here, however, we tread on the confines of prophecy, a field on which at present we do not mean to enter, leaving it for another occasion. We simply add, in confirmation of what has now been advanced regarding the Abrahamic covenant, that as the covenant is called everlasting, and the land also an everlasting possession, so circumcision is called everlasting: " My covenant shall be in your flesh for an everlasting covenant" (v. 13). But we know for certain, that this was not intended to be in the strict sense perpetual. Baptism, the Apostle tells us, is Christ's circumcision; and circumcision outwardly *should* have been dropped when Christ appeared. It is the sin of the Jews to continue it, and it cannot now be the pledge of blessing to them.

www.ingramcontent.com/pod-product-compliance
Lightning Source LLC
Chambersburg PA
CBHW062124160426
43191CB00013B/2192